S0-ATE-825

Crystal L. Downing

Changing Signs of Truth

A Christian Introduction to the Semiotics of Communication

IVP Academic
An imprint of InterVarsity Press
Downers Grove, Illinois

InterVarsity Press
P.O. Box 1400, Downers Grove, IL 60515-1426
World Wide Web: www.ivpress.com
E-mail: email@ivpress.com

InterVarsity Press® is the book-publishing division of InterVarsity Christian Fellowship/USA®, a movement of students and faculty active on campus at hundreds of universities, colleges and schools of nursing in the United States of America, and a member movement of the International Fellowship of Evangelical Students. For information about local and regional activities, write Public Relations Dept., InterVarsity Christian Fellowship/USA, 6400 Schroeder Rd., P.O. Box 7895, Madison, WI 53707-7895, or visit the IVCF website at <www.intervarsity.org>.

Scripture quotations, unless otherwise noted, are from the New Revised Standard Version of the Bible, copyright 1989 by the Division of Christian Education of the National Council of the Churches of Christ in the USA. Used by permission. All rights reserved.

Figure 6.1 on page 171 is used by permission. (p*EC.F6707.B638 p v.1, Houghton Library, Harvard University)

While all stories in this book are true, some names and identifying information in this book have been changed to protect the privacy of the individuals involved.

Cover design: Cindy Kiple
Interior design: Beth Hagenberg
Cover images: cross and graffiti: © manuel velasco/iStockphoto
    Jesus sign: © Ben Blankenburg/iStockphoto
    Jesus Saves: © Skyhobo/iStockphoto
    church sign: © LOU OATES/iStockphoto

ISBN 978-0-8308-3966-7

Printed in the United States of America ∞

Library of Congress Cataloging-in-Publication Data

Downing, Crystal.
  Changing signs of truth : a Christian introduction to the semiotics
of communication / Crystal L. Downing.
     p. cm.
  Includes bibliographical references and index.
  ISBN 978-0-8308-3966-7 (pbk. : alk. paper)
  1. Communication—Religious aspects—Christianity. 2.
Semiotics—Religious aspects—Christianity. 3. Signs and symbols. 4.
Christianity and culture. I. Title.
  BV4319.D69 2012
  230.01'4—dc23

                                                        2012005239

P	20	19	18	17	16	15	14	13	12	11	10	9	8	7	6	5	4	3	2	1
Y	29	28	27	26	25	24	23	22	21	20	19	18	17	16	15	14	13	12

For my father,
who left this life soon after
he entered this book.

CONTENTS

Part IV: Communication in a Pluralistic World

List of Illustrations

ACKNOWLEDGMENTS

This book was made possible by the generous support of Messiah College, which granted a sabbatical to begin the project, a scholarship chair to finish it, and funding for two Smith Scholar interns—Alyssa Lord and Abigail Long—who provided invaluable help not only in my research but also with my prose. Equally generous have been Messiah colleagues who donated time and patience while addressing my many questions. Because the "science of signs" ranges over multiple disciplines, I benefited from the expertise of Sharon Baker, Mike Cosby, George Pickens, Emerson Powery, Meg Ramey, Brian Smith, David Weaver-Zercher and John Yeatts in the Bible and religious studies department; Susanna Caroselli, David Kasparek and Ted Prescott in the art department; John Beaney, Lois Beck and Kim Yúnez in the modern languages department; Joseph Huffman and David Pettegrew in the history department; Ted Davis in science history; Carolyn Kreamer in nursing; Jenell Paris in anthropology; Kate Simcox in communication; Valerie Smith in theater; Tim Schoettle in philosophy; Doug Miller in exercise physiology; and Gene Chase in math. I am also thankful for my colleagues in the English department—including our brilliant administrative assistant, Gina Hale—who provide intellectual and emotional nourishment that energizes both my scholarship and my teaching. To that end, I need to thank my amazing students, several of whom I cite in the following pages.

I am also grateful to Regent College, in Vancouver, for inviting me to teach a graduate seminar in semiotics and Christianity during the summer of 2011. Intensely interesting conversations among a marvelous group of students added depth to this book's argument. Even more credit goes to my editor at IVP Academic, Gary Deddo, who helped me grapple with changes in Christian doctrine over the centuries. Thanks also goes to Victorianist

Tara Moore, whom I consulted about changing signs of Christmas, and to my women's writing group, "The Pinklings," whose moniker illustrates one of the points of this book: that new signs are constructed from the old. Last, but never least, I thank my husband, David C. Downing, who showers me not only with intriguing word origins but also with continual signs of love.

PREFACE TO THE PROBLEM

Christ, Culture and Communication

Christians who want to change the world—whether locally or globally—must ask themselves the following questions:

How do I know when to adapt to culture and when to resist it?
How might I change the status quo without being changed by it?
When should I challenge the status quo of Christianity itself?

These questions have become especially pronounced in the twenty-first century. Because the second millennium closed with increased openness toward faith among secular intellectuals, antagonists to Christianity felt the need to intensify their attacks on religion.[1] Called the New Atheists, they have written bestsellers with disconcerting titles:

The End of Faith
The God Delusion
God Is Not Great: How Religion Poisons Everything
God—The Failed Hypothesis: How Science Shows That God Does Not Exist[2]

Equally disturbing have been attacks coming from different beachheads of

---

[1]For openness to Christianity among academics, see Crystal Downing, *How Postmodernism Serves (My) Faith: Questioning Truth in Language, Philosophy and Art* (Downers Grove, IL: IVP Academic, 2006), esp. pp. 213-14.

[2]Sam Harris, *The End of Faith: Religion, Terror, and the Future of Reason* (New York: Norton, 2004); Richard Dawkins, *The God Delusion* (New York: Houghton Mifflin, 2006); Christopher Hitchens, *God Is Not Great: How Religion Poisons Everything* (New York: Hachette, 2007); Victor J. Stenger, *God—The Failed Hypothesis: How Science Shows That God Does Not Exist* (Amherst, NY: Prometheus, 2007). For a helpful introduction and response to the New Atheism, see John F. Haught, *God and the New Atheism: A Critical Response to Dawkins, Harris, and Hitchens* (Louisville: Westminster John Knox, 2008).

Christianity itself. Some emergent Christians have launched mortars into the trenches of ancient creeds, seeking to wipe out dogma they no longer consider relevant. In response, traditionalists mount retaliatory strikes, bombarding all camps of the emerging church indiscriminately. And both sides lob grenades at the North American megachurch, disgusted by its consumerist showmanship.[3] Meanwhile, Eastern Orthodox Christians believe that emergent as well as traditional Protestants have strayed from the path of true Christianity. And, as Pope Benedict XVI emphasizes a return to indulgences—the practice that instigated Martin Luther's Reformation—both Protestants and Eastern Orthodox Christians wonder whether the Roman Catholic Church is issuing a call to arms rather than to unity in Christ.[4] All brandish swords of the spirit, accusing their opponents of being either too tolerant or too intolerant of cultural change.

In *Changing Signs of Truth*, I hope to turn these swords into plowshares, negotiating the antagonism between Christianity and culture, as well as among Christians themselves. Of course, scores of books have already been written on the relationship between faith and culture. The granddaddy of them all, H. Richard Niebuhr's *Christ and Culture* (1951), was so influential that HarperSanFranciso published a fiftieth anniversary edition in 2001. Readers obviously valued how Niebuhr explains the five responses to culture displayed by different Christian denominations: Christ Against Culture, the Christ of Culture, Christ Above Culture, Christ and Culture in Paradox and Christ Transforming Culture.[5] Christians in the twenty-first century continue to invoke Niebuhr's categories, some approvingly, others in order to challenge them.[6]

---

[3]For a good overview of the tensions between traditionalists and the emerging church and of their common disdain for megachurch tactics, see Jim Belcher, *Deep Church: A Third Way Beyond Emerging and Traditional* (Downers Grove, IL: InterVarsity Press, 2009).

[4]See Jennifer Reeger, "Indulgences Regain Relevance Under Pope Benedict," *Tribune-Review News Service*, February 25, 2009.

[5]H. Richard Niebuhr, *Christ and Culture* (San Francisco: HarperSanFrancisco, 2001).

[6]For endorsements of Niebuhr, see James Emery White, *Serious Times: Making Your Life Matter in an Urgent Day* (Downers Grove, IL: InterVarsity Press, 2004), pp. 69-70; and John G. Stackhouse Jr., *Making the Best of It: Following Christ in the Real World* (New York: Oxford University Press, 2008). For challenges to Niebuhr, see Craig A. Carter, *Rethinking Christ and Culture: A Post-Christendom Perspective* (Grand Rapids, MI: Brazos, 2006); Graham Ward, *Christ and Culture* (Oxford: Blackwell, 2005), pp. 21-22; D. A. Carson, *Christ and Culture Revisited* (Grand Rapids, MI: Eerdmans, 2008); Andy Crouch, *Culture Making: Recovering Our Creative Calling* (Downers Grove, IL: IVP Books, 2008), pp. 178-83. See also Ray S. Anderson, who notes that *Christ and Culture* "misses the mark as essentially a product of modernity," in *An Emergent Theology for Emerg-*

In contrast, *Changing Signs of Truth* approaches the issue in new *terms*—quite literally. Of the many books written on Christ and culture, none, to the best of my knowledge, has centered its discussion on the power of signs—the *terms* we use—to change thought and behavior. Of course, it has long been known that effective rhetoric—the language we use—can generate change. This is because, as James Davison Hunter notes in *To Change the World*, "Language . . . provides the categories through which people understand themselves, others, and the larger world."[7] Communicators committed to a particular message, however, often forget that "every message is made of signs."[8]

To become an effective communicator, one must understand both verbal and visual signs: where they came from, how they function, when or why they change. And the Christian communicator must go one step further, analyzing how signs have functioned within the church in order to assess when and how they should be altered for the good of both Christ and culture.

This book is for anyone who wants to grasp a plowshare of cultivation rather than a sword of division. It is for anyone who wants to understand why signs of Christ have changed over the ages. It will demonstrate how the cultures Christians seek to change have powerfully influenced the signs they use. Hence, rather than function as yet another introduction to the art of persuasion, this book gets underneath rhetoric to the very way words work: as *effects* of the cultures we seek to *affect*.[9] In the process, however, *Changing Signs of Truth* provides strategies for how to effectively ascertain and communicate the essentials of Christian faith in our pluralistic culture.

In sum, while the New Atheists believe (or at least hope) that Christianity is on the edge of extinction, this book will suggest how Christians might be on the edge of distinction.

By providing an introduction to semiotics, the study of signs, it will offer a new way to think about changing culture: what I call (re)signing truth.

---

ing Churches (Downers Grove, IL: IVP Books, 2006), p. 58n. 12.

[7]James Davison Hunter, *To Change the World: The Irony, Tragedy, and Possibility of Christianity in the Late Modern World* (New York: Oxford University Press, 2010), p. 33.

[8]Roman Jakobson, "Language in Relation to Other Communication Systems," in *Selected Writings*, vol. 2, *Word and Language* (The Hague, Netherlands: Mouton, 1971), p. 698.

[9]As one communication theorist notes, "Contemporary rhetorical theory is naïve when it presumes that the culture of good reasons can be attained simply through the study and practice of public speaking. In rhetorical theory we rarely find an adequate account of social and political forces and determinations." See Maurice Charland, "Rehabilitating Rhetoric: Confronting Blindspots in Discourse and Social Theory," in *Contemporary Rhetorical Theory: A Reader*, ed. John Louis Lucaites, Celeste Michelle Condit and Sally Caudill (New York: Guilford, 1999), p. 471.

INTRODUCTION TO THE SOLUTION

(Re)signing Truth

I was barely eighteen and already possessed by demons.

At least I was not alone. Quivering on her bed across the room, Christy, my college roommate, struggled to comprehend our bizarre experience.

Earlier that evening we had responded to fliers placed throughout the first-year women's dorm, inviting us to hear a speaker in one of the lounges talk about a Spirit-filled life. Since both of us had chosen a Christian college for just such opportunities, we pushed aside piles of homework to attend this important event.

Somewhat surprised that only two other students showed up, we settled down on the lounge floor, ready to soak up insight. I still remember the feel of the wall against my back as I leaned away from the speaker's spit-spewing speech, trying to escape his sermon as much as his saliva. For he told us that demons, right at that very moment, were fighting for our souls. And, in order to resist them, we needed to develop a stronger relationship with the Holy Spirit.

He then informed us what *signs* to look for: anytime we couldn't concentrate in church, a demon was harassing us; anytime our minds wandered during prayer, a demon had overtaken us; anytime our stomachs hurt, a demon had invaded us; anytime we had headaches, demons had infiltrated our brains. To exorcise these signs of Satan we needed to exercise the far-stronger sign of the Spirit by speaking in tongues.

I was in agony—and not just over a demonic headache. For I had heard other Christians argue that speaking in tongues was itself a sign of the devil.

Whom was I to trust? How could I judge the correct way to interpret these distressing signs?

While this dilemma (if not evil spirit) was roiling around in my head, the speaker thrust a finger to the ceiling and pronounced, veins throbbing on his temples, "Some of you will leave here doubting what I have told you. That, my friends, is the surest sign you have a demon: the demon of doubt!"

Slowly climbing the stairs to our dorm room, Christy and I felt darkness pressing down on our shoulders. What should we think? Crawling onto our beds we looked up the Bible verses the speaker had given us, choking back tears as well as questions, for fear of the demon of doubt.

And then came a moment of grace: our floor's Resident Assistant stopped by while making her nightly rounds. After hearing our account, she said, with a shake of the head and wave of the arm, "Forget that speaker! He's famous for his extremist views. That's why so few students showed up." Our R.A. offered no Bible verses, no prayer. But what she gave us was enough: her authority as a more adept reader of signs, providing an interpretation that harmonized with our own traumatized intuitions.

THE DEMONS OF CULTURE

That night, Christy and I were exposed to a Christian subculture that read signs quite differently than anything we had ever experienced. More dramatically than in any Bible course, we discovered that signs, even among Christians, can have radically different meanings. This book, then, is about the reading of signs and the trauma they can generate. Since all signs take their meaning from the particular culture or subculture in which they are embedded, this book is also about reading culture.

I start with my "demon" experience because many Christians see contemporary American culture as overrun with demons—if not literally, then at least figuratively. Some Christians despair over signs of rampant promiscuity, indulgent perversion and the decline of family values. Others worry about signs of mindless militarism, an eroding environment and radical social injustice. Concern over signs of unbridled self-interest unites both camps, which probably would agree that American culture could use a good exorcism or two. Choosing which signs to exorcise is the problem.

Of course, any analysis of society has to read cultural signs. Most readers, however, look more at what the signs point to than at the signs themselves.

So I have written *Changing Signs of Truth* to fill a gap in the conversation between Christianity and culture. For the less we understand how signs work, the more powerfully they can control us.[1]

DEFINING A "SIGN"

Though it will take most of this book to explore the complexity of signs, we can start with the classical meaning. Latin rhetoricians defined a sign as *aliquid stat pro aliquo* or "something that stands for something else."[2] The first time I realized that one thing could stand for another thing I was traumatized. At age seven, I decided that I was old enough to collect my two-year-old brother, Garth, from the nursery after Junior Church. Knowing my parents enjoyed socializing on the sidewalk after "big church," I steered the waddling toddler toward the chatting adults.

To my horror, Garth wrapped his arms around the first pair of male legs that he encountered. Ears aflame with embarrassment, I pried his arms from the baffled man, only to suffer a repeat performance as Garth grabbed another pair of legs not the least bit attached to my father. I fought back tears as the toddler pawed every male knee he encountered. Obviously, it had not occurred to me that a two-year-old would not read signs the way a seven-year-old could. For Garth, any suit-clad leg was "Daddy," and he embraced each sign with abandon, oblivious to other important signs that distinguished one daddy from another.

This book is written for Christians who want to be more than toddlers in their faith. To a certain extent, of course, all of us are toddlers before God, whom Jesus described with the sign "our Father." We grab on to the little that has been revealed to us, praying that as we grow in grace and knowledge we will perceive more and more of the Person attached to the sign. But to get to that point we need to become more sophisticated at reading the knees that we can see.

READING THE SIGNS THAT DRIVE US

When my computer crashed during the writing of this book, a tech-support

---

[1]As rhetorician Michael Calvin McGee puts it, "Human beings are 'conditioned,' not directly to belief and behavior, but to a *vocabulary* of concepts that function as guides, warrants, reasons, or excuses for behavior and belief" (emphasis mine). See "The 'Ideograph': A Link Between Rhetoric and Ideology," in *Contemporary Rhetorical Theory: A Reader,* ed. John Luis Lucaites, Celeste Michelle Condit and Sally Caudill (New York: Guilford, 1999), p. 428.

[2]See Thomas A. Sebeok, *The Sign and Its Masters* (Austin: University of Texas Press, 1989), p. xxiv.

person tried to calm me down by asking, "What is your book about?" When I impatiently replied "signs," he blinked twice before looking out the window and pointing to the busy thoroughfare beyond his shop. "You mean like street-signs?" he asked, wondering, perhaps, if I found "Yield" to be enticingly provocative. His response reinforces the need for this book: people fail to think about the signs that they follow every day, most especially those signs that guide the way they understand and communicate truth. As one specialist in sign-theory explains, "All forms of social, cultural, and intellectual life can be viewed as sign systems: as forms of communication, and therefore as verbal or nonverbal languages."[3]

To understand the concept of a "sign system," consider the fact that even street signs reflect cultural conventions that sometimes differ from place to place. When I moved to Pennsylvania from California, I laughed the first time I saw the little red and white stop-sign that swings out from the driver's side of a school bus to demand cars both in front and behind to halt whenever the bus stops. "How cute!" I thought, soon finding it considerably less cute on days when, late to work, I must obey the sign as a school bus stops in front of every house where a child resides: a tradition that reflects the rural roots of the area where I live. Far more efficient are other stop-signs that differ from California signs: those at intersections that qualify their message—"STOP except for right turn"—signs that struck my mother during her first visit as unsafe.

In this book you will discover that, like stop-signs, many theological signs Christians hold dear are qualified by their contexts, both in place and time. Some Christians earnestly hold on to ancient signs—like speaking in tongues or transubstantiation—while others give up on those Christian traditions. Who is right? Do we surrender to traditional readings of a sign, multiplying their presence as with stop-signs on school buses, or do we qualify those signs, noting that, in certain circumstances right turns are safe?

READING SIGNS ALONG THE WAY

To negotiate heavy traffic, responsible drivers must be adept at reading signs—not only stationary signs nailed onto poles and cemented into concrete but also signs that come and go: turn signals that blink from adjacent cars, as well as signs of distraction, fatigue, intoxication and rage from other drivers.

---

[3]David Robey, introduction to Umberto Eco, *The Open Work,* trans. Anna Cancogni (Cambridge, MA: Harvard University Press, 1989), p. xx.

Similarly, to negotiate the driving forces of culture, responsible Christians must become skilled sign-readers, able to distinguish among diverse cultural powers in order to assess their threat and respond appropriately.

Unfortunately, both defensive drivers and defensive Christians are often more aware of other people's signs than of their own. Some drivers feel outrage when a car pulls out of a driveway immediately in front of them, while assuming their own right to pull into traffic or change lanes when the need arises. So also some Christians feel outrage at the direction culture is taking while never considering how their own protestations end up subverting not only their message, but also the cause of Christ.[4]

This book seeks to negotiate the aggressive forces of culture through responsible deciphering and deployment of signs. It discusses how signs work in order to argue that Christians might influence the flow of culture by changing their signs of truth. This does not mean it will call into question Christian truth itself.

The Christian journey focuses upon truth as embodied in Jesus Christ. He is the unchanging destination and the Bible is the time-honored map. However, like any map, the Bible is a network of signs that offers multiple intersecting routes to the final destination: law and grace, free will and determinism, faith and works, mercy and justice, tradition and change. Furthermore, reading a map differs considerably from the lived experience of driving roads while attending to the signs along the way—signs that indicate some roads are more efficient, scenic, hazardous or congested than others.

The experience of driving a route with map in hand is like living in culture with Bible in hand. Even the most detailed map cannot tell drivers how to handle new construction, geological changes, storms, detours and accidents. Therefore, without giving up on the final destination or the guidance of the original map, Christians must venture out on new routes as the signs of culture change, sometimes altering their own signs to aid those who have never studied the map. "The true quality of a sign," as Raymond Williams explains, "is that it is effective in communication." Hence, "as a function of continuing social activity [a sign] is capable of modification and development."[5]

---

[4]Think, for example, of the "God Hates Fags" signs that members of Westboro Baptist Church display at funerals. Wikipedia has a good overview of Westboro's demonstrations: http://en .wikipedia.org/wiki/Westboro_Baptist_Church.

[5]Raymond Williams, "Language as Sociality," in *The Raymond Williams Reader*, ed. John Higgins (Oxford: Blackwell, 2001), p. 203.

(RE)SIGNING TRUTH

This negotiation between an unchanging destination and changing signs along the way I call "the (re)signing of truth."[6] *Resigned* to the truth of the map, Christians, embedded in an ever-changing culture, must sometimes *re-sign* how to get to our final destination.

I have coined *(re)signing,* then, to capture the argument of this book:

• The parentheses in *(re)signing* place the emphasis on "signing," indicating that the signs Christians use reflect the influence of both Christ and culture.

• Our "signing," then, expresses who we are and what we value.

• For any Christian who values effective communication, however, the parenthetical (re) is essential, expressing two necessary components of our "signing"—resigning and re-signing:

    1. As Christians, we are *resigned* to essential truths revealed by God.

    2. As communicators we recognize the need to *re-sign* those truths, generating fresh signs that make ancient truths meaningful to contemporary audiences.

Quite understandably, some readers may dislike the apparent passivity of my phrase "resigned to." It calls to mind a "lukewarm" believer who comments, with a sigh, "Well, I guess I'm resigned to the teachings of Christianity."

In contrast, I wish to reinvigorate the word by resurrecting its original definitions, arguing that "Yield" is, indeed, a provocative sign. In 1366, when "resign" first appeared in English, it meant "to yield up (oneself, etc.) with confidence *to* another for care or guidance."[7] The Latin word "confidence" in the definition is telling, implying that surrendering oneself must be done with faith: *con-fideo.* By 1450, when *De Imitatione Christi* (usually attributed to Thomas à Kempis) was translated into English, "resignation" meant "a giving up of oneself to God" *(OED).*

Such resignation fuels the questions driving this book. How do we give ourselves up to God without giving up on culture? How do we know when to resign ourselves to traditional signs of the Church universal, believing in their signifi-

---

[6]After I finished the first draft of this book, I discovered that another Christian writer has employed the pun (re)signing. I will discuss how he uses the term in my conclusion.

[7]Unless otherwise noted, all word origins throughout this book come from the definitive source for English etymologies, *The Oxford English Dictionary Online,* henceforward cited in the text as *OED.*

cance against all odds, and, harder yet, how do we know when we should depart from the use of traditional signs, regarding them as no longer guiding seekers to the goal of radical discipleship? At the same time, how do we ascertain when the desire to give new signs to Christian truth—to re-sign it—merely operates as an unnecessary resignation to trendy, often ephemeral, cultural values?

(RE)SIGNING CHRIST AND CULTURE: ACCOMMODATION VERSUS SEPARATION

As noted in the preface, J. Richard Niebuhr outlined five ways that Christians respond to such questions: Christ Against Culture, the Christ of Culture, Christ Above Culture, Christ and Culture in Paradox and Christ Transforming Culture.[8] My colleague Milton Gaither wryly asserts that Niebuhr needed another category—"Christ Following Culture"—in order to identify those believers seeking to make Christianity seem *neat, groovy, hip, phat, cool, hot, wicked*—or *whatever*.[9] My italicized words illustrate the problem with making Christianity sound "up to date": contemporary signs turn tacky all too quickly. The embarrassed harumph and rolled eyes of an adolescent whose mom has just used his teenage slang illustrates that adding new tar to old tarmac can get pretty sticky.

Worse, some Christians can get so caught up in making the road attractive to seekers that they lose sight of the final destination: a countercultural life in Christ. As Southern Baptist theologian John Hammett astutely notes, the church "always faces the twin dangers of cultural captivity and cultural irrelevance." However, in his worry over cultural assimilation, Hammett opts for what Niebuhr calls "Christ against culture."[10]

Niebuhr illustrates "Christ against culture" with Anabaptist Mennonites, who "represent the attitude most purely, since they not only renounce all participation in politics and refuse to be drawn into military service, but follow their own distinctive customs and regulations in economics and education."[11] I am not the first to question Niebuhr's pigeonholing of Mennonites, who are often the best communicators I know, energetically en-

---

[8]H. Richard Niebuhr, *Christ and Culture* (San Francisco: HarperSanFrancisco, 2001).
[9]Milton Gaither, "Beyond Mimesis: Higher Education, Rock and Roll, and Christian Tradition," Presidential Scholars Lecture, Messiah College, November 1, 2001.
[10]Quoted in Jim Belcher, *Deep Church: A Third Way Beyond Emerging and Traditional* (Downers Grove, IL: InterVarsity Press, 2009), p. 170.
[11]Niebuhr, *Christ and Culture*, p. 56.

gaging culture through educational and political activism.[12] Nevertheless, it
is true that Old Order Mennonite and Amish Christians, committed to the

Figure I.1. Scripture sign on Mennonite gate

biblical truth "Be ye separate" (2 Cor 6:17 KJV),
demonstrate their sepa-
ration from culture with
numerous signs: using
straight pins rather than
buttons or zippers on their
clothing; driving horse-
drawn buggies rather
than cars; abstaining from
electricity; renouncing
tires on their tractors. In
addition, Mennonites in
my home state of Pennsylvania often put Bible signs at the edge of their farms
as a testimony to how Christ, rather than culture, guides their lives.

Displaying such signs, these Anabaptists fulfill scriptural admonitions:

> You shall love the LORD your God with all your heart, and with all your soul,
> and with all your might. Keep these words that I am commanding you today
> in your heart. . . . Bind them as a *sign* on your hand, fix them as an emblem on
> your forehead, and write them on the doorposts of your house and on your
> gates. (Deut 6:5-9, emphasis mine)[13]

Most evangelicals, while emphatically affirming the first two verses of this
passage, consider the last verse outdated, regarding gate-signs unnecessary.
Rather than posting signs of "Christ against culture," they choose what Niebuhr
calls "Christ transforming culture." Unfortunately, as Craig Carter argues,
"Christ transforming culture" can easily "lead to the accommodation of Christianity to the culture"[14]—to what my colleague calls "Christ following culture."

---

[12]See, for example, Craig A. Carter, *Rethinking Christ and Culture: A Post-Christendom Perspective*
(Grand Rapids, MI: Brazos, 2006).
[13]See also Deut 11:18-20. Thanks to my student Alyssa Lord for drawing my attention to this biblical basis for Mennonite gate signs.
[14]Carter, *Rethinking Christ and Culture*, pp. 24-25. Andy Crouch notes that "initially the call for
'transforming culture' was embraced by Niebuhr's fellow mainline Protestants, but it has become
the rallying cry for more conservative Christians as well." Andy Crouch, *Culture Making: Recovering Our Creative Calling* (Downers Grove, IL: IVP Books, 2008), p. 180.

German theologian Jürgen Moltmann calls the tension between accommodation and irrelevance "the identity-involvement dilemma":

> The more theology and the church attempt to become relevant to the problems of the present day, the more deeply they are drawn into a crisis of their own identity. The more they attempt to assert their identity in traditional dogmas, rights and moral notions, the more irrelevant and unbelievable they become.[15]

Rather than endorsing one of these two positions—accommodation versus separation—*Changing Signs of Truth* suggests how believers might operate on the edge between cultural captivity and cultural irrelevance. It is not about employing the trendy signs of culture to make Christianity seem relevant. It is about demonstrating that Christianity always has relevance—no matter the time, no matter the culture. This demonstration, however, requires us to reconsider and recalibrate signs that made sense to one generation and/or culture but that obscure or deflect Christian truth in another. Let me give some concrete examples.

(RE)DESIGNING CLOTHING

Most American Christians do not wear caftans—even though these sheath-like robes are much closer to the clothing of Jesus and his disciples than anything we can buy at the local mall. Similarly, most women today do not wear head-coverings, even though Paul encourages it: a biblical admonition the Amish and Old Order Mennonites take much more seriously than do most other Christians (1 Cor 11:4-10). I, in fact, still remember the day my mother (re)signed Christian truth about head-coverings.

In my parents' bedroom was a mysterious closet—great for hide and seek—that was entirely dedicated to hats. An air of sanctity pervaded the closet—not only due to its mothball incense or the scolding we received when hats got crushed as hide-and-seek turned into contact sport. More importantly, we knew that the hats were signs of Mother's obedience to a biblical principle: "Judge for yourselves: is it proper for a woman to pray to God with her head unveiled?" (1 Cor 11:13). Every Sunday Mother would don a hat, and when she became a Teaching Leader for Bible Study Fellowship, she wore a hat midweek as well. She became known as "the hat lady" among my playmates, for their mothers had given up hats years before.

---

[15]Jürgen Moltmann, *The Crucified God* (New York: Harper & Row, 1974), p. 7.

Then, one day, Mother stopped wearing hats. Though still resigned to the truth of Scripture and obedience to God, she considered the sign of a hat no longer necessary for her faith. External circumstances and secular culture helped mold her decision. First, a leak in the closet roof ruined her collection, making her wonder if money for replacements might be better spent on people who could barely afford clothes, let alone hats. Second, hats in church had become so out of fashion that she had become a sign of something passé rather than a living, vibrant truth.

Figure I.2. Collin's tattoos

(RE)DESIGNING THE BODY

Let me give a more edgy example than women's hats. My nephew Collin has several large tattoos, something I was taught dishonored the "temple of the Holy Spirit" (1 Cor 6:19), due to the proscription stated in Leviticus 19:28. But Collin's tattoos indicate his commitment to "glorify God in your body" (1 Cor 6:20), with a cross etched on one of his pectorals, and his back licked with tongues of fire that proclaim his HOPE in Jesus.

Collin's tattoos are both a sign of Christ and of culture, his generation more ready to embrace body art than mine. Collin has (re)signed truth: resigned to following Christ, he, quite literally, has re-signed discipleship of the body.[16] It would seem that sometimes we follow the signs of Christ, sometimes the signs of culture. And sometimes we do both simultaneously.

(RE)SIGNING THE BODY OF CHRIST

Like individual bodies, sometimes the body of Christ—or at least a part of the body—decides to re-sign truth. I still remember my peers exchanging "St. Christopher medals" on the grammar school playground as signs they were "going steady." Then, in 1969, the medals hanging around their necks

---

[16]Many times "new" practices echo, often unknowingly, ancient Christian paradigms. For example, fifteenth-century Ethiopians tattooed "their foreheads with the words 'Father, Son and Holy Spirit,'" a tradition (re)signed by contemporary Ethiopian Christians, many of whom tattoo a blue cross on their chins or foreheads. See Diarmaid MacCulloch, *Christianity: The First Three Thousand Years* (New York: Penguin Viking, 2010), p. 283.

lost signifying power, the Roman Catholic church having gone through a process of (re)signing. Though resigned to the importance of Christopher in Church tradition, the Vatican re-signed its Calendar of Saints, removing the feast day of Christopher, since his sainthood seemed based on legend more than historical documentation.

At the time, I, a priggish Protestant, thought to myself, *It's about time they got rid of those superstitious Christophers around their necks!* I failed to recognize that I had quite similarly resigned myself to problematic signs of saintliness within my own evangelical tradition. My St. Christopher was smoking and drinking—or rather the lack thereof. I assumed that Christians who imbibed could not be earnest about their faith, and that cigarettes signaled belief gone up in smoke. Rather than a St. Christopher, these signs had turned into an albatross hanging around my neck.

SIGN OF THE ALBATROSS

"Instead of the cross, the Albatross / About my neck was hung." With these words the narrator of Coleridge's famous poem "The Rime of the Ancient Mariner" (ca. 1798) tells us what happened after he arbitrarily killed an albatross that had guided his ship through treacherous waters. Rather than killing an albatross, judgmental Christians often kill the grace guiding the ship of Christianity (think of the Holy Spirit's classic depiction as a bird). Once killed, the guiding spirit of grace becomes the albatross of self-righteousness hanging around our necks like a chain.

As a result of his violent act, Coleridge's Ancient Mariner is haunted by demons more terrifying than those I encountered my first year of college. They are exorcised only when the Mariner responds with a "spring of love" toward signs he originally found disturbing. First seeing water snakes as "a thousand thousand slimy things," he recognized their "beauty" and "blessed them unaware" (lines 238, 283-85). By this exercise of love, the Mariner is released from the sign of his selfishness:

> The selfsame moment I could pray;
> And from my neck so free
> The Albatross fell off, and sank
> Like lead into the sea. (lines 288-91)

Similarly, only when I exercised love for a user of water-snake–like signs did my albatross fall. For me the sign-user was C. S. Lewis, whose writings enriched my faith not long after my brief bout with demons. When I discovered that this brilliant follower of Christ not only smoked but also drank—often both at the same sitting—I "blessed [the signs] unaware" and was released from my albatross of judgmental self-righteousness.

This book is about blessing the signs of culture unaware. I say "unaware" because I do not at all mean the conscious advocacy of tobacco and beer. C. S. Lewis would probably have lived longer if he had cut back on both. Instead, I echo the Ancient Mariner's "I bless them unaware" to say that Christians are called to love the whole world, which includes the cultures in which we are embedded. For only by loving culture can we become effective communicators within it.

BLESSING CULTURE

The word *culture* comes from a Latin word that means "to till, cultivate, take care of"—actions associated with love rather than contempt. In fact, by 1483 "culture" had become aligned with "worship," based on the idea of "cultivating" a relationship with God. We still retain the concept of "worship" in our word "cult."

Culture as an act of worship preceded the word *agriculture* by 120 years; the *agri-* root, meaning "field," was added to *culture* in 1603. And long before English speakers thought to coin a word about tilling a field, they regarded culture as the tilling of one's "mind, faculties, or manners." The idea of cultivating a relationship with God and cultivating oneself are closely related *(OED)*.

The word *culture,* however, carries negative connotations for many Christians. Instead of an activity aimed at growth, it has become a place: the field of contemporary society where Christian faith gets plowed under. It is an "agri" of dirty soil, bearing crops of intemperance, self-indulgence and violence, breeding the "thorns" that "choke the word" of God (Mt 13:22).

Rather than talk about culture as a field to which Christians react, either by washing their hands of it or by working with and within it, I want to focus on the crops themselves: the signs that are generated by our cultural fields, signs that either nourish the soil or deplete it. By analyzing how we might rotate crops, I want to return us to the idea of culture as an activity rather than a place. Of course, all activity occurs in some kind of field, whether a domestic, commercial, religious, educational, artistic, athletic or governmental locale. Rather than obsessing about the dirt in these fields, I want to encourage the activity of Christian cultivation—by which I mean not only Christians sowing new seeds but also the cultivation of ourselves as Christians, which means growth and change. As any farmer can tell you, soil becomes depleted of nutrients if the same crop is planted over and over. I would say the same thing about signs: using the same signs over and over will make them less helpful to those who need spiritual nourishing.

Furthermore, some cultural signs assumed to be weeds or thorns choking out the Word of God might have beneficial effects. Just think of drums and electric guitars in church, which some Christians disdained—especially when they first appeared—as signs of thorny paganism. But, as many Christians today will attest, such instruments can enrich and deepen the worship of God. When they do so, these so-called pagan signs function like the "beneficial weeds" organic gardeners intersperse with their crops in order to keep insects at bay. Practicing "companion planting," these gardeners study which weeds help seeds reach fruition and which impede their growth.[17]

In *Culture Making*, Andy Crouch notes that God, the very first cultivator, asks us "to imitate him by cultivating the initial gift of a well-arranged garden, a world where intelligence, skill and imagination have already begun to make something of the world."[18] On his opening page, Crouch reports that Christians committed to "engaging culture" have been "looking, with surprising success, for hopeful *signs* of God in the world outside the church and also finding, with depressing frequency, *signs* of the enduring emptiness of that same world."[19] My book focuses on those signs, providing lessons on accurately reading them, understanding where they come from and knowing how to reinforce or change them.

SIGNS OF COMMUNICATION

Signs, of course, are the means by which we communicate. They indicate that we are more than vegetables, that we have spirit, or, in the Latin, *anima*. What distinguishes humans from other animals, however, is the ability to create new

---

[17]Credit goes to my research assistant, Abigail Long, for suggesting the analogy of "companion planting."
[18]Crouch, *Culture Making*, p. 108.
[19]Ibid., p. 9, emphasis mine.

signs. Though certain creatures like chimpanzees and dolphins can be taught to use a narrow range of signs, only humans can generate signs about signs, as manifest in academic disciplines, effective sermons, art and the media. This is our crowning glory, making us only "a little lower than God" (Ps 8:5). Communication theorist Quentin J. Schultze, in fact, encourages Christians to think of themselves as "cocreators" with God: "We are marvelously made creatures who imitate God's own creative ability to cultivate creation."[20]

I endorse Schultze's emphasis on communication as "cocreation," seeing it as part of Crouch's call to "culture making." To effectively do both, however, we need a sophisticated understanding of how signs work. Without this understanding, attempts can backfire, such that secular culture ends up marring the maker. For example, in 2009 a Christian publisher planned to market a book called *Love Is in the Mix* filled with recipes and family-values insights from Kate Gosselin, star of a popular "reality television" show called *Jon & Kate Plus Eight*. However, after several adulterous affairs came to light, the Gosselin marriage spiraled out of control with vitriolic accusations and nasty arguments. Fortunately, the book was halted mid-production. But what if it had come out immediately before the tawdry behavior of the Christian couple was exposed? It would have provided ammunition for those who denounce Christianity as hypocritical.[21]

Christian books based on television stars all too often exemplify "Christ following culture": Christians using secular signs in order to seem relevant (or make money). (Re)signing Christians, in contrast, create and communicate *new* signs that provoke people to think in *new* ways about ancient truths. *Changing Signs of Truth*, then, is predicated upon a basic assumption of communication studies, as summarized by James Boyd White:

> Language is not stable but changing[,] and . . . it is perpetually remade by its speakers, who are themselves remade, both as individuals and communities, in what they say. . . . Our subject is rhetoric, if by that is meant the study of the ways in which character and community—and motive, value, reason, social structure, everything, in short, that makes a culture—are defined and made real in performances of language.[22]

---

[20]Quentin J. Schultze, *Communicating for Life: Christian Stewardship in Community and Media* (Grand Rapids, MI: Baker Academic, 2000), p. 21.
[21]"Christian Publisher Still Plans Kate Gosselin Book," *USA Today.com*, posted June 25, 2009.
[22]James Boyd White, *When Words Lose Their Meanings* (Chicago: University of Chicago Press, 1984), pp. x-xi.

To exemplify a performance of language that helped change culture, I offer you the new signs created by theologian John Wyclif (ca. 1320-1384).

COCREATION AND CULTURE-MAKING: THE (RE)SIGNING OF JOHN WYCLIF

Often called "The Morning Star of the Reformation," Wyclif challenged signs of the Church 150 years before Martin Luther nailed his protests to the Wittenberg door. Rather than simply denounce signs of Christianity that disturbed him, he, like Luther, cultivated new signs, supervising a translation of the Bible into the language of the common people. The *OED*, in fact, credits Wyclif with coining many new English signs, including a new application of the word *resign*. As we have seen, early definitions of "resign" aligned the word with "submit." But in 1380 Wyclif denounced Christians that "resign not their benefits gotten thus by simony," which is the buying or selling of official positions in Church leadership (*OED*, my updated spelling). By attacking this perverted sign of Christianity, Wyclif employs "resign" to mean the relinquishment of something one has benefited from, as in "I resign!" delivered before a boss can yell "You're fired!"

Though many leaders in the Church shared Wyclif's disdain for simony, most were not ready to give up on other signs Wyclif attacked, such as the doctrine of transubstantiation, wherein Eucharist bread and wine are believed to transform into the flesh and blood of Jesus.[23] Therefore, as often happens when a Christian speaks out against an ancient sign of Christianity, Church leaders denounced Wyclif, just as they would later excommunicate Luther.

Several of Wyclif's Oxford University colleagues came to his defense, asserting that many of Wyclif's tenets were based in Christian orthodoxy, "though their expression might admit of a wrong interpretation."[24] In other words, they recognized that Wyclif was (re)signing truth: resigned to orthodox Christianity, Wyclif wanted to re-sign it, offering new signs that traditionalists considered unorthodox. Nevertheless, in response to his culture

---

[23]As MacCulloch notes, in addition to Wyclif's denunciations of transubstantiation, Church leadership was greatly disturbed by Wyclif's argument that "since all authority to rule or the right to own property (*dominium*) was in the hands of God, only those in a state of grace could enjoy them," and therefore, "it was more likely that rulers chosen by God like kings or princes were in this happy condition than was the pope" (*Christianity*, p. 568).

[24]Reginald Lane Poole, "Wyclif," in *Encyclopedia Britannica: A New Survey of Universal Knowledge*, vol. 24 (Chicago: University of Chicago Press, 1949), p. 823.

making, the (re)signer was fired—quite literally: after Wyclif died of a stroke in 1382, the pope ordered that his bones be exhumed and burned to oblivion.

SIGNS OF *CHANGING SIGNS:* AN OVERVIEW

Inspired by Wyclif, this book provides an education on signs in order to delineate how Christians can (re)sign without getting fired. And just as Wyclif took great pains in his translation to make Scripture understandable to English speakers, I have taken great pains in my organization of this book to make sign-theory accessible. I therefore urge you to read the chapters in order, for each builds on its predecessor to offer a more and more complex theory of the sign and its relevance to the communication of Christian faith.

Part one, "Signs of Christ and Culture," focuses on how we understand and respond to signs: those of culture and those of Christ. Chapter one, "Signs of the Times," discusses a problem often manifest in contemporary society: idealizing either signs of the past or signs of the future, usually associated with the problematic words "conservative" and "liberal." Proposing, instead, a faith that functions on the edge between past and future, conservative and liberal, I introduce the primary metaphor of the book: a coin on edge. The chapter ends by giving the example of a famous (re)signer who kept the coin on edge: William Tyndale.

Chapter two employs examples from the life of Jesus to argue that to follow Christ is to follow his example of (re)signing. I then apply this principle to the Bible, which, like Jesus, is the Word of God. This chapter therefore demonstrates that I practice what I preach: I am resigned to an ancient Christian tradition of re-signing tradition.

The problem, of course, comes in identifying not only which traditions need re-signing, but also when and how change should occur. Therefore, part two, "How Signs Work," provides an introduction to the "science of signs." It identifies not only how signs work, but also how signs identify us—an issue everyone who identifies with Christ must consider. As part of this process, chapter three introduces "semiotics," the scholarly study of signs, tracing its historical connections to both classical rhetoric and the early church. I end the chapter focusing attention on one of the two grandfathers of semiotics, Ferdinand de Saussure, who had a profound impact on twentieth-century scholarship.

Chapter four begins with an incident from *The Silver Chair,* one of C. S. Lewis's Narnia chronicles, in order to illustrate structuralism, which developed out of the theories of Saussure. Because structuralism influenced disciplines that focus on communication—linguistics, anthropology, literature and psychology—the chapter introduces some of the most famous structuralist scholars in those fields. It closes with a case study, showing how structuralism might help us understand the (re)signing of Christmas down through the millennia.

Structuralism even affected Marxism, which is discussed in chapter five. The academic discipline of cultural studies, in fact, was ignited by the encounter between structuralism and Marxism. This chapter considers signs from twenty-first-century culture—like sexting, teeth-whitening treatments, self-esteem and shopping—in order to explain what the "cultural materialists" have to say about the relationship between signs and their contexts.

Unfortunately, both structuralists and cultural materialists dismiss religion, regarding it either as one structure among many structural truths or as an insidious form of ideology. Thus, part three, "Changing Signs of Faith," offers approaches to the sign more consonant with Christian thought. Chapter six introduces deconstruction, which developed in reaction to structuralism. The father of deconstruction, Derrida, opened up communication to what he called the "messianic," and this chapter will explain how and why. As an example of fruitful deconstruction, Derrida offers the name of Charles Sanders Peirce, the second grandfather of semiotics. Chapter seven therefore explains the theories of Peirce, applying some of his most famous insights to help us understand changing signs within the history of Christianity. In chapter eight I show how Peirce's theory of the sign reinforces a fundamental doctrine of Christianity: the Trinity. I thus demonstrate how semiotics can provide a new way to communicate the truth of Christianity.

Part four, "Communication in a Pluralistic World," builds on all that came before in order to suggest how semiotics might change the way we think about Christian rhetoric. Chapter nine grapples with signs of tolerance versus intolerance in order to address the tension between religious pluralism and Christian faith. It argues that the fundamental doctrine of Christianity, the gift of salvation, can reorient how we fruitfully communicate the truth of Christianity in a pluralistic world. Chapter ten introduces the semiotic theory of Mikhail Bakhtin in order to discuss how signs reflect the experience of our bodies. As a Russian Orthodox Christian, Bakhtin provides a theory of communication based upon the incarnation, a theory I illustrate with the changing signs of Christ's atonement down through the ages. Bakhtin illustrates the best ideas gleaned from theorists introduced earlier in my book, which is why I present him last.

The conclusion ties the various strands of the book together, offering practical guidelines for "recovering our creative calling" through the (re)signing of truth.[25] After discussing the human resistance to new signs, I suggest how individual Christians can surmount such resistance in order to develop rhetoric that functions "on the edge." I finish with ten principles, based on insights from earlier chapters, that guide effective (re)signing.

RIME OF A NOT-SO-ANCIENT (RE)SIGNER

Lest you are unsure about the direction of this book, let me make explicit what motivates its narrative. As summarized by the chastened Mariner in Coleridge's famous poem, *Changing Signs of Truth* sets sail according to a seaworthy belief:

> He prayeth best, who loveth best
> All things both great and small;
> For the dear God who loveth us,
> He made and loveth all. (lines 614-17)

Written with prayer and love, *Changing Signs of Truth* brings together the signs of culture with those of Christ in order to argue for a faith that creatively re-signs the truth to which it is resigned.

---

[25]The quoted phrase is the subtitle of *Culture Making* by Andy Crouch.

Part I

Signs of Christ and Culture

1

SIGNS OF THE TIMES

On the Edge of Cultural Change

For many Christians, contemporary culture is going down the drain faster than dirty dishwater. Politicians, cheating on constituents as well as spouses, appear more interested in their privileges and perks than the welfare of America. Business leaders bilk investors out of billions while gilding their own nest-eggs. Hollywood celebrities check in and out of rehab faster than finches at a bird-feeder. And media pundits wallow in the mud, slinging dirty denunciations at anyone who disagrees with their political opinions.

Summarizing contemporary culture in an essay titled "Signs of the Times," one cultural critic put it this way: "public principle is gone; private honesty is going; society, in short, is fast falling in pieces; and a time of unmixed evil is come on us." This apt statement appeared, however, in 1829, describing the English culture of its author, Thomas Carlyle (1795-1881).[1] With apologies to Bob Dylan, it would seem that the times are *not* a-changin'. Despite the fact that advances in technology alter the tools with which people commit abusive and destructive acts, "public principle" and "private honesty" have long been lamented. Nevertheless, we continue to hear pronouncements, like those of Carlyle, about the superiority of the past.[2]

---

[1]Thomas Carlyle, "Signs of the Times," in *The Collected Works*, vol. 3 (London: Chapman and Hall, 1858), p. 100. Born in Scotland, Carlyle was raised in a strict Calvinist home but lost his faith before he moved to London, where he became a celebrated intellectual and very powerful influence on Victorian sensibilities.

[2]Take, for example, a statement made in November 2009 by an emeritus professor of public policy: "Personal restraint and dignity have gone out the window. Something is awry with our culture and our character." Robert J. Bresler, "Dress for Success? It's No Longer a Standard," *The Patriot-News* (Harrisburg, PA), November 4, 2009, A-17.

Before we can explore the (re)signing of Christian truth, we need to consider this human tendency to idealize the past. At the same time, we must assess the equal but opposite tendency—especially strong among secular humanists—to idealize the future. Both idealizations, I will argue, impede the cause of Christ. As an alternative, I will suggest how a life-changing Christianity might function on the edge between future and past.

SIGNS OF PAST TIMES: THE GREATEST GENERATION

The title of Tom Brokaw's bestselling book, *The Greatest Generation*, tells it all: the people that lived through the Great Depression and World War II were far greater than the self-serving, stimulation-addicted leaders of today.[3] This assumption leads many to believe that the only (re)signing Christians should consider is a resigning from present decadence, achieved through a return to the family-values and personal integrity of the "greatest generation."

Any study of 1940s America, however, necessitates an asterisk after *Greatest* in Brokaw's title. Doris Kearns Goodwin's title for the same era is perhaps more appropriate: *No Ordinary Time*. Indeed, there were extraordinary acts of heroism and self-denial during World War II—as in our own times. But there were also extraordinary injustices in America. Goodwin tells of U.S. army posts in which black military personnel were not allowed to eat inside buildings where refreshments were regularly served to white soldiers.[4]

I had an experience in 1999 that reinforces Goodwin's disturbing scenario. While visiting Munich, my husband and I met an elderly German who told us he had been a prisoner of war in the 1940s, interned in a camp in a southern U.S. state. He recalled that German prisoners were allowed to attend local movies but that their black American guards could not enter the theaters due to the color of their skin. The white skin of an American enemy was more welcome than the black skin of an American serving his country.

Even apart from racism, the greatest generation wasn't always so great. My father-in-law tells of returning to his ship, the U.S.S. *West Virginia*, after its bombing in Pearl Harbor, only to witness American sailors from other ships stealing watches and wallets off of the dead bodies of crew members.

When people despair over the self-serving agendas of politicians these

---

[3]Tom Brokaw, *The Greatest Generation* (New York: Random House, 1998).
[4]Doris Kearns Goodwin, *No Ordinary Time: Franklin and Eleanor Roosevelt: The Home Front in World War II* (New York: Touchstone, 1995), p. 422.

days, they often forget notoriously corrupt congressmen in the past. In 1919, for example, congress voted an Eighteenth Amendment into the United States Constitution which prohibited the manufacture, sale and transportation of alcohol. However, soon after Prohibition went into effect (1920), senators and congressmen were secretly buying alcohol that they had made illegal for the rest of the country. In fact, office space was made available in official government buildings so that politicians could easily purchase something that they had forbidden to everyone else.

MYSTIFYING PAST SIGNS

When people idealize the past, they "mystify" it: a word many scholars use to denote the smokescreen that covers over actual problems. Unfortunately, even the most biblically literate Christians often mystify the past while denouncing signs of their own times. In his lectures on Genesis, Martin Luther (1483-1546) despaired, "in our age, in these dregs of the world, there is such great wickedness, and there are such manifold instances of fraud and deceit that you do not know what to do for anyone." He contrasted such signs of his times with the age of the Old Testament, when "there was not such a large number of vagabonds and scoundrels in the world as there is today." John Calvin (1509-1564) made a similar assessment of Old Testament times, belittling his own sixteenth-century France in comparison to the age of Abraham: "At that time, there was greater honesty than is, at present, to be found among the prevailing perfidy of mankind."[5] I wonder, however, whether he would call it "honesty" when Abraham lied multiple times about his wife Sarah, telling Pharaoh in Egypt as well as King Abimelech in Gerar that she was his sister, willing to have them sleep with her "so that it may go well with me" (Gen 12:10-19; 20:1-6). One does not need to be a scholar of ancient Hebrew to come up with examples of wickedness among the patriarchs; one need only read the Bible.

So why do we idealize "the good ol' days"? The behavior of young adults might give us a clue. As a college professor, I notice that each generation of students gets nostalgic about the era of its childhood, sentimentalizing signs of a time when life seemed more innocent. They throw parties where they

---

[5]Martin Luther, "Lectures on Genesis Chapters 15-20," and "Lectures on Genesis Chapters 21-25," in *Luther's Works*, ed. Jaroslav Pelikan and Helmut T. Lehman, 55 vols. (Philadelphia: Fortress, 1955-1976), 3:245; 4:282. John Calvin, *Commentaries on the First Book of Moses Called Genesis*, vol. 1 (Grand Rapids, MI: Eerdmans, 1948), p. 470.

don retro-fashions, and some become avid fans of television shows set in the era of their childhood. Meanwhile, parents bemoan the self-indulgence of their children's generation while idealizing their own youth as being more authentic: "When I was in college, we got along just fine without microwaves, refrigerators, televisions and DVD players in our dorm rooms." Or, as my father told me a generation earlier, "I walked through a mile of snow and ice for the privilege of attending school."

Signs of childhood times inevitably seem more innocent than contemporary signs (at least for those who grew up in nonabusive homes). But perhaps rather than the *times* being more innocent, it was the ability to *read signs* that was more innocent. Children in loving homes conclude that their parents are signs of adulthood: signs of fairness, stability and integrity.

My parents so emphasized fairness in the way they doled out both punishments and presents that I was shocked to discover that life is not fair, that adults, even fellow Christians, can be petty, selfish, manipulative and dishonest. It was not the times that had changed, however; the change was in my exposure to new signs. I was slowly learning that, to understand my times, I needed to understand signs—both past and present—rather than merely long for "the good ol' days."

In 1646, Sir Thomas Browne aptly summarized the human impulse to disparage the present in favor of the values of the past:

> It is the humour of many heads to extol the days of their forefathers, and declaim against the wickedness of times present. Which notwithstanding they cannot handsomely do, without the borrowed help and satire of times past; condemning the vices of their own times, by the expressions of vices in times which they commend, which cannot but argue the community of vice in both.[6]

This is one among many "Commonly Presumed Truths" that Browne discusses in his book *The Epidemic of False Doctrine*. I would suggest that the wickedness of present signs, in contrast to the past, is "a commonly presumed truth" that needs (re)signing—in the full sense of the term as I have introduced it. In other words, we need to resign ourselves to the fact that every generation contains "manifold instances of fraud and deceit," with "vaga-

---

[6]Sir Thomas Browne, *Pseudodoxia Epidemica: Enquiries into Very Many Received Tenets and Commonly Presumed Truths*, quoted in George Eliot, *Middlemarch* (New York: Signet, 2003), p. 468.

bonds and scoundrels" in abundance. At the same time, we must recognize that change in the present—the re-signing of truth—is always built on signs of the past. Rather than "either/or" thinking, pitting a preferable past against the pernicious present, I will urge "both/and" thinking: past and present in constant communication with each other.

PROBLEMS WITH THE CHRISTIAN PAST

Communication between past and present is easier said than done. For one thing, different Christians idealize different pasts. When Protestants speak of "the importance of the past," they often refer to the theology of sixteenth-century Reformers like Luther and Calvin. This may seem ironic to Roman Catholics, who look to a tradition established well over a thousand years earlier, when the sign "pope" was first applied to the bishop of Rome in the last half of the fourth century.

Eastern Orthodox Christians, in contrast, consider the bishop of Rome just one bishop among many. They define their past through doctrine established by the first seven ecumenical councils (gatherings of bishops), held between the fourth and eighth centuries, before their "Great Schism" with the Roman Church in 1054. The first council, which determined that Jesus was "begotten, not made," was convened in 325 by the Emperor Constantine, who founded the city of Constantinople (present day Istanbul). Three of the seven ecumenical councils were held in Constantinople, which the Eastern Church considers more significant to the history of Christianity than Rome.

Mennonites look to an even earlier past: that which preceded the first ecumenical council. As far as they are concerned, Emperor Constantine, by making Christianity acceptable to the Roman Empire, paved the way for the tainting of Christianity by political power. Hence, a sign of Mennonite theology is language about "pre-Constantinian Christianity" and "anti-Constantinianism."[7] Unlike Constantine, who killed his enemies and even some of his uncooperative family members, Mennonites refuse to go to war, identifying with the earliest Christians who did not fight back when they were persecuted by emperors that preceded Constantine.

Pentecostal Christians align themselves with a yet more ancient past: the

---

[7]For the complexity of Anabaptist responses to Constantinianism, see J. Alexander Sider, *To See History Doxologically: History and Holiness in John Howard Yoder's Ecclesiology* (Grand Rapids, MI: Eerdmans, 2011), chaps. 2-3.

Day of Pentecost described in the second chapter of Acts. Asserting that speaking in tongues still operates as the sign of the Holy Spirit in the twenty-first century, Pentecostals could argue that they endorse a more biblically based view of Christianity than does the first ecumenical council, which established a new sign not found in Scripture: Jesus was "of one substance" with the Father. The Greek word we translate as "of one substance" *(homoousios)* appears nowhere in the New Testament. But speaking in a Spirit-inspired "tongue" *(glossa)* appears multiple times.[8]

(Re)signing Christians recognize all these pasts as signs of the Church universal, even when they feel uncomfortable with the beliefs and practices of some denominations that value them. To denounce any of these Christian traditions limits the Spirit by implying that only one form of relationship with God is possible. After all, if humans manifest different kinds of love, relating differently to siblings, friends, children, parents, spouses and grandparents, how much more so must our Creator relate differently to the diverse people who turn toward Christ with love!

Like the blind men healed by Jesus in radically different ways, Christians see the light in radically different ways. While some blind men needed Christ's physical touch (Mt 9:27-31; 20:29-34), Bartimaeus was healed simply through hearing Christ's words (Mk 10:46-52; Lk 18:35-43). Others needed much more than words or touch. Jesus therefore instructed a man born blind to "wash in the pool of Siloam" after he put mud on the sightless eyes (Jn 9:1-7). In contrast, Jesus led another blind man out of town and then spat directly on his eyes before laying hands upon him. Even then the healing wasn't complete, causing Jesus to lay his hands upon the eyes a second time (Mk 8:22-26). Obviously, as God incarnate, Jesus could have healed each blind man with a much more efficient snap of the fingers, freeing himself up for even more signs and wonders. Instead, it would seem that Jesus related to each blind man according to his individual needs.[9]

Even to this day Jesus gives (in)sight to his followers in different ways.

[8]In addition to Acts 2:1-13, see Acts 10:46; 19:6, as well as 1 Cor 12–14. This does not mean that Pentecostals do not endorse the Apostles Creed. It means that they base their identity on pre-ecumenical principles. My colleague Douglas Jacobsen actually establishes Pentecostalism as one of the four primary yet distinct streams of Christianity: Eastern Orthodoxy, Roman Catholicism, Protestantism and Pentecostalism. See Douglas Jacobsen, *The World's Christians: Who They Are, Where They Are, and How They Got There* (Malden, MA: John Wiley & Sons, 2011).
[9]I use this same example in *How Postmodernism Serves (My) Faith: Questioning Truth in Language, Philosophy and Art* (Downers Grove, IL: IVP Academic, 2006), pp. 205-6.

Protestants tend to come to the light simply through hearing the Word, while Christians in other traditions respond through different senses, such as incense, icons, genuflection, prostration, kneeling, fasting or washing in pools of ecstatic utterance.[10]

Because Christian denominations appeal to different pasts to validate diverse practices, two problems arise, connected like opposite sides of the same coin:

1. Pronouncing the superiority of one particular idealized past

2. Denouncing the immediate past

PRONOUNCING PAST(ORAL) IDEALS

A student in California once complained to me about visiting a church whose worship service was "unbiblical." When I asked what the problem was, he responded with exasperation, "There was no sermon!" He would have done well to read *Pagan Christianity? Exploring the Roots of Our Church Practices*, which shares his concern about biblical truth. The authors, Frank Viola and George Barna, cite numerous scholarly studies to illustrate how Christianity has been corrupted by the signs of culture. And one of the signs they discuss is the pastoral sermon. However, their research reveals that sermons were *not* a part of early church practices.

Viola and Barna note that the word "sermon" appears nowhere in Scripture. The concept "was borrowed from the pagan pool of Greek culture," which valued the "sophists," intellectuals in the fifth century B.C.E. who were famous for their rhetorical flair.[11] Like Christian preachers centuries later, the sophists dressed in special robes for what they called "homilies," explicating Homer the way preachers today explicate the Bible.[12]

So why do people today think the sermon is essential to "biblical Christianity"? According to Viola and Barna, the Roman culture in which Western

---

[10]Jamie Smith convincingly argues that such Christian pluralism reflects "the original goodness of creation: a creation where many flowers bloom and many voices are heard, where God is praised by a multitude from 'every tribe and language and people and nation' (Rev 5:9), singing songs in a diversity of tongues, even worshiping through a diversity of theologies." James K. A. Smith, *The Fall of Interpretation: Philosophical Foundations for a Creational Hermeneutic* (Downers Grove, IL: InterVarsity Press, 2000), p. 33.

[11]Frank Viola and George Barna, *Pagan Christianity? Exploring the Roots of Our Church Practices* (Carol Stream, IL: Tyndale House, 2008), p. 89. Further quotations from this book will be cited in the text.

[12]See David C. Norrington, *To Preach or Not to Preach? The Church's Urgent Question* (Carlisle, UK: Paternoster, 1996), p. 22.

Christianity developed greatly prized the art of rhetoric (p. 90), in which many of our church fathers were professionally trained. Augustine (354-430), who taught rhetoric before he converted to Christianity, coined the phrase "The Sermon on the Mount" to describe the words of Jesus from Matthew 5–7, thus aligning the nonbiblical concept of sermonizing with Jesus.

Sermons (at least as we know them today) were unknown to the early church because pastors were unknown. Viola and Barna make the dramatic point that "there is not a single verse in the entire New Testament that supports the existence of the modern-day pastor": a salaried, seminary-trained church leader who writes and delivers sermons. In fact, "there seems to be more biblical authority for snake handling (see Mk 16:18 and Acts 28:3-6) than there is for the present-day pastor," a word that appears in only one verse: Ephesians 4:11.[13] The New Testament, according to Viola and Barna, does not make functional distinctions between the roles of pastors, bishops and elders, teaching instead that the church is a body of believers who meet for mutual teaching, exhortation and edification rather than to passively sit and listen to a paid professional deliver a sermon.

So are pastoral sermons a bad thing? Yes, say Viola and Barna, who describe the practice as "a polluted stream [that] made its entrance into the Christian faith and muddied its waters" (p. 93). They want to get back to the pure waters of New Testament Christianity, what they call "God's way for His church" (p. 119), before pagan signs contaminated it.

Note how Viola and Barna, like the student in California, desire uncorrupted "biblical" Christianity. However, like opposite sides of the same coin, the authors and the student have different ideas about what is "biblical." The student, of course, was a bit naive about "biblical Christianity," whereas Viola and Barna cite vast amounts of scholarship to back their understanding of the early church. Nevertheless, they parallel each other by desiring a Christianity free of pagan signs. Ironically, this hunger for culturally untainted Christianity echoes pagan signs!

THE PAGAN PASTORAL

In the third century B.C.E., the Greek poet Theocritus wrote stories ideal-

---

[13]The Greek word that Paul employs—*poimeen*—appears eighteen times in the New Testament, but is always translated "shepherd(s)" except in the Ephesians passage. Viola and Barna, *Pagan Christianity?* p. 106.

izing life among shepherds in Sicily. Uncorrupted by civilization, these shepherds lived together in harmony, not only with each other but also with nature. Two centuries after Theocritus, the pre-Christian Roman poet Virgil similarly mystified rural life, putting his ideal in an area of Greece that he called Arcadia. This kind of literature came to be called "the pastoral," since "pastor" means shepherd. Throughout history, then, pastoral mystifications—which have always been fictions—demonstrate dissatisfaction with signs of present times.[14] As Charles Taylor notes in *A Secular Age*, "most epochs posit a golden age somewhere in the past; and sometimes this is seen as something which can, in favourable circumstances, be recovered."[15]

Christians who seek to recover the lifestyle of the early church reflect the pastoral impulse. However, as anyone who has studied church history can tell you, dissension and division marked the church from the start. Just look at the troubles described in the book of Acts: the deceit and punishment of Ananias and Sapphira (Acts 5:1-11), the "dissension and debate" that Paul and Barnabas experienced with Christians from Judea (Acts 15:1-11), followed by a "disagreement . . . so sharp" between Paul and Barnabas themselves "that they parted company" (Acts 15:36-40).

By the early second century, as some Protestant historians explain it, "the gospel of free grace" had turned into a polluted stream of legalism. Christians were "calculating which sins committed after baptism, if any, could be formally remitted, what tariffs should be in place for particular misdemeanours and so on."[16] In the third century, Christians vociferously disagreed over the sacrament of baptism, arguing whether people returning to the church after falling away should be baptized again. Even the first ecumenical council, at Nicaea in 325, reflected intense division within the church: many Christians of the era endorsed the biblically based teaching of Arius (ca. 250-336), who argued that Jesus, the Son of God, was subordinate to, rather than "one substance" with, the Father.[17]

---

[14]For a fuller discussion of the pastoral tradition manifest in society today, see Crystal Downing, "Witnessing the Amish: Plain People on Fancy Film," in *The Amish and the Media*, ed. Diane Zimmerman Umble and David L. Weaver-Zercher (Baltimore: Johns Hopkins University Press, 2008), pp. 24-41.

[15]Charles Taylor, *A Secular Age* (Cambridge, MA: Harvard University Press, 2007), p. 119.

[16]Rowan Williams, *Why Study the Past? The Quest for the Historical Church* (Grand Rapids, MI: Eerdmans, 2005), p. 37. Though Williams agrees that such things were happening in the second-century church, he astutely argues that we must assess their significance in light of the times.

[17]For a lucid account of the "bitter, political maneuvering" during the Council of Nicaea, see Mark

This is not to say that Christians in the first three centuries of the church are not admirable. Their willingness to be martyred for the sake of Christ puts to shame the comfortable Christianity of our own times. But, as martyrdom implies, early church times were less than idyllic. Archbishop of Canterbury Rowan Williams therefore cautions Christians against pastoral mystifications, which he defines as "the temptation to look for a period of Christian history in which the ordinary ambiguities or corruptions of human history have not obscured the truth of the gospel."[18]

While Viola and Barna urge a return to a church unsullied by culture, I would argue that Christianity has *always* been influenced by signs of the times: sometimes positively, sometimes negatively. Rather than naively mystifying "the undivided Church of the first five centuries,"[19] we should acknowledge that Christians have been (re)signing truth from the very start: resigned to following Christ, they have re-signed how such discipleship takes place, often using signs of their times. All Christians today who value their pastors' sermons should welcome such (re)signing.

How, then, do we know which signs to accept and which to renounce? That question motivates the rest of this book. But first we need to consider another problem with how Christians regard the past: vilification of predecessors.

DENOUNCING THE IMMEDIATE PAST

While some people idealize the ancient past, others authenticate their present beliefs by vilifying their immediate predecessors. This occurs, I think, because many people need to define themselves in contradistinction to the culture that molded their own sensibilities. The hippies of the 1960s and '70s provide a good example. Stock phrases from that Vietnam era—"Don't trust anyone over thirty," "Make love not war," and "Down with the Establishment"—indicate distrust of their parents' generation. Other phrases, such as "Flower Power" and Joni Mitchell's "We've got to get back to the Garden," aligned hippie distrust of "the Establishment" with the pastoral desire for Eden, where no one selfishly grabs after forbidden fruit. It is no coincidence that many hippies joined the Jesus movement, which offered hope in a Second

---

Noll, *Turning Points: Decisive Moments in the History of Christianity* (Grand Rapids, MI: Baker, 1997), pp. 58-62.

[18]Williams, *Why Study the Past?* p. 102.

[19]Rowan Williams quotes this phrase to challenge the pastoral mystification that generates it (ibid., p. 50).

Adam, whose death and resurrection showed us the way back to the garden.

Like hippies refusing to trust anyone over thirty, earnest believers sometimes define their faith in contrast to what came before. I started thinking about this in ninth grade, when I first encountered the phrase "anti-Semitism." I was shocked when I heard the term defined, for I had always been told that the Jews were "God's chosen people," holding a very special place in God's heart. Reiterating the "chosen people" phrase—a sign of the Jews—my parents had convinced me that Jews were smarter and more talented than generic Anglo-Saxon Protestants. After all, look at all the Jews who are actors, doctors and lawyers! Anti-Semitism therefore made absolutely no sense to me.

To my adolescent mind, Roman Catholics were much more deserving of suspicion. Unlike the Jews, Catholics worshiped idols and believed in magic, as when my ten-year-old friend kissed the huge statue of Mary in her church. Outside, I even saw priests and nuns (gasp) smoking. No *true* follower of Jesus Christ would so sully the temple of the Holy Spirit!

As is embarrassingly obvious, I had picked up an attitude toward Catholics that mimicked, in many ways, medieval attitudes toward Jews. Because Protestants define themselves in contradistinction to their Roman Catholic "parents," they vilify those parents in order to avoid regarding themselves as delinquent children—much as hippies vilified the "Establishment" values of their parents. Similarly, since the Western church—what we now call Roman Catholic—defined itself against Judaism, it tended to vilify its "parents": those Jews who did not follow Christ.[20]

Protestants, therefore, tend to idealize what their Roman Catholic "parents" rejected. Indeed, it was only after a radical Protestant came to power in seventeenth-century England—Oliver Cromwell—that a three-hundred-year law banning Jews from the country was overturned. Of course, Cromwell's Puritans defined themselves against their religious "parents" as well, attacking high church Anglicans with word and sword. Though Protestant, Anglicans reeked of popish incense—at least to the Puritans, who sought to nose out "unbiblical" Christianity. I have visited small churches in western England where Cromwell's troops literally tried to wash away signs of the old. By whitewashing images painted on Anglican church walls, Puritans believed they were getting rid of idolatrous signs.

---

[20]As early as the 240s c.e., Cyprian, Bishop of Carthage, was vilifying the Jews in his *Testimonies Against the Jews.*

SIGNS OF ENLIGHTENED TIMES:
VILIFYING CHRISTIANITY ALTOGETHER

While the medieval church repudiated Jews, Protestants repudiated Catholics, and the Puritans repudiated Anglican Protestants, advocates of secular
humanism repudiated Christianity altogether. In the eighteenth-century
"Neoclassical Era"—also known as "the Enlightenment" and "the Age of
Reason"—cultural leaders mystified classical Greek and Roman cultures as
paragons of rational thinking and civilized order. They contrasted such enlightened thinking with the irrational behavior and blind superstitions of the
Christian Middle Ages. The term "Middle Ages," in fact, was coined in the
eighteenth century as the sign for an embarrassing interruption between
Greek and Roman cultures and the "Renaissance"—or "rebirth"—of classical
values in fifteenth- and sixteenth-century Europe.

Idealizing ancient pagan cultures, eighteenth-century intellectuals saw
their own era as the maturation of a classicism reborn after the backwardness
of medievalism. Their architecture imitated the symmetrical colonnades of
the Greeks and the domes of the Romans, while their literature imitated the
odes, epigrams and elegies of the same ancient forebears.

Thomas Jefferson, America's most famous Neoclassical architect, chose
classical styles for several monumental buildings, such as the state capitol in
Richmond, Virginia, which imitated an ancient Roman temple still standing
in southern France. Most telling—and controversial—was Jefferson's
design for the University of Virginia, which eliminated Christianity both in
its curriculum and architecture. While earlier universities in America
usually put a church or chapel at the center of the campus—both architec-
turally as well as intellectually—Jefferson put a library, designed as a Neoclassical rotunda, at the center of his campus. Doing so, he illustrated his
Enlightenment belief that educated reason, untainted by Christianity,
should supplant religion as the source of truth. Jefferson, in fact, cut out any
sign of the supernatural—all of Christ's miracles, including the resurrection—from his personal Bible. And he described the doctrine of the
Trinity as "abracadabra . . . hocus-pocus . . . a deliria of crazy imaginations."[21]

---

[21]On the rotunda, see Mark R. Schwehn, "Christianity and Postmodernism: Uneasy Allies," in
Christianity and Culture in the Cross Fire, ed. David A. Hoekema and Bobby Fong (Grand Rapids,
MI: Eerdmans, 1997), pp. 155-56. About Jefferson's Bible, see Stephen Prothero, *American Jesus:
How the Son of God Became a National Icon* (New York: Farrar, Strauss & Giroux, 2003), pp. 24-25.
The words of Jefferson are quoted in D. L. Homes, *The Faiths of the Founding Fathers* (Oxford:

Ironically, I have heard Christians opine that our country should return to the Christian values of our founding fathers such as Thomas Jefferson. Obviously, rather than understanding Jefferson's signs, such laments manifest a cultural cliché: idealizing the past as superior, just as Jefferson idealized the Greek and Roman past as superior. All of us, instead, should heed the words from Ecclesiastes: "Do not say, 'Why were the former days better than these?' For it is not from wisdom that you ask this" (Eccles 7:10).

MYSTIFYING PROGRESS: KANT AND HEGEL

The Neoclassical values of the Enlightenment led to an equal but opposite problem: mystifying the future. Since (re)signing truth has to do with change for the future, we need to consider this problem before we can seek a balance between two extremes: idolizing the past and idealizing the concept of progress.

Immanuel Kant (1724-1804) began his famous 1784 essay "What Is Enlightenment?" with the statement "Enlightenment is man's emergence from his self-incurred immaturity." For him, unthinking submission to the church perpetuated immaturity, whereas exercise of reason led to mature understanding of the truth. While tradition stifled progress, independent thought encouraged it.

Influenced by Kant, G. W. F. Hegel (1770-1831) developed a model of human progress toward absolute knowledge, which he equated with God. Individual minds, inevitably "alienated" from the universal spirit of absolute knowledge, attain self-consciousness the closer they get to this absolute. This process of advancement has become known as "the Hegelian dialectic": progress occurs when accepted signs of truth (an established "thesis") are challenged by contrary signs (an "antithesis") until the best of both are united in a higher understanding of truth: a "synthesis."[22] Once accepted, however, this "synthesis" eventually turns into an unquestioned dictum: an established "thesis" about the truth of things. Therefore, out of that new "thesis" must arise an "antithesis" until a new "synthesis" is achieved. For Hegel, this process pulls humans closer to Absolute Mind and hence toward freedom and wholeness.

Oxford University Press, 2006), p. 87.

[22]A philosopher named Heinrich Chalybäus (1796-1862) developed the terms *thesis, antithesis* and *synthesis* to explain Hegel, who uses triadic constructs: abstract-negative-concrete and immediate-mediated-concrete. In his *Phenomenology of Spirit* (1807), Hegel suggests that the progress of history would reach its fulfillment in the Prussian state.

THE SYNTHESIS OF FLORENCE NIGHTINGALE

Let me give a practical example of dialectical progress, even though far removed from Hegel's sense of Absolute Mind. In 1845, when Florence Nightingale announced that she felt divinely called to nursing, her upper middle-class family was horrified. In their culture, surgeons had little better status than barbers, and nurses garnered only slightly more respect than prostitutes.[23] Everyone agreed that a proper woman like Florence should concentrate on making a financially advantageous marriage in order to live the life of a decorous lady. That, then, was the "thesis" for respectable women in 1845.

Nightingale defied this "thesis," not only by going to Turkey as a nurse during the Crimean War (1854), but also by attacking the "thesis" of female respectability. In a fictional tale called *Cassandra*, she exposes the problematic thesis of her day: "a woman cannot live in the light of intellect. Society forbids it."[24] Making brilliant advances in the discipline of nursing, including the use of sophisticated diagrams to chart medical data, Nightingale embodied an "antithesis" to contemporary understanding of female capabilities.

Thanks to her, a "synthesis" was reached by the twentieth century, such that a woman might be a respectable wife and mother (the Victorian thesis) even while a professional nurse (the Nightingale antithesis). Unfortunately, if inevitably, this synthesis turned into a problematic thesis: nursing, like mothering, became respectable *women's* work. Still to this day, U.S. nursing programs tend to be 97 percent female, even as nurses continue to earn far less money and respect than doctors.[25] It would seem that our culture's current thesis about the "proper" gender of nurses needs to be challenged by some antithetical movement.

(RE)SIGNING HEGEL: KARL MARX

My example of Florence Nightingale may be closer to the theory of Karl Marx than to that of Hegel. According to Friedrich Engels, Marx appropriated the idea of dialectical process from Hegel, but he re-signed it. While Hegel put *mind* first in order to emphasize how consciousness shapes society, Marx put *economic conditions* first in order to emphasize

---

[23]See Kristine Swenson, *Medical Women and Victorian Fiction* (Columbia: University of Missouri Press, 2005).

[24]Florence Nightingale, *Cassandra* (Old Westbury, NY: The Feminist Press, 1979), p. 37.

[25]I thank Carolyn Kreamer, chair of the Nursing Department at Messiah College, for this statistic, as well as for calling my attention to Nightingale's employment of the polar area diagram.

how society shapes consciousness. Hegel, in other words, focused on progress in the production of ideas, whereas Marx focused on progress in the production of material goods.[26] Marx's view is therefore called "dialectical materialism."

Marxism establishes capitalism as the thesis of nineteenth-century European culture: bourgeois businessmen own modes of production like factories, hiring working-class people—the proletariat—to make money that benefits not the workers but the capitalist bourgeoisie. The proletariat goes along with the system because capitalist assumptions have molded their minds, *alienating* them from their own self-interest. The bourgeoisie thus perpetuate what Marx calls a "mystification": a concept of reality that obscures the truth.

Consonant with Hegel's dialectic, Marxism therefore looked to the future, when antithetical elements within the thesis stage would lead to a new synthesis. For Marx, this meant that contradictions and inequities within capitalism itself would destabilize it, leading to communism, where all humans participate equally in sowing and reaping the material benefits of production. Ironically, as his critics have long noted, Marx merely created his own mystification. Rather than idealizing the past, he idealized the future. Communism is as much a pastoral fiction—if even set in the future—as the ones described earlier in this chapter.

In sum, Marx, like his predecessors Kant and Hegel, illustrates an equal but opposite problem than that outlined at the start of this chapter. While religious traditionalists often mystify the past, Enlightenment humanists tend to mystify the future. And both kinds of mystification have influenced Christian thought.

DEMYTHOLOGIZING CHRISTIANITY: YOUNG HEGELIANS AS HIGHER CRITICS

Some intellectuals influenced by Hegel, often called the Young Hegelians, mystified the future of Christianity, believing that faith in supernaturalism impeded human progress toward Absolute Mind. David Friedrich Strauss (1808-1874) and Ludwig Feuerbach (1804-1872), for example, followed the

---

[26]It is Engels who aligned Marxism with the Hegelian dialectic. Engel's Marx was not the first to re-sign the Hegelian dialectic in material terms; he is just the most famous. See Diané Collinson, *Fifty Major Philosophers: A Reference Guide* (New York: Routledge, 1987), p. 99.

example of Enlightenment thinkers like Thomas Jefferson by eliminating all supernatural encumbrances from the Bible. Doing so, they became part of a German movement known as the "Higher Criticism."

In 1835 Strauss published *The Life of Jesus, Critically Examined*, asserting that Gospel writers invented the miracles to idealize Jesus as the Messiah. Four years later, Feuerbach argued "that Christianity has in fact long vanished not only from the Reason but from the Life of mankind."[27] While for Strauss Christ's miracles reflected an irrational mystification of the past, Feuerbach regarded all religion as an outworn mystification. In his book *The Essence of Christianity* (1841), Feuerbach argues that God is merely a projection of human need: sensing love and justice within themselves, humans imagine an origin outside of themselves. Not surprisingly, Marx read Feuerbach, whose philosophy influenced Marx's oft-(mis)quoted pronouncement: "religion is the opiate of the masses" (1843).[28]

Decades later, Strauss published *The Christ of Belief and the Jesus of History* (1865), establishing a dialectic that still functions among many scholars today: the thesis of Christ's divinity, undermined by the antithesis of Enlightenment reason, is synthesized by Christians who want to follow Jesus without believing in the supernatural. Known as "demythologizers," such Christians often feel quite enlightened in their de-mystification of the past, while remaining naive about their equal but opposite mystification of the future. Believing in human progress, they have merely substituted a doctrine of Enlightenment humanism for belief in the divinity of Jesus.

THE DEVELOPMENT OF FUNDAMENTALISM: COMPETING UNIONS

This cultural tension between those who mystify the past and those who mystify the future came to a head in the early twentieth century. It is worth recounting, for it explains the antagonism that many Christians still feel today, not only between Christ and culture, but also among Christians themselves.

In 1891, Charles Briggs, the first professor of biblical theology at Union Theological Seminary in New York, delivered an address that questioned

---

[27]Ludwig Feuerbach, preface to *The Essence of Christianity*, trans. George Eliot (New York: Harper & Row, 1957), p. xliv.

[28]In context, Marx quite clearly meant that religion, like a drug, helps relieve the anguish of the working class. Karl Marx, *Critique of Hegel's "Philosophy of Right,"* ed. Joseph O'Malley (Cambridge: Cambridge University Press, 1970), p. 131.

biblical inerrancy. Responses to him were polarized—and polarizing—putting Union Theological Seminary at the center of a debate that eventually became known as "the modernist-fundamentalist controversy." Modernists, of course, tended to be those mystifying progress, while fundamentalists mystified tradition.[29]

Someone from a different Union, however, planted the seed that grew into the sign "Fundamentalist." In 1910 one of the founders of Union Oil, a dispensationalist Christian named Lyman Stewart, decided to finance a series of pamphlets that would offset the liberalizing effects of the Higher Criticism. He called the series *The Fundamentals: A Testimony to the Truth.* That same year, the "Doctrinal Deliverance of 1910" was passed by the General Assembly of the Presbyterian Church in the USA, declaring five beliefs as essential to Christian faith:

the virgin birth
an inerrant Bible
the bodily resurrection
the legitimacy of miracles
atonement through Christ's death

Borrowing a sign from Stewart's pamphlet titles, people began calling these doctrines the "Five Fundamentals." The word *fundamentalist* was coined in 1920 "to describe those ready 'to do battle royal for the Fundamentals.'"[30]

Many evangelical Christians still hold to most of these fundamentals, but would never use the sign "fundamentalist" to describe themselves. This illustrates a key point of my book: Christian signs change over time, usually in response to cultural influences. In the case of "fundamentalism," connotations of the sign shifted due to those Christians who applied "inerrancy" to the scientific accuracy of Scripture—even though the Bible was obviously not intended to be a scientific treatise. Composed, instead, as an account of God's love, expectations and salvation for humanity, the Bible

---

[29]The Briggs scandal led to only one of many heresy trials between 1878 and 1906. His case, as George Marsden notes, just happens to be "the most spectacular," with the Presbyterian Church suspending him from the ministry, even though he "was a traditionalist in most of his theology." See George M. Marsden, *Understanding Fundamentalism and Evangelicalism* (Grand Rapids, MI: Eerdmans, 1991), p. 38.

[30]Ibid., p. 57. The development of fundamentalism was far more complex than presented in my brief summary, and I recommend Marsden's lucid and fair-minded overview for a fuller account.

was nevertheless promoted as a sign of scientific truth.

Union Theological Seminary was once again central to the sign-change. In 1921, William Jennings Bryan delivered a series of lectures at Union, aligning the evils of Darwinian evolution with those of the Higher Criticism. He followed up these popular lectures by working to ban the teaching of evolution in public schools. This led to the infamous Scopes "Monkey" Trial of 1925. Supported by the World Christian Fundamentals Association, Bryan prosecuted John Scopes for teaching evolution in a Tennessee school. But his inability to explain how the Bible could be inerrant about science, along with the media storm generated by the trial, led to a discrediting of fundamentalism among many Christians.

In response, fundamentalists dug in their heels, many turning inerrancy into the most important of the five fundamentals. For them Christians *must* believe that the Genesis account of a universe created in six twenty-four-hour days is more scientifically accurate than alternate theories, even when endorsed by Christian scientists. Refusing conclusions based on recent fossil evidence, these fundamentalists mystified past interpretations of Genesis, especially the interpretation generated in the seventeenth century by Irish Protestant James Ussher (1581-1656), who published a timeline of the Old Testament in 1650. Basing his timeline on the stated ages of the patriarchs and the number of "begats" chronicled in the Old Testament, as well as upon the suggestions of earlier scholars, Ussher argued that the Earth was created the evening before October 23, 4004 B.C. By holding up Ussher as their source for biblical truth, fundamentalists were obviously selecting one particular interpretation of the past to mystify. Doing so, they ignored the fact that great fathers of the faith did not see the need to endorse a literal six-day creation in order to establish the truth of Scripture.[31] While thinking they were protecting the Bible as an inerrant source of truth, they were actually proclaiming a *human interpretation* of the Bible as inerrant.

Enlightenment humanists—or "modernists"—reacted by mystifying a future when humans would evolve beyond such simplistic thinking. That left many Christians caught between these two mystifications: fundamentalists idealizing the past, modernists idealizing the future. Some decided that if Young Earth Creationism were a "fundamental" of Christianity, then they could no longer be Christians. Others, especially in mainline churches, joined

---

[31]For examples, see Crystal Downing, *How Postmodernism Serves (My) Faith: Questioning Truth in Language, Philosophy and Art* (Downers Grove, IL: IVP Academic, 2006), pp. 64-65.

the demythologizing camp, holding on to the ethical truths of Scripture while abandoning "old-fashioned" supernaturalism. And those who continued to believe in the "signs and wonders" of Christ, but who were also convinced by the empirical data of science, decided that they must get rid of the sign "fundamentalist."[32] Believing the gist of the Genesis account—that God brought the universe and all within it into existence—they no longer felt compelled to endorse numbers that do not appear in Scripture: six twenty-four-hour days in the year 4004 B.C. Though resigned to the fundamentals, they re-signed how to describe themselves: as evangelical Christians.

RIGHTING WHAT'S LEFT OF FUNDAMENTALISM: POLITICS

The sign "fundamentalist" thus changed meaning since its original reference to the modernist-fundamentalist debates. And it continues to change. In our own day it has become a sign of any person—whether liberal or conservative—who so mystifies their position that they refuse to value people who disagree with them. Take, for example, New Atheists Richard Dawkins and Daniel Dennett, whom evolutionary biologist Stephen Jay Gould describes as "Darwinian fundamentalists."[33] Gould's phrase is a new application for an old practice: proclaiming the inerrancy of one's own understanding of truth. New Atheists and Young Earth Creationists are merely opposite sides of the same coin.

Fundamentalism becomes especially pronounced in the political arena. On the one hand, I have been around otherwise intelligent Democrats—advocates of future change—who contemptuously denounce all "backward-looking" signs of Republican thought as un-Christian stupidity. On the other hand, I know Christians who seem more passionate about their Republican agenda than their call to take up the cross daily. The certitude manifest in both kinds of Christians —convinced of the absolute truth of their party's position—demonstrates what one specialist in sign theory calls the "Fundamentalist Fallacy, . . . instantiated when one assumes that his/her own philosophy is the only valid philosophy . . . (and demands a universal agreement on such a statement)."[34]

---

[32]Dinesh D'Souza argues that "Fundamentalism is a meaningless term outside" the context of the Modernist-Fundamentalist debates. Significantly, he argues for the legitimacy of evolution, saying "it seems improbable that the small group of intelligent design advocates is right and the entire community of biologists is wrong." See *What's So Great About Christianity* (Carol Stream, IL: Tyndale House, 2007), pp. 151, 150.

[33]Stephen Jay Gould, "Darwinian Fundamentalists," *New York Review of Books*, June 12, 1997.

[34]Umberto Eco, "Semiotics and the Philosophy of Language," in *Reading Eco: An Anthology*, ed. Rocco Capozzi (Bloomington: Indiana University Press, 1997), p. 7.

AVOIDING THE FUNDAMENTALIST FALLACY

This book is written for those who want to follow Christ more than to mystify signs, including the problematic signs "liberal" and "conservative." Indeed, some liberals are the most conservative people I know, having never changed a political opinion in decades. Nevertheless, when they use the "C-word"—*Conservative*—they nearly groan with disdain.

The "L-sign" generates equal disgust among those at the opposite end of the political spectrum. I met someone who, when she heard I taught college, said, "Oh, I thought you were a Christian." When I assured her I had committed my life to Christ, she narrowed her eyes warily and remarked, "But aren't all college professors liberal?"

Because the signs *Liberal* and *Conservative* have become sullied through problematic attitudes and practices, I will avoid using them for the remainder of this book. Inaccurate and alienating, they close down communication rather than open it up: a fact recognized by people at both ends of the spectrum, many of whom acknowledge the need for new signs.[35]

Only slightly better are the terms "the Left" and "the Right"—signs coined by the cultural critic with whom I began this chapter: Thomas Carlyle, author of "The Signs of the Times." In *The French Revolution: A History* (1837), Carlyle noted that during an assembly convened soon after the fall of the Bastille (1789), revolutionaries in favor of conserving the president's agenda sat at his right hand, while those who wanted to change it sat to his left. Carlyle thereafter referred to "the Left" and "the Right" to describe their differing positions.[36]

Thanks to Carlyle's signs, people who want to conserve tradition tend to be aligned with the political "right" while people who advocate change tend to be aligned with the political "left." When the right starts to mystify the past and the left idealizes the future, both can turn fundamentalist all too quickly: op-

---

[35]A self-identified "progressive," theologian Catherine Keller renounced "the enfeebled signs 'left' and 'liberal'" in 2007. See John D. Caputo and Catherine Keller, "Theopoetic/Theopolitic," *CrossCurrents* 57, no. 1 (Winter 2007): 108. From the other end of the political spectrum, Thomas Sowell makes a similar comment: "Most liberals are not liberal and most conservatives are not conservative. We might be better off just calling them X and Y, instead of imagining that we are really describing their philosophies." See Thomas Sowell, "The Evolution of the Term 'Conservative,'" *National Review Online*, September 16, 2010, www.nationalreview.com/articles/246682/evolution-term-conservative-thomas-sowell. At the end of 2010, "A high-minded group of political types . . . formed a group called No Labels that is dedicated to improving today's poisonous, hyper-partisan atmosphere." See Dale McFeatters, "'No Labels' Movement Looks to Have Little Chance," *The Patriot-News* (Harrisburg, PA), December 20, 2010, A-11.

[36]Thomas Carlyle, *The French Revolution: A History* (New York: Modern Library, 1960), p. 174.

posite sides of the same coin. In contrast, *Changing Signs of Truth* calls for Christians to be on the edge between. For only on the edge can we (re)sign truth.

CHRISTIANS ON THE EDGE OF THE COIN

I want you to imagine a coin—let's use a quarter—standing on edge. Both sides are covered with signs. The dominant sign on one side—an image of George Washington's head, complete with pigtail—has lasted since 1932 when designed by John Flanagan, who put an eagle on the reverse side. Change came, however, in 1999 when the U.S. Mint began to release quarters commemorating the fifty states of the union. Instead of the eagle, an image significant to a particular state or territory appears. And in 2010, the U.S. Mint started the whole process over again, putting even newer images collected from the states and territories, while retaining an image of the first U.S. president on the obverse. One side therefore represents tradition while the other side represents change. We might schematize it this way:

Figure 1.1. A quarter on edge

Now, imagine yourself shrunk down to the size of an ant, standing on the fluted edge between the left side and the right side. This is the position of (re)signing truth: resigned to the headship of Jesus Christ, you maintain trust in the sign to the right, where the words "In God We Trust" still appear. But your position on the edge also enables you to look to the left, where you can enjoy and celebrate the re-signing of the coin. Just as each state of the union determines its own sign on the quarter, so each new era or state of culture determines new signs for the faith.

Balancing on the edge of the coin between signs of the right and signs of the left takes constant vigilance. It is far easier to allow the coin to fall onto one side or the other so that the reverse or obverse is obliterated, face down in dirt like a coin tossed in a garden. Standing on the exposed surface of the coin—whether the right surface or the left surface as it faces up in the dirt—fundamentalists think they rise above the grime of culture: it's just that those standing on the left surface see those fearful of change as beneath them (in both senses of "beneath"), while those standing on the right surface see majority culture underneath them (in the direction of hell) as abandoning all restraint.

A position on the edge looks to both past and future, to tradition and change. In his appropriately titled *Why Study the Past?* Rowan Williams makes a similar point:

> It will not do to have a simple progressivist myth which allows you to say that we know more of Christ than any earlier age; nor will it do to say that we have only to submit what we think we know of Christ to the judgement of our fathers and mothers in faith. . . . [T]he Christian past is unavoidably part of the Christian present in such a way that we have to be extra careful not to dismiss, caricature or give up the attempt to listen.[37]

This, I believe, reflects Paul's tactic when he discusses food offered to idols in his first letter to the Corinthians. There he encourages a new-found freedom, since "no idol in the world really exists" (1 Cor 8:4). However, he also has compassion for those on the other side of the coin: "some have become so accustomed to idols until now, they still think of the food they eat as food offered to an idol" (1 Cor 8:7). He therefore encourages the Corinthians to stay on the edge of the coin by acknowledging that one side is not superior to the other: "We are no worse off if we do not eat, and no better off if we do" (1 Cor 8:8). In fact, he goes so far as to say, "If food is a cause of their falling, I will never eat meat, so that I may not cause one of them to fall" (1 Cor 8:13): like the fall of a coin onto one side or the other.

Paul, of course, was in the position of defining Christianity at its very start, so he could get away with such edgy thinking. How might we, two thousand years later, stay balanced on the edge? The remainder of this book offers multiple examples throughout church history, and I close this chapter with a stellar one: William Tyndale (ca. 1494-1536).

THE EDGY WILLIAM TYNDALE

Educated at Oxford and Cambridge, ordained priest William Tyndale was a master of linguistic signs, not only in English, but also in French, Spanish,

---

[37]Williams, *Why Study the Past?* p. 28.

Italian, Latin, Hebrew and Greek. So when he encountered fellow priests "unlearned" in the basic signs of the Bible, he became disturbed, especially at those who seemed more committed to "tithes, mortuaries, offerings, customs, and other pillage," as he put it, than to proclaiming God's Word.[38]

Tyndale therefore decided to translate the Latin Bible into English, making it accessible to readers uneducated in Latin. In other words, resigned to the truth of Scripture, he decided to re-sign it—which inevitably changed it. For, rather than merely transliterate the Latin Vulgate, the official Bible of the church for over a thousand years, Tyndale consulted ancient Hebrew and Greek manuscripts, invoking a different Christian past. This sent the Bible in a new direction, like a coin rolling on edge.

TYNDALE'S CULTURE MAKING

Significantly, Tyndale's ability to (re)sign truth changed culture, providing a superb example of what Andy Crouch means by "culture making."[39] Tyndale's poetic renderings of Greek and Hebrew phrases generated signs that are still being employed to this day—and not just by Christians. Speakers and writers of many faiths use phrases that Tyndale invented, doing so not because the coinages are biblical but because they are beautiful. People think, talk and write differently because Tyndale (re)signed, coining into English the following familiar phrases (and many more):

my brother's keeper	fight the good fight
flowing with milk and honey	it came to pass
broken-hearted	gave up the ghost
to have a clear conscience	the spirit is willing
let there be light	the powers that be
a law unto themselves	eat, drink and be merry

RESISTING TYNDALE'S NEW SIGNS

Despite the beauty of these coinages, church leaders stamped down the coin upon which Tyndale was balancing. They argued that if common people read the Bible for themselves in their native English they might interpret it incor-

---

[38]William Tyndale, preface to his 1530 translation of the Pentateuch, quoted in David Daniell, *William Tyndale: A Biography* (New Haven: Yale University Press, 1994), p. 75.
[39]Andy Crouch, *Culture Making: Recovering Our Creative Calling* (Downers Grove, IL: IVP Books, 2008). Crouch does not discuss Tyndale.

rectly. Therefore, only clergy educated in Latin should have control of Scripture. Ironically, what upset some leaders the most were translations that have proved more accurate than those to which they had grown accustomed. Tyndale's knowledge of Greek led to changes in words that had functioned as sacred signs for a thousand years:

Greek word	Past translation	Tyndale's more accurate translation
presbuteros	priest	elder/senior
ekklesia	church	congregation
agape	charity	love
metanoeo	do penance	repent

Tyndale's new signs challenged an ages-old tradition represented by the middle column. According to that tradition, salvation came through works of *penance* and *charity*, mediated through the redemptive activities of the *Church* as overseen by *priests*.

Enraging the traditionalists even more, Tyndale published theological works that built upon the signs of the third column, arguing that justification before God comes not through sacraments of the Catholic Church but through *repentance* based on *love* of Christ and nurtured by a *congregation* of believers overseen by *elders*, not priests.[40] Proclaiming him a heretic, the Church burned not only Tyndale's New Testament (in 1527), but also his body. In 1536 Tyndale was burned at the stake—after being strangled.

RESISTING NEW SIGNS TODAY

Some evangelicals who would denounce Tyndale's treatment nevertheless differ little from those who "fired" him. For example, an uproar occurred early in 2011 with the publication of Today's New International Version of the Bible (TNIV). Protesters to the updated version cited "politically correct" gender-inclusive alterations, as when the traditional "I will make you fishers of men" now reads "I will send you out to fish for people" (Mt 4:19). The Council of Biblical Manhood and Womanhood argued that the change from

---

[40]See, for example, *The Parable of the Wicked Mammon* (1528) as discussed in Daniell, *Tyndale*, pp. 155-73. Tyndale's first full translation of the New Testament was published in 1526; his Pentateuch (the first five books of the Old Testament) in 1530.

"men" to "people" alters "the theological direction and meaning of the text."[41]
Ironically, by replacing "men" with "people," Today's New International Version gets closer to the wording of ancient manuscripts. In the Greek and Hebrew in which the original texts were written, plural pronouns imply *both* genders: "people" rather than just "men." Hence, it would seem that protesters prefer to retain the signs they are used to rather than to get closer to the truth. Just as Tyndale got in trouble for his more accurate translations, so the committee of translators for the TNIV got in trouble for its (re)signing.[42] Indeed, consonant with (re)signing, the committee also generated disdain from people on the other side of the coin because it didn't get rid of male pronouns for God.

(RE)SIGNING ON THE EDGE

Clearly, (re)signing truth is not for the faint of heart. People on both sides of the coin will attempt to knock down someone who stays on the edge: those on the right will lob the word "liberal" at Christians on the edge, while those on the left will attack using the reviled word "conservative."

Staying on the edge therefore necessitates not only balance but also movement forward. Think of your ant-sized body rolling the quarter through culture like an acrobat rolling a barrel through an arena. The fluting on the edge of the coin provides footholds, ridges that visually connect the resigning to tradition on one side to the re-signing change of the other. As soon as you stop taking the next step onto the next lip of the fluting, the coin falls either to the right or to the left. Staying on the edge is about rolling through the signs of the times, attempting to be in them without being of them.[43]

Significantly, Thomas Carlyle, who coined "right" and "left," inherited the phrase "signs of the times" from Tyndale's translation of Matthew 16:1-3. When the Pharisees and Sadducees challenge Jesus "to show them a sign from heaven," Tyndale has Jesus answer, "O ye ypocrites ye can discerne ye fassion of the skye:

---

[41]Quoted in "New Bible Aims for Neutrality," *The Patriot-News* (Harrisburg, PA), March 18, 2011, A-9.

[42]In their desire for accuracy, the translators have been meeting yearly since 1965 to discuss "advances in biblical scholarship and changes in English." Ibid.

[43]Pope Benedict XVI demonstrated "edgy" thinking in 2010 when he (re)signed the Catholic ban on condom use. Though still prohibiting contraception, the pope suggested that condoms should be allowed if they might help prevent the spread of AIDS. Significantly, the name of the book that presents this Catholic (re)signing is *Light of the World: The Pope, the Church and the Signs of the Times* (by Peter Seewald and Pope Benedict XVI [San Francisco: Ignatius Press, 2010]).

and can ye not discerne ye *signes of the tymes?*"[44] In the next chapter we will take a closer look at Jesus, who demonstrated that only by changing signs can we change the times.

---

[44]I quote from "William Tyndale's Translation" as it appears on Wesley Center Online, http://wesley.nnu.edu/fileadmin/imported_site/tyndale/mat.txt.

2

SIGNS OF GOD'S WORD

Following Jesus

With veins throbbing at his temples, the traumatized male growled between his teeth, "You are a liberal who is undermining God's Word." With that daunting accusation, a student attacked one of my colleagues for heresy. Why? Because my colleague suggested in the classroom that the God of the Jews is the same God worshiped by Christians.

Worried that his professor ignored the difference between Judaism and Christianity, the student had some reason for his anger. But the professor was not eliminating difference. Instead, as a trained theologian, she was attempting to avoid a heresy dating back to the second century after the resurrection. At that time a sincere follower of Jesus named Marcion (ca. 85-160) taught that Christians should not consider the Hebrew Scriptures (the Old Testament) as God's Word because the vengeful Jewish God differs so dramatically from the loving Christian God. Marcion's teachings were denounced by many other Christian leaders, and Tertullian (ca. 160-220), an influential leader in the church, wrote a whole treatise to refute Marcion. Eventually, Marcionism was officially rejected by the church as heresy.[1]

My colleague's angry student illustrates why we need to avoid using the accusatory signs "liberal" and "conservative," which function as stop-signs to communication. When we dismiss ideas as liberal or conservative, we sacrifice the opportunity not only to listen and learn, but also to change the

---

[1]Tertullian took Marcion to task for more than his view of Scripture. Marcion also eschewed the incarnation as "a disgrace to God" because the human body is "stuffed with excrement." Jaroslav Pelikan, *The Christian Tradition: A History of the Development of Doctrine*, vol. 1, *The Emergence of the Catholic Tradition (100-600)* (Chicago: University of Chicago Press, 1971), p. 75.

thoughts of those with whom we disagree. Ironically, by taking a stand on the "conservative" side of the religious coin, the student mimicked his enemies on the other side: those "liberals" who regard signs of the past as no longer valuable. The student read Hebrew Scriptures not as relevant truth about the God of Abraham, Isaac and Jacob, but only as signs anticipating Christ.

Christians on the edge, of course, read it both ways, acknowledging that we still worship Yahweh even as we study the changing signs by which Yahweh is revealed: from God's tongue speaking out of the burning bush in the Pentateuch to God's tongues burning above speakers at Pentecost. Pentecost itself illustrates the (re)signing of truth: the tongues of fire recorded in Acts 2 were new signs given to followers of Jesus who had worshipfully re-signed themselves to the traditional celebration of Pentecost, a Jewish festival held seven weeks and a day after Passover.

Christian leaders in the fourth century therefore operated on the edge when they established—at the Council of Carthage (397 c.e.)—that the Bible should include both Hebrew Scriptures and the gospel message.[2] The signs "Old Testament" and "New Testament," in fact, indicate a commitment to (re)signing: resigned to the idea that the Jewish God is the same as the Christian God, Christians re-signed how we are to know that God— through Jesus, the Son of God incarnate. "Testament," meaning covenant or promise, implies that the same God who covenanted with Abraham covenants with us. But the word "new" implies that God's old covenant has been given new signs. Same God, new signs. This chapter will therefore focus on God's Word in two senses—Jesus Christ as the Word of God and the Bible as the Word of God—to demonstrate that Christianity has always been a (re)signing faith.

THIS SHALL BE A SIGN FOR YOU

Luke's first proclamation of the "good news," or the "gospel," identifies a baby as a sign:

> But the angel said to [the shepherds], "Do not be afraid; for see—I am bringing you *good news* of great joy for all the people: to you is born this day in the city of David a Savior, who is the Messiah, the Lord. This will be a sign for you:

---

[2]I thank my colleague Emerson Powery for pointing out to me that the famous bishop of Alexandria, Athanasius (ca. 293-373), was the first known Christian to list—in 367 c.e.—the same twenty-seven New Testament books of the Bible that Protestants consider canonical today.

you will find a child wrapped in bands of cloth and lying in a manger." (Lk 2:10-12, emphasis mine)

Recited every Christmas, this passage has become so familiar that people rarely stop to think about the phrase "this will be a *sign* for you." A sign of what? If, indeed, a sign is "something standing for something else," what does the baby in the manger stand for?

The original audience of the "good news"—whether shepherds or readers of Luke's Gospel—would have recognized "this will be a sign for you" as part of Jewish tradition, repeated often in the Hebrew Scriptures: Exodus 13:9; Joshua 4:6; 1 Samuel 2:34; 14:10; 2 Kings 19:29; Isaiah 37:30; 38:7; Jeremiah 44:29 (and many other variations). The phrase therefore signaled ancient truths, each "sign" standing for God's Word. And we are to assume the same about the "sign" lying in a manger.

Resigned to this traditional approach to truth, Luke's earliest Jewish readers were also confronted with a re-signing of truth. For the sentence immediately preceding "This will be a sign for you" implies that a weak, vulnerable newborn, so poor that it must lie in a feeding trough, is a sign of "the Messiah."

(RE)SIGNING THE MESSIAH

"Messiah," meaning "the anointed one" ("Christ" in Greek), had long been a Jewish sign "for a royal figure as agent of divine deliverance."[3] Daniel describes an appearance by the angel Gabriel, who predicts the coming of "an anointed prince" (Dan 9:26). When the Persian king Cyrus is mentioned two verses later, we get a hint that he may be the predicted "Messiah"—a hint endorsed when Isaiah describes Cyrus as God's "anointed" or "Messiah" (Is 45:1). By enabling the Jews to return to Jerusalem and rebuild their temple, Cyrus brought salvation for the Jews: salvation from pagan Babylonia. Due to the importance of this event, the Hebrews ended their Scriptures with a passage describing Cyrus—a passage which is repeated, nearly word for word at the start of Ezra:

> In the first year of King Cyrus of Persia, in fulfillment of *the word of the* LORD spoken by Jeremiah, the LORD stirred up the spirit of King Cyrus of Persia so that he sent a herald throughout all his kingdom and also declared in a written

---

[3]David Noel Freedman, ed., *The Anchor Bible Dictionary* (New York: Doubleday, 1992), 1:920.

edict: "Thus says King Cyrus of Persia: The LORD, the God of heaven, has given me all the kingdoms of the earth, and he has charged me to build him a house at Jerusalem, which is in Judah. Whoever is among you of all his people, may the LORD his God be with him! Let him go up." (2 Chron 36:22-23, emphasis mine)

At the time of Jesus' birth several hundred years later, Jerusalem, along with its temple, was once again ruled by a foreign power. The Jews, therefore, were awaiting another Messiah, one who, graced with the power and wisdom of Cyrus, might save them from Roman rule. This explains the despair of the men on the Emmaus road after Christ's crucifixion: "[W]e had hoped that he was the one to redeem Israel" (Lk 24:21). Only when the resurrected Jesus broke bread with them did they recognize his (re)signing: resigned to the truth of "Moses and all the prophets," Jesus re-signed it when "he interpreted to them the things about himself in all the scriptures" (Lk 24:27). Jesus turned old truths into new signs: signs of himself.

They should have seen it coming. After all, Jesus got in trouble due to his (re)signing of Jewish law, seen most dramatically when he re-signed the fourth commandment. In a controversy recounted in all three Synoptic Gospels, Jesus had to defend himself for picking grain on the sabbath. His defense, elaborated by Mark, has become famous: "The sabbath was made for humankind, and not humankind for the sabbath; so the Son of Man is lord even of the sabbath" (Mk 2:27-28). Soon afterwards, encountering a man with a withered hand, Jesus asked his critics, "Is it lawful to do good or to do harm on the sabbath, to save life or to kill?" When his detractors gave no answer, Jesus "was grieved at their hardness of heart" and proceeded to heal the cripple. The Pharisees, resenting Jesus' re-signing of truth, "immediately conspired with the Herodians against him, how to destroy him" (Mk 3:4-6). Then as now, religious people often resist change, worried that it might destroy truth.

RESISTING CHANGE VERSUS FULFILLING TRUTH

Jesus did not want to destroy anything, least of all the truth:

Do not think that I have come to abolish the law or the prophets; I have come not to abolish but to fulfill. For truly I tell you, until heaven and earth pass away, not one letter, not one stroke of a letter, will pass from the law until all is accomplished. (Mt 5:17-18)

So what does Jesus mean when he says that not one letter will pass from the law until heaven and earth pass away?

Here is my theory: When Jesus says he will fulfill rather than abolish the law, he refers to (re)signing. Rather than mystifying one side of the coin or the other—by endorsing the saving power of the law on the one side or by renouncing the law on the other—Jesus resigns himself to God's law while at the same time re-signing it. Doing so, Jesus recognizes that to be human is to be embedded in a particular society. Humans understand God according to the language—the traditional signs—of their culture. Jesus was embedded in culture as well; to resist this idea would be to endorse a basic heresy of Christianity. In 451, the Council of Chalcedon established that Jesus was fully human as well as fully God. Hence, to deny that Jesus was embedded in signs of his times would be to deny his humanity.

The culture in which Jesus lived and moved and had his being was, of course, Jewish. As a Jew, then, Jesus was not about to abolish the law; for the law provided the signs by which his culture understood God's Word. At the same time, he realized that a sign, no matter how traditional, always stands "for something else." So when the Pharisees turn the sign "honor the sabbath" into an end in itself, they have misinterpreted what it "stands for": reverent acknowledgment that God desires to be in relationship with a flourishing creation. And for God's creatures to flourish, they need a day of rest, a day to worship the One who graciously provides for them and enables their flourishing. Those who legalistically maintain the sabbath, therefore, act as though God desires the *flourishing of the sign itself* rather than of what it stands for.

Committed to the flourishing and nourishing of God's people, Jesus held on to Jewish truths about the Messiah, but he gave different signs of how the Messiah—"God's anointed"—saves. As theologian M. Shawn Copeland puts it,

> From the beginning of his ministry, Jesus preached a message that was familiar enough so that those who came to hear him could recognize their religious tradition. At the same time, that message was edgy, distinctive enough to make them uncomfortable, even as it stirred their heart to want God more, and to want to be more for God and for others.[4]

---

[4]M. Shawn Copeland, "To Follow Jesus: Slave Narratives and Spirituals," *America*, February 26, 2007, p. 10. Copeland also notes, as does *The Anchor Bible Dictionary*, that "scholars maintain that during the Judaism of Jesus' day, there was no uniform idea of the Messiah" ("To Follow Jesus," p. 11).

The message was "edgy" because Jesus operated on the edge between tradition and change. Rather than abolish tradition, Jesus fulfilled it by giving it new signs.[5]

(RE)SIGNING THE TEMPLE

While Cyrus made possible the rebuilding of an architectural temple in Jerusalem—the site of animal sacrifices to atone for sin—the Gospel writers resigned the locale of salvation, placing it in Christ's own body. Significantly, Matthew's account of (re)signing the sabbath also refers to (re)signing the temple. First Jesus reminds his critics that, due to slaughtering animals on the sabbath, "the priests in the temple break the sabbath and yet are guiltless." Then he makes an extraordinary claim: "I tell you, something greater than the temple is here" (Mt 12:5-6). To many listeners of his day, these words qualified as blasphemy. After all, the temple, with the ark of the covenant at its center, was where the Spirit of God resided. How could Jesus—a human like any human who hungers, thirsts, tires and dies—provide a better place to meet God's Spirit than the temple? Outraged, those who "gave false testimony" against Jesus on the night of his betrayal misrepresented his signs: "We heard him say, 'I will destroy this temple that is made with hands, and in three days I will build another, not made with hands'" (Mk 14:57-58).

Both Matthew and Mark report these accusations as "false," reinforcing that Jesus did not plan to "destroy" the ultimate sign of God's presence among the Jews. Jesus does not give up on the value of the Hebrew temple; he merely re-signs it. This explains his anger over temple money changers in a passage that John interprets with a phrase from the Psalms: "[Jesus] told those who were selling the doves, 'Take these things out of here! Stop making my Father's house a marketplace!' His disciples remembered that it was written, 'Zeal for your house will consume me'" (Jn 2:16-17, quoting Ps 69:9). Then, when the offended parties ask him for a *sign*, or miracle, to legitimize his actions, Jesus establishes *his body* as the sign:

> The Jews then said to him, "What *sign* can you show us for doing this?" Jesus answered them, "Destroy this temple, and in three days I will raise it up." The Jews then said, "This temple has been under construction for forty-six years, and will you raise it up in three days?" But he was speaking of the temple of his

---

[5]For an easy, though insightful, read about the (re)signing of Jesus, see Bruxy Cavey, *The End of Religion: An Introduction to the Subversive Spirituality of Jesus* (Oakville, ON: Agora, 2005).

body. After he was raised from the dead, his disciples remembered that he had said this; and they believed the scripture and the word that Jesus had spoken. (Jn 2:18-22, emphasis mine)

Here we see where the false accusers got the idea that Jesus said, "*I will* destroy this temple*.*" But rather than "*I will,*" the unspoken words in "Destroy this temple" are "If you": "*If you* destroy this temple, in three days I will raise it up." Jesus communicates that destruction is neither his nor God's. The violence to Christ's body was the result of human sin, destroying a temple that God rebuilt in three days through the resurrection of a new kind of Messiah.[6]

(RE)SIGNING THE OLD TESTAMENT

When Christ re-signs the temple, then, he is resigned to ancient Hebrew paradigms. He even quotes from Psalm 118:22 to apply the signs of ancient truth to his re-signed meaning:

What then does this text mean:
"The stone that the builders rejected
has become the cornerstone"? (Lk 20:17)

Jesus is the cornerstone of a re-signed temple: one not made with hands. The cornerstone is "rejected," however, by people who resist the (re)signing of truth.

Luke exemplifies this resistance when he describes Christ's triumphal entry into Jerusalem. As is well known, witnesses welcomed Jesus by jubilantly quoting signs from the Hebrew Scriptures: "Blessed is the king who comes in the name of the Lord!" (Lk 19:38, quoting Ps 118:26). When Pharisees tell Jesus to rebuke the purveyors of such tribute, Jesus responds, "I tell you if these were silent, the stones would shout out" (Lk 19:40). As a child, I imagined such an event the way Saturday morning cartoons might show it: personified rocks with moss for hair and twigs for legs doing a song-and-dance routine along the path where Jesus rode. But this image ignores the ancient sign from the Hebrew Scriptures to which Jesus alludes: "The very stones will cry out from the wall, and the plaster will respond from the woodwork" (Hab 2:11). Clearly, the stones to which Jesus refers during his triumphal entry are not those scattered on the ground. The stones are those

---

[6]I will discuss Christ's atonement, and ways it has been (re)signed through the centuries, in chapter ten.

in a *wall*, like the temple walls, which most likely include plaster and woodwork. By anthropomorphizing these stones, saying they would "shout out" if disciples were silenced, Jesus implies the re-signing of temple walls with human flesh.

Not long after his triumphal entry, of course, Jesus was nailed to the cross in another act of (re)signing. Yielding to ancient Hebrew paradigms for the forgiveness of sin, Jesus re-signed the atonement, his body becoming a sign of sacrifice and temple simultaneously. This simultaneous union of sacrifice and temple anticipates one of the key doctrines developed by the early church: Jesus was fully human—the flesh sacrificed in atonement for sin—as well as fully God, whose presence graced the temple.[7]

No wonder the Synoptic Gospels all recount the tearing of the temple curtain at the moment of Christ's death (Mt 27:51; Mk 15:38; Lk 23:45). The curtain covered the entry to the Holy of Holies, which contained the ark of the covenant: the sign of God's presence. Jewish law established that no one could enter the Holy of Holies except the high priest, himself allowed entrance only once a year: on the Day of Atonement (Yom Kippur) to pour the blood of sacrificed animals on the mercy seat covering the ark. Hence, when Jesus poured out his blood on the mercy seat of the cross, the barrier to the most holy place in Jerusalem was ripped open, allowing anyone—male or female, Jew or Greek, slave or free—access to God's presence (see Heb 10:19-20; Gal 3:28).

Significantly, the ark that represented the fullness of God's presence contained ancient signs of covenant: the ten commandments on tablets of stone, a jar of manna and Aaron's rod. With the tearing of the temple curtain, these signs would be (re)signed. The blossoming rod of Aaron (Latin *virga*) would become re-signed as the Virgin Mary (Latin *virgo*), both producing fruit without biological fertilization (Num 17:8; Lk 1:34). The stone upon which the commandments were written now cried out that Jesus was the new temple filled with the presence of God (see Jer 31:33). The manna that fed the Israelites wandering through the Wilderness of Sin (Ex 16) would become the bread of Christ's body, broken to save us from our wildness of sin.

---

[7]Jesus' functioning as both sacrifice and temple also subverts the problematic dismissal of Judaism by those Marcion-like Christians who relegate the Hebrew Scriptures to a testament about legalism in contrast to the New Testament message of grace. For, like all (re)signing, there is continuity with the past even as its signs change.

In the Gospel of John, Jesus makes this latter (re)signing explicit: "I am the bread of life. Your ancestors ate the manna in the wilderness, and they died. . . . I am the living bread which came down from heaven. Whoever eats of this bread will live forever; and the bread that I will give for the life of the world is my flesh" (Jn 6:48-51). No wonder Jesus tells his disciples, "Is there anyone among you who, if your child asks for bread, will give a stone?" (Mt 7:9). The stones of the temple contain at their heart—in the Holy of Holies open to all—the manna/bread of salvation.

(RE)SIGNING ADULTERY

Jesus (re)signs stones in one of the most famous stories in the New Testament: the woman taken in adultery. Scribes and Pharisees, having caught the woman in the midst of the act, appeal to Jewish law in order to test Jesus: "Now in the law Moses commanded us to stone such women. Now what do you say?" (Jn 8:5). What follows next is one of the great mysteries of the Bible: "Jesus bent down and wrote with his finger on the ground"—twice! (Jn 8:6, 8). He obviously made signs in the dirt, but what were they? If a sign is "something standing for something else," what was Jesus indicating?

Interpretations are plentiful. A fourteenth-century English play about the woman taken in adultery has Jesus write the sins of each accuser in the dust. Jesus says to the accusers, "Loke which of yow that nevyr sinne wrought, / But is of liff clennere than she, / Cast at her stonys and spare her nowght" [Look which of you has never sinned, But has a cleaner life than she, Cast at her stones and spare her not]. Each accuser then recognizes how signs drawn in the dirt reveal that his life is no cleaner than the woman's.[8] Christ's signs "stand for" the sins we all commit—just as the cross will stand for the sins we all commit.

I heard another intriguing interpretation of Christ's signs during a Bible study led by Mark Foreman, father of the famous Foreman brothers in the band Switchfoot. Mark suggested that Jesus drew arbitrary doodles in the dirt to distract attention from the woman, who, if "caught in the very act of committing adultery" (v. 4) was probably naked. Christ's signs "stand for" the need to renounce prurient interest in the naked sins of others.

Distracting salacious focus from a nakedly sinning woman, Jesus might

---

[8]"The Woman Taken in Adultery: From N Town," in *Medieval Drama*, ed. David Bevington (Boston: Houghton Mifflin, 1975), p. 467.

also have been writing the Jewish law in the dirt. Leviticus 20:10 prescribes that "*both* the adulterer and the adulteress shall be put to death"—not just the woman (see also Deut 22:22). Taken as such, the signs in the dirt "stand for" the accusers' sinful manipulation of the law, by which they exclude a male—like themselves—from culpability.

All these interpretations, however, are rendered moot by the fact that no one knows what signs Jesus drew. Perhaps we are not told because the story is not so much about what the dust-signs stand for as it is about the very act of (re)signing itself. Notice that Jesus does not denounce Jewish law about stoning adulterers; rather, he reinterprets it: "Let anyone among you who is without sin be the first to throw a stone at her." His sinless flesh, of course, will become the temple stones that contain the Mercy Seat of God, enabling him to tell the woman, "Neither do I condemn you. Go your way, and from now on do not sin again" (Jn 8:7, 11).

ADULTERIZING THE BIBLE: INERRANT OR ERRATIC?

Ironically, the story of the woman taken in adultery is not included in the most ancient Gospel manuscripts. Later Christians apparently added it to John's narrative. It first appears in a Latin manuscript in the fourth century, and does not show up in Greek until the sixth century, even though Greek was the language used by the writer of John's Gospel. What do we make of this?

People on both sides of the coin often conclude that the story of the woman taken in adultery adulterates the Bible. On one side of the coin, Christians who advocate biblical inerrancy set the story aside in an effort to honor the original God-inspired text. Harold Lindsell, who argued for an inerrant Bible in *The Battle for the Bible,* places John 8:1-11 in a footnote for his edited version of the *Harper Study Bible.*[9]

On the other side of the coin, skeptics scoff at the idea that the Bible is divinely inspired. Pointing at other inconsistencies and late additions in Scripture, they argue that Christians have disingenuously identified their human efforts as the divine "Word of God." This seems to be the tack taken by Bart Ehrman, author of the bestselling *Misquoting Jesus* and its more

---

[9]Harold Lindsell, *The Battle for the Bible* (Grand Rapids, MI: Zondervan, 1976); Harold Lindsell, ed., *Harper Study Bible* (Grand Rapids, MI: Zondervan, 1965), p. 1598.

scholarly predecessor, *The Orthodox Corruption of Scripture*.[10] Identifying the many places where scribal errors and deliberate changes made by Christian copyists have been incorporated into sacred Scripture, Ehrman dismisses the "holy" part of the Holy Bible.

How should we respond to Ehrman's thoroughly erudite scholarship? After all, he has educated himself in the original languages of the Bible and has studied and compared numerous ancient documents in order to pinpoint not only the hundreds of changes made to biblical manuscripts but also contradictions within the biblical text. To argue for biblical inerrancy in response makes Christianity seem intellectually untenable to scholars familiar with the most ancient texts. Isn't the point of the Bible to do the opposite: to draw people into relationship with God? Ehrman himself, a one-time evangelical committed to inerrancy, responded to his discoveries by becoming a self-proclaimed agnostic. For him God's Word had become reduced to mere human words.

Christians on the edge, I would suggest, respond neither with inerrancy nor with agnosticism. Following the Word of God, they offer, instead, the (re)signing of truth.

FOLLOWING THE (RE)SIGNING WORD

New Testament writers seem quite conscious that they are (re)signing truth. Though examples are many, I will only mention a few, in the order in which they appear in the Bible.

1. The Acts of the Apostles. The Greek word for "sign" appears thirteen times in the book of Acts, which is filled not only with "signs and wonders" but also with examples of (re)signing truth. After tongues of flame appeared during Pentecost, Peter gives a sermon in which he proclaims that the multiple linguistic signs (speaking in tongues) fulfill a proclamation from the prophet Joel, whom he quotes at length. To follow Christ, in other words, involves the (re)signing of Hebrew truth.

Not much later, Peter offered another sign, changing once again the truth he had recently asserted. While Pentecost established that Christ fulfilled Judaism, Peter's visit to Caesarea opened Christianity up to non-Jews. This

---

[10]Bart Ehrman, *Misquoting Jesus: The Story Behind Who Changed the Bible and Why* (San Francisco: HarperOne, 2005); *The Orthodox Corruption of Scripture: The Effect of Early Christological Controversies on the Text of the New Testament* (New York: Oxford University Press USA, 1996).

time signs of change were in a sheet rather than in tongues of flame. As re-counted in Acts 10, the hungry Peter enters a trance while praying on a roof. In his trance he sees a sheet filled with animals that God had proclaimed "profane or unclean." When a voice tells him to "kill and eat," Peter refuses, seeking to hold fast to sacred law. But the voice explains, "What God has made clean, you must not call profane" (Acts 10:9-16). In other words, signs have been radically re-signed: from unclean to clean! Peter therefore shares the good news of God's re-signing with Cornelius and other Gentiles: "You yourselves know that it is unlawful for a Jew to associate with or to visit a Gentile; but God has shown me that I should not call anyone profane or un-clean" (Acts 10:28).

This does not mean, however, that the Hebrew God has been superseded by the Christian God, as Marcion proclaimed. It means that signs of what it means to follow the God of Abraham, Isaac and Jacob have changed. As Peter puts it, "I truly understand that God shows no partiality, but in every nation anyone who fears him and does what is right is acceptable to him" (10:34).

2. Paul's letter to the Romans. In his letter to the Romans, Paul quotes from Genesis 15:6 to suggest that Christians should follow the example of Abraham:

> We say, "Faith was reckoned to Abraham as righteousness." How then was it reckoned to him? Was it before or after he had been circumcised? It was not after, but before he was circumcised. He received the *sign* of circumcision as a seal of the righteousness that he had by faith while he was still uncircumcised. The purpose was to make him the ancestor of all who believe without being circumcised and who thus have righteousness reckoned to them, and likewise the ancestor of the circumcised who are not only circumcised but who also follow the example of the faith that our ancestor Abraham had before he was circumcised. (Rom 4:9-12, emphasis mine)

By establishing circumcision as a "sign" of "righteousness" through "faith," Paul makes faith the ultimate goal. Therefore, whether or not one has the "sign" is not as important as what the sign "stands for": faith. In other words, resigned to the truth of Abraham's faith, Paul changes the sign. As a result, Christian practice changes; circumcision is no longer considered necessary. An old commandment has been preserved by changing the sign.

3. The letter to the Hebrews. The letter to the Hebrews could be studied as a lesson in (re)signing. Its unknown author appeals extensively to stories and passages from the Septuagint, the Greek translation of Hebrew Scripture, in order to re-sign them. However, rather than arguing that Yahweh has been superseded by the Christian God, the author is resigned to the God of the Hebrews. Therefore, as professor Timothy Bryan observes, the writer "plunges his readers/hearers into the ancient world of Abraham; the priestly, sacrificial cult of the Israelites in the wilderness; the psalmists' cries; and Jeremiah's prophetic utterances of covenantal renewal." These examples of God's words and actions, in other words, apply to Christians. Endorsing the relevance of the Hebrew Scriptures to Christian belief, the writer to the Hebrews refers to three passages quoted nowhere else in the New Testament:

> Psalm 11:4—to emphasize the *new* priesthood of Jesus
> Jeremiah 31:31-34—to emphasize the *new* covenant mediated by Jesus
> Psalm 40:6-8—to emphasize the *new* sacrifice of Jesus[11]

Bryan's repetition of the word "new" indicates that Jesus fulfills rather than supplants the faith of his Hebrew fathers. Indeed, Christianity began not as an alternate religion but as a re-energized expression of Judaism. The letter to the Hebrews, then, establishes that new signs are predicated on the truth of the old.

4. The letters of John. This tension between old and new is made explicit in the first letter attributed to John. Notice how John starts out by denying any change to the word of God, but then totally reverses himself:

> Beloved, *I am writing you no new commandment*, but an old commandment that you have had from the beginning; *the old commandment is the word* that you have heard. Yet *I am writing you a new commandment* that is true in him and in you, because the darkness is passing away and the true light is already shining. (1 Jn 2:7-8, emphasis mine)

Why the apparent contradiction? Perhaps because John is (re)signing truth: old teachings are endorsed even as they are being revised.[12]

---

[11]Timothy Bryan, "The Letter to the Hebrews," *Cokesbury Adult Bible Studies: Teacher* 16, no. 4 (Summer 2008): 5, emphasis mine.

[12]As New Testament scholar Emerson Powery informed me, commentaries differ in their assessment of John's word "commandments." The sign could refer to "Scripture" or "Law"; "Word of God" or "teachings of the community." Any of these definitions, however, support my point about (re)signing.

Take, for example, the Old Testament alignment of God with light. The Psalms alone provide plenty of examples:

> The LORD is my light and my salvation;
>   whom shall I fear? (Ps 27:1)

> For with you is the fountain of life;
>   in your light we see light. (Ps 36:9)

> O send out your light and your truth;
>   let them lead me. (Ps 43:3)

> Your word is a lamp to my feet
>   and a light to my path. (Ps 119:105)

As though alluding to these verses, the Gospel of John establishes Jesus as God's Word by aligning him with light:

> In the beginning was the Word, and the Word was with God, and the Word was God. . . . What has come into being in him was life, and the life was the light of all people. The light shines in the darkness, and the darkness did not overcome it. (Jn 1:1, 3-5)

This may explain why, unlike the other Gospels, John shows Jesus explicitly identifying himself with the light:

> I am the light of the world. Whoever follows me will never walk in darkness but will have the light of life. . . .
>   As long as I am in the world, I am the light of the world. (Jn 8:12; 9:5)

> The light is with you for a little longer. Walk while you have the light, so that the darkness may not overtake you. If you walk in the darkness, you do not know where you are going. While you have the light, believe in the light, so that you may become children of light. (Jn 12:35-36)

As we have seen, the letter attributed to John similarly reflects this (re) signing of God's light. Furthermore, like Paul with circumcision, John proceeds to relate such (re)signing to the practice of discipleship. Immediately after the old commandment made new (quoted above), we read, "Whoever says, 'I am in the light,' while hating a brother or sister, is still in the darkness. Whoever loves a brother or sister lives in the light, and in such a person there is no cause for stumbling" (1 Jn 2:9-10). Darkness and light now signal the absence or presence of love, a love most fully revealed in the atoning work of the cross. And it is with love that we follow God's Word, loving the light more than the signs that point to the light.

BOTH SIDES OF THE BIBLICAL COIN

Like Jesus, whom John identifies as both Word and Light, the Bible as the Word of God is both fully human and fully divine. Thus, while skeptics stand on one side of the coin to say that God's Word is fully human, and inerrantists stand on the other side of the coin to say that God's Word is fully divine, Christians on the edge affirm both/and rather than either/or thinking. As Niels Bohr, the Nobel Prize–winning physicist famously put it, "The opposite of a true statement is a false statement, but the opposite of a profound truth can be another profound truth"—like, I would suggest, these opposite truths: Jesus was fully human; Jesus was fully God. Educational theorist Parker Palmer comments on Bohr's insight with the following comment: "truth is a paradoxical joining of apparent opposites, and if we want to know that truth, we must learn to embrace those opposites in one."[13] Where better to embrace paradoxical opposites than on the edge of the coin?

Evangelical Bible scholar Peter Enns, for example, stands on the edge by paralleling the paradox of Jesus with the paradox of the Bible. He notes that just as some Christians have rejected the paradox of the incarnation, some Christians reject the paradox of Scripture:

> The ancient heresy of Docetism stated that Christ was fully divine and only *seemed* to be human (the Greek verb *dokein* ["to seem"] is the root of the word Docetism). The Council of Chalcedon rightly concluded that if Christ only appeared to be human, then the death and resurrection are not real. . . . What some ancient Christians were saying about Christ, the Docetic heresy, is similar to the mistake that other Christians have made (and continue to make) about Scripture: it comes from God, and the marks of its humanity are only apparent, to be explained away.[14]

Resigned to the Bible as God's Word, Enns goes on to demonstrate how the New Testament writers, following the example of Jesus, often re-signed it

---

[13]Parker Palmer, *The Courage to Teach: Exploring the Inner Landscape of a Teacher's Life* (San Francisco: Jossey-Bass, 2007), p. 65. I thank my student Karissa Graybill for drawing my attention to Palmer's allusion to and commentary on Niels Bohr.

[14]Peter Enns, *Inspiration and Incarnation: Evangelicals and the Problem of the Old Testament* (Grand Rapids, MI: Baker Academic, 2005), p. 18.

in unusual ways. In addition to quoting Hebrew Scripture out of context, sometimes they changed the words of the Bible to fit their own purposes. For example, in Romans 11:26-27, Paul quotes from Isaiah 59:20:

> And so all Israel will be saved; as it is written:
> "*Out of Zion will come the Deliverer;*
>   he will banish ungodliness from Jacob.
> And this is my covenant with them,
>   when I take away their sins." (emphasis mine)

In the original Hebrew, however, Isaiah states that the redeemer will come *to* Zion rather than *out of* Zion.[15] Enns explains this, as well as many other blatant changes to Scripture, in terms of Jewish interpretive practices. Revelation occurs, in other words, via signs of the times. Jesus and New Testament writers interpreted Scripture as did scholars of their day, who took a totally different approach to interpretation than we do today.

Here is another example I gleaned from a Sunday school workbook.[16] Isaiah 40:3 proclaims, "A voice cries out: 'In the wilderness prepare the way of the LORD, make straight in the desert a highway for our God.'" The Gospel writers, however, quote the phrase differently, so that the voice cries out not *about* the wilderness, but *in* the wilderness: "This is the one of whom the prophet Isaiah spoke when he said, 'The voice of one crying out in the wilderness: Prepare the way of the Lord, make his paths straight'" (Mt 3:3; see also Mk 1:2-3; Lk 3:4-6; Jn 1:23). All four Gospels (re)sign the truth of Isaiah such that the statement becomes fulfilled in John the Baptist.

Does this mean we should follow the example of Jesus and New Testament writers by quoting verses out of context or changing grammar and punctuation? Of course not! For we are embedded in times that value different signs. Think of it this way: it would be absurd to insist that Jesus, God's Word, wore a pin-striped suit and silk tie in order to preach the truth. So also, to insist that the Bible, God's Word, preaches the truth dressed in signs of twenty-first-century thought is ridiculous. Peter Enns explains in reference to Genesis:

> It is wholly incomprehensible to think that thousands of years ago God would

---

[15]Ibid., p. 139.
[16]Jack Gilbert, "The Highway for God," in *Cokesbury Adult Bible Studies: Teacher* 19, no. 2 (Winter 2010-2011): 27.

have felt constrained to speak in a way that would be meaningful only to Westerners several thousand years later. To do so borders on modern, Western arrogance. Rather, Genesis makes its case in a way that ancient men and women would have readily understood—indeed, the *only* way.[17]

While some people might accuse Enns of being a "liberal," he is merely following the example of godly Christians down through the centuries. C. S. Lewis, for example, felt the need to "rule out the view that every statement in Scripture must be historical truth." Nevertheless, he believed "that the over-all operation of Scripture is to convey God's Word to the reader . . . who reads it in the right spirit."[18] For Lewis, "the right spirit" is not one that seeks to either prove or disprove the Bible's scientific and historical accuracy: opposite sides of the same coin. For him, the right spirit is on the edge; it is a spirit that believes in the resurrection of Jesus while aware that the Bible has certain inconsistencies in the way it points to the same ultimate reality. The right spirit opens itself to the Holy Spirit, seeking in the Bible truths for life lived in relationship with our creator and redeemer.[19]

Lewis was merely following the example of Luther and Calvin, who themselves followed the example of early church fathers by ascribing to a principle of "accommodation": "God spoke to his people as a parent speaks to a child," accommodating the truth to their understanding.[20] For example, because Old Testament authors believed that the sun moved around the earth, they were inspired to write that God stopped the sun in its movement to help Joshua conquer the Amorites (Josh 10:12-13). They understood truth according to the signs of their times.

As confirmed by the incarnation, God meets people in and through the signs of their times. To deny this is to commit the Docetic heresy.

---

[17]Enns, *Inspiration and Incarnation*, p. 55.

[18]Letter to Clyde S. Kilby (July 5, 1959), in *The Collected Letters of C. S. Lewis: Narnia, Cambridge, and Joy, 1950-1963*, ed. Walter Hooper (San Francisco: HarperSanFrancisco, 2007), 3:1043-44. Lewis cited "the apparent inconsistencies between the genealogies in Matt i and Luke iii," as well as discrepancies "between the accounts of the death of Judas in Matt xxvii 5 and Acts i 18-19."

[19]Here's how Rowan Williams explains it: "The inspiration of Scripture . . . is not a matter of the Holy Spirit holding a writer's hand as a book is written; it is the present reality of a divine mediation that makes recognition possible as we now encounter the strangeness of the story." See *Why Study the Past? The Quest for the Historical Church* (Grand Rapids, MI: Eerdmans, 2005), p. 29.

[20]Joseph T. Lienhard, *The Bible, the Church, and Authority: The Canon of the Christian Bible in History and Theology* (Collegeville, MN: Liturgical Press, 1995), p. 81.

CERTITUDE ABOUT THE WORD: AUGUSTINE

According to Augustine (354-430), one of the most influential shapers of Western Christianity, we can only be certain about one infallible truth in the Bible: the Love of God. At the end of the fourth century, he wrote a treatise called *On Christian Doctrine* in which he argues, "Whoever, therefore, thinks that he understands the divine Scriptures or any part of them so that it does not build the double love of God and of our neighbor does not understand it at all."[21]

Nevertheless, some Christians seem more passionate about protecting the holiness of an inerrant sign (the Bible) than about humbly considering how to be transformed by what the sign points to (God's holy character and loving acts). Augustine aligns this problem with slavery:

> He is a slave to a sign who uses or worships a significant thing without knowing what it signifies. . . . However, he who does not know what a sign means, but does know that it is a sign, is not in servitude.[22]

In other words, recognizing something as "a sign," even without fully understanding what it means, is far preferable to worshiping the sign as holy in and of itself.

THE RULING OF THE WORD: THE CANON

When my mother, Joy, was attending Wheaton College, she had two different classmates tell her "God told me that you are to be my wife." These men, as intensely earnest about their walk with Christ as was Joy, claimed to know God's word. Now, either God was condoning polygamy for the twentieth century, or else these fellows were motivated by their human spirits more than the Holy Spirit. Nevertheless, each believed God had given him a "sign." Joy could only respond to each, "God has not given me the same sign." (Indeed, she married neither, for which I am quite clearly grateful.)

Realizing that even the most earnest believers develop competing signs for God's Word, our church fathers recognized the need for a "canon," which means "measuring rod" or "ruler." Christians need something that rules over interpretations of God's work on earth. It's similar to the development of the

---

[21]Augustine, *On Christian Doctrine*, trans. D. W. Robertson Jr. (New York: Liberal Arts Press, 1958), book 1, para. 40, p. 30.
[22]Ibid., book 3, para. 13, pp. 86-87.

foot-long ruler. Before twelve inches became standardized in Scotland during the twelfth century C.E., people determined length by a man's foot (hence the word *foot*). A barn in one village might therefore differ in size from a barn elsewhere—depending upon the size of the builders' feet. One story suggests that a ruler, King Henry I of England (ca. 1068-1135), provided the standard for the twelve-inch ruler—based on his extraordinarily large feet (!). Whether or not this story is true matters less than the recognized need for a universal standard of measurement.

So also with standardization of the biblical canon. In the early centuries of the church, many Christians read as Scripture the *Revelation of Peter, Shepherd of Hermas* and the *Gospel of Thomas*, even though the latter was denounced as heretical by the influential theologian Origen (ca. 185-254). Later Christians therefore saw the need for an agreed-upon standard to "measure" Christian truth. But, as with carpenters' feet in early English history, different Christians had different "sizes" of measuring rods. The first Christian to use the sign "New Testament," Irenaeus of Lyons (who died around 202), argued for four Gospels because "there are four zones of the world in which we live, and four principal winds." Jerome (ca. 347-420), who translated the Bible into Latin, argued for 22 books in the Old Testament because "there are 22 letters in the Hebrew alphabet."[23]

Hence, just as the English decided to follow one person's foot size for greater consistency in architecture, so church leaders decided to establish better criterion than meteorology and numerology for the architecture of the biblical canon. Rather than the somewhat subjective measurement of "inspiration"—think of my mother's "inspired" suitors—our forefathers based the inclusion of a book in the canon on three more tangible considerations:

1. Was the text written by an apostle or the disciple of an apostle?

2. Did the text teach correct doctrine?

3. Was the text used for teaching and worship in churches throughout the Roman Empire?[24]

The fourth-century Council at Carthage thus established a ruler—the

---

[23]Quoted in Lienhard, *The Bible, the Church, and Authority*, pp. 25, 59.

[24]I quote these three questions directly from Michael R. Cosby, *Interpreting Biblical Literature: An Introduction to Biblical Studies* (Grantham, PA: Stony Run Publishing, 2009), p. 415. As Cosby notes, these three considerations were outlined by the first great historian of Christianity, Eusebius, around 325 C.E.

biblical canon—to guide the building of Christian truth the way a stan-dardized ruler was developed to guide the building of British barns.

To dismiss the Bible as no longer relevant to Christianity, then, is compa-rable to airplane designers dismissing the standard measuring devices in their field. Though both standards were established by humans (Christians, of course, seeking the guidance of the Holy Spirit), both are absolutely nec-essary for the effective construction of anything new. (Hint: avoid boarding a plane designed by people who didn't use standardized measurements.) The new, then, is built according to guidelines established by our predecessors. As Luke Timothy Johnson summarizes in his helpful book on the Bible, "An unlimited canon is no measure, any more than a foot ruler can gain inches and still be a foot ruler. Because it is closed, the canon can perform the function of mediating a specific identity through successive ages of the church."[25]

In recognition of this truth, Reformed Christians wrote the following into their Confession of 1967:

> The Scriptures, given under the guidance of the Holy Spirit, are nevertheless the words of men, conditioned by the language, thought forms, and literary fashions of the places and times at which they were written. They reflect views of life, history, and the cosmos which were then current. The church, therefore, has an obligation to approach the Scriptures with literary and historical under-standing.[26]

HOW, THEN, DO WE KNOW IT IS THE WORD OF GOD?

Right now some exasperated readers may feel like the student at the be-ginning of this chapter, wanting to say, "You are a liberal . . . oops . . . You are a . . . a . . . scoundrel undermining truth!" I understand this response. After all, how do we know the difference between God's Word and human words, between holy signs and human signs? How do we know whether new signs are of Christ or from culture, whether they reflect holy deity or human desire?

It will take me the rest of this book to fully answer these sign-ificant ques-tions. For now let me offer two suggestions. First, if we genuinely believe that

---

[25]Luke Timothy Johnson, *Scripture and Discernment: Decision Making and the Church* (Nashville: Abingdon, 1996), p. 36.
[26]Quoted in Shirley C. Guthrie, *Always Being Reformed: Faith for a Fragmented World* (Louisville: Westminster John Knox, 1996), pp. 28-29.

the Holy Spirit still moves among God's people, having guided the process of canon formation itself, we must be open to new signs.

Second, if we genuinely believe that the Holy Spirit still moves among God's people, we should believe that the Spirit enables us to identify truths that transcend the biblical inconsistencies identified by C. S. Lewis and the manuscript errors identified by Bart Ehrman. Rather than giving up on the truth of Christianity, as did Ehrman, we might endorse (re)signing: resigned to Scripture as God's Word to those who listen in faith, we acknowledge the possibility of a faithful re-signing. This acknowledgment arises from the testimony of Scripture itself. Nowhere does the Bible proclaim its own scientific inerrancy, but everywhere it demonstrates the (re)signing of truth.[27]

How, then, do we recognize signs of God's Word? To answer this question, we need to better understand how signs work. Significantly, when Jesus is presented to us as a "sign" in the manger, and then repeatedly does "signs and wonders" as an adult, early manuscripts employ the same Greek root for "sign": *sēmeion*. Variations of this word, sometimes translated "miracles," sometimes "wonders," appear over seventy-five times in the Greek New Testament. From this same Greek root comes the word *semiology*, which means "the study of signs."

Part two of this book will introduce the field of semiology and the influential cultural theorists who developed it, applied it and challenged it. This will lay a foundation for the *sēmeion* that the builders rejected, so that we might rejoice in a temple not made with hands: a temple that (re)signs truth.

---

[27]As John Yeatts notes, "The Bible logically should be the source for a theory of its own authority. Yet, the Bible does not claim to be inerrant." See *Revelation*, Believers Church Bible Commentary (Scottdale, PA: Herald, 2003), p. 432.

Part II

How Signs Work

3

IDENTIFYING SIGNS

From Rhetoric to Semiotic

When I decided in my twenties that I no longer wanted to be identified as a dumb blonde, I had myself fitted for glasses—though I really didn't need them—and started pulling my hair back into a tight bun that never held its place, inevitably sliding down to the nape of my neck. The caricature below captures this identifying stage in my life: the time when I wanted to be perceived as intellectual. It was drawn at a state fair where a group of friends decided to have our "portraits" done by the resident caricaturist. After asking what activity we wanted to be shown doing, he drew one of us surfing, an-

other cycling, a third cooking. When it came my turn, I removed my ineffectual glasses to say, with a touch of condescension, that I wanted to be shown reading. The cartoonist made fun of my arrogance, turning my activity of reading into a sign of how he read me: as a female failing to understand what men really want in a woman. The sign of the question mark by my nose gives it away.

At the time I was disgusted. How dare this sexist cartoonist misinterpret my signs! Today, however, I think that perhaps he

Figure 3.1. Caricature of Crystal Downing

interpreted me all too well. After all, one becomes an intellectual not by appropriating ready-made signs like glasses, buns and books, but by creating new signs—in response to the old—in order to help people think in new ways. In contrast, I was so caught up in superficial signs of intelligence that I resented anyone who did not validate my signs—just as the Pharisees resented Jesus for not validating their signs.

Rather than brandishing signs in order to browbeat others, Christians on the edge attempt to understand not only what motivates the signs they use but also how those signs affect others. For them, the creating of new signs directs attention not to the self but to the significance of life in Christ.

What follows, then, is a lesson in identifying the signs that identify us.

THE LESSON BEGINS

Please identify this sign:

X

"Ummm," you say, flipping a few pages forward to see if things get a bit more sophisticated, "well, it is, quite obviously, of course, the letter X."

"Yes and no," I respond. After all, if I had written out the sound—"ex"—rather than the alphabet image, you probably would not have thought of "the letter X." Instead, popping into your head might be the image of someone who repeatedly refers to "the Ex": a spouse who is no longer.

If I had presented the X as follows—

$$2 \times 3 = 6$$

—you would have identified it as "the multiplication sign" and not a letter at all. Context makes a difference, just as the letter "x" makes a difference to the word *context*. Substituting an "n" for the "x" in *context* delivers a much different content.

By now you've gotten my point. No "X" stands alone with autonomous, universal meaning. It can be enticingly positive, marking the site of treasure on a map, or discouragingly negative, marking the wrong answer on a test. At the end of a letter it signals "a kiss," but on a bottle it once meant "poison." It might be interpreted identically by two individuals who, at the same time, give it different value, as when the "XXX" on a tawdry storefront warns one viewer, "Stay away!" while another it tempts, "Come on in!"[1]

---

[1]At this point I originally wrote the following: "When a teacher places an X over a paragraph in a

SIGNS OF XMAS

For Christians, "X" can be distressful. I still feel queasy any time I hurriedly write "Xmas" instead of "Christmas," remembering how my parents would groan every time they saw the abbreviation, despairing, "Look how those people have taken the Christ out of Christmas." The "X," for them, was a sign of absence or, worse, of contemptuous crossing out. Christ, divorced from Christmas, was an "Ex" no longer espoused by our culture. When businesses started telling employees to substitute the greeting "Happy Holidays" for "Merry Christmas"—the ultimate "ex-ing" out—many Christians despaired over the triumph of secular culture.

But there is another way to read the "X" of Xmas. As is well known, early Christians used "X" to represent Christ. *Chi*, or "X" in Greek, was the first letter of the title "Christ." Early Christians, in fact, used "X" *(chi)* as part of an acronym that symbolized their faith. The Greek letters—*iota-**chi**-theta-upsilon-sigma*—stood for the phrase "Jesus Christ, God's Son, Savior," but they also spelled out the Greek word for "fish." During the time of persecution, then, Christians would draw the "sign of the fish" to indicate to other believers their commitment to follow Jesus. This has become known as the *Ichthus*, which is the latinized spelling of the Greek word for "fish."

Figure 3.2. Ichthus: the sign of the fish

In the third century, Tertullian (the challenger of Marcionism discussed in the preceding chapter), (re)signed *ichthus* with baptismal meaning: "But we small fishes, named after our great ICHTHUS, Jesus Christ, are born in water and only by remaining in water can we live."[2] The "X" in Xmas therefore has an ancient and godly heritage, standing for Christ, who was born in a manger.[3]

---

student essay, the sign might have different meanings. On the one hand it could indicate that the paragraph is irrelevant to the essay's thesis; on the other hand it could mean almost the opposite: that the paragraph redundantly reiterates the thesis." Upon reading this passage, however, my husband crossed it out with an "X."

[2]Quoted in Everett Ferguson, "When Did the Cross Supplant the Ichthus (Fish) as a Symbol of the Christian Faith?" on ChristianHistory.net (posted February 26, 2009), www.christianitytoday.com/ch/asktheexpert/ask_whythecross.html.

[3]The *OED* notes that the abbreviation "Xmas" was used as early as 1551.

Ironically, the part of "Xmas" that infuriated some nineteenth-century Christians was not the "X" but rather the second syllable. The word "mass" was a sign of Roman Catholicism, and some evangelicals in Victorian England repudiated anyone who would use the "popish" word "Christmas." Philip Gosse (1810-1888), a well-respected marine biologist and lay pastor for a Plymouth Brethren congregation, regarded the celebration of Christmas as inimical to biblical Christianity and hence "nothing less than an act of idolatry." As his son Edmund recounts, "He would denounce the horrors of Christmas until it almost made me blush to look at a holly-berry." When Philip discovered that his cook had made a plum-pudding to celebrate the holiday, he "flung the idolatrous confectionery" into the trash, leaving "an impression on [Edmund's] memory which nothing will ever efface."[4]

THE CONTEXT OF XMAS

The sign "Xmas," like the "X" that begins it and the "mas" that ends it, means different things in different contexts. While some nineteenth-century Christians repudiated Christmas as too unbiblical, some twenty-first-century secularists go to the other extreme, denouncing it as too Christian. Some cities in both England and America therefore discourage any public decoration that alludes to Christ's birth: signs of mangers, magi or Marys.

It is easy to get angry over this dismissal of "the things of God," wanting to snatch back the coin and flip it over. Christians on the edge, however, might respond differently. Perhaps we should welcome current cautions concerning Christmas, for they imply the power of the sign. By being told not to use religious images or the common holiday greeting, people are reminded that the word "Christmas" references more than an excuse to pile on pounds as well as presents—or to place gargantuan plastic Santas on front lawns. The word itself reminds them that the celebration began as a mass to celebrate Christ's birth. Like the Christmas pudding Philip Gosse tossed into the trash, the sign "Merry Christmas" may make a stronger impression when people attempt to throw it away.

UNDERSTANDING SIGNS: SEMIOTICS

To stay on the edge, therefore, Christians need to understand how signs make

---

[4]Edmund Gosse, *Father and Son: A Study of Two Temperaments*, ed. Peter Abbs (London: Penguin, 1983), pp. 111-12.

and change meaning. What follows, then, is an introduction to semiotics, the scholarly study of signs. Practitioners, called semioticians, analyze *how* signs make meaning and *what* gives them value. While linguists focus on the wording and working of languages, semioticians range over broader territory, analyzing, in addition to words, the nonlinguistic signs of culture, from fashion to flirting. One introduction to semiotics, in fact, is called *Of Cigarettes, High Heels, and Other Interesting Things*.[5]

Semioticians note that even pre-literate children are sign-readers. I realized this one snowy day while sitting in the backseat of a car with my two-year-old godson, Jude, who was contentedly inspecting each one of his Cheerios before gingerly placing them on his tongue. Though traveling in treacherous conditions, his parents and I were having a lively conversation until the car started to slide on a steep hill. We immediately stopped talking and Jude, astutely reading our unspoken signs of worry, started crying. When we reinstated the calm tones of adult conversation, Jude returned to his cereal inspection. Though not attuned to our verbal signs, Jude quite clearly understood extra-linguistic tones.

ZOOSEMIOTICS: NO LAUGHING MATTER

Even nonhuman animals transmit and respond to signs, as every pet-owner can attest, leading some scholars to specialize in what they call "zoosemiotics." In this growing field, zoosemioticians analyze how animal communication functions in mating rituals, food discovery, warning signals, domination tactics and so on.[6]

My first lesson in zoosemiotics was both amateurish and traumatic. The summer after my sophomore year of college, a local wildlife park offered me a job as a cashier with the stipulation that I must help out in one of the shows. Though never having held a cat or dog before, I was required to carry a forty-pound "baby hyena" (named Fang!) onto a stage.

A zoosemiotician might explain how the hyena picked up signs of my terror and then generated its own sign, its tail suddenly standing straight up in the air. Not knowing how to interpret this sign, I experienced a shock—

---

[5]Marcel Danesi, *Of Cigarettes, High Heels, and Other Interesting Things: An Introduction to Semiotics* (New York: St. Martin's, 1999).
[6]The word *zoosemiotics* was coined in 1963 by semiotician Thomas Sebeok (1920-2001). See his book *Perspectives in Zoosemiotics* (The Hague, Netherlands: Mouton, 1973).

and the new and sudden interpretive insight—when my arm under his belly became "slimed." Ironically, when I first came out on stage holding Fang, I was introduced to the audience as an "animal trainer." This illustrates what semiotician Jean Baudrillard calls "the simulacrum": a sign for which no original exists. I was being used as a "sign" of professionalism even though I had no professional training.[7]

Few readers, however, need a degree in zoosemiotics to understand the significance of a tail pointing straight up into the air: it was a natural sign of an ensuing biological function. They might say the same about the audience's ensuing laughter when I dropped Fang and fell on top of him to prevent his escape. A semiotician, however, would argue that even laughter reflects culturally conditioned semiotic systems. As Vic Gatrell notes in his history of laughter, aristocrats in the eighteenth century considered excessive laughter to be a sign of the lower classes. Lord Chesterfield (1694-1773), whose *Letters to his Son* is considered a "classic" statement of "proper" behavior for a gentleman, describes "frequent and loud laughter" as characteristic of "folly and ill-manners."[8] Like adult burping, then, which some cultures consider a compliment to the cook, the significance of laughter varies from culture to culture.

This, then, is the purview of semiotics. Though burping and laughter may have biological causes, *as signs* they have different meanings in different contexts. (When it comes to the so-called laughter of hyenas, however, I cede all speculation to experts in zoosemiotics.)

HOW SEMIOTICS WORKS

The semiotician assesses differences in signs as they become manifest in divergent locations and/or eras. The "common semiotic account," as Harvard humanities professor Homi Bhabha puts it, acknowledges a sign's "discursive embeddedness and address, its cultural positionality, its reference to a present time and a specific space."[9] Semiotics, in other words, is as much about a sign's context as it is about its content.

---

[7]Baudrillard indicts theme parks for inculcating "the order of the hyperreal and of simulation." See "The Precession of Simulacra," in *The Norton Anthology of Theory and Criticism*, ed. Vincent B. Leitch et al., 2nd ed. (New York: Norton, 2010), p. 1565.

[8]Kenneth Baker, "Mirror Images," review of *City of Laughter: Sex and Satire in Eighteenth-Century London*, by Vic Gatrell, *Times Literary Supplement*, September 1, 2006, p. 27.

[9]Homi K. Bhabha, "The Commitment to Theory," in *The Norton Anthology of Theory and Criticism*, ed. Vincent B. Leitch et al., 2nd ed. (New York: Norton, 2010), p. 2370.

To distinguish that they are talking about a sign rather than the thing to which it refers, some semioticians put lines (rather than quotation marks) around a word or letter, as in /X/ or /Xmas/.[10] Most importantly, they analyze how relationships among signs contribute to their significance, from the signs in a cartoonist's caricature to a study of how 9-11-01 gave new meaning to the sign of the American flag. In fact, semioticians might analyze why /9-11/ became a sign for the multiple events on that fateful day: the fall of New York's World Trade Center, the bombing of the Pentagon, the downing of Flight 93. People were using /9-11/ within weeks of the horrific events—due not simply to media dissemination, but also to the sign's double coding:

1. /9-11/ signaled the day many people felt they lost a sense of protection as Americans.

2. /9-11/ reminded many people of the sign for crisis, wherein one dials 9-1-1 "in case of emergency."

This double-coding gave /9-11/ extra wallop, seeming the perfect sign with which to capture the devastating crisis. In fact, a new genre of literature has been marked with this sign, some university campuses offering courses in "9-11 Fiction."[11] Before 2001, people would have assumed such a class studied literature about emergencies—or perhaps about phone books.

ANCIENT FOUNDATIONS OF SEMIOTICS

The analysis of signs is as old as discussions about communication itself. In fact, as Don Paul Abbott notes in the journal *Rhetorica,* "a remarkable number of semioticians preface their works with a history of rhetoric": the art of influencing the thought and behavior of an audience.[12] And effective rhetoric, as Maurice Charland notes, depends upon an astute understanding of signs: "Rhetorical force arises in the deployment of signs in

---

[10]See, for example, Umberto Eco, *A Theory of Semiotics* (Bloomington: Indiana University Press, 1979). This technique is not practiced as much as it once was, but I find it helpful, employing it throughout the remainder of the book for the sake of clarity.

[11]Thanks to my student Alyssa Lord for drawing this to my attention.

[12]Don Paul Abbott, "Splendor and Misery: Semiotics and the End of Rhetoric," *Rhetorica* 24, no. 3 (2006): 304. In 1970, a group of semioticians in Belgium, calling themselves Group Mu, published a book suggesting that rhetoric is a subset of semiotics. For its English translation, see Jacques Dubois et al., *A General Rhetoric,* trans. Paul B. Burrell and Edgar M. Slotkin (Baltimore: Johns Hopkins University Press, 1981).

concrete historical situations, where signs rework and configure both affect and interest."[13] Overviews of both semiotics and rhetoric, then, usually start with the ancient Greeks, whose word for "sign"—*sēmeion*—is the root of *semiotics.*

Plato's *Cratylus* (fourth century B.C.E.) is often singled out because it addresses the difference between "natural" and "conventional" (human-made) signs. To understand Plato's point, think of goose bumps, which everyone would consider a *natural* sign of a chill. Humans did not invent goose bumps the way they invented whoopee cushions. But English-speaking humans did invent /goose bumps/, making it an *arbitrary* sign that has become conventional. English philosopher John Locke (1632-1704) discusses "arbitrary" signs in his *Essay Concerning Human Understanding* (1690), noting that there is no "natural connection" between words and the ideas that they "sign." If there were, "there would be but one Language amongst all Men." Instead, each language reflects "a voluntary Imposition, whereby such a Word is made *arbitrarily* the Mark of such an Idea."[14] For instance, some Brits arbitrarily coined /goose flesh/ in the early nineteenth century, perhaps influencing the American /goose bumps/, both based on the bumpy flesh of a freshly plucked goose.[15] And even though few of us have ever seen a nude goose, we perpetuate the sign because it has become a conventional way to signal not only a chill, but also fear or excitement.

Plato was wary of conventional (human-made) signs, knowing that savvy rhetoricians and poets can manipulate them in ways that might distract people from truth. He therefore attacked the "sophists": itinerant teachers that would hire themselves out to teach the art of persuasive rhetoric. In Plato's mind, as one semiotician puts it, the sophist only "sells the signs and insignia" of knowledge rather than authentic wisdom.[16] In fact, largely thanks

---

[13]Maurice Charland, "Rehabilitating Rhetoric: Confronting Blindspots in Discourse and Social Theory," in *Contemporary Rhetorical Theory: A Reader,* ed. John Louis Lucaites, Celeste Michelle Condit and Sally Caudill (New York: Guilford, 1999), p. 467.

[14]John Locke, *An Essay Concerning Human Understanding,* book 3, chap. 2, in *Literary Criticism and Theory: The Greeks to the Present,* ed. Robert Con Davis and Laurie Finke (New York: Longman, 1989), p. 301, emphasis mine.

[15]The first recorded use of /goose-flesh/ was by Coleridge in 1810 *(OED).* According to my colleagues in the Modern Languages Department, the German word for "goose bumps" translates into "goose skin," the French word into "chicken flesh," and the Spanish word into "chicken skin."

[16]Jacques Derrida, "Plato's Pharmacy," in *The Norton Anthology of Theory and Criticism,* ed. Vincent B. Leitch et al., 2nd ed. (New York: Norton, 2010), p. 1721.

to Plato, /sophistry/ became a sign of "trickery, dishonesty, and persuasive but fallacious reasoning."[17]

Sophistry, of course, is still alive and well. Think, for example, of the radical difference between politicians' platform rhetoric and their actual practices once they get elected. Or consider all those commercials in which a drop-dead gorgeous woman stops in her tracks to watch an expensive car (and presumably its driver) glide down the street. Such an artificially constructed *sign* of sexiness distracts people from truths not only about the car's safety and pollution standards, but also about issues and ideas of greater importance than the automobile one drives.

Plato's famous pupil Aristotle (384-322 B.C.E.) was more sanguine about conventional signs, formulating an influential text in support of rhetoric. Considered "the most important single work on persuasion ever written,"[18] Aristotle's *Treatise on Rhetoric* not only discusses the words a speaker uses, but also the signs that make the speaker seem credible and trustworthy to his listeners. For him, signs have rhetorical power when the rhetor excels in three areas:

1. *logos:* an astute pattern of reasoning

2. *pathos:* sensitive appeal to audience emotion

3. *ethos:* manifest credibility[19]

For Aristotle, then, as noted by Kenneth Burke, the successful orator "will seek to display the appropriate 'signs' of character needed to earn the audience's good will."[20]

By the century that preceded Christ, an education in rhetoric was considered essential for any upper-class male. One such male, Cicero (106-43 B.C.E.), synthesized what he had learned from Plato and Aristotle to compose

---

[17]James Fieser and Norman Lillegard, *A Historical Introduction to Philosophy: Tests and Interactive Guides* (New York: Oxford University Press, 2002), p. 29.

[18]James L. Golden, Goodwin F. Berquist, William E. Coleman, Ruth Golden and J. Michael Sproule, eds., *The Rhetoric of Western Thought from the Mediterranean World to the Global Setting,* 9th ed. (Dubuque, IA: Kendall Hunt, 2007), p. 67. In his book *On Interpretation,* Aristotle notes that words are, "before all else," signs; quoted in Umberto Eco, *The Limits of Interpretation* (Bloomington: Indiana University Press, 1990), p. 113.

[19]As Patricia Bizzell and Bruce Herzberg note, *logos, pathos* and *ethos* are the qualities Aristotle aligns with "artistic" rhetoric. In contrast, Aristotle's "inartistic" rhetoric appeals to empirical evidence. See *The Rhetorical Tradition: Readings from Classical Times to the Present,* ed. P. Bizzell and B. Herzberg, 2nd ed. (New York: Bedford/St. Martin's, 2001), p. 171.

[20]Kenneth Burke, *A Rhetoric of Motives* (New York: Prentice-Hall, 1950), pp. 55-56.

seven of his own treatises on rhetoric, two of which became extremely influential in the centuries that followed the classical period: *De Inventione* and *De Oratore*. Though not knowing Christ, Cicero had a profound influence on those who did.

CHRISTIAN CONTRIBUTORS TO SEMIOTICS: TERTULLIAN AND AUGUSTINE

A brilliant orator and stylist, Cicero may be partially responsible for the move away from Greek as the preferred language for biblical truth among Western Christians. Though trained in Greek, Cicero defended the power of Latin to fulfill Aristotle's five components of effective oratory: invention, arrangement, style, memory and delivery. Perhaps due to Cicero's influence, the classically trained Tertullian (ca. 160–ca. 220 C.E.) began inscribing Christian theology in Latin, becoming known as the "father of Latin Christianity" and the first known Christian to employ the sign /Trinity/ (*trinitas* in Latin). Since the New Testament was written in Greek—still considered the language of well-educated citizens in his day—Tertullian thus became a (re)signer of truth.[21]

Familiar with the writings of Tertullian and Cicero (not to mention Plato and Aristotle), Augustine (354-430) was one of the most influential contributors to the development of Western Christianity. Because Augustine taught as well as studied rhetoric, it makes sense that his writings reflect *logos* not only as Aristotle defined it, but also as the Gospel of John defined it: "In the beginning was the *Logos*, and the *Logos* was with God, and the *Logos* was God" (Jn 1:1). Augustine actually established a parallel between the Word made flesh and words that flesh out our thoughts:

> How did He come except that "the Word was made flesh, and dwelt among us"? It is as when we speak. In order that what we are thinking may reach the mind of the listener through the fleshly ears, that which we have in mind is expressed in words and is called speech. . . . In the same way the Word of God was made flesh without change that He might dwell among us.[22]

---

[21]This is my own theory since little is known about Tertullian's education. While the importance of Cicero to the Roman Empire in Tertullian's day supports my theory, Diarmaid MacCulloch speculates that "the switch to Latin in Christian Rome may have been made by one of the bishops at the end of the [second] century, Victor (189-99)." See *Christianity: The First Three Thousand Years* (New York: Viking, 2010), p. 136.

[22]Augustine, *On Christian Doctrine*, trans. D. W. Robertson Jr. (New York: Liberal Arts Press, 1958), book 1, para. 12, p. 14.

Often quoted in rhetoric books, Augustine's theological work *On Christian Doctrine* discusses how to effectively communicate the *Logos* of Scripture. However, before he addresses the issue of eloquent preaching, Augustine focuses on how signs work, defining a sign as "a thing that causes us to think of something beyond the impression that the thing itself makes upon the senses." And, like Plato, Augustine finds it important to distinguish natural signs *(signa naturalia)* from conventional signs *(signa data)*, noting that "even signs given by God and contained in the Holy Scriptures" are *signa data*, "since they were presented to us by the men who wrote them."[23] In other words, language—even that in the Bible—cannot capture the fullness of God, who far transcends all human signs.

This might explain why Augustine so valued his mystical experience of God: as a validation that believers can commune with their uncreated Creator apart from the mediation of signs. As he recounts in his *Confessions*, "I was swept away to you by your own beauty, and then I was torn away from you by my own weight and fell back groaning toward these lower things."[24] Among "these lower things" are *signa data*, which can never encompass God's nature. Nevertheless, how we understand God's self-revelation through the incarnation of Christ is through the *signa data* of biblical accounts: created signs that cause us to think of the Uncreated that exists above and beyond all signs.

Augustine therefore argued that an astute reading of Scripture necessitated not only informed assessment of literal versus figurative language but also appreciation for the Bible's historical contexts. Only by understanding signs, then, can a communicator develop persuasive rhetoric about the gospel message. It is no wonder that the famous semiotician Umberto Eco identifies Augustine as "the first explicitly to propose a 'general semiotics.'"[25]

CHRISTIAN CONTRIBUTORS TO SEMIOTICS: BOETHIUS, ABELARD AND AQUINAS

In the century after Augustine, a Roman senator named Boethius (ca.

---

[23]Ibid., book 2, para. 1, 3, pp. 34, 35. T. L. Short takes issue with the common translation of *signa data* as "conventional signs," noting that "Augustine called the crowing of cocks and the cooing of doves *signa data*." Can these be conventional, he asks? See T. L. Short, *Peirce's Theory of Signs* (New York: Cambridge University Press, 2007), p. 24.

[24]*The Confessions of St. Augustine*, trans. Rex Warner (New York: New American Library, 1963), 7.17.153.

[25]Eco, *Limits of Interpretation*, p. 113.

480-524), later beatified by the Roman Catholic Church, committed himself to translating Plato and Aristotle into Latin, thus providing Latin Christians their primary access to Greek philosophy for seven centuries. Writing commentaries on the rhetoric of Aristotle and Cicero, as well as inscribing his own *Overview of the Structure of Rhetoric,* Boethius distinguished between conventional and natural signs as did his forebears. His work influenced a movement centuries later that became known as Christian Scholasticism: the attempt to reconcile Christian doctrine with the reasoning style of Aristotle.

One early Scholastic, Peter Abelard (1079-1142), read Boethius as well as Aristotle, adding layers of complexity to earlier distinctions between natural and conventional signs. A century later, the most influential Scholastic of them all, Thomas Aquinas (ca. 1225-1274), added even more layers of complexity, considering "every utterance endowed with meaning" to be a sign.[26] Like Augustine, whom he often cites, Aquinas was especially interested in the signs of Scripture, stating in his *Summa Theologica,* one of the most influential texts of Western Christianity, that "the things signified by the words can be themselves signs of other things."[27]

And I could go on. As noted by Jonathan Culler, former president of the Semiotic Society of America, "semiotics has helped to reveal . . . that what had previously been sneered at as medieval scholasticism was in many respects a subtle and highly developed theory of signs."[28] Great ancestors of our faith recognized that following Christ necessitated an understanding of how signs work—and they were willing to learn from non-Christian philosophers to increase that understanding. So might we.[29]

---

[26]The phrase is Eco's summation of Aquinas (ibid., p. 117). Eco creates charts, looking much like family genealogies, to illustrate how Augustine, Boethius, Abelard and Aquinas distinguish natural from conventional signs. See his pp. 115-19.

[27]Thomas Aquinas, "Question 1, Tenth Article: Whether in Holy Scripture a Word May Have Several Senses?" from *Summa Theologica,* in *Literary Criticism and Theory: The Greeks to the Present,* ed. Robert Con Davis and Laurie Finke (New York: Longman, 1989), p. 147.

[28]Jonathan D. Culler, *The Pursuit of Signs: Semiotics, Literature, Deconstruction,* augmented edition (Ithaca, NY: Cornell University Press, 2001), p. 22.

[29]As theologian Derek W. H. Thomas notes, "In her best moments, [the church] has plundered Philistinism and emerged with booty to better defend and assert what is core belief: think of Augustine's use of Plato, Aquinas's employment of Aristotle, Calvin's engagement with Cicero or John Owen's interest in Maimonides." See "The Doctrine of the Church in the Twenty-First Century," in *Always Reforming: Explorations in Systematic Theology,* ed. A. T. B. McGowan (Downers Grove, IL: IVP Academic, 2006), pp. 338-39.

THE DEVELOPING SCIENCE OF SIGNS

The word "semeiotic" and the related "semeiology" did not appear in the English language until the seventeenth century *(OED)*. John Locke employed "*semiotika*" in 1690 to refer to "the doctrine of signs" he was exploring in his "Essay Concerning Human Understanding."[30] Though "semeiology" usually referred to physical gestures like waving goodbye or blowing a kiss, it also referred to the assessment of medical symptoms: heartburn, a high temperature, a rash. In fact, some scholars locate the origin of semiotics in ancient science: "Semiotics grew out of symptomatology, or medical semeiotics. . . . In this sense, Hippocrates and Galen, with their early studies of signs and symptoms, were among the very first semioticans [*sic*]."[31]

It was not until the twentieth century that the words *semiotics* and *semiology* broadened to encompass the study of all kinds of signs: human as well as animal, natural as well as conventional, words as well as gestures. Significantly, the "science of signs" developed separately in the minds of two scholars: the American philosopher Charles Sanders Peirce (1839-1914), who employed the word "semeiotic,"[32] and the Swiss linguist Ferdinand de Saussure (1857-1913), who employed the word "semiology." It wasn't until the 1970s that the International Association for Semiotic Studies made Peirce's term, without the second "e," primary.[33]

Nevertheless, it was Saussure's approach to the sign that became primary in the twentieth century, impacting not just rhetoric, but also anthropology, psychology, philosophy, theology and art criticism. The remainder of this chapter will focus on Saussure's theory of signs, while the next two chapters will discuss how his semiology revolutionized twentieth-century thought. Part three will introduce Peirce's view of the sign, discussing how it contributes to the (re)signing of Christian truth.

---

[30]Robert Stam, Robert Burgoyne and Sandy Flitterman-Lewis, *New Vocabularies in Film Semiotics: Structuralism, Post-structuralism and Beyond* (New York: Routledge, 1992), p. 3.

[31]Susan Petrilli and Augusto Ponzio, *Semiotics Unbounded: Interpretive Routes Through the Open Network of Signs* (Toronto: University of Toronto Press, 2005), p. xxi.

[32]T. L. Short notes that "the term 'semeiotic' is almost certainly a transliteration of the Greek word that Locke used, at the end of his 1690 *Essay*, to name a new 'doctrine of signs'" (*Peirce's Theory of Signs*, p. 2). The phrase "science of signs" was first employed by Charles W. Morris in *Foundations of the Theory of Signs* (Chicago: University of Chicago Press, 1938), pp. 1-2.

[33]In his writings, Peirce sometimes used "semeiotic," other times "semiotic." Anthropologist Margaret Mead added the "s" to Peirce's "semiotic," following the example of "ethics" and "mathematics." See Stam, Burgoyne and Flitterman-Lewis, *New Vocabularies*, p. 4.

SO SURE OF SAUSSURE

Unlike most teenagers, who worry more about their complexions than inflections, the adolescent Saussure immersed himself in Latin, Greek and Sanskrit. By age twenty-one he had already published a scholarly work, the "Primitive System of Vowels in Indo-European Languages," and by twenty-three he had earned his doctorate. After spending a decade teaching Sanskrit, Gothic and Old High German in Paris, he accepted a position at the University of Geneva. It was there that Saussure unwittingly changed the way scholars think about signs—unwittingly because he never published his theories about semiology. Instead, some of his students, sure of his brilliance, published notes they took during Saussure's course on General Linguistics—after he had died.[34] It puts him in good company. Aristotle's *Rhetoric* was also put together by students who had heard his lectures. Both Aristotle and Saussure would be amazed to know how much ink has been spilled, type-ribboned, carbon-papered, ditto-machined, mimeographed, Xeroxed, ink-jetted, emailed and Twittered about their lectures. Every teacher should be so lucky.

SAUSSURE'S DICHOTOMY: DIACHRONIC VERSUS SYNCHRONIC

In his *Course on General Linguistics,* Saussure challenged the traditional approach to linguistic signs. Before Saussure, the study of language, known as "philology," focused on historical changes in language. Calling this a "diachronic" ("through time") approach to language, Saussure advocated, instead, a "synchronic" ("at one time") approach. He therefore studied the differences among signs at one particular moment in history in order to assess how signs make meaning through their contrasts with each other.

Take, for example, the difference between a diachronic and a synchronic analysis of women's fashion. A diachronic study might look at the change from the not-so-secret Victorian "bustle" to a Victoria's Secret "bustier" in order to assess the increasing sexualizing of women's clothing over time. In contrast, a synchronic study might analyze how the belly-baring low-rise jeans of early twenty-first-century fashion affected the length of contempo-

---

[34]The French lectures were given between 1906 and 1911 and published posthumously in 1915. I use the first English translation: Ferdinand de Saussure, *Course in General Linguistics,* trans. Wade Baskin (New York: Philosophical Library, 1959). Clarifications for the *Course* were made available in 1996, when a manuscript written by Saussure was discovered in his house in Geneva.

raneous shirts and belts, one sign affecting others in the fashion system. Indeed, with the onset of low-rise jeans, fashionistas lost interest in beautifully crafted waist-cinching belts that they once valued highly. No matter how expensive, no matter how much it was complimented in the past, a belt's value was determined by its relationship to the current fashion system: there is no universal standard of belt beauty. Similarly, for semiologists like Saussure, words make meaning only in contemporary "relationship to other words," such that, like belt-value, "reference is arbitrary or accidental."[35]

Arbitrary synchronic reference might be illustrated by something I noticed in first grade. Reading groups were assigned arbitrary names: the Robins, the Finches, the Bluebirds. The terms only had meaning within the context of Mrs. McGrath's classroom, since other teachers used different names for their reading groups. But within the synchronic system of Mrs. McGrath's room, most children understood the meaning of Bluebird, Robin and Finch: one name referenced an advanced reader, one an average reader and one a struggling reader. The words, though arbitrary, took on significance *in relation to each other* within a particular context. Indeed, if I had said "I am a Bluebird" in another context—as in my Sunday school class—the listeners might interpret a different meaning altogether: that I belonged to "the Bluebirds," a program for young Camp Fire Girls (which changed its name in 1989 to "Starflight"). This reflects what a famous analyst of semiotics once called "the various relationships between code and context."[36]

For Saussure, then, signs are like coins that have no value in themselves, but only in relation to "the code" of a synchronic system. As he notes, "it is not the metal in a piece of money that fixes its value. . . . Its value will vary according to the amount stamped upon it and according to its use inside or outside a political boundary."[37] In 2007, for example, when I tried to spend an old shilling in England, it was refused wherever I offered it. Though at one time the very same coin purchased products or services, it had lost its synchronic exchange value. Though the *metal* was the same, the British monetary *system* had changed, such that shillings were no longer *coded* as legal tender. Reflecting this coin analogy, Saussure avoids referring to a sign's

---

[35]Robert Scholes, *Semiotics and Interpretation* (New Haven: Yale University Press, 1982), p. 146.
[36]Roman Jakobson, "The Development of Semiotics," in *The Framework of Language* (Ann Arbor: University of Michigan Press, 1980), p. 22.
[37]Saussure, *Course in General Linguistics*, p. 118.

meaning, discussing only its *value* within a particular *system*—just as /Bluebird/ had a different value in Mrs. McGrath's classroom than it did in Camp Fire Girls.

SAUSSURE'S *LANGUE* AND *PAROLE*

Saussure is most interested, then, in the *system* that generates value for a sign. He calls this linguistic system *langue,* which means "tongue" in French, and each act of communication that arises from it a *parole,* or "word" in French. For him, the "science of signs" focuses on the *langue* (pronounced "long") that generates each *parole* (pronounced "pa-ROW"). (I provide the pronunciation for non–French speakers so they might avoid the mistake I made my first semester of grad school, when I told a world-class critic, "I am intrigued by the distinction between "lang-gew" and "pa-roll-ee.")

One introduction to semiotics explains the distinction as follows: "*Langue* can be thought of as a communal cupboard, housing all the possible different signs which might be pulled out and utilized in the construction of an instance of *parole.*"[38] Though helpful, this cupboard analogy can be misleading, sounding as though *langue* cupboards contain signs the same way kitchen cabinets contain products. In other words, just as one person's cupboard contains Twinkies while another person's contains Tahini, so also one *langue* contains /God/ while another contains /Dios/. If this were so, Saussure belabors the obvious: different languages have different vocabularies. Brilliant!

A more accurate way to understand *langue* is to think of a kitchen cupboard filled not with edible products but with ingredients by which edibles might be constituted. One cupboard might contain whole wheat flour and yeast, while a second contains cake flour, baking powder and sugar. Clearly, different ingredients will result in different end products: yeast bread is possible from the first cupboard but not the second, while cake is possible from the second cupboard but not the first.

For a linguistic example, think of the common observation that Eskimos have many different words for snow. This does not mean their cupboard has a larger vocabulary for precipitation than that of a Hawaiian who has never seen snow. It means that their context—in frozen northern climes—has

---

[38]Paul Cobley and Litza Jansz, *Introducing Semiotics,* ed. Richard Appignanesi (Lanham, MD: Totem, 1997), p. 15.

stocked their cupboard with numerous ingredients that make subtle distinctions. These create the possibility for one *parole* that describes light fluffy snow at night; another that describes wet morning snow; yet another for snow that crunches under foot and so on. In contrast, the Hawaiian who doesn't need to make distinctions about snow, because it makes no difference in his lifestyle, might respond, "Hey, snow is snow!"

Langue, then, provides the "conditions of possibility" by which *paroles* are cooked up. Even then my analogy is deficient, for it implies that people can reach into *langue* and mix up ingredients to make signs. Instead, as Niall Lucy puts it, "These rules or conditions [of possibility] cannot be accessed directly; they can only ever be inferred, on the basis of signs in actual use"[39]— just as I infer the presence of flour and sugar (if even in pre-mixed form) in the cupboard of someone who has made me a birthday cake.

CONDITIONS OF POSSIBILITY

Saussure himself provides a good example for "conditions of possibility," noting that "in some languages it is not possible to say 'sit in the *sun*.'"[40] Speakers of such languages might ask, "What do you mean IN the sun? First of all, you are on earth, and second of all, you would burn to oblivion if you even approached the sun, let alone sat IN it!"

Obviously, the "conditions of possibility" in one *langue* allow for idiomatic *paroles* that make no sense to someone conditioned by another *langue*. Indeed, when I was studying Spanish, I discovered that the American idiom "He toots his own horn" is sometimes translated into Spanish as "No necesita una abuela," which means, "He doesn't need a grandmother." In other words, a person so brags about his own achievements that he doesn't need a grandmother to proclaim his accomplishments. We see that, even when trying to communicate the same meaning, different *langues* produce radically different *paroles*.

While the phrase "conditions of possibility" explains difference, it also might account for similarity. Take, for example, the nearly simultaneous development of semiotics in America (via Peirce) and France (via Saussure): the *langue* (cupboard) of Western culture had expanded its ingredients in such a

---

[39]Niall Lucy, *A Derrida Dictionary* (Oxford: Blackwell, 2004), p. 111.
[40]Saussure, *Course in General Linguistics*, p. 116.

way that it made possible two new theories about signs.[41] Such parallel development has many other examples:

- In the 1660s, Isaac Newton and G. W. Leibniz both invented calculus while living in different countries.

- In 1837, W. F. Cook and C. Wheatstone invented the telegraph in England even as Samuel Morse was inventing it in the U.S.

- A decade later, the theory of natural selection developed at the same time in the minds of two Brits: Charles Darwin and Alfred Wallace.

- Alexander Graham Bell and Daniel Drawbaugh independently but nearly simultaneously invented models of the telephone in the 1870s.

- The invention of computer chips happened contemporaneously in two different American companies in 1958.

- Two European scientists, one from France and one from Germany, discovered GMR (giant magneto-resistance) independently but in the exact same year (1988).[42]

"Conditions of possibility" also account for historical repetitions within a culture. Take, for example, the Arab Spring of 2011. Within months after helping Egyptian protesters oust Hosni Mubarak from autocratic rule, the military was mimicking the tactics of the oppressor it replaced. As one newspaper summarized, "the secretive council of top generals that rule the country is looking too much like the regime it replaced." Why? Because Egypt, like all societies, is ruled by a *langue* that shapes ideas about leadership. Similarly, soon after revolutionaries killed the dictator of Libya, Moammar Gadhafi, a pro-democracy activist lamented, "They killed Gadhafi's regime, but Gad-

---

[41]Peirce coined the word "semiosis" in 1907, while Saussure first applied "semiology" to the study of linguistic signs in 1916 *(OED)*. Though Peirce started conceptualizing his semeiotic in the 1860s, critics see him systematizing it just as Saussure was articulating his views in the first decades of the twentieth century. See Ronald Schleifer, "Semiotics and Criticism," in *Literary Criticism and Theory: The Greeks to the Present*, ed. Robert Con Davis and Laurie Finke (New York: Longman, 1989), p. 902.

[42]C. S. Peirce discusses "great discoveries made independently and almost simultaneously," giving similar examples in "Evolutionary Love," in *Philosophical Writings of Peirce*, ed. Justus Buchler (New York: Dover, 1955), pp. 373-74. Daniel Drawbaugh, who once lived ten minutes from my current home, is famous in Pennsylvania. Jack Kilby of Texas Instruments Inc. and Robert Noyce of Fairchild Semiconductor Corp. both patented chip designs in 1958, as cited in *The Patriot-News* (Harrisburg, PA), February 23, 2007, p. A2. About the parallel GMR discoveries, see the Nobel Prize website, http://nobelprize.org/nobel_prizes/physics/laureates/2007/press.html.

hafi's culture, Gadhafi's mentality, is still in their mind."[43] Saussure could not have said it better. A *langue* that had dominated Libya for over forty years established the condition of possibility for revolutionary *paroles*. This, then, explains why societies don't immediately embrace American democracy after rulers like Saddam Hussein of Iraq are eliminated. As far as Saussurean semiologists are concerned, only the most naive person would think that killing a dictator could change the way an entire culture thinks. The problem, as they say, is "systemic": humans perceive truth and correct behavior according the *langue* (the system generating signs) in their cultures. Only through a change in *langue*, as may eventually happen in Egypt and Libya, will there be a change in signs.

For Saussure, then, ideas do not exist independently from the signs we use; instead, our *langue* gives form to those signs, and hence to ideas, in the first place. As he puts it in his *Course in General Linguistics*, "Without language, thought is a vague, uncharted nebula. There are no pre-existing ideas, and nothing is distinct before the appearance of language."[44]

SAUSSURE'S SIGNIFIER AND SIGNIFIED

In his analysis of language, Saussure focused primarily on the differences made by sounds in a word. For instance, rather than diachronically studying the etymology of the word "pan," he might look synchronically at how its meaning operates in contradistinction from the word "pat." The /n/ versus /t/ creates the difference: we understand /pan/ because it is not /pat/—just as we understand the difference between /content/ and /context/ due to the x. (This illustration implies Saussure was an English speaker, which he wasn't. But I didn't think his French examples would be very helpful.)

What *is* helpful is Saussure's idea that a sign has two parts: a signified concept in the mind and the signifier that generates the concept. When I use the signifier "elephant," for example, you picture in your mind a huge gray pachyderm with big ears and long trunk; you don't visualize a furry rodent with long ears and bushy tail. The "signified" of "elephant" is the former, not the latter. Hence, Saussure compares the sign to "a sheet of paper: thought is

---

[43]"Brutality in Egypt Harkens to Old Regime," *The Patriot-News* (Harrisburg, PA), July 18, 2011; Tara Bahrampour (*Washington Post*), "Sinking Feeling," *The Patriot-News* (Harrisburg, PA), October 22, 2011.
[44]Saussure, *Course in General Linguistics*, p. 112.

the front and the sound the back."[45] The two cannot be divided; if you have one side of paper, you'll always have the other side. Similarly, if you have a signified, there is always a signifier connected to it. In English, therefore, *pan* is a signifier while *pyxn* is not, since the latter does not generate a specific concept as its signified reference.

Of course, context may change the "thought-image" that is on one side of the sheet of paper. When we speak (or think) /pat/ and /pan/ in the kitchen we probably reference different things than when we speak or think them in a theater. In the kitchen, /pat/ and /pan/ most likely refer to what we do to the dough for bar-cookies: pat it down into the pan. When employed during a theatrical performance, in contrast, we may refer to the actors having the script "down pat," but we nevertheless "pan" their bad acting. One /pan/ relates to something crumbly, the other to something crummy.

Bad punning (if not panning) aside, I want to make clear that, for Saussure, context controls meaning: there is no universal, absolute signified that a signifier points to. If you say in a kitchen "Give me the pan," your English listener will not start yelling "Your acting is horrible." But the listener might refuse to give you the pan because your cooking is horrible.

This does not mean that a theater and a kitchen each have different linguistic system or *langue*. It's the same cupboard that opens onto different contexts. It reminds me of the house that my husband's parents owned for many years. In the upstairs hall was a closet used for linens, medicine and toiletries. Right next to the closet was a bathroom that contained a small cabinet door halfway up the wall that opened into the very same closet. People in the bathroom usually pulled out different "ingredients" (toilet paper, washcloths, shampoo) than people in the hall, who usually opened the door to get bed linens or medicines. The same closet/cupboard, then, supplied different ingredients in different contexts (bathroom versus hall)—and sometimes led to embarrassing encounters when both doors (the one in the hall and the one in the bathroom) were opened at once. But that is a different story.

(NOT) SO SURE ABOUT CHRISTIANITY

Notice how Saussure's emphasis on sound (*pat* versus *pan*) relates to my coinage *(re)signing*. You may wonder whether to pronounce it with a Z-

---

[45]Ibid., p. 113.

sound, as in "resign from a job" or whether to maintain the hissing S-sound, as in the word "sign." Roland Barthes (1915-1980), a cultural critic influenced by Saussure, discusses the sound difference between /s/ and /z/ in his aptly titled *S/Z* (1970). He calls Z "the letter of mutilation: pho-netically, Z stings like a chastising lash, an avenging insect." This is cer-tainly how he feels about those who promote reZignation to traditional doctrines of Christianity.[46]

On the other side of the coin are Christians who consider it quite appro-priate that a "hiss-sound" accompanies re-Signing. They interpret any change to the way their church has always done things to be a sign of the serpent in the garden. Many of us have probably heard the tale of a 1950s Christian who resisted the newly published Revised Standard Version Bible with the words "If King James English was good enough for Jesus, it's good enough for me!"[47] Though the story may be apocryphal, I can attest that a church not far from my house recently put up a brand new sign to advertise that it uses the KJV.

Hence, while Saussure would suggest that we know the difference be-tween /resign/ and /re-sign/ by the difference in sound, I blur that distinction by writing (re)sign. Which is exactly my point! Christians on the edge must balance between both sides of the coin: resigned (Z-sound) to ancient doc-trines of the church, we seek to re-sign (hiss-sound) them. We do so in order to maintain their potency amidst new signs of the times.

NEW SIGNS OF FAITH

In contrast to announcing "KJV," some churches put up signs reflecting con-temporary times. On my way to work I pass a church billboard proclaiming, "God always answers knee-mails," thus invoking "email" in order to imply its inadequacy. In Saussure's terms, the sign /knee-mail/ was synchronically generated, reflecting the *langue* of the times. Indeed, a 1950s Christian would be baffled by the sign, having never heard of email.

---

[46]Roland Barthes, *S/Z: An Essay,* trans. Richard Miller (New York: Hill and Wang, 1974), p. 106. Barthes aligns any kind of religious doctrine with "censorship" in "From Work to Text," trans. Stephen Heath, in *The Norton Anthology of Theory and Criticism,* ed. Vincent B. Leitch et al., 2nd ed. (New York: Norton, 2010), p. 1328.

[47]Stanley Malless and Jeffrey McQuain offer a slightly different take on the story: "If the King James Version was good enough for St. Paul, it's good enough for me." See *Coined by God: Words and Phrases that First Appear in the English Translations of the Bible* (New York: Norton, 2003), p. xiii.

Or think of a billboard sign many churches displayed several years ago:

Got Jesus?

Except for the Amish, who do not watch television or flip through magazines while standing in grocery-store check-out lines, most Christians "got" the sign. It was a re-signed *parole* based on the signs of the times. The *parole* began as an advertising campaign by the Milk Advisory Board. Famous people appeared in magazine advertisements sporting a prominent milk mustache, having (supposedly) just drunk from the large glass of milk held in their hands. Captioned beneath is the phrase "Got Milk?"

The phrase "Got Jesus?" only makes sense within the sign-system of the times, implying that Jesus is even better for you than milk. Response to this re-signing was mixed. Some Christians thought it a clever way to make Jesus relevant to contemporary culture; others thought it reduced Jesus to a consumer commodity. Either way, it exemplifies synchronic meaning, the sign making little sense diachronically. If a church had signed "Got Jesus?" in the 1930s, most viewers—Christian and secular alike—would be disturbed, assuming the congregation had no decent sense of grammar. The *langue* of the times had no place for such a *parole*.

CHANGING SIGNS OF THE TIMES: A GAY DISTINCTION

As Saussure notes, "language changes, or rather evolves, under the influence of all the forces which can affect either sounds or meanings."[48] Rather than study the historical forces that generate such evolution, however, he wants us to assess how each cupboard synchronically generates signs in people's minds. He therefore regards his linguistics as psychological rather than historical.

Nevertheless, he acknowledges that, over time, signifiers often become attached to new signifieds. Take, for example, /gay/. I still remember cringing when my Grandma Tuty, laughing at something my father said, would turn to me and say, "Your father is so gay!" In adolescent high seriousness I would carefully explain the word's new meaning, but Tuty would respond with, "*Gay* is a perfectly good word to describe a happy-go-lucky person. I am using it the way it is *supposed* to be used!"

Aside from the fact that "happy-go-lucky" was not a sign most people

[48]Quoted in Jonathan Culler, *The Literary in Theory* (Stanford, CA: Stanford University Press, 2007), p. 117.

would connect to my father, Tuty's "supposed to be used" is accurate only within the synchronic *langue* of her youth. Nevertheless, Tuty wanted to hold on to the old signified when she used the signifier "gay." Saussure, however, said that separating the signifier from the signified within a particular synchronic system is like trying to detach one side of a sheet of paper from another. Like it or not, we must be sensitive to how changes in *langue* alter the signified meaning of the signifiers we use.

Nevertheless, Tuty's desire to freeze the meaning of a word is common. In his *Philosophy of Rhetoric*, I. A. Richards attributes this desire to "the Proper Meaning Superstition," contrasting it with an awareness of context: "What a word means is the missing parts of the contexts from which it draws its delegated efficacy."[49] Like ingredients drawn from a cupboard, meaning is drawn from a sign's context. Richards, however, did not think that Saussure provided the best means to understand how context affects meaning.

NOT SO SURE ABOUT SAUSSURE:
THE MEANING OF MEANING

In *The Meaning of Meaning,* coauthored with C. K. Ogden, I. A. Richards criticizes Saussure, not only for "neglecting entirely the things for which signs stand" but also for ignoring "the process of interpretation."[50] In other words, when Saussure discusses how the cupboard of *langue* generates signs, he looks mainly at the way signifiers constitute signified concepts in listeners' minds. Context, therefore, is primarily a human's position within a particular *langue:* the *langue* of Grandma Tuty's adolescence generated "happy-go-lucky" as the signified meaning of "gay," whereas the *langue* of my adolescence generated "homosexual male" as the signified meaning of "gay." Ogden and Richards, in contrast, want to also include the world beyond language.[51]

---

[49]I. A. Richards, *The Philosophy of Rhetoric* (Oxford: Oxford University Press, 1971 [1936]), pp. 11, 35.

[50]C. K. Ogden and I. A. Richards, *The Meaning of Meaning: A Study of The Influence of Language upon Thought and of the Science of Symbolism* (New York: Harcourt, Brace & World, 1923), pp. 6, 5 n.2.

[51]For a more thorough critique of Saussure's dichotomies, see Paul Ricoeur, *The Rule of Metaphor: Multi-disciplinary Studies of the Creation of Meaning in Language,* trans. Robert Czerny et al. (Toronto: University of Toronto Press, 1977), pp. 120-25. Discussing Richards's *Philosophy of Rhetoric* approvingly (pp. 76-87), Ricoeur critiques "semiotics" throughout his book, always equating it with Saussure's semiology: "Whereas the sign points back only to other signs immanent within a system, discourse is about things. Sign differs from sign, discourse refers to the world. Difference is semiotic, reference is semantic" (p. 216). Though he briefly mentions Peirce's "icon" (p. 34), Ricoeur does not consider the difference between Saussure's dyadic and Peirce's triadic sign.

Ogden and Richards therefore prefer the semeiotic of C. S. Peirce to the semiology of Saussure. While Saussure tends to think in dyadic terms—*langue/parole*, signifier/signified, synchronic/diachronic—Peirce views reality in triadic terms. One Peirce-inspired triad, still taught in rhetoric and communication programs around the world, has become known as "the semiotic triangle." Rather than reducing a sign to a voiced signifier and its mental signified, the triangle reflects the interdependent relationship among *things* in our world, the *signifiers* we use to communicate them to others, and the *concepts* molded by and about both. The contrast with Saussure might be visualized as follows:

Signifier ←-------------------------------→ Signified

Figure 3.3 Saussure's dyadic view of the sign

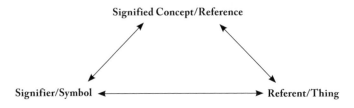

Signified Concept/Reference

Signifier/Symbol ◄-----------------------► Referent/Thing

Figure 3.4 A triadic view of the sign

Ogden and Richards place their version of the semiotic triangle at the beginning of *The Meaning of Meaning*, titling the chapter that contains it "Thoughts, Words, and Things."[52] They do so in order to communicate the interdependence of all three: things in the world generate concepts that become communicated with words/signifiers, but at the same time signifiers/words affect how we see things in the world, which inevitably changes our concepts about them, changes that we attempt to put into new words: words that inevitably alter our concepts.[53]

---

[52]Ogden and Richards, *Meaning of Meaning*, p. 11.

[53]Reflecting their own contexts during the heyday of logical empiricism (1920s-1930s), Ogden and Richards believed that only "words" about empirically verifiable "things" qualified as legitimate language. For them, religious language was superstitious nonsense created from metaphors that must be avoided. Ogden, in fact, argued for a "Basic English" that necessitated no more than 1000 words in order to refer to the things in our world.

In chapter seven I will explain the origin of the semiotic triangle in the thought of Charles Sanders Peirce.[54] Before then, we must consider the far-reaching influence of Saussure. It could be argued that Saussure had more impact on the humanities and the social sciences than any other thinker in the twentieth century. The next three chapters will discuss how and why.

---

[54]Ogden and Richards (*Meaning of Meaning*) summarize Peirce's thought in an appendix, pp. 279-90.

4

UNDER SIGNS

Structuralism

In *The Silver Chair*, one of C. S. Lewis's Narnia chronicles, Aslan sends a young schoolgirl, Jill Pole, on a quest to find a lost prince. When she asks the lion how to accomplish such a task, he replies, "These are the *Signs* by which I will guide you in your quest." He proceeds to list four signs, the third of which states, "you shall find writing on a stone in that ruined city, and you must do what the writing tells you." Discouraged by the rigors of her journey and nearly forgetting the signs, Jill falls into a labyrinth-like trench that eventually dead-ends. Only later does she discover that she was embedded in the sign itself: the trench was a huge letter "E" carved into a stone plateau. Her discovery comes from the heights of a giant's castle where she can look down on the plateau in order to interpret the writing dug into it.[1]

This chapter will examine theorists who seek to decipher cultural signs from the heights of their academic castles. Influenced by Saussure, they assess how signs guide human movement through the trenches of life. The history of advertising makes such movement obvious. Get your hands on a magazine from the 1940s and look at the ads. You'll notice products advertised in ways that would repulse many people today. In the background of some ads you'll see multiple factory chimneys spewing out smoke: the sign today of environmental blight. But in the 1940s, factory smoke signaled the power and potential of industrial America. The sign, shaped by cultural values, molded human behavior, for it led people to buy products aligned with factory smoke. That, of course, is the whole point of advertising: using positive signs that appeal to

---

[1]C. S. Lewis, *The Silver Chair* (New York: Collier, 1970), pp. 19-21, 102-4, emphasis mine.

consumer interest. It's just that a positive sign in one era can seem so outrageous in the next that it looks almost like a joke. Take, for example, the following advertisement from the early part of the twentieth century:

Figure 4.1. Blatz beer ad for babies

Like Jill and her companions, then, we often understand how a sign has controlled our thought processes and behavior only after we are beyond it. This happens quite noticeably with fashion. Looking through old photo albums or yearbooks, many of us explode with laughter, commenting, "Can you believe how we dressed back then? Look at that absurd hair!" At the time, however, we didn't think our black netting, iron-on Holly-Hobby patches or mullets the least bit absurd. Like Jill Pole looking down on the trench that once directed her movements, we become aware of a sign's control over our fashion choices only with the distance of time.[2]

The labyrinthine sign which molded the behavior of Jill Pole and company spelled out UNDER ME. Once conscious of the sign, they were able to get UNDERneath it, where they discovered a realm under the spell of a witch—much as people today are under the spell of advertising, buying things they do not need with money they do not have.[3]

---

[2]The most famous theorist to apply semiology to the analysis of both advertising and fashion is Roland Barthes (1915-1980). See his books *Mythologies,* trans. Annette Lavers (New York: Farrar, Straus & Giroux, 1972); and *The Fashion System,* trans. Matthew Ward and Richard Howard (Berkeley: University of California Press, 1990).

[3]Significantly, one of the world's first known ads, a billboard from 1000 B.C.E. Thebes, involves a coin: "In large letters [the poster] offered a gold coin for the capture of a runaway slave." Marcel Danesi, *Of Cigarettes, High Heels, and Other Interesting Things: An Introduction to Semiotics* (New York: St. Martin's, 1999), p. 184.

THE STRUCTURE *UNDER* THE SIGN

Saussure, as we have seen, believed that *under* signs was a system of differences *(langue)* that controls each speech act *(parole)*. In fact, he asserted that "in language there are only differences. . . . The idea or phonic substance that a sign contains is of less importance than the other signs that surround it."[4] Think, for example, of conversations you may have had about the color of an object. One person says, "it's purple," another responds, "no, it's violet." Then others attempt greater accuracy by suggesting *heather*, then *lavender*, or maybe even *mauve*. Arguments ensue. Hair is pulled. Well, probably not that. But often one person fumes with exasperation, "What's the difference? It's just PURPLE, OK?!" Such a response exposes the actual problem: it's *all* about difference! Rather than identifying universal color concepts, each person has made her distinction *in relation to* the color signs used by others—as lighter, darker, grayer, pinker and so forth. A system of differences *under*girds the color-sign each uses.

Influenced by Saussure's emphasis on systems—or *structures*—of difference, Russian-born linguist Roman Jakobson coined the term "structuralism" in 1929. He also cofounded what has become known as the Prague School of Structuralism: an influential group of linguists and literary critics who assessed how the focus on systems of difference might revolutionize the study of communication.[5]

COMMUNICATION PARADIGMS OF ROMAN JAKOBSON (1896-1982)

According to semiotician Umberto Eco, Roman Jakobson's "entire scientific existence was a living example of a Quest for Semiotics."[6] In his Jill Pole–like quest, Jakobson formulated a paradigm of six communication functions that arguably became, by the end of the twentieth century, "the single most quoted source in modern communication theory."[7] He diagrams his communication paradigm as follows:

---

[4]Ferdinand de Saussure, *Course in General Linguistics*, trans. Wade Baskin (New York: McGraw-Hill, 1959), p. 120.

[5]Also called the Prague Linguistic Circle, the Prague School focused on the communication functions of language and art. I had the privilege of taking a graduate course from René Wellek (1903-1995), a member of the Prague School who became a professor at Yale.

[6]Quoted in Thomas Albert Sebeok, *Semiotics in the United States* (Bloomington: Indiana University Press, 1991), p. 76.

[7]Briankle G. Chang, *Deconstructing Communication: Representation, Subject, and Economies of Exchange* (Minneapolis: University of Minnesota Press, 1996), p. 176.

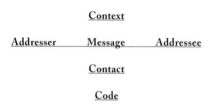

Figure 4.2. Jakobson's communication paradigm[8]

To understand the various functions on this chart, think of the simple message "It is lunchtime." This seemingly self-evident statement communicates different ideas depending on which one of the components charted above is most emphasized:

- Emphasis on Context: This is "the referential function," in which a fact is stated. Think, for example, of the statement "It is lunchtime," which indicates the time of day and its associated feeding frenzy. By "context," then, Jakobson means the transmission of information about the world in which one is situated (one's context).

- Emphasis on Addresser or Sender: Rather than simply state a fact, this "emotive function" transmits the attitude and/or emotion of the speaker. The phrase thus might really be communicating "Yippee! It's finally lunchtime!" or "I'm so hungry!"

- Emphasis on Addressee or Receiver: The sender expects, perhaps even commands, the receiver to do something, such that "It is lunchtime!" actually means "Make me lunch right now" or "Stop the car at that McDonald's." Jakobson calls this the "conative function."

- Emphasis on Contact: The statement is made to emphasize relationship between the Sender and Receiver, such as might happen after an awkward pause in conversation. The statement often signals interpersonal contact through a question at the end, such as "It's just about lunchtime, isn't it?" Jakobson calls this the "phatic function."

- Emphasis on Code: This "metalingual function" focuses on clarification of terms. For instance, a woman may look at the clock and pronounce, "It's time for our prandial ritual." When the addressee responds, "What

---

[8]Roman Jakobson, "Closing Statements: Linguistics and Poetics," in *Style in Language*, ed. Thomas Sebeok (Cambridge, MA: MIT Press, 1960), p. 353.

do you mean?" he seeks guidance in the "code," not realizing that the word *prandial* means "relating to a meal." When the speaker responds, "I mean it's lunchtime," she has decoded her statement for her vocabulary-challenged listener.

• Emphasis on Message: This is "the poetic function," as Jakobson calls it, by which language draws attention to its sound (as well as other qualities of form). An overworked secretary, for example, might announce, "It is la-la-la-la-lunchtime," making us think about the jubilant alliteration of the "l" sound as much as (if not more than) the meaning of the words. Such repetition can, in the hands of a poet, achieve the "conversion of a message into an enduring thing."[9] Think of the endurance of a word coined by Shakespeare, /bump/, which most likely caught on due to the appropriate bouncing sounds of the *b* and *p*.

The way sound affects communication, as in the childlike joy in a repeated *la-la-la* and the bouncing sounds of *bump*, intensely interested Jakobson, for sound promotes "the palpability of signs." He gives the example of the slogan "I like Ike" during Dwight D. Eisenhower's campaign for president (1952). The phrase became popular due to the "palpability" of the thrice-repeated "I" sound.[10] Effective public speakers, in other words, pay attention to *sound* as key to their message.

Most political messages that "endure" reflect the palpability of sound. Consider the following famous examples:

• The repetition of "fear" and the iambic rhythm in Franklin D. Roosevelt's "The only thing we have to fear is fear itself" (1933).

• The multiple word repetitions and hard "c" and "k" sounds in John F. Kennedy's "Ask not what your country can do for you; ask what you can do for your country" (1961).

• The power of the famous speech Martin Luther King Jr. delivered in 1963, when he repeated at least ten times "I have a dream" and "Let freedom ring." Not only does each phrase have an iambic dimeter rhythm, but together their endings create a slant rhyme: *dream* and *ring*.

---

[9]Ibid., p. 371.
[10]Ibid., pp. 356-57.

MESSAGE MESS-UP

Jakobson's focus on sound as part of the "message" function of communication also explains *mis*communication. Consider an incident during my second visit to England. Stopping in a tea shop around 2:30 p.m., I said to the attendant at the counter "steak and kidney pie, please." She curtly responded with "Name a cookie." Baffled, I repeated my order more slowly, eliciting from her an even louder "Name a cookie!" Trying to figure out why I was required to order dessert first (Oreo? Chocolate Chip?), I repeated my request one more time, only to have her shout in exasperation "NAME A COOKIE!!" Then, turning in disgust, she entered the kitchen only to bring back the cook, who pronounced in slow syllables, as though I were a bit daft, "Kitchen closed! *No more cooking!*" Her translation exposed a failure of communication based on phonological principles: a sound that meant "cooking" to one English speaker meant "cookie" to another.

Like Jill Pole who eventually explores where the sign UNDER ME directs her, Jakobson burrows under signs to assess structures of phonological differences. As one book on semiotics aptly puts it,

> Undergirding the protean variety of sounds in natural languages, Jakobson argued, was a small set of binary phonological oppositions or distinctive features, i.e. the presence or absence of a distinctive trait: vocal cord vibration, lip-rounding, nasalization, and so forth. Jakobson classified all the distinctive oppositions operating in the world's languages into a series of twelve such oppositions.[11]

Consider the opposition between the sounds *t* an *d*, for example. Concentrating on your mouth and voice, slowly say *tip* and *dip* out loud. Notice how your tongue presses against your teeth at the start of both, making them comparable. Now put both hands around your throat and say *tip* and *dip* out loud, noticing what makes them different: vocal chord vibrations are more intense (and lower in your throat) when you sound the *d* than when you sound the *t*. Jakobson therefore bundled *t* and *d* together, to signal their similarity and difference. We can chart the relationship as follows:

$$\frac{t}{d}$$

---

[11]Robert Stam, Robert Burgoyne and Sandy Flitterman-Lewis, *New Vocabularies in Film Semiotics: Structuralism, Post-structuralism and Beyond* (New York: Routledge, 1992), p. 15.

This "binary opposition," as he calls it, echoes Saussure's belief that "the entire mechanism of language . . . is based on oppositions,"[12] such as that between *resign and re-sign.* This is important for understanding Jakobson's influence. Not only did his word *structuralism* all but replace Saussure's word *semiology,* but his "consistent binarism," as we will see, affected most academic disciplines that study culture and communication.[13]

Furthermore, while Saussure assessed differences generated by sound variations *within* any one *langue (pat* versus *pan),* Jakobson assessed differences of value *between* languages or dialects. Doing so, he did two things: (1) he helped initiate a new discipline called *phonology,* which studies how sound creates meaning; (2) he implied that "structuralism" involved the comparison of different linguistic systems—like lining up multiple cupboards ("structures") in order to assess what each can cook up.[14]

STRUCTURAL ANTHROPOLOGY: CLAUDE LÉVI-STRAUSS (1909-2009)

Jakobson profoundly influenced the field of anthropology through his impact on Claude Lévi-Strauss, whose relatives influenced the development of blue jeans.[15] Educated in philosophy at the Sorbonne in Paris, Lévi-Strauss switched to anthropology after doing research in Brazil with his wife, a trained ethnographer. He switched once again when he heard Jakobson lecture on the writings of Saussure: he became a structuralist, applying linguistic paradigms to ethnographic study.

In contrast to traditional anthropologists, then, Lévi-Strauss argued that

---

[12]Obviously influencing Jakobson's binary thinking, Saussure suggested "an algebraic formula a/b in which a and b are not simple terms but result from a set of relations." Saussure, *Course in General Linguistics,* p. 122.

[13]Thomas Albert Sebeok notes that, even after Jakobson fell in love with the work of Charles Sanders Peirce in the early 1950s, he never gave up on his "consistent binarism." See *Semiotics in the United States,* p. 79.

[14]Julia Kristeva (who is discussed later in this chapter), aligned Jakobson with the "tendency towards the establishment of a typology of signifying systems" (comparing different structures) as opposed to semioticians who wanted to develop a universal semiotic that transcends all sciences. She exemplifies the latter with Danish linguist Louis Hjelmslev (1899-1965) and American semiotician Charles W. Morris (1903-1979), both of whom wanted "to unify in a gesture of metaphysical mastery all possible modes of discourse." See Julia Kristeva, "The Semiotic Activity," *Screen* 14 (1973): 34.

[15]Murray Krieger, who established the School of Criticism and Theory at the University of California, Irvine, told me of the connection between Claude Lévi-Strauss and the nineteenth-century designer of Levi jeans. I had the privilege of studying with Krieger my first year in grad school.

scholars must study cultures "at the sign level."[16] For him, a truly rigorous anthropology focuses on modes of communication, analyzing the *system* that gives signs value *in relation to each other.* Thus even "marriage regulations and kinship systems" are "a type of communication."[17] As he explains in his book *Structural Anthropology,* "The error of traditional anthropology, like that of traditional linguistics, was to consider the terms, and not the relations between the terms."[18]

Inspired by the "consistent binarism" of Saussure and Jakobson, Lévi-Strauss analyzed tribal communication according to oppositions. They can be charted as follows, indicating that the top term gains its value through its distinction from the bottom term:

human	culture	male	friend	native	pretty
animal	nature	female	enemy	foreign	ugly

Lévi-Strauss argues that all tribal truths are based on oppositions like these, affecting every aspect of communication: not only verbal language, but also gift exchange, cooking rituals, story-telling and so on. Signs of communication therefore foreground tensions in a society—including our own. Indeed, Lévi-Strauss believes that all humans think according to such oppositions; for him the mind has evolved a structure that thinks according to binaries.[19]

Consider, for example, the oppositions that are part of Christian tradition, where the top term is always preferable to the lower term. Jakobson describes the upper term in such binaries as "unmarked"—as though it were the natural or preferable way to function—while the lower term is "marked" as deficient:

salvation	grace	faith	heaven	Christ	angels
damnation	law	works	hell	Satan	demons

While cynics might reference these oppositions as proof that Christianity

[16]Claude Lévi-Strauss, *The Raw and the Cooked: Introduction to a Science of Mythology,* vol. 1, trans. John and Doreen Weightman (New York: Harper & Row, 1969), p. 14.
[17]Quoted in Dan Sperber, "Claude Lévi-Strauss," in *Structuralism and Since: From Lévi-Strauss to Derrida,* ed. John Sturrock (New York: Oxford University Press, 1979), p. 23.
[18]Claude Lévi-Strauss, *Structural Anthropology* (Harmondsworth, UK: Penguin, 1972), p. 46.
[19]Lévi-Strauss begins *The Raw and the Cooked* with a set of binaries: "The aim of this book is to show how empirical categories—such as the categories of the raw and the cooked, the fresh and the decayed, the moistened and the burned, etc., which can only be accurately defined by ethnographic observation . . . —can nonetheless be used as conceptual tools with which to elaborate abstract ideas and combine them in the form of propositions" (p. 1).

parallels primitive mythologies, Lévi-Strauss asserts that scientific minds function the exact same way. Just think of the binaries reiterated by the New Atheists:

evolution	science	empiricism	materialism	reason
creationism	religion	superstition	supernaturalism	faith

For Lévi-Strauss, therefore, the civilized thinker parallels "the savage mind"—a phrase that names one of his most famous books.[20] In both cases, signs enter the mind like coins entering a sorting machine. Because all humans have the same mental slots to sort the sense, all machines produce similar rolls of coin wrapped in similar colors of paper. However, because the signs entering the machines differ from society to society, the similar-looking rolls have different contents: a mind in one tribe might produce an orange tube of pennies; that in another society produces an orange tube of pence. This means that one person pops out language about Genesis, another about Darwin, but both have merely produced orange tubes about the origins of life. While the structure is the same, the content is as different as the signs that enter the coin-machine brains.[21]

While people on either side of the coin may disdain my parallel between Genesis and Darwin, Lévi-Strauss provides a foothold for Christians who want to be on the edge. He ends his "Structural Study of Myth" with these words:

> [T]he kind of logic in mythical thought is as rigorous as that of modern science[;] . . . the difference lies not in the quality of the intellectual process, but in the nature of the things to which it is applied. . . . [M]an has always been thinking equally well; the improvement lies, not in an alleged progress of man's mind, but in the discovery of new areas to which it may apply its unchanged and unchanging powers.[22]

The writers of the Bible, then, were "thinking equally well" as evolutionary biologists; they just had access to different kinds of signs.[23]

---

[20]Claude Lévi-Strauss, *The Savage Mind* (Chicago: University of Chicago Press, 1968). The structural anthropology of Lévi-Strauss differs dramatically from theories of anthropologists like Evans-Pritchard (1902-1973), who suggested that the minds of the Sudanese people he studied functioned differently than the minds of Europeans.

[21]I take all responsibility for any weaknesses in the coin-machine analogy, which is my own. I also employ it in my book *How Postmodernism Serves (My) Faith: Questioning Truth in Language, Philosophy and Art* (Downers Grove, IL: IVP Academic, 2006), pp. 125-26.

[22]Claude Lévi-Strauss, "The Structural Study of Myth," *Journal of American Folklore* 68 (October-December 1955): 444.

[23]This does not mean that Lévi-Strauss was sympathetic to Christianity. As René Girard notes,

STRUCTURAL PSYCHOLOGY: JACQUES LACAN (1901-1981)

Saussure, Jakobson and Lévi-Strauss influenced French-born psychiatrist Jacques Lacan, who served up Freud with a structuralist twist. While Freud asserted that unconscious desires are accidentally revealed through language, as in a "Freudian slip," for Lacan, "language creates the unconscious" in the first place: language molds the way we think.[24] Furthermore, as in Saussure, Jakobson and Lévi-Strauss, Lacan sees language structured according to binary oppositions. His point is illustrated by something he calls "the laws of urinary segregation," by which he means separate restrooms for males and females.[25] Let me exemplify with an embarrassing incident from my own life.

On my way to teach a class on *Macbeth* for a university in California, I rushed into a restroom. Once inside the door I became baffled. A woman had her back to me, closely facing a wall that had no mirror on it. I wondered what this signified. Was she crying? Drawing graffiti? Feeling shame or despair? And then I noticed the urinal at her feet. I suddenly realized that the person with hair down to her shoulder blades was a he. Fortunately, I was able to slip out before *he* discovered that the person who had entered the restroom behind his back was a *she*.

My process of interpretation was based on various structuralist principles:

1. Restrooms in that building follow a structural system: every other floor has a facility for females; the intervening floors are designated "male." Their difference is based on their relation to each other. I had simply forgotten which floor I was on.

2. The restroom doors on each floor look exactly alike. Aside from their structural relations, the only difference between the doors is a tiny sign on the wall adjacent to each. The signifiers *women* and *men* control the signified reality inside. In my hurry, I had failed to look at the signifier.

3. These signifiers therefore establish the signified reality for anyone who enters. This is especially pronounced in the mathematics building on the

---

"Lévi-Strauss is almost as eager to castigate religion as to extol language." See "Differentiation and Undifferentiation in Lévi-Strauss and Current Critical Theory," in *Directions for Criticism: Structuralism and Its Alternatives*, ed. Murray Krieger and L. S. Dembo (Madison: University of Wisconsin Press, 1977), p. 114.

[24]Malcolm Bowie, "Jacques Lacan," in *Structuralism and Since: From Lévi-Strauss to Derrida*, ed. John Sturrock (New York: Oxford University Press, 1979), p. 126.

[25]Jacques Lacan, "The Instance of the Letter in the Unconscious: Reason Since Freud," in *Écrits*, trans. Bruce Fink (New York: Norton, 2002), p. 417.

same campus. Built at a time when architects assumed only males major in math, the restrooms on *every* floor have urinals (except for the floor where secretaries have their offices). The signified—male restroom or female restroom—is determined by arbitrary signifiers outside each door: "male" or "female." Inside, however, the restrooms are exactly the same, urinals and all.

4. As a result of this signifying system, I interpreted a long-haired male to be female due to culturally coded assumptions:

   a. the structural assumption that I was on the right floor and therefore in a woman's restroom

   b. the traditional, though often inaccurate, assumption that long hair signals the female gender

Assumption "a," of course, influenced assumption "b." For it's only because I thought I had entered a women's room that I "recognized" the hair as belonging to a female.

In his writings, appropriately called *Writings (Écrits)*, Lacan uses the phenomenon of such "urinary segregation" to illustrate that culturally constructed and therefore arbitrary signifiers *precede* our understanding of signified reality. Hence, while Lévi-Strauss emphasized the universal structure of the human mind, like similarly built mechanisms within coin machines, Lacan was more interested in the coins (signifiers) inserted into the machines, arguing that the coins make the machine run.

LACAN'S COIN(AGE): THE NAME OF THE FATHER

For Lacan, these coins, or signifiers, bear "*le nom du père,*" or "the name of the father." I quote Lacan's original French because *le nom du père* sounds, in French, just like *le non du père* or "the no of the father." Lacan employs this pun to make a semiotic point: our understanding of reality arises from the signs of the language we speak. Conventional signs are reinforced by the authority of culture the way behavior in a family is often regulated by the father who says "No!" These "laws" of the cultural father are mediated through signifiers: the names of things, or "the name of the father."

Lacan does not mean, of course, that fathers meet in secret societies to cook up the truths of culture. He means that language controls the way we think the same way fathers (at least before the widespread phenomenon of single-parent homes) control the way we act. My mother's greatest threat when I misbehaved was "Just wait until your father gets home!" That got me into line right away, having learned from experience the strength of his spanking hand. The *no* of my father was signaled when my mother appealed to the *name* "your father."

Once again, Lacan is talking about much more than parental disciplining techniques. By learning linguistic signs, children are initiated into the realm of "the symbolic" policed by "the No of the father." For example, think of the sign of a tan. For many centuries in Western culture the "name" /tan/, was a "No!" If someone called you (named you) "tan," it was an insult, because sun-darkened skin showed you were lower class: a person forced to work outside to make a living. Because the pampered wealthy had white skin, Europeans from the sixteenth through eighteenth centuries would try to make themselves even paler, often smearing white (and highly toxic) paste on their faces to prove their superior status.[26]

However, by the time I was growing up in the last half of the twentieth century, white skin was a "No!" It was the sign of "a pasty-faced geek" who had to sit in a cubicle all day. The wealthy, in contrast, could afford to bask in the sun. They had the money to build swimming pools, join country clubs, take Caribbean cruises. A tan was now a sign of status, and people all over America would rather "work on" their tans than work in a cubicle.

Signs of beauty thus radically changed over the centuries, people *seeing* beauty according to *le nom du père*. /Tan/ has no universal connection to attractiveness, its value based instead upon another binary opposition: rich versus poor. Beautiful skin is defined by those who have wealth (and hence power) in any given culture: *le nom du père*. Figure 4.3 illustrates it:

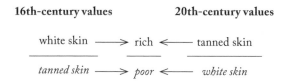

16th-century values   **20th-century values**

white skin ——→ rich ←—— tanned skin

tanned skin ——→ *poor* ←—— *white skin*

Figure 4.3. Inverting the "tan" binary

---

[26]Note this statement made by an upper-class female character in a 1778 novel: "the sun, too, is monstrous disagreeble!—I dare say I shall be so tanned I sh'n't be fit to be seen this age." Fanny Burney, *Evelina: or the History of a Young Lady's Entrance Into the World* (Oxford: Oxford University Press, 1982), p. 279.

Notice how figure 4.3 reflects Saussure's idea that value is based on differences, or oppositions, within a system. Though the tan illustration is my own, Lacan might add this: "white skin" was the big "S" in Shakespeare's day; it was the Signifier that established signified value (wealth and hence beauty). However, by the twentieth century, "tan skin" was the big "S" Signifier in Western culture. By explicitly writing S/s in his writings, Lacan (re)signed Saussure's binary (in which the top term always has priority):

$$\frac{\text{Signified}}{\text{signifier}} \qquad \frac{\text{Signifier}}{\text{signified}}$$

Saussure's Binary   Lacan's Binary

The second column, with the Signifier on the top part of the binary, illustrates Lacan's sense that Signifiers *create* their signified meaning. In contrast, Saussure seemed to believe that a Signified concept precedes the signifier, if even intangibly, until the signifier gives it substance.

STRUCTURALIST FEMINISM AND JULIA KRISTEVA

Many feminist critics appropriated Lacan's theory because it explained why women so often have low self-images: *le nom du père* controls the capital "S" Signifiers that shape the way females think about themselves.[27] Consider, for example, how some people use different Signifiers when talking to baby girls than to baby boys: "You are so pretty" versus "You are so alert"; "Look at how she clings to my finger" versus "He's got quite a grip"; "Oh, you've got a boo-boo" versus "Hey, tough guy, you're alright." These Signifiers, according to Lacanian feminists, *create* the signified reality, such that females come to think of their identities in terms of how they appear, to whom they are attached and how they've been victimized. Other signs in culture—like restrooms in mathematics buildings—serve to reinforce this symbolic system overseen by *le nom du père*. Hélène Cixous (b. 1937), who knew Lacan, refers to those who reinforce "the Name-of-the-Father" as "cops of the signifier."[28]

---

[27]In contrast, many feminists repudiate Lacan, since "like Freud's theory, Lacan's theory takes patriarchy as a given." Vincent B. Leitch et al., eds., "Jacques Lacan," in *The Norton Anthology of Theory and Criticism*, ed. Vincent B. Leitch et al., 2nd ed. (New York: Norton, 2010), p. 1162.

[28]Hélène Cixous, "The Laugh of the Medusa," in *The Norton Anthology of Theory and Criticism*, ed. Vincent B. Leitch et al., 2nd ed. (New York: Norton, 2010), p. 1958.

Cixous's French contemporary, Julia Kristeva (b. 1941), was influenced by most of the structuralists discussed so far. After serving as a research assistant at Lévi-Strauss's Laboratory of Social Anthropology, she became a practicing psychoanalyst influenced by the thought of Lacan. Considered one of the foremost French feminists of the twentieth century, Kristeva has even challenged feminism itself, discussing how it, as well, might be controlled by the "name of the father."

Think, for example, of movies like *Charlie's Angels* (2000, 2003) or *Laura Croft: Tomb Raider* (2001, 2003), in which drop-dead gorgeous women punch, kick, jump and shoot as well as any man. On the surface, the films seem "feminist," demonstrating the amazing power of women. But, in actuality, signs of power in such movies are still defined by macho-male standards: the scantily clad women function as sexy objects of desire even as they mimic testosterone-driven actions. Similarly, the female CEO of a Fortune 500 company, while dressing and acting not at all like Charlie's Angels or Laura Croft, may still be led to protect the male-dominated system that gave her the power. In other words, even feminists might get stuck in a trench, functioning UNDER the signs of their cultural father.

Kristeva's answer to this problem is "semiotic" communication. Her word "semiotic," however, means something different than what we have encountered so far. For Kristeva, "the semiotic" refers to existence before a child enters into "the symbolic" realm of language that is policed by "the name of the father." The semiotic, for her, is tied to pre-linguistic communication, as when a baby coos in his mother's arms in response to his mother's nonverbal humming.

Not all is lost with the entry into speech, however. Kristeva believes we can access the semiotic by generating the musicality of poetry.[29] Reminding us of the "palpability" of sound valued by Jakobson, the semiotic, according to Kristeva, "gives us a vision of the human venture as a venture of innovation, of creation, of opening, of renewal."[30] Remember this idea, for it will become

---

[29]Julia Kristeva titled her first book *Séméôtiké* (1969), parts of which were translated and published in *Desire in Language: A Semiotic Approach to Literature and Art,* ed. Leon S. Roudiez, trans. Thomas Gora, Alice Jardine and Leon S. Roudiez (New York: Columbia University Press, 1980). She develops her distinction between "the semiotic" and "the symbolic" in *Revolution in Poetic Language,* trans. Margaret Waller (New York: Columbia University Press), pp. 19-106.
[30]Kristeva made this statement in an interview, quoted in "Julia Kristeva," in *The Norton Anthology of Theory and Criticism,* ed. Vincent B. Leitch et al., 2nd ed. (New York: Norton, 2010), p. 2069.

important to the conclusion of *Changing Signs of Truth*. Before then, we need to consider how structuralism led to the exact opposite idea: that people cannot escape the control of language.

ABOVE AND BEYOND SAUSSURE: RADICAL STRUCTURALISM

Inspired by Lévi-Strauss and Lacan, many structuralists radicalized Saussure's constructs. While Saussure assumed that signifiers elicit signified concepts that are already part of human consciousness (if even amorphously), these structuralists taught that the signs of culture established those concepts in the first place.[31] Signs, then, don't merely shape thought the way advertisements do; signs actually *create* thought. Hence, while Saussure held that any *parole* reflects a "completely free act of choice" based on ingredients extracted from the *langue* cupboard,[32] radical structuralists came to the logical conclusion that "choice" is not free when ruled by a linguistic structure.

Think again of *The Silver Chair*. Deep in the structure of the underworld, far beneath the sign UNDER ME, Jill and friends discover a Black Knight. Believing himself to be an independent agent in control of his thoughts and behavior, the knight is actually UNDER the spell of a witch. Calling her his "heavenly Queen," he blithely states, "I am well content to live *by her word*," believing he has a choice in the matter. As the knight tells Jill and friends, "*Her word* shall be my law." (Significantly, some scholars translate Lacan's *le nom du père* with "the *law* of the father.") However, as Lewis makes very clear, the knight's very desire to follow the "word" of the Queen is part of her spell over him. As hard-core structuralists might explain it, human desires are not freely chosen. Instead, we function UNDER a spell cast by linguistic structures: we think according to the way capital "S" Signifiers control our perception. Indeed, any time someone sits *in* the sun or goes to a tanning salon, despite all the warnings about skin cancer, they demonstrate behavior controlled by the Signifier *Tan*.

Significantly, the Queen in *The Silver Chair* starts to enchant Jill Pole. As a result, Jill "couldn't remember the *names* of the things in our world": she has started to replace her English Signifiers with the witch's Signi-

---

[31]Structuralists were merely following Saussure's own words: "No ideas are established in advance, and nothing is distinct, before the introduction of linguistic structure." But, as T. L. Short notes, Saussure is inconsistent on this issue, other times suggesting "thought's intentionality, independent of language." See T. L. Short, *Peirce's Theory of Signs* (Cambridge: Cambridge University Press, 2007), p. 17.
[32]Michael Holquist, *Dialogism: Bakhtin and his World*, 2nd ed. (New York: Routledge, 1990), p. 60.

fiers. C. S. Lewis explains the spell with a profound structuralist insight: "and of course, the more enchanted you get, the more certain you feel that you are not enchanted at all."[33] As Lacan famously put it, "the unconscious is the Other's discourse."[34] Jill's unconscious was being molded by the language of the Queen, an "Other" whose discourse already controlled the Black Knight.

QUESTIONING STRUCTURAL MACHINATIONS

The problem with radical structuralism is obvious: it seems to turn humans into machines. Signs enter our coded brains to get us to act, much as coins enter a gumball machine to produce insipid candy-coated treats. Structuralists, however, seemed to operate as though they were the great gumball machine repairmen in the sky, regarding all people's minds as mechanistic except their own. How does Lévi-Strauss know that his theory about the universal structure of human perception is true and not just coded by the system of signs in which *he* is entrenched? What makes Lacan think he can float above Signifiers, established by *le nom du père*, in order to read what's UNDERneath? Where is the castle that allows these structuralists to rise above the signs dug into the plateaus of life?

Before we explore how Marxists and poststructuralists responded to these significant questions (in chapters five and six), we need to consider how structuralism might aid Christian thought. One theorist, for example, has appropriated Saussurean terms to quite rightly argue that Christians should function as signifiers of God's love: "God the signified can be known through the lives of Christians, and that meaning is clarified, defined, and redefined through the continual accretion of signifiers."[35]

Structuralism might also explain changes to Christianity over the millennia. This is important, because, to stay on the edge, (re)signing Christians need to consider how and why signs of faith function differently in different eras.

CHRISTMAS OUT OF THE CUPBOARD

The comparison of different linguistic systems (cupboards) might explain the

---

[33]Lewis, *Silver Chair*, pp. 136, 139, 138, 153.
[34]Jacques Lacan, "Seminar on 'The Purloined Letter,'" in *Écrits*, trans. Bruce Fink (New York: Norton, 2002), p. 10.
[35]Jeffrey Ringer, "Hilton, St. Augustine, and Semiotics," *Christianity and Literature* 63, no. 1 (Autumn 2003): 16.

opposing attitudes toward Xmas mentioned in chapter three. Different eras, as we shall see, cook up the sign /Christmas/ differently.

Early believers, for example, did not celebrate Christmas until the fourth century. The theologian Origen (ca. 185-232) argued against any celebration of Christ's birth, noting that "of all the holy people in the Scriptures, no one is recorded to have kept a feast or held a great banquet on his birthday. It is only sinners (like Pharaoh and Herod) who make great rejoicings over the day on which they were born into this world below."[36] He therefore aligns any kind of birth-celebration with paganism.

Does this mean it is not Christian to celebrate Christmas? Yes—at least according to Origen. However, Origen's response to Christmas was based on the *langue* of his day, when the signifier "Christian" signified people persecuted by the dominant culture. Moreover, the people who did the persecuting always celebrated the births of their pagan lords. For Origen, then, a birthday celebration honoring Christ would be as offensive as a strip-tease in church today.

The *langue* cupboard changed in 312 C.E. when Constantine became the first Roman emperor to align himself with Christianity. While the emperor before him (Diocletian) tortured Christians mercilessly, Constantine proclaimed—via the Edict of Milan in 313 C.E.—that Christianity was now lawful in the Roman Empire. Not only did he return property that had been confiscated by Diocletian, he exempted Christian clergy from paying taxes, allowing them the same privilege given priests in Roman temples. In fact, Constantine granted the bishops of Rome "more power than he gave Roman governors"![37] The signifier *Christian* no longer signified "persecuted for Christ."

In fact, Constantine synthesized signs of his times with signs of Christ, joining together two distinct cupboards: the pagan political realm with the realm of Christ-followers. He directed construction of the first permanent buildings for Christian worship, modeling them after halls constructed for business and legal activities. And the clergy inside started dressing like Roman officials, their vestments functioning as signs of leadership.[38]

Constantine, in other words, united the *langue* of pagan politics with the message of Christ's death and resurrection. This, then, paved the way for the

---

[36]Quoted in "Origen," *The Catholic Encyclopedia*, on the New Advent website, www.newadvent.org/cathen/.

[37]Frank Viola and George Barna, *Pagan Christianity? Exploring the Roots of Our Church Practices* (Carol Stream, IL: Tyndale House, 2008), p. 120.

[38]Janet Mayo, *A History of Ecclesiastical Dress* (New York: Holmes & Meier, 1984), pp. 14-15.

uniting of Christ's birth with a pagan holiday. As one scholar notes, "Evidence suggests that by 336 Christmas was being observed in Rome on 25 December. The day seems to have been chosen so that the Christian festival could compete with the pagan festival of *Natalis Solis Invicti,* thanksgiving for the rebirth of the sun."[39] Though controversial at first, the celebration of Christ's birth on a pagan holiday eventually became an accepted sign of Christian truth: the signified had a new signifier (December 25).

WE THREE KINGS OF ORIENT ARE . . . SEMIOTIC

After Constantine changed the *langue* of Christianity, new signs of Christmas developed, such as three magi joining the shepherds to worship the Christchild in his manger: an event not in the Bible. Matthew, in fact, is the only Gospel to mention the magi, due, I would argue, to the *langue* of Judaism in which Matthew was immersed. As even inerrantists note, "the strongly Hebraic character of the book identifies its author as a Jewish Christian writing for Jewish readers" in order to prove that Jesus fulfilled Hebrew expectations of a savior born from the line of David.[40] Matthew therefore begins with a genealogy of Jesus, identifying his ancestors as signs generated from the correct *langue.* And the Gospel contains repeated allusions to and quotations of Hebrew Scriptures. For example, when the wise men inform Herod that they are looking for "the Messiah" in Bethlehem, they tell him, "for so it has been written by the prophet: 'And you, Bethlehem, in the land of Judah, are by no means least among the rulers of Judah; for from you shall come a ruler who is to shepherd my people Israel'" (Mt 2:5-6, citing Mic 5:2). Evangelical Bible scholar Robert Gundry argues that the wise men were introduced by Matthew to prove that Jesus fulfilled "messianic prophecies."[41] Though Gundry doesn't use semiotic language, he essentially argues that Matthew's signs were generated out of the *langue* (cupboard) of Jewish hope. The truth of the gospel, then, lies in the fulfillment of that hope.

By the third century, Tertullian had (re)signed *magi* into "kings,"[42] based

---

[39]David Parker, *Christmas and Charles Dickens* (New York: AMS, 2005), p. 21.

[40]Harold Lindsell, "Introduction to the Gospel According to Matthew," *The Harper Study Bible* (Grand Rapids, MI: Zondervan, 1965), p. 1435.

[41]Robert Gundry, *Matthew: A Commentary on His Literary and Theological Art* (Grand Rapids, MI: Eerdmans, 1982), p. 37.

[42]David Lyle Jeffrey, ed., *A Dictionary of Biblical Tradition in English Literature* (Grand Rapids, MI: Eerdmans, 1992), p. 472.

on his reading of Hebrew Scriptures: "May the kings of Tarshish and of the isles render him tribute, may the kings of Sheba and Seba bring gifts" (Ps 72:10); "Nations shall come to your light, and kings to the brightness of your dawn" (Is 60:3). The *langue* (cupboard) of the Hebrew Scriptures, in other words, provided the "conditions of possibility" by which new signs might be cooked up.

By the eighth century, the number of "kings" had been limited to three.[43] Matthew, of course, does not designate how many men "from the East" (Mt 2:1)—or "the Orient"—visit the holy family, establishing only that they offered three gifts. Obviously, the sign /three gifts/ affected the sign of the wise men. This accords with Saussure's view that signs take their value from other signs within a system: just think of the example in chapter three whereby low-rise jeans affected the length of belts.

The eighth century also gives witness to the addition of animals in the nativity scene. As one eighth-century document explains it,

> Then was fulfilled that which was said by Isaiah the prophet, "The ox knows its owner, and the donkey its master's crib." Therefore, the animals, the ox and the ass, with him in their midst incessantly adored him. Then was fulfilled that which was said by Habakkuk the prophet, saying, "Between two animals you are made manifest."[44]

Once again, the "conditions of possibility" within the ancient Hebrew *langue* gave rise to new signs not mentioned in the Gospels.

By the eleventh century, masses celebrating Christ's birth sometimes included mini-dramas that represented the magi chatting with the shepherds on their way to the manger, even though Luke makes no mention of magi, and Matthew makes no mention of shepherds, having the magi visit not a manger but a house (Mt 2:11).[45] Nevertheless, these (re)signed truths were perpetuated by the development of the "crèche," or nativity scene, usually attributed to St. Francis of Assisi (ca. 1181-1226), which places angels, magi, shepherds and animals together in adoration of the Christ child.

---

[43]Jeffrey's *Dictionary* (Ibid.) notes that the three wise men are described in a treatise called *Excerpta et Collectanea*, attributed to the Venerable Bede (ca. 672-735).

[44]From the eighth-century *Gospel of Pseudo-Matthew*, quoted in Laura Hobgood-Oster, *Holy Dogs and Asses: Animals in the Christian Tradition* (Chicago: University of Illinois Press, 2008), p. 48.

[45]See the "*Incipit Ordo ad Repraesentandum Herodem* [The Service for Representing Herod]" from Fleury, France, in *Medieval Drama*, ed. David Bevington (Boston: Houghton Mifflin, 1975), p. 64.

This sign became so firmly established that, to this day, many churches present living Nativities with actors portraying the holy family, shepherds and magi all together around a manger, with live animals in the background. (I'll never forget the time a girl portraying Mary started to cry because the goat behind her began eating her mantle!) How should we respond, knowing such scenes do not accord with Gospel accounts? Should we renounce these signs because they do not reflect biblical narratives? "Yes we should!" proclaimed earnest Christians in seventeenth-century England.

SIGNS OF CHRISTMAS: PURITAN HUMBUG

Influenced by Luther's and Calvin's denunciations of Roman Catholicism, many early Protestants associated Christmas celebrations with "the Whore of Babylon," their name for the Roman Catholic Church (taken from Rev 17:5).[46] When the Puritans ruled England (1649-1660), they passed laws banning Christmas carols, Christmas pies and the decoration of houses with boughs of holly. They even banned Christmas services, declaring Christmas Day a working day, "Parliament setting an example by sitting on 25 December."[47] Why? Because for Oliver Cromwell and his Puritan followers, these traditions were not biblical. For them, any (re)signing of truth based on signs of the times was sinful.

Ironically, the Puritans became famous for their own "nonbiblical" behavior, like long sermons inside church buildings: something Frank Viola and George Barna establish as unscriptural, as we saw in chapter one.[48] Nevertheless, because the Puritans controlled Parliament during the mid-seventeenth century, their anti-Christmas sentiment became associated with status and power: *le nom du père*. As a result, the *langue* changed, such that the celebration of Christmas became associated with the lower classes (just as a tan was associated with the lower classes). Hence, for almost two hundred years after Puritan rule, it was not unusual for business owners to expect their employees to work Christmas day.[49]

And then something extraordinary happened that entirely changed the signs of Christmas.

---

[46]Martin Luther established this connection in his 1520 treatise "On the Babylonian Captivity of the Church," which asserted that the pope was the antichrist.
[47]Parker, *Christmas and Charles Dickens*, p. 46.
[48]Viola and Barna, *Pagan Christianity?* p. 89.
[49]Parker, *Christmas and Charles Dickens*, pp. 47-48.

THE CELEBRATION OF CHRISTMAS: CHARLES DICKENS

In 1843 Charles Dickens published *A Christmas Carol,* in which he aligns employers who demand work on December 25 with Scrooge, a "squeezing, wrenching, grasping, scraping, clutching, covetous old sinner." In the process, Dickens's novel re-signed Christmas "as a good time: a kind, forgiving, charitable, pleasant time . . . when men and women seem by one consent to open their shut-up hearts freely, and to think of people below them as if they really were fellow-passengers to the grave."[50]

This sign of Christmas was so new that it led one cultural critic in the early twentieth century to describe Charles Dickens as "The Man Who 'Invented' Christmas."[51] Even scholars who regard this description as exaggerated, admit that *"A Christmas Carol,* more than anything else, . . . persuaded the fashionable to resume Christmas merry making."[52] In other words, as one biographer puts it, Dickens "almost single-handedly created *the modern idea* of Christmas."[53] Dickens helped re-design the cupboard producing signs of Christmas.

But, of course, he didn't do it by himself. For Saussure, individuals never produce new signs out of the blue; new signs are always baked up out of a cupboard's ingredients. Anything "original," then, is simply a new combination of old ingredients: a new recipe for truth. Once the new recipe becomes popular, however, cupboard users stock up on those particular sign-making ingredients, which helps reconfigure the cupboard.[54] Shelves are moved to make room for more cornmeal and cream of tartar, changing the potential signs that can be produced from it. In this light, a structuralist would argue that a change in ingredients had already preceded Dickens.

Indeed, in the decade before Dickens invented Scrooge, Charles Lyell

---

[50]Charles Dickens, *A Christmas Carol* (New York: Weathervane Books, 1977), pp. 5, 9.

[51]The essay was published in 1903 by F. G. Kitton. See Parker, *Christmas and Charles Dickens,* pp. 14-16.

[52]Parker, *Christmas and Charles Dickens,* p. 113.

[53]Peter Ackroyd, *Dickens* (London: Sinclair-Stevenson, 1990), p. 34, emphasis mine. In 1937 D. L. Murray noted that, as early as the 1840s, Dickens was "hailed as a national benefactor" for his re-creation of "Christmas as a secular festival." See "The Submerged Dickens," *Times Literary Supplement,* December 19 & 20, 2008, p. 22. I similarly discuss this issue in Crystal Downing, "Finding Satisfaction in Great Expectations," in *The Ignatius Critical Edition of* Great Expectations (San Francisco: Ignatius, 2010), pp. 599-613.

[54]"The community is necessary if values that owe their existence solely to usage and general acceptance are to be set up; by himself the individual is incapable of fixing a single value." Saussure, *Course in General Linguistics,* p. 113.

(1797-1875) had published several scholarly volumes about his geological investigations, concluding that the earth was significantly older than allowed for by a creation event in 4004 B.C., the date English Christians had promoted ever since Bishop Ussher suggested it at the start of Puritan rule.[55] In conjunction with Enlightenment skepticism about the possibility of supernatural events and the reliability of the Bible (see chapter one), Lyell's scholarship led to suspicions about the legitimacy of Christianity itself. These suspicions generated a recipe for agnosticism. In fact, /agnosticism/ was coined in 1869 by Dickens's contemporary Thomas Henry Huxley from shelves that held fewer and fewer ingredients that contributed to Christian truth. Dickens, then, provided hope in human love at a time when Christ's love was in question. He did so, however, by re-signing, rather than (re)signing truth.

In *A Christmas Carol*, Dickens appropriates traditional signs of the Bible story and re-signs their significance. The ghost of Marley bemoans to Scrooge, his former business partner, "Why did I walk through crowds of fellow-beings with my eyes turned down, and never raise them to that blessed Star which led the Wise Men to a poor abode? Were there no poor homes to which its light would have conducted me!"[56] The Star now signifies the poor rather than the Christ-child. I wish more people today considered helping the poor during the Christmas season. But Dickens entirely leaves out where the sign came from. In other words, Dickens re-signs the Christmas message without resigning himself to its original significance. He and his fellow Victorians were cooking up truth according to the ingredients of an entirely new *langue*.[57]

FROM FAMILY VALUES TO CULTURAL STUDIES

When Dickens ends *A Christmas Carol* with Bob Cratchit's son Tiny Tim pronouncing "God bless Us, Every One," he implies that blessing is mediated through family. Not only does a transformed Scrooge bless Cratchit's poverty-stricken circle with gifts, but he becomes "a second father" to the

---

[55]Charles Lyell, *Principles of Geology*, 3 vols. (London: John Murray, 1830, 1832, 1833). See the "Fundamentalism" section of chap. 1 for a brief discussion of Bishop Ussher.

[56]Dickens, *Christmas Carol*, p. 31.

[57]For more about the Victorian faith crisis, see Downing, "Finding Satisfaction in Great Expectations," pp. 61-70. Not all Victorians, of course, had given up on Christ. For good overviews of active Christians in nineteenth-century England, see Julie Melnyk, *Victorian Religion: Faith and Life in Britain* (Westport, CT: Praeger, 2008); and Timothy Larsen, *Crisis of Doubt: Honest Faith in Nineteenth-Century England* (Oxford: Oxford University Press, 2006).

crippled Tim. And on Christmas Day Scrooge joins the family of his own nephew, where "He was at home in five minutes. . . . Wonderful party, wonderful games, wonderful unanimity, won-der-ful happiness!" This has become the new sign of Christmas!

As one scholarly introduction to the novel explains it, "Scrooge's gradual awakening to a more generous sense of responsibility toward his dependents and fellow beings illustrates the redemptive power of imaginative sympathy"[58]—not, quite clearly, the redemptive power of Christ. Just as the Israelites set up a golden calf to allay their fears during Moses' absence (Ex 32:1-4), people in the nineteenth century set up "family values" to allay their fears about morality as they faced the absence of Christian faith.

Ironically, then, this Victorian cupboard stocked with doubts about Christianity continues to generate signs used today by people on opposite sides of the same coin: those on the left who want to get rid of /Christmas/ altogether versus those on the right who (inaccurately) regard "family values" as inherently Christian (see Lk 14:26).

Clearly, to understand signs, one must understand the historical contexts generating them. This, in fact, is the emphasis of the theorists I discuss in the next chapter: students of culture and communication who turned "cultural studies" into an academic discipline.

---

[58]Heather Henderson and William Sharpe, eds., *The Longman Anthology of British Literature,* vol. 2B: *The Victorian Age,* 3rd ed. (New York: Pearson, Longman, 2006), p. 1464.

5

Ideology and Cultural Studies

As a little girl, I was allowed to skip Sunday night worship only once a year: when the classic film *The Wizard of Oz* made its annual television debut. The conclusion I reached—that this film was worthy enough to substitute for evening service—helped sear its images into my psyche. I was especially enamored of the Emerald City, always hopeful when Dorothy and her companions were finally granted access to the chamber of the Great Oz.

The wizard's huge egg-like head, however, reminded me of the Humpty-Dumpty nursery rhyme, when all of the king's horses and all of the king's men couldn't put Humpty together again. While it never occurred to me that horses' hooves were unlikely tools for reassembling an egg, my association of the Great Oz with the signs of Humpty-Dumpty foreshadowed the tentative nature of the egg-headed wizard. Indeed, viewers soon discover that the Great Oz is merely a projection controlled by a bumbling good-hearted man behind a curtain. The egg-like Oz, then, turns out to be something people believe in that is controlled by someone with power.

This revelation accords with a fundamental assumption of Marx: that people with power control the way we view reality. Hence, the goal of Marxism is to pull aside the curtain, exposing the fact that our perceptions and beliefs are merely false projections, like the egg-head on the throne. Marx and his collaborator, Friedrich Engels (1820-1895), called such false projections "ideology." Hence, while structuralists believe that linguistic systems generate signs that control the way people think, Marxists assert that ideology controls the way people think.

To understand the difference, think of the moment in *The Wizard of Oz* when Dorothy and her companions discover the projectionist behind the curtain. The structuralist would say that the projection of the egg-head is generated by the structure of the cupboard-like booth, all its gears and knobs providing "conditions" for "possible" signs. The Marxist, in contrast, would focus on the people who built and control the booth: people who want to create projections that serve their own best interests. Despite this difference, the parallels between structuralism and Marxism are strong enough that, as we shall see, some cultural critics came to the conclusion that ideology is best understood by discussing the relationship between linguistic structures and the people with power inside.[1] Before we discuss these critics, however, it is necessary to understand the Marxist concept of ideology and its power over signs.

SIGNS OF IDEOLOGY

To understand the effect of ideology on signs, consider this list of binary oppositions:

noble	versus	clownish
gentleman	versus	villain
courteous	versus	vulgar
kind	versus	lewd
quality	versus	quantity

Many Christians today would say that an effective witness for Christ embodies the characteristics listed in the left-hand column while avoiding those on the right. Contemporary Marxists, however, would point out the disturbing history of the terms.

In the early sixteenth century, *clown* was the term for a "countryman, rustic, or peasant" who made a living by working outdoors.[2] The word, however, became tinted with—and tainted by—the attitude of the rich, who laughed at peasants not only for their lack of refinement, but also for their appearance: noses burned red and hair bleached into straw from hours in the sun, clothing patched and shoes ill-fitting due to limited financial resources.

---

[1]Cultural critic Stuart Hall outlines the effect of structuralism on Marxism in "Cultural Studies: Two Paradigms," *Media, Culture, and Society* 2 (1980): 57-72. Marxist literary critic Fredric Jameson became famous through his synthesis of structuralism with Marxism. See *The Political Unconscious: Narrative as a Socially Symbolic Act* (New York: Routledge, 2002).

[2]This and all quotations until the end of this section are extracted from the *OED*.

This, of course, led to the present-day signs employed by circus clowns.

More dramatic is the change to the fourteenth-century sign *villain* (origi-nally spelled "villein"), which is etymologically related to the word *village*. It denoted "a peasant, country labourer, or low-born rustic" who lived in a village while working as a serf for a feudal lord. But because people of priv-ilege suspected the integrity of uneducated villagers, the denotation of the term changed. Contributing to the change in denotation was "The Peasants' Revolt" of 1381: a rebellion of poor serfs against unjust taxation and the "vil-leinage" system of serfdom. Rioting peasants burned palaces, beheaded offi-cials and sacked London boroughs. An exasperated King Richard II told one group of rebels, "Villeins ye are still, and villeins ye shall remain."[3] By this he meant, "You will not be freed from serfdom," but it is easy to see how the idea of "villainy" became associated with the violent actions of these rebelling vil-lagers—especially in the minds of the upper classes who levied the taxes and wrote the histories.

In the same way, the value-neutral word for commoners, the *vulgar*, took on the negative attitudes of the upper classes, who contrasted "vulgar" be-havior with their own "courteous" behavior. But "courteous" merely referred to the conventional behavior and manners of "court": an artificial etiquette in which the vulgar were uneducated. Similarly, a *noble* person had the money, power and education to act like a member of the nobility—making it impos-sible for a poor person to ever be considered noble.

Even the word "gentle" originally meant "well-born, belonging to a family of position." In fact, a priest who influenced the 1381 Peasants' Revolt asked in a sermon, "When Adam delved and Eve span, who was then the gen-tleman?" He was making the point that people with cultural privilege—gentlemen—do not seem to be part of God's original plan. Nevertheless, fourteenth-century peasants, unable to be "gentle," were instead described as "lewd," a word that originally denoted anyone who could not read. They were "lewd" rather than "kind," because they were not the same *kind* of people as aristocrats, who had money for education. Indeed, "kind" in its earliest ninth-century definition meant "the station, place, or property belonging to one by birth." Developing out of this idea was the definition we assume today: kindness is a quality shown by certain individuals. However, until around

---

[3]Winston S. Churchill, *The Birth of Britain: A History of the English-Speaking Peoples*, vol. 1 (New York: Dodd, Mead, 1956), p. 383.

1600, the "character or quality" of being kind was a sign of one's status. Indeed, "to grow out of kind" meant "to lose the character appropriate to one's birth and family." Hence, because the majority of people in medieval culture (the *vulgar*) were *lewd,* their *quantity* was contrasted with people of *quality:* those born into the aristocracy. Up through the nineteenth century, working-class people often referred to their wealthy employers as "the quality."[4] We could chart the binary oppositions as follows, where the top is valued over the bottom:

rich	quality	noble	gentleman	courteous	kind
poor	quantity	clown	villain	vulgar	lewd

Examples like these lead Marxist critics to conclude that linguistic signs are molded by people with economic power. Or, in the language of Marxist cultural criticism, *hegemony* affects the meaning of signs.

THE HEDGING OF HEGEMONY

Coming from a Greek word for "leader," the term "hegemony" means "predominant authority" *(OED).* The Russian revolutionary Vladimir Lenin (1870-1924) employed the word to describe the power of those who controlled the "modes of production," which meant, in his day, those who owned the factories in which the lower classes worked. To put it in the language of Marxist-Leninism, the working class "proletariat" needed to wrest hegemony away from the capitalist "bourgeoisie": those who made money from the factories. Revolt, however, was impeded by the fact that those with hegemony controlled not just the nuts and bolts of the economic system, but also the way people *thought about* the system. Those with hegemony perpetuated an ideology—comprised of ideas, perceptions and practices—that made the capitalist economic system seem inevitable. They were the wizards of Oz who created a huge egg-like projection that people believed to be the *real* Oz.

---

[4]Note this statement in a 1778 novel: "she thought I was a woman of quality: and I make no doubt but she was miserable when she discovered me to be a mere country gentlewoman." Fanny Burney, *Evelina: or the History of a Young Lady's Entrance Into the World* (Oxford: Oxford University Press, 1982), p. 284. In the eighteenth century, the word *gentleman* was starting to change, such that in his famous *Dictionary of the English Language* (1755), Samuel Johnson followed the primary definition of *gentleman*—"A man of birth"—with an emerging definition: "A man raised above the vulgar by his character or post."

THE HOUSE-LIKE STRUCTURE OF IDEOLOGY

For another analogy, imagine a house built on a cement slab for its foundation. The house is what Marx called the "superstructure" of society, which is built on an economic "foundation" or "base." And the building materials are a society's religion, politics, law, philosophy, arts and so on. Holding all these materials together is ideology: the nails, cement and glue of the superstructure. Meanwhile, those with hegemony are like landlords that maintain the building's structure because it is lucrative for them. They therefore add extra nails and glue to keep the (super)structure from collapsing. The "renters" inside (proletariat) define their lives according to the building around them, their perception controlled by the window placement: they see what the house design allows them to see.[5] They therefore operate according to what Engels called "false consciousness": a distorted view of reality from within the superstructure maintained by their bourgeoisie landlords.[6]

To extend the analogy, consider an unintentionally humorous "Hints from Heloise" that I read in my local paper. A woman wrote Heloise offering the following hint:

> I usually watch the news at night to see what the WEATHER is going to be the next day so that I can dress accordingly. However, sometimes the weatherperson is not on the mark. We recently moved to a house that has a garage, which we always park our vehicles in, so I don't find out that the weather has changed until I am on my way to work. . . . So, now before I change out of my pajamas, I step out onto the back deck to check the weather. This has saved me several times from being cold the whole day![7]

Basically, this woman reports that reality outside her house differs from the way she perceives it from within her house. Her house is therefore a (super)structure where voices with power (television newscasters) report a false reality. She can only access the scientific truth by exiting her house. Similarly, Engels

---

[5]As Marx explained in *A Contribution to the Critique of Political Economy* (1859), "The mode of production of material life conditions the social, political and intellectual life process in general. It is not the consciousness of men that determines their existence, but, on the contrary, their social existence determines their consciousness." Quoted in Vincent B. Leitch et al., eds., "Karl Marx and Friedrich Engels," in *The Norton Anthology of Theory and Criticism*, 2nd ed. (New York: Norton, 2010), p. 648.

[6]For an elaboration of "false consciousness" consult Georg Lukács, *History and Class Consciousness* (Cambridge, MA: MIT Press, 1971).

[7]"Heloise," *The Patriot-News* (Harrisburg, PA), April 2, 2007, C-4.

believed that "ideology would end when men realized their real life-conditions and therefore their real motives, after which their consciousness would become genuinely *scientific* because they would then be in contact with reality."[8]

Escaping ideology, of course, is not as easy as exiting a house, because most people are not conscious of the ideology that holds up their perceptions. However, Marx and Engels theorized that, when conditions got bad enough, laborers would "step out onto the back deck" (as it were) to witness the cold-hearted exploitation of capitalism. Once the working class recognized that the rich get richer off the sweat and toil of industrial labor, the proletariat would turn against the superstructure that once blinded them to their own exploitation. To destroy the superstructure, however, jackhammers of revolution must break apart the economic base upon which it rests. Only by undermining capitalist hegemony could the proletariat live in a paradise of egalitarian communalism—communism—with no roof impeding their view of reality.

Not long after the Russian Revolution, however, the Marxist paradise—like all paradises—appeared to be a snake-infested Eden. Stalin imposed economic egalitarianism with despotic brutality far beyond the "dictatorship" of the proletariat advocated by Lenin.

THE GRAMMAR OF GRAMSCI (1891-1937): THE RHETORICAL TURN

Decades before the demise of Soviet communism in the early 1990s, socialists began to question not just Stalin, but the economic determinism of Marx: the idea that economy controls ideology. One of the most influential of these questioners, Antonio Gramsci, helped found the Communist Party in his native Italy shortly before Mussolini came to power. Gramsci's defiance of Mussolini landed him in jail, where he spent the last nine years of his life (re)signing the grammar of communism. Resigned to Marx's desire for a radically egalitarian society, he re-signed how it might be achieved, leading to what has been called "the rhetorical turn" in Marxism.[9]

---

[8]This summary of Engels is by Marxist critic Raymond Williams, who notes that the word *ideology* gets used in different ways in Marxist theory: sometimes to mean "illusion" or "false consciousness," and sometimes simply to mean "world view." See Raymond Williams, *Keywords: A Vocabulary of Culture and Society* (New York: Oxford University Press, 1983), pp. 157, 156. For "ideology" as a "world view," see Raymond Williams, *Marxism and Literature* (Oxford: Oxford University Press, 1977), pp. 109, 132.

[9]Maurice Charland, "Rehabilitating Rhetoric: Confronting Blindspots in Discourse and Social Theory," in *Contemporary Rhetorical Theory: A Reader,* ed. John Louis Lucaites, Celeste Michelle Condit and Sally Caudill (New York: Guilford, 1999), p. 470.

Trying to figure out why workers around the world had not risen up to overthrow their exploiters, Gramsci questioned the Marxist understanding of hegemony. While traditional Marxists saw ideology determined by an economic base shored up by those with hegemony (the bourgeoisie), Gramsci saw ideology infused throughout society, perpetuated by the *hegemony of signs* that permeated culture.

For an analogy, think again of the house described in the "Hints to Heloise." The owner reported that she had a better view of authentic reality (the weather) from outside on her deck. The traditional Marxist would explain that she escaped the "false consciousness" perpetuated by bourgeois rhetoric; by getting outside the superstructure of the rhetorical house she finally saw truth. Such thinking, as contemporary rhetorical theorist Raymie E. McKerrow notes, perpetuated the Enlightenment assumption that rhetoric is "subservient" to "universal standards of reason."[10] And, for traditional Marxists, universal reason endorses Marxism. In contrast, suggests McKerrow, rhetoric itself shapes what we consider reasonable. Reminding us of the structuralists discussed in chapter four, McKerrow challenges those who presuppose "the possibility of meaning outside specific historical contexts of rhetorical practices."[11]

Here is how we might visualize it: think of the Hints from Heloise woman living in a continuously smoggy city. Stepping out onto the deck, she might be totally unaware of the many particles in the air that impede her view. Indeed, when I lived in the Los Angeles area, I would often be shocked by the occasional clear day, when suddenly I could see the nearby mountains that had been obscured by smog for weeks on end. My perception of reality had been impeded by particulate elements that permeated the air, not one of which could be vacuumed up for a better view. Even if I razed my house to the ground, the smog would still be there, affecting my vision. Analogously, particulate signs, generated by multiple cultural factories, contribute to the smog of language, which has hegemony over my view of reality.

This idea, influencing the "rhetorical turn" in Marxism, was suggested by Gramsci as early as the 1930s. For him and those he influenced, there are no

---

[10]Raymie E. McKerrow, "Critical Rhetoric: Theory and *Praxis*," in *Contemporary Rhetorical Theory: A Reader*, ed. John Louis Lucaites, Celeste Michelle Condit and Sally Caudill (New York: Guilford, 1999), p. 441.

[11]Ibid., p. 456. McKerrow is quoting Steven Mailloux, "Rhetorical Hermeneutics," *Critical Inquiry* 11 (1985): 630.

revolutionary "winds of change" that enable Marxists to entirely eliminate the smog of language. We all, Marxists included, understand reality according to the rhetorical formations of our culture.

THE SMOG OF MANUFACTURED CONSENT: GIRLS GONE WILD

For a historical example of semiotic smog, think of the "Girls Gone Wild" phenomenon in the early twenty-first century. Joe Francis, the capitalist behind the scheme, trolled parties where he got tipsy females to display their breasts for his video camera. He made nearly $30 million a year by selling the videotapes, while the female flashers usually received a tank-top for their services. Nevertheless, the women willingly submitted to their own degradation. Why? Because their view of reality was permeated by an ideological smog, making them believe that their worth was enhanced when they were treated as fun-loving objects of display.

Of course, since most Americans were disgusted by the "Girls Gone Wild" enterprise, the phenomenon did not achieve what Gramsci called "cultural hegemony." However, values that *do* have hegemony in our culture—the enticement of being "on camera," the idealization of youthful sexy bodies, alcohol's ability to loosen inhibitions, the power of celebrity, the authority of millionaires like Francis—certainly influenced the participants' response.[12] Gramsci coined the phrase "manufactured consent" to explain the way people agree to activities that do not serve their own best interests.

Cultural signs reflect and perpetuate manufactured consent. In 2008 I was disturbed when my newspaper reported an incident in which a thirteen-year-old girl sent her boyfriend a photo of her naked breasts, which he then sent to his friends.[13] Since then, such behavior has become so common that a new word was coined for it: "sexting." Gramscian hegemony is manifest in the fact that the girls *think* they are in control of their own bodies, *freely* offering them to the male gaze, when, in actuality, cultural signs cause them to think this way.

Hegemony, for Gamsci, permeates multiple institutions of culture, controlling what people regard as "natural" or "common sense." For example, it was "common sense" in the nineteenth century that only males should be

---

[12]Even when an occasional videotaped woman sobers up and seeks legal action, Francis points out that she willingly signed a "model release form" in advance. "'Girls Gone Wild' Case," *The Patriot-News* (Harrisburg, PA), April 11, 2007, A-2.

[13]Anne McGraw Reeves, "Cell Phones Might Give Teens Too Much Power," *The Patriot-News* (Harrisburg, PA), November 11, 2008, B-1.

allowed to vote. Even Queen Victoria, the female ruler of England for sixty-four years, shared the hegemonic assumption that women should not be allowed at the polls, describing "woman's rights" as "dangerous & unchristian & unnatural."[14] During her reign (1837-1901), it was also considered only "natural" that a divorced father be awarded custody of the children.

By the middle of the twentieth century, of course, such "manufactured consent" about the roles of women had changed, such that it seemed only "common sense" that females should vote and that mothers be awarded child custody. Rather than solely built on an economic base, then, hegemony arises out of various cultural institutions: family, religion, the arts, education, entertainment, the media. Instead of economic "base" and social "superstructure," Gramsci therefore preferred to talk about *cultural* hegemony, wherein institutions within the culture sustain the ideology of the ruling class.

GRAMSCI'S ARCHITECTURE OF CHANGE

Radical structuralists, as we saw in chapter four, pretty much eliminated the possibility of changing the structure in which one was embedded. Marxists, however, are committed to change. Therefore, since political revolution no longer seemed viable as a vehicle of change, Gramsci—as interpreted by his followers—came up with another means. Here's how I would illustrate their strategy for changing society.

Think of a medieval cathedral, the roof held up by multiple pillars representing the multiple institutions of culture: education, religion, art, entertainment, advertising, leisure, sports. Surrounding these pillars are various signs of culture reinforcing its ideology—like stained glass windows in cathedral walls. However, as anyone who has studied medieval architecture can tell you, a high cathedral roof puts incredible pressure on the pillars and walls holding it up, often necessitating flying buttresses to keep the walls from buckling. Similarly, cultural institutions hold up the ruling-class ideology, while the ideological roof puts pressure on—has hegemony over—the institutions themselves. As a result, new signs are constructed on the outside of traditional institutions to help keep the structure standing, just as flying buttresses were added to shore up the walls of Notre Dame Cathedral in Paris.

---

[14]Letter to William Gladstone, 6 May 1870; quoted in *The Longman Anthology of British Literature: The Victorian Age*, ed. Heather Henderson and William Sharpe, 3rd ed. (New York: Pearson Longman, 2006), p. 1655.

Were you to knock down one of Notre Dame's buttresses, the building would not fall: it has too many reinforcements. Similarly, Gramsci believes that the institutional pillars and buttresses upholding cultural hegemony are too numerous to undermine. Unlike Marx and Engels, he did not think it possible to exit an ideological superstructure to get a view of reality from a vantage point of objective perception. He therefore argued that Marxist intellectuals must encourage the construction of a new ideological space attached—like an add-on to a cathedral. Supporting the addition will be communist signs—beliefs, attitudes, values, practices—attractive enough that people can easily transition from within the original space to the new "chapel" addition—just as people transitioned from an all-male franchise in the nineteenth century to female suffrage in the twentieth without undermining the entire political system. Eventually, the new add-on will attract enough people that original parts of the cathedral will be refurbished in its style, new signs effacing the old. After multiple such "makeovers," Marxism will gain hegemony over the entire space, demolishing parts of the cathedral no longer used.

My analogy of changing a medieval cathedral reflects Gramsci's Marxist antagonism toward Christianity, which he believed sustained an oppressive capitalist ideology. Under the refurbished system, as he puts it in his *Prison Notebooks,* the Communist Party "takes the place of the divinity."[15] By changing the cathedral shape through added spaces, Gramsci hoped to change the shape of religious belief: from redemption that is focused on the cross, as in the floor plan followed by most medieval cathedrals (fig. 5.1), to redemption through communism, as signaled by the "C" (fig. 5.3).

Of course, Gramsci was not talking about literal architecture. But he was interested in signs, having studied linguistics at Turin University. I therefore suspect that Gramsci would enjoy how the signs on the next page capture his idea that hegemony cannot be escaped, only re(de)signed. Because his idea of "cultural hegemony" foregrounds how a society's rhetoric perpetuates the truths of culture, he is often cited by analysts of popular culture.[16]

---

[15]Antonio Gramsci, *Selections from the Prison Notebooks,* trans. and ed. Quintin Hoare and Geoffrey Nowell Smith (London: Lawrence and Wishart, 1971), p. 133.

[16]See, for example, Robert Goldman, "Hegemony and Managed Critique in Prime-Time Television," *Theory and Society* 11, no. 3 (May 1982): 363-77; Gaye Tuchman, *The T.V. Establishment* (Englewood Cliffs, NJ: Prentice Hall, 1974), pp. 165-67; and Tony Bennet, "Popular Culture and the 'Turn to Gramsci,'" in *Cultural Theory and Popular Culture: A Reader,* ed. John Storey (New York: Prentice Hall, 1995), pp. 217-24. Stuart Hall, Director of the Centre for Contemporary Cultural Studies at the University of Birmingham from 1968-1979, regards Gramsci as a kind of

Figure 5.1. The shape of medieval cathedrals

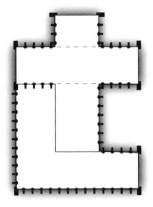

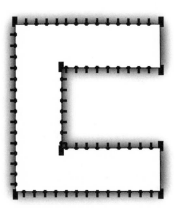

Figure 5.2. An add-on to medieval cathedral shape

Figure 5.3. The hegemonic shape of communism

ALTHUSSER (1918-1990): CHANGING "NATURAL" SIGNS

Influenced by Gramsci, French communist Louis Althusser was one of the first theorists to explicitly combine Marxism with structuralism. Having studied the structural anthropology of Lévi-Strauss (chapter four), he focused on the semiotic structures that shape ideology. For him, ideology is "a *system* of representations, perceptions, and images that precisely encourages men and women to 'see' their specific place in a historically peculiar social formation as

grandfather to cultural studies, crediting him for the "displacement" of Marxism in the twentieth century. See Stuart Hall, "Cultural Studies and Its Theoretical Legacies," in *The Norton Anthology of Theory and Criticism*, ed. Vincent B. Leitch et al., 2nd ed. (New York: Norton, 2010), p. 1787.

inevitable, natural, a necessary function of the 'real' itself."[17] In other words, ideology for Althusser, as for Gramsci, is most powerful when no one recognizes it as ideology, when people regard their everyday thoughts as "natural."

Think of the "natural" desire for white teeth. It seems only "common sense" to get teeth as white as possible. But upper-class wannabes in Shakespeare's day often darkened their teeth by rubbing them with pitch: the exact opposite of people today who slide slimy whitening strips into their mouths. To us, it seems almost laughable that people once desired black teeth. What possibly could motivate such bizarre behavior?

The answer is simple: the same thing that motivates bizarre behavior today! People want to adorn themselves with signs of cultural hegemony. In the sixteenth century, only the rich could regularly consume expensive sugar products from the New World, an indulgence that turned their teeth black. People who could not afford sugar therefore found cheaper alternatives—like pitch—in order to imitate signs of class privilege.[18] Similarly, people today mimic wealthy celebrities who can afford extravagant dental procedures by purchasing the far less costly whitening strips.

Anyone who argues that white teeth are more "natural" than black would be hard-pressed to explain why, in our era, middle-class males as well as females dye their hair to get rid of their "natural" gray, simultaneously paying extravagant orthodontia bills to change their children's teeth from "natural" growth patterns. Althusser would argue that straight white teeth and youthful dyed hair are signs that reflect the system, or structure, of capitalism and thus perpetuate distinctions between the working class and the ruling elite.

THE ALTER CALL OF ALTHUSSER: INTERPELLATION

Althusser was also influenced by Lacan (chapter four), and hence became intrigued by what he called "the structural unconscious": the psychological effects of language. He suggested that individuals in a society develop their sense of selfhood—their "subjectivity"—through their *subjection* to hegemonic signs: a Marxian way to talk about the "name of the father."[19]

---

[17]James H. Kavanagh, "Ideology," in *Critical Terms for Literary Study,* ed. Frank Lentricchia and Thomas McLaughlin (Chicago: University of Chicago Press, 1990), p. 310.

[18]Bill Bryson, *Shakespeare: The World as Stage* (San Francisco: HarperCollins, 2007), p. 55.

[19]Althusser's student Michel Foucault (1926-1984) picked up on this suggestion and elaborated it in his highly influential cultural criticism: "Foucault draws on *subject* as a verb. Individuals get

By way of analogy, think of an abusive father who repeatedly calls his child names: "You're so stupid; you're such an idiot." Studies have shown that smart children subjected to this kind of verbal taunting start believing it—to such an extent that their scores on aptitude tests actually get worse and worse. Their identity is so tied to the signs with which their parents have identified them that they become what they are called.[20] Their subjectivity, in other words, reflects the language to which they have been subjected.

For Althusser, individuals are subjected not just to the language of their parents but also to that of multiple institutions, what he calls "ideological state apparatuses."[21] Rather than a father calling a child names, institutions like the media, education, politics, sports and religion call out to citizens with their signs of truth. Althusser calls this a process of "interpellation"—a word that means to "summon" or "hail." For him, a culture's ideology is hegemonic when it successfully "summons" citizens not simply to think and act in certain ways, but to think *about themselves* in certain ways.[22]

Interpellation alters both self-perception and behavior. For example, consider how Americans were "summoned" to "SHOP!" after 9-11, as though consumerism is patriotic. The fact that the majority of Americans are willing to pay astronomical credit card rates and fees for luxuries they can't afford proves the success of ideological state apparatuses. Of course, most of these shoppers do not regard their SUVs or plasma TVs as luxuries at all—which proves the success of the ideology all the more. I'll never forget the passion with which a woman in Santa Barbara once announced at a Bible study, "I have a right to own a house with hardwood floors!" Her interpellation as a consumer seemed to outweigh Christ's summons "to take up your cross [hardwood or not] and follow me."

Althusser therefore identifies "communications" as one ideological state

---

to occupy subject positions (the various roles existing within a discourse or an institution) only through a process in which they are 'subjected' to power." "Michel Foucault," in *The Norton Anthology of Theory and Criticism*, ed. Vincent B. Leitch et al., 2nd ed. (New York: Norton, 2010), p. 1471.

[20]N. Sachs-Ericsson, E. Verona, T. Joiner and K. Preacher, "Parental Verbal Abuse and the Mediating Role of Self-Criticism in Adult Internalizing Disorders," *Journal of Affective Disorders* 93, no. 1 (2006): 71-78.

[21]See Louis Althusser, "Ideology and Ideological State Apparatuses (Notes Toward an Investigation)," trans. Ben Brewster, in *The Norton Anthology of Theory and Criticism*, ed. Vincent B. Leitch et al., 2nd ed. (New York: Norton, 2010), pp. 1335-61.

[22]Ibid., p. 1356.

apparatus.[23] However, he does not mean that a Bureau of Cultural Hegemony controls microwave towers, sending out subliminal messages as we sleep. He means that the media, like other cultural institutions, transmit attitudes, values and beliefs that shape our very sense of self. We feel "authentic" when we fulfill this sense of self, oblivious to the fact that the way we imagine an authentic self was shaped by the signs and practices of culture. For Althusser as for Gramsci, signs of the times affect signs of "common sense." Consider the following example.

THE COMMON SENSE OF SELF-ESTEEM

To most Americans, the encouragement of self-esteem is a matter of common sense. Reinforced by signs in the media, education, politics and even church, the importance of self-esteem seems only natural. Althusser, however, might suggest that we have been interpellated by culture to perceive our identities this way. Indeed, advertising, one of the most insidious of ideological state apparatuses, literally calls out to us from billboards and televisions—"Because you're worth it!" "Do it for YOU!" "Pamper yourself!" "It's all for YOU!" "You deserve it!" "Be all that you can be!"—convincing us that consuming certain products and services will enhance our self-esteem.

The hegemony of self-esteem has also altered the signs of education—almost as dramatically as aristocratic superiority altered the word *villain*. The sign of a "C," a grade that once meant "satisfactory," now registers as failure to most students and their parents. However, rather than worry about the lack of preparation signaled by a C, some parents protest about the grade's effect on their child's self-esteem. They have been so interpellated by an ideology of capitalist consumerism that they see education as a product to buy, for which they demand consumer satisfaction, rather than as a privilege requiring responsibility and sacrifice.

CALLING OUT ALTHUSSER: PROBLEMS WITH INTERPELLATION

The concept of interpellated subjection, though insightful, is problematic. Althusser regards it as so deterministic that he, like other radical structuralists, seems to eliminate the concept of free will and hence of change. Just as children repeatedly called "stupid" become less intelligent, so all of us take on

---

[23]Ibid., p. 1345.

the subjectivities that "ideological state apparatuses" subject us to.

In fact, for Althusser, the hegemony of ideology even controls rebellions against it.[24] For an example, think of the famed movie *Titanic* (1997). Leonardo DiCaprio plays Jack, a young man who wins passage on the *Titanic*'s 1912 voyage in a poker game. On board ship, he meets the charming Rose (Kate Winslet), whose mother plans to marry her off to the wealthy but despicable Cal. As Rose falls in love with Jack, she discovers that the poor people in steerage have much more fun than the rich snobs luxuriating on decks above. We see the laborers dancing and partying together in class solidarity, while the wealthy passengers look bored to death as they eat off expensive china and engage in stultifying small talk. Then, after the *Titanic* hits an iceberg, the wealthy Cal—who almost always wears black—cheats his way onto a lifeboat, whereas the poor Jack—who almost always wears white—risks his life to save others, ultimately dying so that Rose might live. Get it? All the signs point to wealthy capitalists as bad; poor laborers as good. Indeed, I heard someone deliver a paper at an academic conference arguing that *Titanic*, which signals the relation between higher and lower classes with the higher and lower decks of the ship, subverts the hegemony of capitalism.

I think Althusser would have been disgusted. He would most likely respond that the subversive elements of *Titanic* actually reinforce capitalist ideology. For by showing those in steerage to be happier and to have more integrity than the wealthy people above, the film maintains capitalist hegemony by eliminating any motivation for revolt. Why would the proletariat down below overthrow a system that keeps them happier and healthier than those with capital above? The filmmakers, it would seem, have been so interpellated by bourgeois ideology that even when they attempt to be subversive they end up perpetuating the status quo.

THE WILLING OF WILLIAMS:
THE DEVELOPMENT OF CULTURAL STUDIES

I use the example of *Titanic* in honor of Raymond Williams (1921-1988),

---

[24]Althusser intensifies Gramsci's assumption that "any apparent dialogue and debate is merely a means for the acceptance of the perspective emanating from the center" of the hegemonic culture. See Craig Brandist, "Gramsci, Bakhtin and the Semiology of Hegemony," *New Left Review* 216, March 1, 1996, p. 103.

whose work helped turn "cultural studies" into an academic discipline.[25] As one of the first literary critics to regard film as worthy of academic study, Williams challenged the humanist privileging of high culture (as in *Li-ter-a-ture*, usually pronounced with four syllables) over low culture (as in *moo-vies*, usually pronounced like the call of a cow). Regarding the difference between *high* and *low* culture as elitist—the signs "high" and "low" tell it all—Williams encouraged analysis of popular culture, not *instead* of Li-ter-a-ture, but in *addition* to it. For him, all fictions—from *Titanic* on screen to Titania in *A Midsummer Night's Dream*—reflect their historical and hence ideological contexts. Hegemony affects all modes of cultural production.

Williams, however, was not an ideological determinist like Althusser. The structuralists and Marxists who influenced Althusser both regarded "structure" as static and unbending, like the cupboard I have aligned with structuralism and the house I have aligned with Marxism. Though acknowledging the power of ideology, Williams asserts the possibility of free will in the midst of hegemony—especially manifest in the creation of new signs through the arts. For Williams, ideology is more like a "home" than a house or a cupboard.

Unlike a house, we usually identify "home" with the changing people who occupy a house, a town, a state or a country. Just think of how people talk about "flying home" from another country, even though they may land in a city or state far away from the house where they may end up. They may even say, while still miles from their house, "It's great to be home." Furthermore, unlike a house, "home" constantly changes as people go off to school, give birth, divorce, remarry, provide shelter for foster kids or aging parents, entertain guests, hire service personnel, deal with new neighbors, and host Bible studies or birthday parties.

In the midst of all these alterations and interactions, certain attitudes about the home are either reinforced or challenged as power-relations change among the inhabitants. Middle-aged adults, for example, often report how strange it felt when they first realized that they needed to look after their

---

[25]"Cultural studies has its roots in the cultural analysis of British Marxism, but also," as Jonathan Culler argues, "in semiotics, particularly Roland Barthes' *Mythologies*." Published in 1957, *Mythologies* is a collection of essays that analyze how objects in everyday life function as cultural signs—as when an automobile is treated more as a sign of status and power than regarded as a form of transportation. See Jonathan Culler, *The Pursuit of Signs: Semiotics, Literature, Deconstruction*, augmented edition (Ithaca, NY: Cornell University Press, 2001), p. xiii.

parents rather than vice versa. Nevertheless, their parents' house they still consider their first "home," hegemonic in the way it defined their values, beliefs, and practices—even as they changed.

Here's how Williams explained it in 1977, distinguishing his views from a structuralist emphasis on system:

> A lived hegemony is always a process. It is not, except analytically, a system or a structure. It is a realized complex of experiences, relationships, and activities, with specific and changing pressures and limits. . . . [I]t does not just passively exist as a form of dominance. It has continually to be renewed, recreated, defended, and modified. It is also continually resisted, limited, altered, challenged by pressures not at all its own.[26]

In other words, a lived hegemony is always in the process of (re)signing.

CHALLENGING THE HEGEMONY OF SELF-ESTEEM

If he were still alive, Williams might point out current pressures that both challenge and reinforce the hegemony of self-esteem discussed earlier in this chapter. Many educators, for example, wonder if the self-esteem ideology explains the cheating that has become rampant on contemporary university campuses, where success—at whatever cost—has supplanted learning. And consonant with the cultural hegemony theories of Gramsci and Althusser, family often reinforces this trend, seen when parents call up professors to argue about their child's grade. This has become such a problem that a term was coined to capture parental surveillance of their child's self-esteem: *helicopter parent.*

Ironically, *Scientific American* has published studies indicating that juvenile delinquents and criminals have unusually high self-esteem.[27] Furthermore, a twenty-four-year-long study of student attitudes—from 1982 to 2006—concludes that the "self-esteem movement" has resulted in rampant narcissism among twenty-first-century young adults.[28] Problematically, narcissists "are

---

[26]Williams, *Marxism and Literature*, p. 112.

[27]Roy F. Baumeister, "Exploding the Self-Esteem Myth," *Scientific American* 284, no. 4 (April 2001): 96-101. In September 2009, authorities discovered that one of the books owned by Phillip Garrido, a California man who kidnapped and raped twelve-year-old Jaycee Lee Dugard, holding her for 18 years, was titled *Self-Esteem: A Family Affair*. Greg Hardesty and Kimberly Edds, "Woman, Children Lived Secret Lives in the Open," *The Patriot-News* (Harrisburg, PA), September 2, 2009, A-12.

[28]For a report of the study, see Jean M. Twenge, *Generation Me: Why Today's Young Americans Are*

more likely to have romantic relationships that are short-lived, [be] at risk for infidelity, lack emotional warmth, and to exhibit game-playing, dishonesty, and over-controlling and violent behaviors."[29]

Narcissism, of course, reflects and affects hegemonic signs in our culture. Facebook, MySpace, YouTube and Twitter—welcome forms of communication with powerful potential—also allow people to wallow in their own self-representations. Twitter can reduce narcissism to conformist banality as thousands follow any sign of celebrity movement—whether down the hall or to the mall. And Facebook has generated another semiotic trend, wherein /friend/ is no longer a sign of a loved one; it has become a sign of a person who has been allowed to view one's Facebook page. People's self-esteem thus becomes elevated by the quantity of /friends/ rather than the quality of friendships.[30] And a study published in the *American Journal of Men's Health* reports that college males attract more Facebook friends when they mention beer or post photos of inebriated parties. Not coincidentally, the title of the article is "Expanding Hegemonic Masculinity."[31]

Don't get me wrong. I am not advocating renunciation of Facebook, MySpace, YouTube or even Twitter. Many of my most pleasurable friendship and aesthetic moments in the past several years were generated by creative postings in the social media. Instead, like other educators committed to effective communication, I wonder how these elements of material culture might be appropriated to combat, rather than to inculcate, narcissism in our society. How might the social media be (re)signed? As Raymond Williams notes, "We must not think only of society or the group acting on the unique individual, but also of many unique individuals, through a process of com-

More Confident, Assertive, Entitled—and More Miserable Than Ever Before (New York: Simon & Schuster, 2006). See also Jean M. Twenge and W. Keith Campbell, *The Narcissism Epidemic: Living in the Age of Entitlement* (New York: Free Press, 2009).

[29]Quoted in an Associated Press release, "College Students Think They're So Special," February 27, 2007, www.msnbc.com.

[30]*Prevention* magazine cites a 2009 study by Kodak in which 78% of the people surveyed reported that "it's easier now to stay in touch with friends and family than it was 5 years ago." However, 60% of those surveyed said that "they have fewer meaningful relationships now." *Prevention*, November 2009, p. 20.

[31]Neill Korobov, "Expanding Hegemonic Masculinity: The Use of Irony in Young Men's Stories About Romantic Experiences," *The American Journal of Men's Health* 3, no. 4 (December 2009): 286-99. For an accessible discussion about ways the media shape self-esteem, see Thomas De Zengotita, *Mediated: How the Media Shapes Your World and the Way You Live in It* (New York: Bloomsbury, 2005), especially chap. 2, "The Cult of the Child."

munication, creating and where necessary extending the organization by which they will continue to be shaped."[32] Communication, in other words, has the power to shape the institutions that shape us.

RESIGNED TO "RESIDUAL" SIGNS

In his assessment of culture and language, Raymond Williams talks about "residual" meanings and practices: "The residual, by definition, has been effectively formed in the past, but it is still active in the cultural process, not only and often not at all as an element of the past, but as an effective element of the present."[33] While most Marxist cultural critics dismiss signs of the past, Williams implies that residual values have the potential to challenge the hegemony of dominant culture.[34]

For example, educators who challenge the hegemony of self-esteem decry not simply helicopter parents but the very evaporation of residual educational values: academic discipline, respect for instructor expertise, high grades reserved only for the extraordinary few and so forth. By reiterating values of the past that no longer have cultural dominance, educators' appeals to the "residual," if proclaimed with rhetorical sensitivity rather than disdain, have potential to change attitudes.

Similarly, rather than decry the narcissism generated by Facebook, MySpace and YouTube, Christians should consider how to (re)sign the social media with "residual" values. This necessitates appropriation rather than renunciation, creativity rather than passive submission to technology. It necessitates, in other words, balancing on the edge of the coin: something advocated by German philosopher Martin Heidegger. In "The Question Concerning Technology," he wrote, "we want to have an approach that in no way confines us to a stultified compulsion to push on blindly with technology or, what comes to the same thing, to rebel helplessly against it and curse it as

---

[32]Raymond Williams, "Individuals and Societies," in *The Raymond Williams Reader*, ed. John Higgins (Oxford: Blackwell, 2001), p. 82.

[33]Williams, *Marxism and Literature*, p. 122.

[34]Raymond Williams describes "a reaching back to those meanings and values which were created in real societies in the past, and which still seem to have some significance because they represent areas of human experience, aspiration and achievement, which the dominant culture under-values or opposes, or even cannot recognise." See "Base and Superstructure in Marxist Cultural Theory," in *The Raymond Williams Reader*, ed. John Higgins (Oxford: Blackwell, 2001), p. 172. In contrast, the Althusser-influenced Paulo Freire considers residual values as impediments to cultural revolution. See *Pedagogy of the Oppressed*, trans. Myra Bergman Ramos (New York: Herder & Herder, 1970), p. 158.

the work of the devil."[35] The best way Christian communicators might respond to the often vulgar, lewd or clownish signs of social media is not to flip the coin through harangues about the necessity of courteous, noble and gentlemanly behavior. Instead we (re)sign through a process of "culture making." This phrase, employed by Andy Crouch, reflects his sense that the "only way to change culture is to create more of it."[36]

In an act of culture-making, Christians might enter Facebook, MySpace and YouTube, adding to them signs that creatively reflect residual values. And I mean *creatively*. Putting a sermon on YouTube or Bible verses on Facebook will not attract nonbelievers, who, as soon as they see religious signs, will exit a site with amazing alacrity. But they might look, stay and consider if you have created a stunning image, a beautiful song or a powerful film-clip about self-sacrificial friendship, about the need for clean water in Darfur or about saving the environment.[37] All connect to important residual values: "No one has greater love than this, to lay down one's life for one's friends"; "Do to others as you would have them do to you"; God created . . . and saw that it was good.[38]

RESIDUAL VALUES VERSUS SELECTIVE TRADITIONS: RACISM AND SLAVERY

Unfortunately, as discussed in chapter one, many people would rather idealize the "residual" than practice (re)signing. Williams, in fact, employed the phrase "selective tradition" to describe how societies mystify a certain idea of the past—often inaccurately, as when Christians today talk about returning to the faith of our nation's founders, not realizing that Thomas Jefferson and

---

[35]Martin Heidegger, "The Question Concerning Technology," in *The Question Concerning Technology and Other Essays*, trans. W. Lovitt (New York: Harper Torchbooks, 1977), pp. 25-26.

[36]Andy Crouch, *Culture Making: Recovering Our Creative Calling* (Downers Grove, IL: IVP Books, 2008), p. 67. Significantly, James Davison Hunter aligns Crouch's approach with "cultural materialism": the response to culture made popular by Raymond Williams. See *To Change the World: The Irony, Tragedy, and Possibility of Christianity in the Late Modern World* (New York: Oxford University Press, 2010), p. 28.

[37]For a good example of "culture making" as an act of (re)signing, go to www.youtube.com/watch?v=kDvgavOJyUc. Created by Theran Knighton-Fitt, one of my summer seminar graduate students at Regent College in Vancouver, the YouTube video films Tibetan prayer flags blowing in the wind. Theran then recites a poem on top of the image in order to (re)sign a Christian understanding of the Holy Spirit, who not only breathes a breath of life into us as creatures but also inspires us and our flag-like creations as signs of our love for the Creator.

[38]Jn 15:13; Lk 6:31; Gen 1.

Benjamin Franklin did not believe in the divinity of Christ.[39]

"Selective tradition" is not motivated by accuracy. It reminds me of proof-texting, when people pick and choose Bible verses to reinforce their ideologies. Bigots, for example, have been known to justify racial segregation by quoting Genesis 1:4: "And God saw that the light was good; and God separated the light from the darkness." They have thus selected what Williams calls "a version of the past which is intended to connect with and ratify the present."[40] As he explains, "selectivity is the point; the way in which from a whole possible area of past and present, certain meanings and practices are chosen for emphasis, certain other meanings and practices are neglected and excluded."[41] In other words, to argue for segregation using the fourth verse of Genesis entirely neglects and excludes "God so loved the [whole] world"; "Love your neighbor as yourself"; "There is no longer Jew or Greek, there is no longer slave or free, there is no longer male and female; for all of you are one in Christ Jesus."[42]

Many nineteenth-century abolitionists, in fact, emphasized the "residual value" of these verses when they protested slavery. But because more verses in the Bible condone slavery than condemn it, most antebellum Christians—in the North as well as the South—justified the practice by appealing to the Bible's authority. For example, the pastor of Brooklyn's First Presbyterian Church, Henry Van Dyke, argued that "Abolitionism is evil. . . . [I]t springs from, and is nourished by, an utter rejection of the Scriptures."[43]

In response, a Dutch Reformed professor named Taylor Lewis established the need to (re)sign truth. Though resigned to the truth of Scripture, he suggested that many signs in Scripture reflect the hegemony of their times and must therefore be re-signed for the nineteenth century. To this end he asserted that the pro-slavery Van Dyke

> does not take into view the vastly changed condition of the world; he does not seem to consider that *whilst truth is fixed*, . . . its application to distant ages, and differing circumstances, is so varying continually that a wrong direction given to the more truthful exegesis may convert it into the more malignant falsehood.[44]

---

[39]See Brooke Allen, *Moral Minority: Our Skeptical Founding Fathers* (Chicago: Ivan R. Dee, 2006).
[40]Williams, *Marxism and Literature*, p. 116.
[41]Williams, "Base and Superstructure," p. 169.
[42]Jn 3:16; Mk 12:31; Gal 3:28.
[43]Quoted in Mark A. Noll, *The Civil War as a Theological Crisis* (Chapel Hill: University of North Carolina Press, 2006), p. 3.
[44]Ibid., p. 4.

Most Christians today, including those who mystify an inerrant Bible (see chapter two), would agree with Taylor Lewis that the endorsement of slavery is a malignant falsehood. However, in Lewis's day, as historian Mark Noll points out, the Christians "who took most seriously the authority of Scripture" were the ones arguing that "the Bible sanctioned slavery." Regarding themselves as more authentically biblical, they considered Christians who argued otherwise as intellectual "elites" who manipulated rhetoric and Scripture to serve the abolitionist cause.[45]

CHANGING SIGNS OF SLAVERY: CULTURE MAKING

Why, then, did Christian attitudes change? One important influence, as Noll recounts, was Harriet Beecher Stowe's *Uncle Tom's Cabin* (1851), which "provided one of the era's most powerful examples of the abolitionist appeal to the general spirit of the Bible."[46] As a bestseller, *Uncle Tom's Cabin* illustrates Williams's belief that artifacts of popular culture can instigate change in attitude. In the language of Andy Crouch, Harriet Beecher Stowe was a "culture maker."

Stowe, of course, did not convert everyone to the abolitionist cause. Some Christians denounced abolition all the more as undermining the authority of Scripture, and it took a devastatingly bloody Civil War to overturn the institution of slavery. But just think: what might have happened if more Christians had been willing to (re)sign truth and become Bible-quoting advocates for emancipation?

Clearly, the process of (re)signing truth is neither easy nor swift, explaining why Williams held to "political gradualism," to the disdain of traditional Marxists.[47] Rather than endorse bloodshed, Williams argues for "conversation" whereby "new meanings and values, new practices, new significances and experiences" might develop—as eventually happened for blacks in America.[48] To describe new cultural signs, Williams employs the term "emergent": a word that has been appropriated by "the emergent church."

---

[45]Ibid., pp. 115, 49. As Diarmaid MacCulloch notes, "The long struggle to abolish slavery remained throughout a curious collaboration of fervent Evangelicals . . . with radical children of the Enlightenment, many of whom had no great love of Christianity." *Christianity: The First Three Thousand Years* (New York: Viking, 2010), p. 870.

[46]Noll, *Civil War*, p. 42.

[47]James Aune, *Rhetoric and Marxism* (Boulder, CO: Westview, 1994), p. 98.

[48]Williams, "Base and Superstructure," p. 171.

Eventually, of course, the Abolitionists' "emergent" repudiation of slavery became so incorporated into the ideology of the dominant culture that a hatred of slavery seems only "natural" to most educated people today. Nevertheless, the International Justice Mission (IJM) reports that there is more "human trafficking" (people sold into slavery) around the world today than ever before. A residual value—the financial benefits of slavery—has led to a re-emergent practice. We see that "residual" ideas can sometimes benefit and sometimes warp culture. Similarly, "emergent" meanings can sometimes benefit and sometimes mar culture. In both instances, either/or thinking proves problematic. On the one hand, either idealizing residual values of the past or denouncing them is shortsighted; on the other hand, either idealizing all emergent change or resisting it is naive. Williams, *in other words*, would encourage us to be on the edge between mystification and resistance, changing dominant culture by creating new signs.

FAITH IN THE WORKS OF WORDS

In other words is key to Williams, who wrote an influential book in 1976 called *Keywords*. Like a good rhetorician, Williams approaches words as "condensed social practice, sites of historical struggle, repositories of political wisdom or domination."[49]

His belief might be illustrated through one of the most dramatic changes to cultural hegemony in the twentieth century: the abolition of apartheid. As noted by Professor of Rhetoric Erik Doxtader, reconciliation in South Africa was energized "with a belief that there are words which hold the potential for all things to become new."[50] In his aptly named *With Faith in the Works of Words*, Doxtader recounts the arduous process of (re)signing /reconciliation/ itself, so that it honored justice and mercy for both sides of the political and racial divide. As he notes, "calls for reconciliation disturbed the (given) *signs of the times* by offering words to an opponent or enemy that had been previously deemed unworthy of conversation, irrational, or evil beyond redemption."[51] Though making clear that the two-decade-long process was often contentious and sometimes brutal, Doxtader demonstrates how

---

[49]Terry Eagleton, "Resources for a Journey of Hope: The Significance of Raymond Williams," *New Left Review* 168, March/April 1988, p. 10. For *Keywords*, see n. 8 above.
[50]Eric Doxtader, *With Faith in the Works of Words: The Beginnings of Reconciliation in South Africa, 1985-1995* (East Lansing: Michigan State University Press, 2009), p. ix.
[51]Ibid., p. 18, emphasis mine.

rhetoric can function as a form of collective action: revolution through words rather than with guns.

Few of us, of course, may ever be in positions of political power like people who influenced South Africa's Truth and Reconciliation Commission. Nevertheless, we can be agents of change, if even on a smaller scale, through the signs we use. If, as Raymond Williams notes, "keywords" in culture—like /self-esteem/—have the power to shape and perpetuate cultural values and practices, we must consider how new signs might get people to think differently, potentially influencing change in behavior. For example, when parents hear /helicopter parent/, some might be convicted by the coinage, leading them to assess how hovering over their college students might not serve their children's best interests. As will be explored more fully in the conclusion, coinages can keep us on the edge of the coin: resigned to ancient truths, we can nevertheless work to re-sign them.

Williams, in fact, became famous for (re)signing Marxism, using the word "revalue" to make his point. Resigned to signs created by Marx and Engels, he wanted to give them new values:

> We have to *revalue* "determination.". . . We have to *revalue* "superstructure."
> . . . And, crucially, we have to *revalue* "the base" away from the notion of a
> fixed economic or technological abstraction, and towards the specific activities
> of men in real social and economic relationships.[52]

Williams therefore coined a new sign, /cultural materialism/, to describe his study of specific activities and relationships. Furthermore, he aligned cultural materialism with semiotics: "a fully historical semiotics would be very much the same thing as cultural materialism."[53]

Williams's word "materialism" is telling. Perceiving reality through the lens of Marxist ideology, Williams did not give credence to "residual" signs of the supernatural, focusing only on material culture in order to assess hegemony at particular moments in history. Nevertheless, (re)signing Christians can learn from Williams the way early church fathers learned from pagan rhetoricians. For, as Williams notes, "becoming conscious" of the hegemonic forces controlling signs "can often lead to changing or shifting or

---

[52]Ibid., p. 165, emphasis mine.
[53]Raymond Williams, "Crisis in English Studies," in *The Raymond Williams Reader,* ed. John Higgins (Oxford: Blackwell, 2001), p. 264.

amending them."[54] Antonio Gramsci, whom Williams often cites, described such efforts as "counter-hegemonic."[55]

CHRISTIANS (EN)COUNTERING HEGEMONY

Many Christians today would rather be hegemonic than counter-hegemonic. They think Christian values should control culture rather than be controlled by it. This is understandable, since Christianity was hegemonic in Western society for nearly 1,400 years—from the age of Constantine in the fourth century to the Age of Reason in the eighteenth century. And language reflects that hegemony.

Consider some phrases we still hear all the time:

I swear to God

God only knows

I pray to God that . . .

Hand to God

With God as my witness

Oh my God!!

Like the signs *clown* and *villain*, however, these phrases have lost their original meaning, often employed by people who do not even believe in God. As a result of the hegemony of Enlightenment reason and empirical science that replaced the hegemony of Christian truth, these phrases came to express human earnestness rather than God's sovereignty. These signs were re-signed, not through conscious acts of redefinition but through hegemonic attitudes disseminated, like smog, throughout culture.

How do we re-infuse these phrases with their original sacred significance? Not through hegemony, Gramsci and Williams would argue. If a group of urban politicians decided to return the word *villain* to its original meaning, subsequently addressing rural villagers with, "Hello there, you villains," they'd more likely get poked with pitchforks than create any linguistic change. The intentional re-signing of language must come from the unempowered group in a counter-hegemonic move, villagers calling themselves

---

[54]Raymond Williams, "The Writer: Commitment and Alignment," in *The Raymond Williams Reader,* ed. John Higgins (Oxford: Blackwell, 2001), p. 217.

[55]Unfortunately, as James Aune notes, Gramsci "was unable to theorize systematically . . . how moments of counter-hegemony are made" (p. 73).

villains in defiance of hegemonic attitudes toward words that describe them.

RE-SIGNING FROM THE MARGINS: QUEER AND NEGRO SIGNS

I can think of two examples of counter-hegemonic re-signing in the twentieth century—made, in other words, from people on the margins of power. First is the word "queer." In the late nineteenth century the term started to transition from its five-hundred-year-long definition, "strange, odd, peculiar" *(OED)*, to a sign for homosexuality. Initially, this new sign was derogatory: a contemptuous slur by those with hegemony. In the second half of the twentieth century, however, gays decided to assign positive value to *queer,* appropriating the term as a way to describe themselves, with pride, as counter-hegemonic. Resigned to their homosexuality, they re-signed a word to describe it.

Even more dramatic is the establishment of the NAACP—the National Association for the Advancement of Colored People—in 1909. The name of the organization reflected a move away from the term *Negro,* which had contracted into a racist slur in the mouths of the white majority. However, because racist whites still had hegemony, the sign "colored" also became debased, reflecting, like the word *vulgar,* the disdain of those with power. So, through additional acts of re-signing, the terms "African American" and "Black" were substituted, which, in combination with successes in the civil rights movement, finally achieved linguistic dignity.

It would seem that groups have more power to consciously re-sign truth when they are counter-hegemonic than when they have power. This, of course, seems counterintuitive. Haven't I shown, through words like *vulgar* and *courteous,* that people with the most power control the signs of culture?

Well, yes and no. As Gramsci has taught us, the social group with hegemony often does not know it has it, assuming that truth as it sees it is most "natural": it is only "natural" to desire black teeth; it is only "natural" that suffrage be limited to white males. Individuals with hegemony usually do not consciously practice it. If anything, their hegemony practices on them, controlling the way they think about reality, as when Queen Victoria believed that female suffrage was "unchristian" and slave-owners believed that abolition was "unchristian." The medieval nobility did not self-consciously say, "Let's make ourselves seem better than the villains by elevating the words *noble* and *courteous* into descriptions of superior human characteristics." Instead, their assumptions about the naturalness of their status had hegemony over their perceptions as well as their language.

RESISTING CULTURAL HEGEMONY: POLITICS AND RELIGION

The last thing Christians should desire, then, is cultural hegemony. For power blinds people to their own blindness. Those with hegemony assume "whatever is, is right," to quote Alexander Pope (1688-1744), a British poet who reflected the hegemonic optimism of Enlightenment thinkers: reason will lead to the only truth worth knowing.[56] This explains why the eighteenth-century founders of America wrote into the Constitution a "separation of church and state." Right? No!

The phrase "separation of church and state" appears nowhere in the Constitution. Nevertheless, the phrase has become such a part of American "selective tradition" that people inaccurately assume it appears there, regarding it as a pillar holding up the roof of democracy. In actuality, our country's founders, their ancestors having escaped religious persecution, merely forbade a state-sponsored church. They recognized that when political power beds down with religion, spiritual syphilis corrupts the health of faith. A vital, culture-changing Christianity is always counter-hegemonic.

In *Rethinking Christ and Culture,* Craig A. Carter effectively illustrates the corruption of Christianity by cultural hegemony. Until the fourth century, Christians were on the margins of European culture, often suffering persecution if not martyrdom. Nevertheless, Christianity spread like wildfire, perhaps because of its counter-hegemonic message: Jesus provided access to God for any that believed, no matter their race, gender, class or ethnicity. Believers defied social hierarchies, sharing meals and resources in communitarian acts of worship that would put communists to shame. No wonder those in power wished to stamp out Christianity! It was counter-hegemonic!

Then, after seeing a vision of the cross in 312, the Emperor Constantine reputedly became a Christian: an event, as we have seen, that many regard as a triumph for the faith. Carter, however, argues that Constantine's "conversion" may have been motivated as much by the desire for political hegemony as by the desire for a transformed life. Even though he put an end to the persecution of Christians, Constantine's personal life did not differ very

---

[56]These are the last words from Epistle I of Alexander Pope's unfinished poem "Essay on Man," published in 1734.

much from other emperors, as he murdered not just political rivals but also friends and family who defied him. On the positive side, he recruited Christian bishops to "distribute food to the urban poor, hold trials and settle disputes, and act as his network of advisors on matters of importance to the empire."[57] However, by giving leaders of the church power in the political arena, Constantine set into motion a hegemonic structure that would overshadow the counter-hegemonic truth of Christ. By 528, things had so flip-flopped that, by decree of Emperor Justinian, it became illegal for Roman citizens to *not* be Christians! And what followed is infamous: a church sullied by self-indulgence, corruption and violence, several popes littering Europe with their bastard children.

Many Christians during the medieval era, of course, still followed Christ with heart, soul and mind, loving their neighbors as themselves. But they tended not to be the pillars of hegemony. As Christian historian Lord Acton (1834-1902) put it in his famous letter to an English bishop, "Power tends to corrupt, and absolute power corrupts absolutely." Or, to quote an even more subversive source, "If any want to become my followers, let them deny themselves and take up their cross and follow me. For those who want to save their life will lose it, and those who lose their life for my sake, and for the sake of the gospel, will save it" (Mk 8:34-35). Jesus, here, calls his followers to sacrifice hegemony.

I therefore agree with cultural theorist James Davison Hunter when he argues, "If there is a possibility for human flourishing in our world, it does not begin when we win the culture wars but when God's word of love becomes flesh in us, reaching every sphere of social life."[58]

BIBLICAL HEGEMONY

Lest you think I am manipulating Scripture to fit Marxist hegemony theory, please note that various forms of the word *hegemony* appear in the Greek New Testament. During the *hēgemonia* [reign] of Tiberius Caesar, while Pontius Pilate *hēgemonūo* [was governor] of Judea, John the Baptist went into the

---

[57]Craig A. Carter, *Rethinking Christ and Culture: A Post-Christendom Perspective* (Grand Rapids, MI: Brazos, 2006), p. 81. For more recent scholarship challenging negative views of Constantine, see Peter J. Leithart, *Defending Constantine: The Twilight of an Empire and the Dawn of Christendom* (Downers Grove, IL: IVP Academic, 2010).

[58]James Davison Hunter, "Faithful Presence," an interview by Christopher Benson, *Christianity Today* online, May 2010, p. 5 [accessed August 4, 2010].

wilderness (Lk 3:1-2). A few years later, Jesus stood trial before this same Pontius Pilate, the *hēgemōn* [governor] (Mt 27:2, 11, 14, 21, 27). But Jesus did not seek to wrest hegemony from the *hēgemōn*. Instead, he instructed his disciples that "he who is chief" *[hēgeomai]* must become like a servant (Lk 22:26 KJV).

The epistle to the Philippians uses forms of the word *hēgeomai* six times within a 35-verse passage (between 2:3 and 3:8). Rather than referring to ruling leaders, the word here means *to be ruled by a certain attitude or idea*. The writer encourages the Philippians to "consider" or "regard" an attitude that should guide their practices:

> Do nothing from selfish ambition or conceit, but in humility regard *[hēgeomai]* others as better than yourselves. (Phil 2:3)

> Let the same mind be in you that was in Christ Jesus, who, though he was in the form of God, did not regard *[hēgeomai]* equality with God as something to be exploited. (Phil 2:5-6)

> Yet whatever gains I had, these I have come to regard *[hēgeomai]* as loss because of Christ. More than that, I regard *[hēgeomai]* everything as loss because of the surpassing value of knowing Christ Jesus my Lord. For his sake I have suffered the loss of all things, and I regard *[hēgeomai]* them as rubbish, in order that I may gain Christ. (Phil 3:7-8)

Scripture, then, anticipates theories developed by Gramsci, Althusser and Williams: that ideas can rule as powerfully as human leaders. However, unlike Althusser, who regarded the hegemony of cultural summoning (interpellation) as deterministic, Christians believe they have a choice: to freely respond to God's summons. As the writer to the Galatians puts it, "For you were *called* to freedom, brothers and sisters; only do not use your freedom as an opportunity for self-indulgence, but through love become slaves to one another" (Gal 5:13)—just as Christ freely took the form of a slave for us.

What are the signs of this call? Are we to sell ourselves into slavery to fulfill biblical prescriptions? Obviously not. Our culture, which eschews signs of slavery, makes such a reading of Scripture untenable—even though many Christians once used biblical signs to endorse the slave trade. Fortunately, as we have seen, counter-hegemonic abolitionists worked tirelessly to (re)sign the truth of Scripture. Though resigned to the Bible as God's Word, they regarded slavery as a biblical sign that must be re-signed.

HOW THEN SHALL WE SIGN?

Once again we see that context affects the meaning of signs—even the signs of Scripture. Saussure regarded context as a system of linguistic differences that gave value to signs. The structuralists he influenced regarded context as providing the data with which the mind structures meaning in predictable ways. Marxist cultural critics saw context shaped by hegemonic forces that controlled meaning. Nevertheless, Gramsci and Williams, two fathers of cultural studies, established the possibility of counter-hegemonic change.

How might Christians, then, be counter-hegemonic through acts of "culture making"? To which "residual" values do we appeal without perpetuating "selective traditions"? How do we know which Christian signs must be changed—and when—in order to fit new cultural contexts? How do we negotiate between the "interpellations" of culture and the call of Christ?

To begin addressing such questions, the next chapter considers the semiotics of Jacques Derrida, who responded to both structuralism and Marxism with deconstruction.

Part III

Changing Signs of Faith

6

SIGNS OF DECONSTRUCTION

Maintaining the House of Faith

In the 1960s, just as structuralism became the hottest ticket in town, a new semiotic act—deconstruction—started upstaging it. Jacques Derrida (1930-2004), its preeminent performer, became the Elvis of the erudite, his dance of deconstruction helping to energize *post*-structuralism.[1] In this chapter I will explain the relationship between structuralism and deconstruction, suggesting how deconstruction might prepare Christians to (re)sign truth.[2] I will start with a true story from my own life in order to provide an analogy for what Derrida meant by deconstruction.

A CONSTRUCTIVE ANALOGY: ESCAPING ALLERGENS

While teaching summer school at a research university in California, I agreed to help a student who was allergic to the inside of both classrooms and books. I met with Sue (as I shall call her) at an outdoor picnic table, upon which she placed a huge wooden box with a glass top. Inside was her textbook, which she read through the glass lid, turning the pages by inserting gloved hands into holes cut into the side of the box. Because Sue was both smart and conscientious we had great discussions, and at the end of the term she invited me to have dinner with her family to thank me for my help.

---

[1]Marcel Danesi identifies Derrida as a "semiotician" who proposed a "counter-approach" to signs. See *Of Cigarettes, High Heels, and Other Interesting Things: An Introduction to Semiotics* (New York: St. Martin's, 1999), p. 18.

[2]I am not the first to do so. See John D. Caputo's lucid book *What Would Jesus Deconstruct? The Good News of Postmodernism for the Church* (Grand Rapids, MI: Baker, 2007). For a different approach to deconstruction, see chapter 5 of Crystal Downing, *How Postmodernism Serves (My) Faith: Questioning Truth in Language, Philosophy and Art* (Downers Grove, IL: IVP Academic, 2006).

So one hot summer day I drove into the mountains where Sue lived in a former logging cabin with her mother and sister, both of whom shared her allergies. As I mounted the rickety porch, the door opened only enough to reveal a pair of lips, which asked me to spit out my gum in the woods across the road. After doing so, I remounted the porch, only to have the same lips tell me to go into the shed across the yard, undress and put on the clothes laid out for me. Wanting to be sensitive to the special needs of my hosts, I put on the oversized outfit and shuffled my way back to the porch, discretely trying to keep the woolen slacks from falling to my ankles. This time, instead of the mysterious lips behind the door, a hand shot out—holding a shower cap to cover my hair.

Finally allowed to enter the cabin (feeling *quite* lovely), I noticed that every inside wall was lined with aluminum sheeting, all surfaces of wooden furniture were wrapped in aluminum foil, and a television stood behind thick glass in the fireplace. Fortunately, the women were so friendly that after our organically grown dinner I felt free, despite my fashion dis-ease, to ask, "What are your symptoms that necessitate such drastic measures?" After a long pause while glancing at each other for support, one finally answered with, "We get irritable." My reaction, though unexpressed at the time, was probably the same as yours right now. Though allergies are nothing to sneeze at, I wanted to hear about symptoms considerably more dramatic than irritability.[3]

For me, this story is a parable of how Christians sometimes respond to new signs in culture: as allergens that must be kept out of the house of belief. Seeking to protect themselves from new ways of thinking—especially about Christianity—they turn their faith into an aluminum-lined fortress, expecting all who enter their presence to dress their thought with language that doesn't disrupt their highly controlled beliefs. However, if you were to ask them how elements from the outside world might debilitate their faith, many could only offer their extreme irritability at encountering new signs.

LINING THE FORTRESS: GALILEO AS ALLERGEN

Unfortunately, the history of Christianity is filled with stories of aluminum-

---

[3]I tell this story to a different end in Crystal Downing, "Imbricating Faith and Learning: The Architectonics of Christian Scholarship," in *Scholarship and Christian Faith: Enlarging the Conversation,* ed. Douglas Jacobsen and Rhonda Hustedt Jacobsen (New York: Oxford University Press, 2004), pp. 34-35.

lined fortresses. For centuries, the Church has evicted from the house of faith Christians who refuse to hide new ideas under shower caps. In 1633, Galileo was tried by the Roman Inquisition for saying that the Earth revolved around the sun rather than vice versa. In the minds of the protectors of Christianity, Galileo subverted the Bible, which taught that the sun once stood still (Josh 10:12-14). After all, the Church had published a decree in 1616 "that declared that the earth's motion was physically false and contradicted Scripture."[4] Because Galileo refused to give up his heliocentric view of the solar system, the Church placed him under house arrest until he died in 1642.

Admittedly, Galileo's trial was more subtle than many people realize: he was convicted not for heliocentrism per se, but for his *disobedience* to Church leaders, who commanded him in 1616 "neither to hold nor to defend the thesis that the sun is the immovable center of the universe and that the earth is movable and not at the center."[5] But why make such a command? Perhaps because geocentrism reinforced a whole *system* of signs, the word *system* reminding us of a structuralist view of the sign.

As Cambridge scholar E. M. W. Tillyard famously explains, "The world picture which the Middle Ages inherited was that of an ordered universe arranged in a fixed *system* of hierarchies."[6] To protect *the system,* then, Inquisitors required shower caps for "scientists" entering the house of Christianity.[7] For them, questioning "truth" about the universe might undermine "truth" not only in the Bible, but also about church leadership.[8] Just as the Earth was

---

[4]Maurice A. Finocchiaro, "Myth 8: That Galileo was Imprisoned and Tortured for Advocating Copernicanism," in *Galileo Goes to Jail and Other Myths about Science and Religion,* ed. Ronald L. Numbers (Cambridge, MA: Harvard University Press, 2009), p. 70.

[5]Edward Peters, *Inquisition* (New York: Macmillan, 1988), p. 245.

[6]The medieval church "inherited" the idea from Plato and Aristotle. E. M. W. Tillyard, *The Elizabethan World Picture* (Harmondsworth, UK: Penguin, 1943), p. 14. Giles Brown confirms the interdependence of earthly and heavenly systems in the Middle Ages: "earthly order reflected heavenly order; God's Church was functioning properly only if, in its organization, its habits, and its worship . . . it reflected heavenly practice." See "Introduction: The Carolingian Renaissance," in *Carolingian Culture: Emulation and Innovation,* ed. Rosamond McKitterick (Cambridge: Cambridge University Press, 1994), p. 25.

[7]I use the word *scientist,* even though it did not appear in print until 1834 *(OED),* because it makes the most sense to us today.

[8]This does not mean that Church leaders self-consciously thought about the connection between geocentrism and their own status in the church hierarchy. As we have seen, structuralists assume that one's linguistic system generates thoughts that endorse the system itself. One Marxist critic influenced by structuralism argued that the endorsement of "sign systems" reflects the "political unconscious" that molds the way people perceive reality. See Fredric Jameson, *The Political Unconscious: Narrative as a Socially Symbolic Act,* 2nd ed. (New York: Routledge, 2006), pp. 84-85.

the center of the universe, with the sun, then the moon, then the planets and finally various gradations of stars revolving around it, the pope was the center of the Western Church, with cardinals, then archbishops, then bishops and so forth revolving around him. This, Christians believed, reflected the nature of God, who, at the center of all creation, had various gradations of angels revolving around him, in descending importance like the descending power of Catholic leaders. Reminding us of structuralism, the signs in their system generated value in relation to each other.

The following diagram drawn by a contemporary of Galileo, English physician Robert Fludd (1574-1637), symbolically illustrates the sign-system that had defined Christian truth for centuries. At the center of the universe is Earth, the monkey sitting on top signaling that humans "ape" Mother Nature, represented by the woman chained to the monkey. But Mother Nature herself is attached by a chain to God, represented by the cloud at the top of the diagram. The many concentric circles indicate that every element of the universe has its proper orbit around Earth at its center, all being suspended—and sustained—by the hand of God. This became known as "the great chain of being."[9]

Galileo's radical idea, though not original to him, called into question this entire *system,* and that may be one reason the Church resisted it. Those at the center of Church leadership felt that Galileo's challenge might destroy the entire house of Christianity. In this light we should sympathize with his Inquisitors. At the same time, we need to acknowledge that the system the Church sought to protect was as much influenced by pagan belief as Christian.

Seventeenth-century Jesuits, for example, in their commitment to rigorous reasoning, resisted Galileo because his perspective countered Aristotle's view of the universe, with the Earth at the center. As Jonathan Hill notes, "Jesuits were committed to defending the old Aristotelian cosmology . . . not simply by appealing to religious authority but by making scientific observations that they believed supported [Aristotle's] theory."[10] How often

---

[9]See Arthur Lovejoy, *The Great Chain of Being: A Study of the History of an Idea* (Cambridge, MA: Harvard University Press, 1936). Alexander Pope coined the phrase "the vast chain of being" in his wildly popular poem *Essay on Man,* published in the 1730s. Tillyard notes that "a primate in one class of creation must be an important link in the chain as being closest to the class above it and must also correspond to a primate in another class" (*Elizabethan World Picture,* p. 105).

[10]Jonathan Hill, *What Has Christianity Ever Done for Us? How It Shaped the Modern World* (Downers Grove, IL: InterVarsity Press, 2005), p. 100.

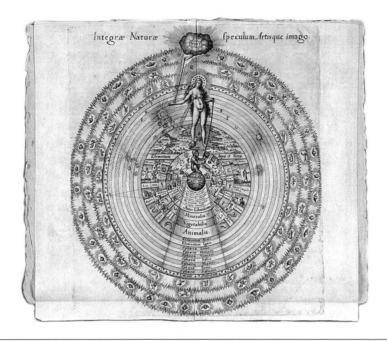

Figure 6.1. Robert Fludd's *Utriusque cosmi maioris scilicet et minoris metaphysica, physica, atque technica historia* (Frankfort? ca. 1624).

today might Christians think they stand for "true" Christianity when what they stand for is a secular tradition—what cultural critic Raymond Williams would call a "selective tradition" (chapter five)—that has little to do with the kingdom of God?

ILLUSTRATING DECONSTRUCTION: SIGNS OF PRAYER

Deconstruction, then, might be seen as the effort to rip away aluminum that shields us from irritating ideas outside our system, or structure, of truth. It tears down signs of belief we feel most passionately about in order to inspect them, to consider where they came from, how they block our vision and hence our understanding of people and ideas outside our house of faith. Sometimes, after such an inspection, a sign-board will be nailed back up as important to our house. But in the process of taking it down, we can—in fact, we *must*—look through the gap in the wall that the sign once covered up in order to understand what is outside our structure of belief.

Deconstruction thus aids in the (re)signing of truth. Identifying with a traditional house of belief and therefore resigned to its truth, we re-sign it in order to maintain it, replacing planks of belief warped by "moth and rust" (Mt 6:19). By doing so, not only will we maintain intellectual spaces where Christianity can thrive amidst the signs of our times, but we will also provide places of entry for all who hunger and thirst outside.

Let me give a practical example of how this might work. My colleague Doug Miller, an exercise physiologist at Messiah College, challenges students to rethink the rhetoric of their prayers before athletic events. Focusing on their common request, "Dear God, help us to win this game," Doug asks them questions about their prayer-signs:

- How exactly do think God will help you win? Will God give you skills you don't have? Or somehow injure your competitors?

- What if the opposing team sends up more prayers for a win than your team? Will God count up the number of prayers and reward the team with the most requests?

- Might not help from God violate the true spirit of competition, falling under the category of receiving unfair outside assistance? Is it therefore ethical for us to desire God to intervene in some miraculous way on our behalf?

- Rather than praying for a win, why not pray that you will play to the best of your ability and training?

- Rather than praying to trounce your opponents, why not pray that your opponents will witness the love of Jesus in and through you, whether you win or lose?

By asking questions like these, Doug tears down aluminum signing, encouraging students not only to inspect the way they pray, but also to look through their *structure* of faith to consider the people outside it.

Occasionally, a student will whip out a shower cap, accusing Doug of being, alas, a "liberal" who wants to destroy the traditional structure of Christianity. Ironically, this attack parallels those missiles lobbed at deconstruction by secular humanists, who accuse Derrida of destroying the traditional structure of Enlightenment rationalism. But, as Derrida himself insists, "deconstruction has nothing to do with destruction." Instead, deconstruction aims to "dismantle . . . metaphysical and rhetorical structures . . . not in order to reject or discard them, but to reconstitute them in another way."[11] Similarly, Doug seeks to preserve the structure of Christianity by getting students to pull down signs of prayer in order to "reconstitute them in another way."

(RE)COVERING THE HOUSE OF CHRISTIANITY: THE INQUISITION

Think of an old historic house: inhabitants sometimes need to replace time-worn planks with fresh, updated material *in order to maintain the house itself.* Covering up rotted wood with aluminum siding may keep the house standing for awhile, but eventually the walls will warp as they crumble underneath its shiny surfaces. This, of course, is what happened to Christians who tried to reinforce the structure of Aristotelian cosmology to keep out the allergen of Galileo: they caused the rot to spread.

Indeed, due to the Inquisition's long-lasting astronomical aluminum, antagonists to Christianity continue to trot out the example of Galileo as reason enough to renounce *all* signs of Christianity. Historian Edward Peters explains how signs of the Inquisition became exaggerated by people antagonistic to Roman Catholicism. In the sixteenth century, Protestants published hyperbolic accounts of sadistic torture by the Inquisitors as part of their propaganda against the Roman Church. But then their propaganda was eventually turned against them as Enlightenment humanists embellished myths about the Inquisition in order to reject *any* form of Christianity: "By the mid-eighteenth century . . . it was universally accepted that *The Inquisition* played a role as an instrument of obscurantism and anti-intellectualism, designed to protect superstitions and fanaticism."[12] And this attitude still abounds. When I communicated my beliefs to a non-Christian professor several years ago, she responded, "How can you be a Christian? What about the Inquisition?!"

Of course, those who use the Inquisition as an overarching indictment of Christianity are not that much different from Galileo's Inquisitors. While one group sought to discredit Galileo, the other group seeks to discredit Christianity: opposite sides of the same coin. Both demonstrate the need for *deconstruction,* which Derrida defines as "an openness toward the other."[13]

---

[11]Quoted in M. H. Abrams, *A Glossary of Literary Terms,* 8th ed. (Boston: Thomson Wadsworth, 2005), p. 59; and M. H. Abrams, "How to Do Things with Texts," in *Critical Theory Since 1965,* ed. Hazard Adams and Leroy Searle (Tallahassee: University Press of Florida, 1986), p. 440.

[12]Peters, *Inquisition,* p. 247.

[13]Quoted in "Dialogue with Jacques Derrida," in *Dialogues with Contemporary Continental Thinkers:*

Significantly, the Greek word for "other" is *allos*—from which we get our word "allergen." *Allos + ergon* means *other-work*. Deconstruction provides openings so that the *other* can *work* on our thought: a pun that Derrida himself employs in his famous essay "Plato's Pharmacy" (1968).[14]

Once again, this does NOT mean abandoning our houses of belief. Neither does it mean allowing our beliefs to be destroyed by outside forces. As religious studies professor Jeffrey Robbins astutely summarizes, "deconstruction isn't something that happens from the zap of a deconstruction gun. Instead, you enter into something fully and, in doing that, you take it beyond its own limits or expose it to its own limitations."[15]

DECONSTRUCTING CLOSED STRUCTURES

Of course, many people are so certain that their house of belief, and only their house, is correct that they refuse to "take it beyond its own limits." This necessitates people on the outside exposing the structural flaws in the house.

Take, for example, agnostics residing in a house constructed out of words like "open-mindedness" who, as soon as they encounter someone speaking of Christ's resurrection, whip out extra shower caps to keep the offensive idea from irritating them inside their so-called open-minded house. Refusing to accept the possibility of supernatural signs, they undermine the language of open-mindedness that holds their house together. So they fortify their defenses with even stronger resistance to "signs and wonders," seeing them as the most insidious of allergens that must be resisted. But the more they fortify their defenses, the more clearly we see traces of closed-mindedness that have entered their "open-minded" structure. Derrida, in fact, uses the word *trace* to describe an element outside a system that enters in (like an allergen) exposing the structure's flaws.[16] By showing how traces of closed-mindedness

---

The Phenomenological Heritage, ed. Richard Kearney (Manchester, UK: Manchester University Press, 1984), p. 124. Derrida did not invent the sign "to deconstruct," which was used by French literary critics before him. However, by promoting "deconstruction," Derrida turned a literary technique into a philosophical concept. See Kevin Hart, *Postmodernism: A Beginner's Guide* (Oxford: Oneworld Publications, 2004), p. 114.

[14]Jacques Derrida, "Plato's Pharmacy," in *The Norton Anthology of Theory and Criticism*, ed. Vincent B. Leitch et al., 2nd ed. (New York: Norton, 2010), p. 1718.

[15]Jeffrey W. Robbins, ed., *After the Death of God: John D. Caputo and Gianni Vattimo* (New York: Columbia University Press, 2007), p. 157.

[16]See, for example, Jacques Derrida, "Structure, Sign and Play in the Discourse of the Human Sciences," in *Critical Theory Since 1965*, ed. Hazard Adams and Leroy Searle (Tallahassee: University Press of Florida, 1986), p. 93. In chapter nine I will discuss the problem with signs

have entered in, I have deconstructed the house of Enlightenment "open-mindedness" from the outside.

Derrida practiced what he preached. Having resided in the house of atheism for decades, he recognized the need to deconstruct his atheism, to "expose it to its own limitations." Even though not sure God existed, Derrida began to pray, *open* to the *possibility* of a God that far exceeds any and all signs of faith. A brilliant book describing this openness is called *The Prayers and Tears of Derrida: Religion Without Religion.* The author, Derrida's friend John D. Caputo, establishes a pun in his title: Derrida prays with *tears* while he *tears* away problematic signs that shore up aluminum-lined structures of thought.[17] He started doing so, early in his career, by exposing the limitations of structuralism.

TEARING OPEN LÉVI-STRAUSS

Derrida catapulted to fame in 1966 when he delivered a paper at a conference meant to celebrate structuralism. Titled "Structure, Sign and Play in the Discourse of the Human Sciences," Derrida's essay focuses on problems with the structural anthropology of Claude Lévi-Strauss (chapter four). Lévi-Strauss, Derrida suggests, writes as though he can innocently enter and exit the aluminum-lined structures of tribal peoples in order to objectively assess their signs.

Derrida gives the example of the preface to *The Raw and the Cooked,* where Lévi-Strauss states that he "sought to transcend the opposition between the sensible and the intelligible by operating from the outset at the level of signs." The word "transcend" is telling, as though Lévi-Strauss can be both inside a structure of signs while simultaneously flying above it. In response, Derrida points out that "the concept of the sign cannot in itself surpass this opposition between the sensible and the intelligible."[18] After all, as Saussure taught us, every sign is made up of the *sensible* "sound-image"—the signifier—and the *intelligible* concept to which it is connected: the signified. In other words, signs themselves contain what Lévi-Strauss seeks to "transcend." Thus, what he wants to keep outside of his structural analysis—the opposition between

---

of tolerance and intolerance more thoroughly.

[17] In his first endnote to the book, Caputo explains that he borrows the pun on "tears" from Mark Taylor's *Tears* (Albany: SUNY Press, 1990). See John D. Caputo, *The Prayers and Tears of Jacques Derrida: Religion Without Religion* (Bloomington: Indiana University Press, 1997), p. 340 n. 1.

[18] Quoted in Caputo, *Prayers and Tears,* p. 85.

the sensible and the intelligible—is already inside it. Derrida thus deconstructs Lévi-Strauss.

Here's another way to think about it. Lévi-Strauss, like many social scientists in the twentieth century, thought he could float above the house of signs in which a tribe or society lives in order to objectively describe it. But he is oblivious to the fact that the house he studies is encased by the larger house of his own cultural signs. (Think of a box inside a box, with the scientist on a broomstick flying in the space between them.) The larger house containing the smaller house is lined with the aluminum of Enlightenment "objectivity" that the scientist takes for granted. Derrida wants to pull down that aluminum in order to inspect it, to assess how much the sign of scientific objectivity is just that: a sign that must be questioned.

Derrida thus draws attention to the allergen that structural anthropologists think will pollute their project: lack of objectivity. Doing so, he forces them to question how they thought they could escape this allergen in the first place. Derrida's deconstruction is especially important to Christians, since "scientific" people—whether in the hard sciences or the social sciences—often denounce Christianity because it cannot be "objectively" verified. Derrida, in contrast, establishes that no one—including the most rigorous scientist—is totally objective.

Philosopher René Girard discusses Lévi-Strauss at length in *Violence and the Sacred,* summarizing the problem with structural anthropology: it "is itself locked into the structure, a prisoner of the synchronic."[19] In other words, Lévi-Strauss seems to ignore the synchronic structure that frames his analysis, the structure that holds together the signs that *he* uses when he analyzes the signs of tribal peoples. Ignoring what Derrida calls "the structurality of structure,"[20] Lévi-Strauss parallels those who dismissed the structure of Galileo's cosmology while oblivious to the structure (Aristotle's cosmology) upon which their assessments were based.

TEARING OPEN SAUSSURE: THE SPEECH/WRITING BINARY

Derrida becomes even more explicit about the relationship between "inside" and "outside" in his watershed book *Of Grammatology* (1967), where he takes

---

[19]René Girard, *Violence and the Sacred* (Baltimore: Johns Hopkins University Press, 1977), p. 98.
[20]Derrida, "Structure, Sign and Play," p. 83.

on Ferdinand de Saussure.[21] Derrida is especially troubled by Saussure's implied elevation of spoken signifiers above written signifiers, as though speech is closer to truth than writing.

I understand Saussure's impulse. Speech certainly feels closer to my mind, the breath of life passing through my mouth to create words. As an adolescent, I experienced an opposition between mouth (the medium of speech) and hand (the medium of writing) at piano recitals. Though from junior high on up I had no trouble giving speeches to the entire student body, I quaked like a leaf at every one of my stormy recitals. Why? Because my hands seemed so much farther from my brain than my mouth. I felt that I could control what I said, but those appendages at the ends of my arms kept flailing over piano keys, randomly hitting wrong notes even when I urged them not to. My spoken words seemed closer to my authentic self than the work of my hands.

Of course, neither Saussure nor Derrida discuss the opposition between mouths and hands—or second-rate piano-playing for that matter. But Derrida does note that the elevation of speech over writing, which goes back at least as far as Plato, does reflect the tension between body and breath: "writing, the letter, the sensible inscription, has always been considered by Western tradition as the body and matter external to the spirit, to breath, to speech, and to the logos."[22] The authentic breath of words comes first, followed up by the secondary task of giving body to those words by writing them down.

Derrida's own words remind me of the Gnosticism that tempted Christians in the early centuries of the church. As discussed in chapter two above, some early Christians elevated spirit over body to such a degree that they believed Jesus, the Logos, only *appeared* to have a body. Influenced by Platonism, these Christians also dismissed the importance of their own bodies, sometimes flagellating them into submission. Such Gnostic dismissals parallel Plato's dismissal of writing. Establishing the spirit of the spoken word as primary, Plato regarded the physicality of writing as an unruly servant, like

---

[21]Jacques Derrida, *Of Grammatology*, trans. Gayatri Chakravorty Spivak (Baltimore: Johns Hopkins University Press, 1976). Derrida titles his preface to the book "Exergue," a word that means *epigraph* or *inscription* in French. In English, however, "exergue" refers to the space on a coin where the date and place of minting is often inscribed, usually below the main design. As we shall see, Derrida refers to the image of a coin multiple times in his writings, his sense of "deconstruction" inspiring my idea of balancing between two sides of a coin.

[22]Ibid., p. 35.

my piano-playing hands. Saussure therefore follows in this Platonic tradition when he states that "language and writing are two distinct systems of signs; the second exists for the sole purpose of representing the first."[23] Derrida summarizes Saussure's belief as follows: "Writing . . . will be the outside, the exterior representation of language."[24] To invoke the metaphor that began this chapter, writing is the allergen outside the house of authentic language.

As far as Derrida is concerned, then, Saussure is nailing up additional aluminum to an ancient house. He sees Saussure merely working in the interest of *"protecting,* and even of restoring the internal system of the language in the *purity* of its concept against the gravest, most perfidious, most permanent *contamination* which has not ceased to menace, even to *corrupt* that system." Writing is "dangerous" for Saussure, contaminating the "purity" of spoken language.[25]

In response, Derrida argues that we can't understand the concept of speech apart from the concept of writing. In fact, Saussure unwittingly implies as much, argues Derrida. When Saussure elevates spoken language over writing, he needs the idea of "writing" in order to establish that spoken language is superior to it. Think of it this way: if there were no males in the world, we would not have a concept of the "female"; we would just have a concept of "humans," all of whom happen to be born with uteruses. So also, without writing we could have no sense of the significance of speech. Therefore something that Saussure thought was outside of authentic language—the allergen of writing—was already inside it, making it possible (just as males make possible the idea of females). Derrida thus deconstructs the purity of Saussure's system.

OPENING A LACAN OF WORMS

Derrida does the same thing with Lacan. As we saw in the preceding chapter, Lacan established that the signifier, policed by the name of the father, creates the signified meaning in our minds, whether voiced or written. Though recognizing parallels between Lacan's thought and his own,[26] Derrida critiqued Lacan. In his mind, Lacan gave too much power to the signifier and the way

---

[23]Quoted in ibid., p. 30.
[24]Ibid., p. 31.
[25]Ibid., p. 34, emphasis mine.
[26]Gayatri Chakravorty Spivak, "Translator's Preface" to *Of Grammatology,* p. lxii.

it controls the unconscious. It's as though Lacan turned signifiers into imperturbable drill sergeants whose barked-out commands control not just the behavior of new army recruits but also the way recruits *desire* to behave. Furthermore, like Lévi-Strauss, Lacan gave too much power to himself, assuming he could step outside the structure of his own unconscious desires in order "to provide objective descriptions."[27]

When Derrida delineates such inconsistencies, he practices deconstruction, which exposes the failure of structures to contain the whole truth—no matter how much aluminum signing we put up. Traces of something from outside the system inevitably worm their way in.

Another way to think of Derrida's deconstruction is to remember the binary oppositions that Roman Jakobson and Claude Lévi-Strauss made so important (chapter four).[28] Three traditional binaries, harkening back to Classical Greece, might be illustrated as follows:

Meaning	Speech	Male
Sign	Writing	Female

When Derrida deconstructs such binaries, he does not invert them, as though signs, writing and females were more important than meaning, speech and males. Instead, he takes them apart, showing that each term is essential for our understanding of the other.

Sign	$\longleftrightarrow$	Meaning
Writing	$\longleftrightarrow$	Speech
Female	$\longleftrightarrow$	Male

We need the "allergen" of what is outside each term in order to assess each by what it is not.

TEARING OPEN COMMUNICATION THEORY

For deconstruction in practice, we might turn to communication theory. In 1989, rhetoric scholar Barbara A. Biesecker invoked Derrida in order to deconstruct a binary that had developed in response to questions such as "What

---

[27]Ibid., p. lvii.
[28]For a fuller discussion of Derrida's deconstruction of binaries, see Downing, *How Postmodernism Serves (My) Faith*, pp. 128-45.

elicits rhetorical discourse?" or "What generates persuasive language?"[29] In 1968, Lloyd Bitzer had published his famous answer, "The Rhetorical Situation," arguing that "Not the rhetor and not persuasive intent, but the situation is the source and ground of rhetorical activity." Context, in other words, generates the need for rhetoric, "not by the direct application of energy to objects, but by the creation of discourse which changes reality through the mediation of thought and action."[30] In reaction to Bitzer, Richard E. Vatz wrote "The Myth of the Rhetorical Situation" in 1973, arguing that a speaker's *interpretation* of a situation, and her creative intentions in response, generate rhetorical discourse.[31]

We might diagram that difference between Bitzer (on the left) and Vatz as follows:

The rhetorical situation	A speaker's intentions
A speaker's intentions	The rhetorical situation

Biesecker, in contrast, deconstructs these binaries, arguing for both/and thinking. A situation always affects a speaker's intentions and a speaker's interpretation always inflects the situation. In fact, Biesecker adds an obvious third element to rhetorical discourse: the audience. This idea of a "third"— creating a triangle of communication functions—will be important to the next chapter. But until then, we can apply Biesecker's deconstruction of Vatz and Bitzer to the idea that there is no allergen-free, autonomous origin of communication. Because any situation is made up of signs, speakers are always in the position of interpreting signs before they create new ones, whereby they formulate new sign-filled situations for their audiences.[32]

TO BE INSIDE THE STRUCTURE: COMMUNICATING BELIEF

Derrida implies that all communication—including his own—functions inside some sign-covered structure or other: "we cannot do without the

---

[29]Barbara A. Biesecker, "Rethinking the Rhetorical Situation from Within the Thematic of '*Différance*,'" *Philosophy and Rhetoric* 22 (1989): 110-30.

[30]Lloyd Bitzer, "The Rhetorical Situation," *Philosophy and Rhetoric* 1 (1968): 6, 4.

[31]Richard Vatz, "The Myth of the Rhetorical Situation," *Philosophy and Rhetoric* 6 (1973): 154-61.

[32]Kenneth Burke, of course, recognized this complexity decades before Biesecker deconstructed the Bitzer/Vatz binary. Not only did he emphasize "identification" between rhetor and audience, but he also noted that "the same rhetorical act could vary in its effectiveness, according to shifts in the situation or in the attitude of audiences." See Kenneth Burke, *A Rhetoric of Motives* (New York: Prentice-Hall, 1950), p. 62.

concept of the sign, for we cannot give up this metaphysical complicity without also giving up the critique we are directing against this complicity."[33] In other words, we have to use signs to talk about the way signs use us, molding the way we perceive and respond to reality. Furthermore, the signs are held together by structures of belief—"metaphysical complicity"— whether belief in Marxism or Methodism, socialism or capitalism, materialism or supernaturalism, "the rhetorical situation" or a "speaker's intentions."[34]

Deconstruction helps us question why we believe as we do. Take, for example, two equally problematic beliefs:

Liberals are naive.
Conservatives are stupid.

People on opposite sides of the political spectrum will take issue with the absolutism of one or the other of those statements, arguing that it is irresponsible to deride an entire group with the assured word "are." The "to be" verb— known as a "copula" because it couples a subject with a predicate—can be offensive.[35]

Now, let us apply that same principle to the way we talk about religious belief. Many Christians have said (or thought) one of the following:

Protestants are going to hell.
Roman Catholics are going to hell.

What troubles most of us about those statements is the certitude signaled by coupling each of the subjects with a damning predicate. How can the people who make these statements have such assurance? They speak as though they have special access to the mind of God when, in actuality, they are merely reinforcing their house of belief.

Does that mean we should abandon our houses of belief? Not at all! Read on!

DERRIDA'S RESISTANCE TO THE COPULA

In his early work, Jacques Derrida would occasionally put an X (that sign again!) over the copula. By doing so, he challenged its universalizing certi-

---

[33]Derrida, "Structure, Sign and Play," p. 85.

[34]Derrida deconstructs Marxism in *Specters of Marx: The State of Debt, the Work of Mourning and the New International,* trans. Peggy Kamuf (New York: Routledge, 1994).

[35]"To be" is not the only copula; it is simply the one most often used. "Seems" and "become," for example, also couple a subject with a predicate: "He seems tired"; "They become angry."

tude.[36] Let me give an example—if even far beneath Derrida's philosophical sophistication.

If I were to proclaim "killing is wrong," you might respond, "Well, it depends on the context. What about killing in self-defense? What about killing in a just war? What about killing chickens for food? What about killing a black widow spider crawling on a child? What about killing a news story that has proven inaccurate?" Your questions situate the sign /killing/ in different contexts that change its value. You thus demonstrate that my "is," the copula of my sentence, does not capture the complete truth.

In response to your insight, then, I could follow the lead of Derrida (and Heidegger before him) by putting an "X" over a form of the "to be" verb:

Killing ✗ wrong

By doing so, I put my copula "under erasure."[37] In other words, I do not suddenly reverse myself by saying "Killing is not wrong." Instead, I hold on to my belief—killing is wrong—even as I signal, with an X, that changes in context qualify my belief. Putting the copula under erasure is a form of deconstruction because it signals openness to other perceptions of truth.

As mentioned earlier, Derrida's "openness toward the other" led him to qualify his own beliefs, symbolized when he famously averred, "I rightly pass for an atheist."[38] Rather than stating "I *am* an atheist," he avoids the "to be" verb altogether. By using the word "pass" rather than a copula, Derrida implies that signs of atheism in his life are only on the surface. However, at the same time, his word "rightly" implies that signs of atheism may accurately capture his identity. Derrida thus asserts his inclination toward atheism while also putting it under erasure, indicating that he is open to something atheists consider impossible: the existence of God.[39]

---

[36]Following the lead of Heidegger before him, Derrida put the copula under erasure in order to indicate the inability of *any* language to fully capture truth, to deliver a "metaphysics of presence." For an example of "X-ing" out the copula, see *Of Grammatology*, p. 44. Derrida grapples with philosophical implications of the copula in his 1971 essay "The Supplement of Copula: Philosophy before Linguistics," republished in Jacques Derrida, *Margins of Philosophy*, trans. Alan Bass (Chicago: University of Chicago Press, 1982), pp. 175-205.

[37]Derrida, *Of Grammatology*, p. 60.

[38]Jacques Derrida, "Circumfession," in *Jacques Derrida,* ed. Geoffrey Bennington and Jacques Derrida, trans. Geoffrey Bennington (Chicago: University of Chicago Press, 1993), p. 155.

[39]For a helpful discussion of the theological implications of Derrida's "impossible," see Richard Kearney, "Deconstruction, God, and the Possible," in *Derrida and Religion: Other Testaments*, ed. Yvonne Sherwood and Kevin Hart (New York: Routledge, 2005), pp. 297-307.

Inspired by Derrida and Caputo, Christian philosopher Keith Putt states, "I rightly pass for a Christian."[40] By avoiding the "to be" verb, Putt acknowledges his repeated failures to follow the example of his savior. Though people might "rightly" assume he has given his life to Jesus, he knows his heart well enough to realize that at times he only "passes" as a Christian. Such awareness leads to humility, to the acknowledgment that, despite the Spirit of Christ within us, we do not have everything figured out. Though we can have confidence in the gift of salvation, belief that we fully understand the mind of God is another matter. Those who think they know precisely how salvation works are like the people in Genesis 11 who built the Tower of Babel certain that they could reach the heavens. In response, God exercised de-construction, giving them conflicting linguistic signs to prevent them from constructing an impermeable fortress. For only the creator of the universe can use the to-be verb with all-encompassing certitude, as indicated by the self-describing name God delivered from the burning bush: "I am Who I am."

DERRIDA'S (RE)SIGNING: DECONSTRUCTION AS HOSPITALITY

Concerned that people would exercise certitude about the way they understood deconstruction, Jacques Derrida (re)signed it: resigned to the need for deconstruction, he repeatedly created new signs for it. One new sign was the familiar word "hospitality."[41] He recognized that too many people offer hospitality to a stranger only if the stranger already shares their fundamental worldview. Like my allergy-prone family dressing me in their own clothes, such hosts welcome people into their company only if the latter are willing to dress their thoughts and conversation in ways that will not irritate them. But how can this be genuine hospitality? As Derrida puts it, "If I welcome only what I welcome, what I am ready to welcome, and that I recognize in advance because I expect the coming of the [guest] as invited, there is no hospitality."[42] True hospitality occurs when one welcomes in the allergens of society.

---

[40]Keith B. Putt, "Rightly Passing for a Christian: Deconstructing Dogma and Doubt," lecture at Messiah College, October 27, 2009. Caputo proclaimed, "I rightly pass as a Christian," in Robbins, *After the Death of God,* p. 136.

[41]See Jacques Derrida, *Adieu to Emmanuel Levinas,* trans. Pascale-Anne Brault and Michael Naas (Stanford, CA: Stanford University Press, 1999), and *Of Hospitality: Anne Dufourmantelle Invites Jacques Derrida to Respond,* trans. Rachel Bowlby (Stanford, CA: Stanford University Press, 2000).

[42]Derrida, "Hostipitality," trans. Gil Anidjar, in Jacques Derrida, *Acts of Religion,* ed. Gil Anidjar (New York: Routledge, 2002), p. 362. The word I put in brackets is the French *hôte,* which means both guest and host. I will discuss the significance of this word-play later.

Derrida thus echoes the teaching of Jesus: "When you give a luncheon or a dinner, do not invite your friends or your brothers or your relatives or rich neighbors. . . . But when you give a banquet, invite the poor, the crippled, the lame, and the blind" (Lk 14:12-13).

As we have seen, deconstruction exposes inconsistencies in the signs lining our houses of belief. But exposure happens best when an element outside our belief system somehow enters inside—without submitting to our control by donning our clothing of thought. For example, if a secular humanist were to genuinely welcome several evangelical Christians to explain why they act the way they do, she might discover that they are not as intolerant as she assumes; she might discover that what she thought was outside her house of tolerance was actually inside it. Similarly, if an evangelical really listened to secular humanists, she might discover that they are as motivated by compassion for humanity as she is; she would discover that the sign of love she thought unique to her house of belief actually occurs outside of it.

Unfortunately, rather than questioning their own signs of belief, people on both sides of the coin tend to think that the outsider is an exception to the rule, as in "She may be an evangelical Christian, but she is really tolerant"; or "He may be a secular humanist, but he exercises integrity in all he does." Such people thus maintain an allergic response to all outsiders except for this one exception. Doing so, they merely add extra nails to their aluminum signing.

Indeed, it must have distressed Derrida to see how people on the left appropriated deconstruction as a tool with which to promote their own political agendas, deconstructing any position with which they already disagreed. In other words, they encouraged open-minded hospitality while eschewing those who disagreed with their definition of open-mindedness. Postmodern theologian Mark A. Taylor implied as much in his obituary for Derrida: "Betraying Mr. Derrida's insights by creating a culture of political correctness, his self-styled supporters fueled the culture wars that have been raging for more than two decades and continue to frame political debate." In contrast, Derrida worked to expose "the unavoidable limitations and inherent contradictions in the ideas and norms that guide our actions, and do so in a way that keeps them open to constant questioning and continual revision."[43]

---

[43]Mark C. Taylor, "What Derrida Really Meant," *New York Times*, October 14, 2004, A29.

FROM HOSPITALITY TO HOSTIPITALITY

Demonstrating his own openness to continual revision, Derrida coined a new sign—hostipitality—by synthesizing the words "hospitality" and "hostility." Noting that both come from the same root word, the French *hôte*—which can mean *host, guest* or *stranger*—he suggests that authentic hospitality necessitates hostility toward the person or idea one welcomes. Otherwise, acts of hosting are nothing more than exchanges of entertainment among friends.

There is nothing wrong with friendship, of course; the Jewish Derrida went so far as to defend his friendship with literary critic Paul de Man (1919-1983) when it was discovered that the latter had once written anti-Semitic articles for the Nazi-controlled press in Belgium. Derrida's position as a Jew illustrates his point. True hospitality must be hostipitality: opening ourselves to those hostile to us, to those totally foreign to us, both in lifestyle and in thought.[44] Significantly, it later came to light that de Man hid a Jewish couple in his Belgian apartment for several days, thus exercising hostipitality toward an ethnicity he had slurred.[45]

Christians should take heed, having been instructed to "extend hospitality to *strangers*" (Rom 12:13). In other words, once we have deconstructed the aluminum in our houses of belief, enabling us to focus on those outside, hostipitality requires us to invite them inside—without dressing them in the clothing of our own thoughts. This means we attempt to understand their radically different beliefs, their radically different practices and especially their radical hostility toward Christianity.

Take, for example, Bruxy Cavey, teaching pastor of The Meeting House, a collection of Brethren in Christ congregations in the greater Toronto area. Though believing that the Bible prohibits homosexual practices he welcomes into his church openly gay and lesbian seekers. By doing so, he maintains his beliefs: not only about homosexuality but also about the all-encompassing love of God.[46] His actions signal radical trust that God will make the truth known to those who seek it. But for this truth to be true, it must apply to seekers on either side of the coin. Those on one side who condemn all signs

[44]Jacques Derrida, "Like the Sound of the Sea Deep within a Shell: Paul de Man's War," *Critical Inquiry* 14 (1988): 590-652.

[45]Shoshana Felman, "Paul de Man's Silence," *Critical Inquiry* 15 (1989): 704-44.

[46]Bruxy Cavey, chapel talks at Messiah College, Grantham, PA, March 2007. Cavey's teachings and sermons can be accessed at www.themeetinghouse.ca/themeetinghouse/myweb.php?hls +10061.

of homosexuality must be *open* to a change of heart—as must those on the other side who denounce as "homophobic" anyone who questions gay marriage. Notice that my emphasis—like that of Derrida—is on *openness*. Both sides can get so caught up in justifying their positions from Scripture that they close themselves off from God's leading.[47]

For an even more radical example, consider Brad Pellish, an evangelical pastor in Arizona. When he learned in 2007 of global sex trafficking and then about child prostitution in his hometown of Phoenix, he felt led to energize his congregation to reach out to prostitutes and exotic dancers. While two years previously members of his congregation would never have dreamed of worshiping side by side with prostitutes, Pellish reports that now "we've got people in the church from the commercial sex industry and they feel comfortable here because they are loved."[48] Resigned to the example of Jesus, who extended hostipitality to publicans and sinners, Pellish has re-signed his evangelical church.

THE (IM)POSSIBILITY OF HOSPITALITY

In his collection of lectures titled "Hostipitality," Derrida describes "hospitality as the possibility of impossibility (to receive another guest whom I am incapable of welcoming, to become capable of that which I am incapable of)—this is the exemplary experience of deconstruction itself, when it is or does what it has to do or to be, that is, the experience of the impossible. Hospitality—this is a name or an example of deconstruction."[49]

So why does he say hospitality is "impossible"? Doesn't that undermine everything I've been talking about for the last several pages? My answer is that the impossibility of hospitality makes this discussion all the more important to Christians. For Derrida also describes God as impossible.[50]

God is "impossible" for Derrida because as soon as people use a name—/God/ or /Allah/ or /Yahweh/ or /Jehovah/—the worshiped One becomes

---

[47]To understand how Christians might (re)sign their rhetoric about homosexuality, see Jenell Williams Paris, *The End of Sexual Identity: Why Sex Is Too Important to Define Who We Are* (Downers Grove, IL: IVP Books, 2011).

[48]Brad Pellish, quoted in Amy L. Sherman, "The Church on a Justice Mission," *Books and Culture,* July/August 2010, p. 27.

[49]Derrida, "Hostipitality," p. 364.

[50]Derrida explored the possibility of the impossible in *Politics of Friendship* (New York: Verso, 1997), and "Comme si c'etait possible, 'Within Such Limits' . . . ," *Revue Internationale de Philosophie* 3, no. 205 (1998): 497-529.

limited to the signs people employ in their houses of faith, bringing God down to the level of their finite understanding. But the Creator of the universe transcends all human signs. The Creator cannot be contained by our constructions, no matter how much aluminum we put up.

Derrida, then, says the same thing about hospitality: it cannot be contained by the signs and conventions—or even logic—of society. Completely pure hospitality gives up everything for the guest, but once it does so, there is nothing left to give, making future hospitality *impossible*. Furthermore, if guests have free reign over a host who exercises no control over them, how can we consider the host hospitable? Rather than hospitality, it's more like a hostile take-over on the part of the guests.

A hostile take-over, in fact, is what worries many Christians. If we open our houses of belief to any outsider—whether a person or an idea—what is to prevent the outsider from taking control of our beliefs and changing them so radically that the house no longer looks like Christianity? Such fears are so fully legitimate that they motivated me to write this book. Troubled by the way some Christians uncritically advocate any form of re-signing, I wanted to figure out how semiotics might help me develop a rhetorically sophisticated, persuasive argument about what believers should resign themselves to as unquestionably essential to Christian faith. By the end of the book I present my conclusions, acknowledging that I rightly pass for a Christian apologist. In preparation for my edgy answer, however, we need to continue exploring the all-too-common fall of the coin onto one side of the issue or the other.

ONE SIDE OF THE COIN: HOSTILITY TO CHANGE

In their book *Pagan Christianity? Exploring the Roots of Our Church Practices*, Frank Viola and George Barna demonstrate how signs of Roman times entered the structure of Christianity. Before the fourth century, for example, Christians met in private homes or "commercial buildings modified for church use."[51] The word "church" (Greek *ekklesia*) literally referred to a "gathering" of people rather than to a specific building. "To the ears of a first-century Christian," as Viola and Barna put it, "calling an *ekklesia* a building would have been like calling your wife a condominium or your mother a

---

[51]Everett Ferguson, *Early Christians Speak: Faith and Life in the First Three Centuries*, 3rd ed. (Abilene, TX: Abilene Christian University Press, 1999), p. 74.

skyscraper!"[52] Hence, in their perspective, the Emperor Constantine sullied New Testament Christianity in the fourth century by building basilicas for worship that followed the design of sanctuaries for pagan deities.[53]

Viola and Barna feel especially hostile about pagan *practices* Constantine introduced to the church. Just as Roman emperors were preceded by lights and aromatic spices when they appeared in public, so Christian clergy, attired like Roman officials, were preceded with candles and incense as they entered their sanctuaries. Even church choirs arose from pagan allergens, for they reflected "Constantine's desire to mimic the professional music used in Roman imperial ceremonies."[54]

Any Christian who finds that majestic choir performances, beautiful church architecture, dignified clerical vestments, or candle-lit processions aid in their worship of God should take pause. Signs of pagan culture might enrich one's walk with Jesus Christ—as happened in churches across America when drums and electric guitars (allergens to traditionalists) entered houses of Christian faith. Openness to signs of the times—hostipitality—might turn hostility into grace.

Christians who fear hostipitality seem to demonstrate one of two things:

1. rickety walls of faith, generating worry lest a strange person or idea might cave them in

2. idolatry of aluminum-lined beliefs, as though God depended upon our signs as props

Dorothy L. Sayers alludes to such problems in a letter to a friend. She compares a Christian who thinks her house of faith "will fall to pieces if [an interviewer] starts asking questions" to an old-fashioned grandmother trying to protect God: "I see [the grandmama], deeply reverent in black bombazine, standing protectively between the pushing interviewer and the frail and aged figure of God in a bath-chair, [saying], 'Now, don't you speak rough to Him—He's very old and shaky, and I wouldn't answer for the consequences.'"[55]

[52]Frank Viola and George Barna, *Pagan Christianity? Exploring the Roots of Our Church Practices* (Carol Stream, IL: Tyndale House, 2008), p. 11.
[53]Other churches were modeled after pagan halls constructed for business and legal activities. See Gregory Dix, *The Shape of the Liturgy* (London: Continuum International, 2000), p. 26.
[54]Viola and Barna, *Pagan Christianity?* pp. 24-25, 274.
[55]*The Letters of Dorothy L. Sayers: 1937 to 1943, From Novelist to Playwright,* ed. Barbara Reynolds (New York: St. Martin's Press, 1997), p. 380.

Sayers, of course, means to assert the opposite: that Almighty God cannot be dethroned through challenges to our faith.

THE OTHER SIDE OF THE COIN: HOSTILITY TO TRADITION

All too often challenges to our faith reflect simplistic premises. Some people who use the language of "deconstruction" and "hospitality" act as though we must suppress all our own beliefs if we want to exercise Derrida's "openness to the other." But hospitality doesn't make much sense without an identifiable home: a house of faith to which we welcome strangers—not in spite of the fact but *because* they might help us deconstruct (not destroy!) its walls. As Derrida notes, "Hospitality is the deconstruction of *the at-home;* deconstruction is hospitality to the other, to the other than oneself." His point is summarized by Caputo: "To be as welcoming as possible to the other while not surrendering the mastery of one's house."[56]

Without an identifiable *at-home,* or house, conversing with the stranger is neither hospitality nor hostipitality; it is only mingling. Derrida implies as much in *Of Grammatology:* "The movements of deconstruction do not destroy structures from the outside. They are not possible and effective, nor can they take accurate aim, except by inhabiting those structures. Inhabiting them *in a certain way,* because one always inhabits, and all the more so when one does not suspect it."[57] This final sentence applies to people on both sides of the coin. A progressive humanist who thinks she has escaped the closed-minded constraints of religious belief "does not suspect" that she also "inhabits" a "structure" of perception: a house of humanist belief in and through which she interprets the world. Her lack of suspicion imprisons her all the more to the construction. Believing that she is totally "objective" about reality (in contrast to those she considers "superstitious religious people"), she makes no effort to understand what is outside her worldview.

In contrast, traditionalists who have self-consciously moved into a particular belief system often fail to inhabit it "in a certain way." That "certain way" is the way of hostipitality, of openness to the stranger. This refers not only to strange persons but also strange ideas, especially when they seem impossible to believe. Indeed, an idea is not entirely "other" to us unless we first consider it "impossible" or unthinkable.

---

[56]Derrida, "Hostipitality," p. 364., emphasis mine. Caputo, *Prayers and Tears,* p. 355n.2.
[57]Derrida, *Of Grammatology,* p. 24, his emphasis.

Consider, for example, the "impossible" idea that Jesus communicates to Nicodemus: "Very truly, I tell you, no one can see the kingdom of God without being born from above." Indeed, Nicodemus responds as though the concept were unthinkable: "How can anyone be born after having grown old?" (Jn 3:3, 4). Jesus then proceeds to undermine Nicodemus's hostility to the idea by explaining his strange new sign.[58]

MESSIANIC HOSTIPITALITY

Jesus exercised hostipitality repeatedly, demonstrating the tripartite definition of *hôte: host, guest* and *stranger*. Luke's Gospel seems especially attentive to the issue of hospitality, recounting ten different meals in which Jesus functions as *hôte*. Especially complex is the incident described in Luke 7:36-50, when Jesus was invited for dinner with a Pharisee named Simon. In the course of the meal, a strange woman entered the house, and Jesus welcomed her as though he were in the position of host rather than guest. When the woman kissed Christ's feet after bathing them with her tears, Simon felt hostility toward the stranger, regarding her as an allergen: "If this man were a prophet, he would have known who and what kind of woman this is who is touching him—that she is a sinner." As though reading the Pharisee's mind, Jesus did two things: first he deconstructed the Pharisee's *hostility*, then he deconstructed the Pharisee's *hospitality*.

Jesus challenged the Pharisee's hostility by telling a story about the forgiveness of debts, getting Simon to admit that "the one for whom [a creditor] canceled the greater debt" will love the creditor more. Then Jesus pointed out that the reviled stranger was more hospitable than the religious host, telling Simon,

> I entered your house; you gave me no water for my feet, but she has bathed my feet with her tears and dried them with her hair. You gave me no kiss, but from the time I came in she has not stopped kissing my feet. You did not anoint my head with oil, but she has anointed my feet with ointment. (Lk 7:44-46)

As Ron Hansen notes, kissing a guest and bathing his feet were "Jewish

---

[58]My thanks to Alyssa Lord for suggesting the example of Nicodemus. I discuss the "born again" sign more thoroughly in my conclusion.

customs associated with the gracious hosting of a meal."[59] The Bible text implies as much by reiterating Simon's status as host: "One of the Pharisees *asked Jesus to eat with him*. . . . [Jesus] was *eating in the Pharisee's house*. . . . Now when the Pharisee *who had invited him* saw it" (Lk 7:36, 37, 39). By praising the stranger as more hospitable than the host, Jesus exposes inconsistency in the Pharisee's structure of hospitality. Doing so, he takes apart (deconstructs) the binaries under which Simon operated:

Pharisee	Host	Creditor	Friend	Hospitality
Prostitute	Guest	Debtor	Stranger	Hostility

In sum, Jesus challenges the terms by which hospitality is understood: the guest (Jesus) plays host to the stranger; Christ's guest, the stranger, acts more host-like than the hostile host of the dinner.

While Christians who consider themselves "progressives" might rightly welcome this story as justification for necessary changes in Christian practices, they must also grapple with the other side of the coin. For immediately after Jesus deconstructs Simon's structure of belief, he identifies himself with God: "Then he said to [the stranger], 'Your sins are forgiven'" (Lk 7:48). This is one of the few places in the Synoptic Gospels where Jesus could be interpreted as unambiguously proclaiming his divinity.[60] While "Son of God" and "Son of Man" had multiple meanings in Christ's day, the forgiveness of sins was regarded by Jews as a prerogative only God could exercise (Mk 2:5-7). Hence, the divinity of Christ—an idea toward which many progressives feel hostile—has entered the story. Rather than exercise hostipitality, many progressives nail up extra aluminum—signs of Enlightenment rationalism—to keep the allergen of supernaturalism outside of their houses of belief.

We can't denounce their closed-mindedness too harshly, however, for Christ's disciples did the same thing.

HOSTIPITALITY TO THE RESURRECTION

According to Luke, Christ's disciples originally considered the resurrection, as reported by females (considered entirely *other* in first-century Jewish

---

[59]Ron Hansen, *A Stay Against Confusion: Essays on Faith and Fiction* (New York: Perennial, 2002), p. 242.

[60]John's Gospel suggests Christ's divinity more adamantly than do the Synoptic Gospels. See, for example, Jn 2:19 and Jn 8:58, as well the "I am" statements in the tenth chapter.

culture) to be impossible: "But these words seemed to them an idle tale, and they did not believe them" (Lk 24:11). Peter, apparently more "open to the other" than his companions, ran to the tomb to verify the unthinkable witness of women (Lk 24:12). Matthew informs us that "some doubted" even after *seeing* the resurrected Jesus in the flesh, presumably regarding it as impossible (Mt 28:17).

Eventually convinced of this "impossible," Peter later encountered another: the unthinkable idea that Gentiles could join Jews in worshiping the impossibly risen Christ. After receiving a vision from God, Peter finally admitted to Gentiles from Joppa, "You yourselves know that it is unlawful for a Jew to associate with or to visit a Gentile; but God has shown me that I should not call anyone profane or unclean" (Acts 10:28). Peter thus exercised hostipitality, willing to worship the Messiah even with those toward whom he was trained to feel hostile.

DERRIDA'S MESSIANIC IMPOSSIBLE: THE EVENT

Significantly, Derrida discusses the Messiah in "Hostipitality": "To wait without waiting, awaiting absolute surprise, the unexpected visitor, awaited without a horizon of expectation: this is indeed about the Messiah as *hôte*, about the messianic as hospitality, the messianic that introduces deconstructive disruption or madness in the concept of hospitality, the madness of hospitality, even the madness of the concept of hospitality."[61]

The *messianic*, for Derrida, refers to an entirely unanticipated "Event," comparable to a revelation of God. For him, a true "Event" totally exceeds any extant religious sign-system, what he calls a "*messianism*," to predict or describe it. This certainly explains what happened in first-century Palestine. Jesus was an "Event" that did not accord with the signs of Messiah as contemporary Jewish scholars (scribes and Pharisees) and political activists (Zealots) understood them (see chapter two). By exceeding the messianism of his day, Jesus made traditionalists mad. Rather than exercise hostipitality, people in power resisted him as an allergen that must be evicted from their house of belief. Nevertheless, without abandoning the house of Judaism, Jesus kept pulling down its aluminum signing in order to open it to a new vision of the Messiah. But the hostility generated by his

---

[61]Derrida, "Hostipitality," p. 362.

new signs—like healing on the sabbath—led to his death.

Through his death, however, Jesus offered the ultimate hostipitality: opening a way for sinful humanity to reconcile with that which is inherently hostile to sin—the absolute goodness of God. Nevertheless, even after the resurrection Jesus repeatedly presented himself as a guest rather than a host. Talking to men on the Emmaus road who apparently regarded resurrection as impossible, the unrecognized Jesus acted in a way that *put the responsibility of hospitality on them:* "As they came near the village to which they were going, he walked ahead as if he were going on. But they urged him strongly, saying, 'Stay with us, because it is almost evening and the day is now nearly over.' So he went in to stay with them" and sat "at the table with them" (Lk 24:28-30). Their sudden recognition of Jesus, when he blessed and broke bread, harmonizes with *Event* as Caputo describes it: "the time of the surprise, a time in which one is struck by the amazing changes that take place before one's eyes or in one's own heart." Caputo goes on: "It is not a time that rides smoothly along the grooves of the potential and the possible, but one that is continually disturbed by the shock of the impossible."[62]

JESUS AS IMPOSSIBLE *HÔTE*

Soon after the Emmaus road Event, Jesus exceeded all expectation by suddenly appearing among his disciples, who "thought that they were seeing a ghost." Rather than outlining the theological significance of this Event, Jesus requested what is usually considered the traditional sign of hospitality: "'*Have you anything here to eat?*' They gave him a piece of broiled fish, and he took it and ate in their presence" (Lk 24:36-43). Only then did Jesus explain how his impossible resurrection fulfilled Hebrew Scripture.

Christ's actions are echoed in the book of Revelation: "Listen! I am standing at the door, knocking; if you hear my voice and open the door, I will come in to you and eat with you, and you with me" (Rev 3:20). By saying "come in to you and eat with you," the speaker identifies himself as guest. But then he follows with a grammatical reversal, "and you with me," putting himself in the role of host. In other words, Jesus invites us to invite him into our hearts, thus deconstructing the binary opposition between host and guest.

---

[62]John D. Caputo, *The Weakness of God: A Theology of the Event* (Bloomington: Indiana University Press, 2006), p. 150.

By fulfilling the opposite definitions of *hôte*—both inviting host and invited guest—Jesus (re)signed truth, opening up salvation beyond the "messianism" of his day. The Roman Church celebrates this Event by lifting the *Host*—a sign of Christ's flesh—during Eucharist. Significantly, the word *host* to describe the Eucharistic wafer comes from the Latin *hostia,* meaning "an expiatory victim offered to the gods, a sacrifice." Jesus, in other words, made salvation possible by taking on himself the multiple signs of Host: generating *host*ility he was taken *host*age and sacrificed *(hostia)*; though crucified as an enemy *(hostis),* Jesus became the host *(hospes)* of salvation, inviting each one of us to be a guest *(hospes)* at his table, where he is lifted up as Host *(hostia).* And we will continue to ingest the sign until Jesus returns as Lord of Hosts *(hostis).*[63]

CHRISTIAN HOSTIPITALITY: LOUIS MASSIGNON

Though welcoming the messianic, Derrida did not consider himself a Christian.[64] Nevertheless, his openness to what he called "*the* Impossible" made Derrida value openness in ardent Christians like Augustine (354-430), Kierkegaard (1813-1855) and, as discussed in his essay "Hostipitality," Louis Massignon (1883-1962).[65]

France's "greatest authority on Islam and Islamic society," Massignon converted to Christianity when he had an overwhelming experience of God's "mad" hospitality: what he called the "visitation of a Stranger."[66] In "Hostipitality" Derrida quotes Massignon's definition of hospitality, "the sweetest Christian duty," as "welcoming the other, the stranger, the neighbor who is closer than all our close ones, without reserve nor calculation, whatever it cost and at any price."[67] And Massignon means "at any price"—willing to sacrifice his life to save others.

---

[63]In the medieval era, *hostis* acquired the sense of "army" (because armies attack enemies) and from that came the idea of "multitude," as in Lord of Hosts. For all these etymologies, see Eric Partridge, *Origins: A Short Etymological Dictionary of Modern English* (New York: Greenwich, 1983), pp. 296-97.

[64]As Richard Kearney notes, "Derrida refrains from responding one way or another to any particular God-claim." See "Deconstruction, God, and the Possible," p. 304.

[65]For discussion of Augustine, see "Circumfession"; for discussion of Kierkegaard, see Jacques Derrida, *The Gift of Death,* trans. David Wills (Chicago: University of Chicago Press, 1995).

[66]Cleo McNelly Kearns, "Mary, Maternity, and Abrahamic Hospitality in Derrida's Reading of Massignon," in *Derrida and Religion: Other Testaments,* ed. Yvonne Sherwood and Kevin Hart (New York: Routledge, 2005), p. 81; Mary Louise Gude, *Louis Massignon: The Crucible of Compassion* (Notre Dame, IN: Notre Dame University Press, 1996), pp. 39-46.

[67]Quoted in Derrida, "Hostipitality," p. 371.

Massignon felt overwhelming love for Muslims, so much so that he didn't want to force them into belief. As he writes in *L'hospitalité sacrée [Sacred Hospitality]*, "The 'conversion' of these souls, yes, it is the goal, but it is for them to find themselves, without their suffering our insistence as an external pressure. It must be the secret birth of a love, shared Love." Massignon goes on to explain that love becomes Christlike when one offers to God the substitution of oneself for non-Christian others: "It is with this vocation for their salvation that we must and wish to sanctify ourselves, aspiring to become additional Christs (like living Gospels), so that they recognize Him through us, and that we safeguard, with this silent and obscure apostleship, the sincerity of our own donation."[68] Massignon's hospitality is thus messianic, trusting that God will do a work far exceeding not only his control but also his limited understanding of how salvation works.

Deconstruction, hostipitality, openness to the other, acknowledging the possibility of the impossible: none are easy to practice. I am reminded of the shock I felt when my earnestly evangelical father admitted that, had he lived in first-century Palestine, he would probably have responded to Jesus more like the Pharisees than the disciples. He thus humbly recognized a psychological need to protect his house of faith (his messianism) from messianic signs that might destabilize it. By identifying himself with those toward whom Christians throughout the centuries have viewed with hostility—Pharisees—my father exercised a form of hostipitality.

SIGNS OF THE END

My father's humble admission illustrates the attraction of aluminum-lined fortresses. Most of us like things to be predictable, tempting us to stuff the radical call of Christ into a religious structure where we can nail down the signs with certitude. This explains why some Christians get caught up in signs about the "end times," trying to figure out when and how the Messiah will come again. Not wanting anything—including the "second coming"—to disrupt their tidy house of signs, they limit the Messiah to the structure of their messianism. But Jesus, who incarnated the messianic, warned that "about that day and hour no one knows, neither the angels of heaven, nor the Son, but only the Father" (Mt 24:36). In other words, we should regard the

---

[68]Ibid., pp. 376n.36, 377.

second coming as *the* Impossible. Thomas A. Carlson explains, "*The* impossible in Derrida (the naming of God, death, justice, the coming of the Messiah, etc.) maintains the irreducible openness of futurity; it always remains to come, and hence remains, in its 'not yet,' always possible."[69]

I suspect that when we finally enter the presence of God (at an end time and in an ending manner that far exceeds our current understanding) we will be shocked by the inadequacy of the signs we have employed in our faith. This is certainly Christ's point as he illustrates the future time "when the Son of Man comes in his glory":

> Then the king will say to those at his right hand, "Come, you that are blessed by my Father, inherit the kingdom prepared for you from the foundation of the world; for I was hungry and you gave me food, I was thirsty and you gave me something to drink, I was a stranger and you welcomed me." (Mt 25:31, 34-35)

Notice that signs of inheriting the kingdom all have to do with hospitality. As on the Emmaus road, welcoming the risen Christ is about welcoming the stranger.

And we will probably encounter even stranger signs at the final Emmaus supper. The redemptive work of Christ may open so many doors that we discover it to be far more welcoming than we ever dreamed possible; salvation, itself, may be the ultimate work of hostipitality! Rather than pharisaically fearing such (im)possible signs, we are called to open ourselves, like Christ's disciples, to *the* Impossible. Then and only then might we discover the second coming of the Messiah to be as messianic as the first.

Until that Event, we need guidelines about exercising hostipitality, keeping us from falling down onto one side of the coin or the other: the problematic binary between hostility to change and hostility to tradition. Fortunately, Christians have been given a book of signs, the Bible, that calls us to stand on the edge, open to the most radical of all Events: God walking among and working within us. That very same book nevertheless indicates that the call exceeds the signs of Scripture, charging us to yield in such a way that (re) signing is inevitable. For not only do we yield—resign ourselves—to the Divine Word revealed in and beyond human words, but in that resignation we yield up signs that blind us to the (Im)possible Other who makes all

---

[69]Thomas A. Carlson, "Postmetaphysical Theology," in *The Cambridge Companion to Postmodern Theology*, ed. Kevin J. Vanhoozer (Cambridge: Cambridge University Press, 2003), p. 58.

things new (2 Cor 5:17). Such yielding prepares us for the next chapter, which introduces a semiotician who establishes "openness to the other" as fundamental to the very way signs work.

7

A PLACE FOR THE COIN

Charles Sanders Peirce

In his sign-shattering book *Of Grammatology*, Jacques Derrida introduces Charles Sanders Peirce (pronounced "purse") while discussing Saussure. In little more than two pages, Derrida presents Peirce's view of the sign, stating that "Peirce goes very far in the direction that I have called . . . deconstruction."[1] He touches only briefly on the rich insight of Peirce, however, in order to better focus on the bankruptcy of Saussure. I, in contrast, want us to invest in Peirce, believing that his intellectual deposits can generate significant interest—especially for Christians on the edge.

THE PURSE OF C. S. PEIRCE: EXTRACTING THE SEMIOTIC COIN

A chemist, mathematician and logician, C. S. Peirce earned the admiration of philosophers like William James, Alfred North Whitehead, Karl Popper and John Dewey—despite the fact he had trouble with his purse, often having to accept charity from friends and colleagues. After his dismissal from a lectureship at the Johns Hopkins University,[2] Peirce focused on writing, composing his fascinating (and often opaque) treatises with "Peirce-istence" and "Peirce-everence" (the puns, for once, are his). Unfortunately, Peirce can be

---

[1]Jacques Derrida, *Of Grammatology*, trans. Gayatri Chakravorty Spivak (Baltimore: Johns Hopkins University Press, 1967), p. 49.

[2]The dismissal was based on "unspecified moral grounds." Many scholars cite the fact that, after his wife left him, Peirce lived with another woman for awhile before he married her, angering the administration at Johns Hopkins. (How signs of the times have changed!) Some biographers imply that Peirce's money mismanagement and truculence—attributable to bipolar disorder—made him a pariah in the academy. See Joseph Brent, *Charles Sanders Peirce: A Life*, rev. ed. (Bloomington: Indiana University Press, 1998), pp. 9-11, 20.

hard to understand: a problem he himself recognized, calling his work "a very snarl of twine."[3] The snarl—approximately 1,650 unpublished manuscripts totaling over 100,000 pages of writing—ended up at Harvard University, where Peirce had been a student.[4] In these numerous manuscripts, along with more than 10,000 pages of published material, Peirce developed his "semeiotic," later dropping the second "e" to create the word *semiotic*. This chapter will extract a valuable coin from the snarl of twine clogging the semiotic Peirce, suggesting how we might invest that coin in the (re)signing of truth.

Peirce's triadic sign. While Saussure's dyadic sign engaged only the signifier (the sound-image) and its signified (the thought-image connected to the signifier), Peirce considered the objects that signs refer to. However, as he puts it, any "sign has *two Objects*, its object as it is represented and its object in itself."[5] The object as it is represented he calls the "representamen." How do these two objects differ? Peirce answers this question with "the interpretant": a person's mental apprehension of the object.[6]

Think, for example, of a burqa-clad woman in an airport. She functions as a sign as soon as she stands out in your mind from all the other bodies swarming the corridors. Obviously, she exists whether you notice her or not; but as soon as she registers on your brain due to her distinctive clothing she becomes a representamen. A representamen of what? That depends on your interpretant, which may differ from the interpretant of another person who notices her in the airport causeway. For some she simply signals strict adherence to Islam, while for others she might represent the threat of terrorism. Indeed, after 9/11/01, the interpretants for many Americans changed. Before the terrorist attacks on that fateful day, people unaware of Taliban expecta-

---

[3]Charles Lock, "Peirce Unbound," *The Semiotic Review of Books* 4 (1993), on SRB archives at www .univie.ac.at/wissenschaftstheorie/srb/srb/unbound.html.

[4]One Peirce scholar estimated that to publish all of Peirce's works would necessitate 104 volumes containing 500 pages each. Edward C. Moore, "Preface," to *Writings of Charles S. Peirce: A Chronological Edition*, ed. M Fisch et al. (Bloomington: Indiana University Press, 1982), 1:xi.

[5]Quoted in C. K. Ogden and I. A. Richards, *The Meaning of Meaning: A Study of the Influence of Language upon Thought and of the Science of Symbolism* (New York: Harcourt, Brace & World), p. 282.

[6]C. S. Peirce, "Logic as Semiotic: The Theory of Signs," in *Philosophical Writings of Peirce*, ed. Justus Buchler (New York: Dover, 1955), p. 99. For the most part, titles of essays in *Philosophical Writings* are those of Buchler, who synthesized selections from both published and unpublished writings that had a similar focus. Derrida cites Buchler's edition. In some of his writings, Peirce substitutes the word "sign" for "representamen," which can cause confusion. I therefore stick to "representamen" throughout my discussion.

tions for women may have seen a burqa as signaling an enticingly exotic culture. When the post-9/11 media made practices of the Taliban better known, people unfamiliar with the diversity within Islam came to view burqas negatively.

To diagram Peirce's view of the sign, scholars sometimes draw triangles to communicate the interdependence of all three elements: the object, the representamen and the interpretant.[7] Just as a triangle necessitates three lines, so Peirce's understanding of the sign necessitates all three elements, each in mutual support of the other (see fig. 7.1).

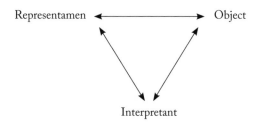

Figure 7.1. Peirce's understanding of the sign

The triangle works this way: you see any *object* as a sign (representamen) that makes sense in your mind (the interpretant). If you are still confused, think of a lion in a zoo. Obviously, it is an object. But the very fact that it is in a zoo means that it is a sign of something; if not, why put it in a zoo? As a representamen, then, it is seen differently by different interpretants. Some see the lion as an awe-inspiring image of dignified power; some see it as a potentially cuddly, if dauntingly huge, cat; some see it as a terrifyingly vicious predator. That does not mean each person *chooses to interpret* the lion differently. Instead each actually *sees* the representamen differently. Peirce's interpretant, then, does not mean "interpretation" or "interpreter." It refers to a sign generated in the mind of the listener/reader/viewer that connects a representamen (sign of the lion) to the object (lion) being represented. It is in this

---

[7]See, for example, Ogden and Richards, *Meaning of Meaning,* pp. 5-6; Umberto Eco, *A Theory of Semiotics* (Bloomington: Indiana University Press, 1979), pp. 59-60; Paul Cobley and Litza Jansz, *Introducing Semiotics,* ed. Richard Appignanesi (Duxford, UK: Icon, 1999), pp. 21, 25; John K. Sheriff, *Charles Peirce's Guess at the Riddle: Grounds for Human Significance* (Bloomington: Indiana University Press, 1994), pp. 34-36; Daniel Chandler, *Semiotics: The Basics* (New York: Routledge, 2002), p. 34; and John Deely, *Basics of Semiotics* (Bloomington: Indiana University Press, 1990), pp. 88-90.

way that "the other" is part of the sign itself, for every interpretant is "other" to the *object* being perceived. Peirce thus establishes what he calls the "triadic relation" of the sign.[8]

Furthermore, because *interpretants* are themselves signs, if even in people's minds, they are triadic as well. Think, again, of the burqa-clad woman. One interpretant regarded her to be an object (Muslim woman) representing "strict adherence" to her faith. But the interpretant "strict adherence" becomes a representamen that generates different interpretants: some read the woman's "strict adherence" to Muslim expectations as indicative of female oppression, others as symbolic of feminist choice.[9] It might be diagrammed as in figure 7.2.

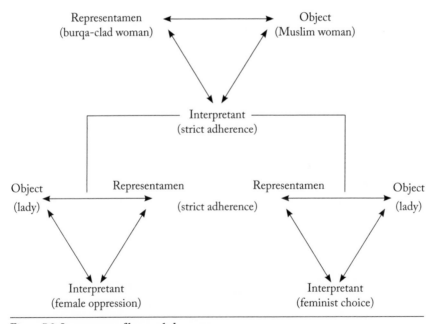

Figure 7.2. Interpretant of burqa-clad woman

These last two *interpretants* will themselves generate new signs in the mind, and so on. Peirce calls this development of thought "semiosis," a word

---

[8]Peirce, "Logic as Semiotic," p. 100.
[9]Phyllis Chester, "The Burqa: Ultimate Feminist Choice? Naomi Wolf Discovers That Shrouds Are Sexy," *Islamist Watch*, August 31, 2009, www.islamist-watch.org.

he coined from the Greek terms for "sign" and "process" *(OED)*.[10]

In sum, while Saussure focuses on a synchronic *system* (the cupboard) from which differences in signifiers generate value at any one time, Peirce emphasizes the diachronic *process* by which signs generate new signs through their triadic relations. This difference impacts the communication of Christian truth in multiple ways, as will be demonstrated in the remainder of this book. To prepare for this impact, however, we need to continue untangling Peirce's snarl of twine in order to get a firm grip on the coin in his purse.

COLLATERAL EXPERIENCE

How we understand a sign is affected by what Peirce calls "collateral experience": a "previous acquaintance with what the sign denotes."[11] For example, if I were to say to an audience, "Saul was opposed to God's purposes," different people would come up with different mental signs (interpretants) for Saul. Someone not familiar with the Bible would probably wonder, "Saul who?" Jews in the audience would most likely think of the King of Israel who tried to kill David. Many Christians might think the same, until I went on to say, "On the road to Damascus, however . . ." At that point, their interpretants—the signs in their minds—would change, even before I finished my sentence. My new sign—"road to Damascus"—suddenly qualifies "Saul." In other words, different communities—Jews, Christians, secularists— have different grounds for understanding (or not understanding) the reference to "Saul." In fact, as we shall see, the idea of "community" is very important to Peirce. A structuralist, in contrast, would explain the difference according to differing systems/structures of truth: the ingredients in

---

[10]Peirce believes that, as a result of semiosis, which he aligns with logical thinking, all of humanity will perceive truth similarly in the far-distant future. But, until then, interpretants reflect their contexts. As one Peirce scholar summarizes, "truth is in the future, but in our consciousness we cannot help but consent to what we perceive to be the case within the particular contexts and language games within which we live." John K. Sheriff *The Fate of Meaning: Charles Peirce, Structuralism, and Literature* (Princeton, NJ: Princeton University Press, 1989), p. 60.

[11]Peirce scholars tend not to discuss "collateral experience," a phrase (along with "collateral observation" and "collateral acquaintance") that is mentioned only several times in Peirce's papers (The *Collected Papers of Charles Sanders Peirce*, vols. 1-6, ed. Charles Hartshorne and Paul Weiss; vols. 7-8, ed. Arthur W. Burkes [Cambridge, MA: Harvard University Press, 1931-1958]). Since it is a very helpful concept for the (re)signing of truth, I have appropriated it. Henceforth I will exercise the common practice of citing Peirce's papers as *CP*, followed by volume and paragraph numbers. In this case, I have quoted from *CP* 8.179. Peirce also refers to collateral experience, observation or acquaintance in *CP* 6.338, 8.178, 8.183, and 8.314.

a Christian cupboard lead to a different recipe for "Saul" than do the ingredients located in a Jewish cupboard. Peirce might respond by asking, "What do we do with the fact that many times people functioning according to the same 'conditions of possibility' generated by a particular *langue* (cupboard) often see the same sign differently?"

He would answer with "collateral experience." For example, when my nine-year-old nephew was told that I had flown to England to receive a "thousand pound" award for my first book, he responded with, "How is she going to carry a thousand pounds onto the plane?" His collateral experience had not yet exposed him to signs for British money: pounds and pence rather than dollars and cents. Therefore his interpretant—the sign in his mind—generated for him the image of multiple wheelbarrows full of heavy coin following me down the jet-way. Ironically, of course, my nephew was more etymologically astute than he realized. The British pound reflects a millennium-old system in which a pound of silver had purchasing power. The impracticality of carrying around many pounds of silver and gold coins led to the invention of signs for the pound: printed bills standing for the heavier silver they represent.[12]

HABITS OF PERCEPTION: CULTURAL DIFFERENCES

As demonstrated by a child's understanding of /pounds/, collateral experience affects interpretants: the signs in our minds. This doesn't mean that anyone can read whatever they want into any sign they see.[13] It's not a matter of choice; it's an issue of the experience—or lack thereof—that has molded our interpretants. This is why we need education: to give us knowledge—whether about the Bible or the British monetary system—that adds sophistication to our interpretants, and hence, in Peirce's mind, gets us closer to the truth. Nevertheless, different cultures educate their citizens differently, creating different "habits" of perception.

By "habit," Peirce doesn't mean annoying practices, like biting one's fingernails. Nor does he mean individualistic routines, like flossing every night while watching re-runs of *Lost*. A "habit" for Peirce is an ingrained way of

---

[12]The *OED* notes that the earliest recorded use of /pound/ for a monetary unit is from a 975 C.E. translation of Matthew's Gospel. See Mt 18:24, where /pund/ is employed in the tenth-century document rather than /talents/.

[13]The semiotician Umberto Eco wrote a whole book to make this point, calling it *The Limits of Interpretation* (Bloomington: Indiana University Press, 1990).

interpreting signs *that is shared by an entire community*, "independent of the vagaries of me and you."[14] Communities shape our interpretants.

"Habits" of seeing—and hence of communicating—can be illustrated linguistically. For example, during my first trip to England as an adolescent, I stopped an elderly woman at a village street market to ask, "Where is the nearest bathroom?" Shifting her wicker shopping basket to the other hip, she snippily replied, "Shouldn't you wait until you get back to your lodgings?" My desperate response, "I can't wait that long," elicited from her, "Why on earth would you want to take a bath this time of day?"

While laughing over this elderly villager with my American friends, I suddenly realized that we were the odd ones. The sign "bathroom" meant for the British just that: a room in which to take a bath. We Americans had totally re-assigned meaning to the sign, turning it into a euphemism: a new sign for a less than lovely function. /Bathroom/ become so normalized in our language that we stopped thinking about its original meaning.

Ironically, my friends and I were appalled at the crass Brits who used the impolite sign "toilet" for the function I had been seeking. But the word "toilet"—normalized for the English and impolite for Americans—was also a euphemism, once referring to the articles on a dressing table with which to make final adjustments to one's appearance. (I still remember my childhood shock when I first sounded-out the phrase "toilet water" on my mother's perfume bottle!) Both "bathroom" and "toilet"—different signs for the same thing—are meant to distract us from thinking about the less comely signs of human elimination. And Americans have developed a "habit" by which the sign "toilet" doesn't distract them enough.

CULTURAL INTERPRETANTS: PEIRCE'S COMPLEXITY

Examples like the above can oversimplify, reducing Peirce's semiotic to "You say 'po-tay-toe,' I say 'po-tah-toe'": "You say 'toilet,' I say 'bathroom.'" As though aware of this problem, Peirce added qualifier on top of qualifier to his

[14]C. S. Peirce, "Some Consequences of Four Incapacities," in *Philosophical Writings*, p. 247. Peirce's idea of "habits" is more complicated than the consensus-building advocated by communitarians, for Peirce believes that "all things have a tendency to take habits." He would thus consider water to be the result of a molecular "habit": two hydrogen molecules habitually adhering to one oxygen molecule (H_2O). See C. S. Peirce, "Synechism, Fallibilism, and Evolution," in *Philosophical Writings*, p. 358. For more on "habits," see also the following essays in *Philosophical Writings:* "How to Make Our Ideas Clear," pp. 28-30; "The Criterion of Validity in Reasoning," p. 123; "Pragmatism in Retrospect," pp. 280, 284.

understanding of the sign (generating his "snarl of twine"). For example, he divides the interpretant into three different types:

1. *The emotional interpretant,* which is the initial awareness of a sign: you give me a rose, and I recognize it as a sign even before I know why you gave it.

2. *The energetic interpretant,* which is the effect the sign has on me. This is often muscular: my joy over the rose causes me to throw my arms around you in a big hug.

3. *The logical interpretant,* which conceptualizes why you gave me the rose: what it signifies in our relationship, whether an apology for the past or hope for the future.[15]

Each stage of the above depends on different habits and forms of collateral experience. For Peirce, the emotional interpretant (#1) is intuitive rather than learned. Necessitating no collateral experience, it simply recognizes that something has been offered. In contrast, the energetic interpretant (#2) depends on a cultural habit that establishes roses as signs of love. Otherwise, I might think that you offered me the rose as a means to perfume a smelly bathroom (toilet?). The final interpretant (#3) depends on my collateral experience of our relationship: Do you have something to apologize about? Have I been depressed about something? Is it a special anniversary?

Even then I could be accused of oversimplifying. As Jonathan Culler soberly notes, Peirce establishes "ten trichotomies by which signs can be classified . . . yielding a possible 59,049 classes of sign."[16] Furthermore, among his one-hundred-thousand-plus pages of theory, Peirce sometimes changes the definitions of his already opaque terms, adding to the confusion.[17] Nevertheless, Peirce can help facilitate the (re)signing of Christian truth, despite inevitable oversimplification of his theories.

PEIRCE'S INDEX, ICON AND SYMBOL

Every introduction to Peirce discusses index-icon-symbol, probably because it

---

[15]C. S. Peirce, "Pragmatism in Retrospect: A Last Formulation," in *Philosophical Writings,* p. 277. The rose example is my own.

[16]Jonathan Culler, *The Pursuit of Signs: Semiotics, Literature, Deconstruction: An Augmented Edition with a New Preface by the Author* (Ithaca, NY: Cornell University Press, 2002), p. 23.

[17]Ogden and Richards, *Meaning of Meaning,* pp. 284-85. Here is an example of Peirce's less-than-lucid prose: "How is it that the Percept, which is a Seme, has for its direct dynamical Interpretant the Perceptual Judgment, which is a Pheme?" How indeed?! Quoted in ibid., p. 286.

is the triad easiest to understand. (Derrida alluded to this triad in *Of Grammatology*.[18]) These three terms describe the three ways that a representamen can refer to its object by establishing an interpretant in a person's mind.

Index. An index is a sign that points to what caused it: the sign of smoke indexes fire, a fever indexes sickness, a hyena tail sticking up in the air indexes . . . well, you know. That's why the index finger is called the index finger: it is the finger that we point with. Our word "indicate," in fact, comes from the Latin "index."

Icon. In contrast, Peirce's icon does not point to its cause. An icon, according to his definition, offers a likeness that visualizes what it refers to, like a photograph.[19] Think of "icons" on a computer screen. A picture of a trashcan or recycle bin resembles the places in your house where you trash or recycle unwanted paper, thus deleting it from your home. Meanwhile, your computer files are signaled by little icons of manila file folders, the resemblance identifying their function. For Peirce, a diagram or chart might also serve as an icon, as when a bar graph shows population amounts in a city from year to year. Though abstract, such a chart still pictures what it refers to.

Symbol. Unlike an index or icon, Peirce's "symbol" parallels what Plato meant by "conventional sign." Symbols are human constructions that look nothing like the ideas or things they represent. All words, therefore, are symbols. /Bee/ for example, looks nothing like the insect buzzing outside my window. Because of their arbitrary status, with no "natural" connection to their objects, symbols can create puns. Think of those witty grade school Valentines depicting a honey bee holding a heart and stating, "Will you bee mine?"

The valentine heart is, of course, another symbol, looking nothing like love. Nevertheless, a fad begun in the 1970s placed the heart symbol on bumper stickers (see fig. 7.3).

I ♥ my dog

Figure 7.3. "I 'heart' my dog"

The fad spread to "I [heart] soccer" or "knitting" or "Jesus"; you name it.

---

[18]Derrida, *Of Grammatology*, p. 336n.6.

[19]Unlike other semioticians, Robert Corrington argues that a photograph is an index as well as an icon, because a photo points to what caused it: the object that it reproduces. See *An Introduction to C. S. Peirce: Philosopher, Semiotician, and Ecstatic Naturalist* (Lanham, MD: Rowman & Littlefield, 1993), p. 144.

Then some people, tired of the craze, started punning on the heart symbol itself (see fig. 7.4).

I ♠ my dog

Figure 7.4. "I 'spade' my dog"

Some who used this sign did not intend the spade to symbolize the truth: that they had spayed their pets. Instead, the entire sticker was an index pointing to the fad that created it by making fun of it. But note the cultural knowledge necessary to understand the joke:

• One must know about playing cards and their symbols for hearts and spades.

• One must know about the homonym between "spade" and "spayed."

• One must know about the "I [heart] my dog" fad.

The joke depends upon habits of perception shared by a community, some of which have lasted for centuries (love identified with a "heart"), some of which last only several decades (the "I heart" bumper stickers). Humor, in fact, is often based on ephemeral habits, explaining why comic elements in Shakespeare often make no sense today.

Effective communicators, then, consider the perceptual "habits" of their audiences, using signs that endorse "reality" as their listeners understand it. A good communicator also knows, however, that collateral experience affects habits of perception, causing some people to see objects as icons, some as indices and some as symbols. This might explain, then, differences in Christian belief. Let me give a real-life example.

SIGNS OF BLASPHEMY

My friend Gina tells of a disturbing moment during her college years. Invited to go home with a friend, she looked forward to meeting his family and accompanying them to church. But when she entered the sacred building Sunday morning, Gina was troubled by what she saw: there, at the front of the sanctuary, was a sign of blasphemy. "How could anyone who takes the Bible seriously allow such a sign in church?" she thought. "This congregation has obviously elevated American culture to the same level as Christ!"

So what was the sign that distracted Gina from worship that Sunday morning? It was an American flag standing close to the cross.

This may come as something of a shock—perhaps even an insult—to readers whose churches display American flags. Am I implying, they wonder, that love of America is blasphemous? Of course not. When I count my blessings, I count the fact that I was born in America. But I also understand what grieved Gina. She grew up in a community that takes very seriously Christ's words "Give therefore to the emperor the things that are the emperor's, and to God the things that are God's" (Mt 22:21). Her church interpreted this to mean that things associated with politics—the realm of the emperor—should not be displayed in a place dedicated to the things of God: the church. Hence, the American flag, a sign of political allegiance, should not be aligned with our commitment to Christ.

THE AMERICAN FLAG: ICON, INDEX OR SYMBOL?

How should Christians who display the flag in church respond? A semiotician influenced by Peirce, Thomas Sebeok (the developer of zoosemiotics), might help with an answer. Sebeok, in fact, used the American flag to illustrate how the same object might be perceived differently, "depending on the circumstance in which it is displayed." In some contexts it will be seen as an icon, in some an index, and in others a symbol. Here's how he puts it:

1. *iconicity* comes to the fore when the interpreter's attention fastens upon the seven red horizontal stripes of the flag alternating with six white ones (together identical with the number of founding colonies), or the number of white stars clustered in a single blue canton (in all, identical to the actual number of States in the Union);

2. in a cavalry charge . . . our flag was commonly employed to imperatively point, in an *indexical* fashion, to a target;

3. the debates . . . on the issue of flag burning present our banner as an emotionally surcharged emblem, being a subspecies of *symbol*.[20]

Though Sebeok says nothing about how the flag would be seen in church, his appeal to icon, index and symbol helps explain why interpretants differ from Christian to Christian: different communities inculcate different habits of perception.

For many, putting a flag near a cross implies that they are comparable

---

[20]Thomas A. Sebeok, "Indexicality," *The American Journal of Semiotics* 7, no. 4 (1990): 13, emphasis mine.

signs, both functioning as indexes, or as icons, or as symbols. Perceiving each as an index would imply that both point to that which gathers the church together: the saving work of Christ. If both are icons, they similarly visualize historical realities, the flag resembling the various flags carried into American wars. But in that case, placing a flag by the cross at the front of the sanctuary implies that historical events of America are as important as those of Christianity, or else that Christianity is an American faith. Millions of Christians in Africa and Eurasia would heartily disagree.

The problem, then, is not with patriotism. The problem is with communication: where we display and how we interpret the signs we use. Indeed, outside of the church, Gina dutifully participated in the Pledge of Allegiance during her public school years, honoring Paul's exhortation to the Romans: "Let every person be subject to the governing authorities" (Rom 13:1). But she also believes, as do I, that Paul's ensuing advice about obeying our political leaders (Rom 13:2-7) is trumped by his very next verse: "Owe no one anything, except to love one another; for the one who loves another has fulfilled the law" (Rom 13:8). Christians under the governing authority of Hitler were therefore justified—yea, righteous—in defying Romans 13:1-7 by hiding Jews from the Nazis. Standing on the edge of the coin, they rendered unto the government a love for *all* the governed.

SIGNS OF THE BIBLE: ICONS, INDICES AND SYMBOLS

As is quite clear, different Christian interpretants will see signs in church differently, depending upon their community's habits of perception and their own collateral experiences. The same, of course, can be said about the way Christians read signs of the Bible.

For example, from the very start of the church, Christians have perceived stories in the Old Testament not only as historical events, but also as signs of New Testament truth. Paul tells the Galatians, for example, to regard the two wives of Abraham as symbols: "Hagar is Mount Sinai in Arabia and corresponds to the present Jerusalem, for she is in slavery with her children. But the other woman corresponds to the Jerusalem above; she is free, and she is our mother" (Gal 4:25-26).

Following Paul's example, third-century theologians like Clement of Alexandria and Origen suggested that the Bible's greatest truths were symbolic. In the next century, John Cassian (ca. 360-435) suggested that the Bible should be read on at least three levels, but it wasn't until the twelfth century that a fourfold system of interpretation was standardized in the Western church: literal, allegorical, tropological and anagogical readings.[21] Take, for example, the fourfold interpretation of /Jerusalem/:

- *Literal* readings assume historical contexts: there was an actual city in Palestine named Jerusalem. In Peirce's terms, Jerusalem is the "object" that functions as a representamen differently, depending upon the interpretant.

- *Allegorical* (also called *typological*) readings focus on how Old Testament truths anticipate New Testament realities: Jerusalem, sanctified by a physical temple at its center, anticipates the Christian church, sanctified by the temple of Christ's body at its center (see chapter two). In Peirce's terms, elements from the Old Testament function as *indices* that point to truths in the New.

- *Tropological* readings focus on the moral implications for the individual believer: Jerusalem represents the soul into which Christ makes his triumphal entry, transforming it into a holy place. Such a reading accords with Peirce's *symbol*.

- *Anagogical* readings look toward the end times and/or heaven: through Christ, God will eventually welcome us into the heavenly Jerusalem.[22] Jerusalem can thus be seen as an *icon* that pictures, if even inadequately, our future home in glory.

Peirce's view of the sign, then, might be seen as continuing an ancient tradition of fourfold interpretation: a literal object can be read as an icon, an index and a symbol. This, then, may explain the different ways biblical truths have been communicated through the ages. Take, for example, the multiple readings of Noah's ark.

---

[21]Robert Con Davis and Laurie Finke, *Literary Criticism and Theory: The Greeks to the Present* (New York: Longman, 1989), pp. 121, 139. In his analysis of signs in the Bible, Augustine also demonstrates multiple ways to read Scripture. See *On Christian Doctrine*, trans. D. W. Robertson (New York: Liberal Arts Press, 1958), book 2, paragraphs 7-8 and 23-26, pp. 37-38, 50-53. In *Summa Theologica*, Aquinas lists the four levels of biblical interpretation: "historical or literal, allegorical, tropological or moral, and anagogical." See Davis and Finke, *Literary Criticism and Theory*, p. 146.

[22]As Henri de Lubac notes, Jerusalem is the most commonly cited example of the fourfold interpretation. See his helpful essay "Doctrine of the 'Fourfold Sense' in Scripture," in *Theological Fragments*, trans. Rebecca Howell Balinski (San Francisco: Ignatius, 1989), p. 115.

FROM NOAH'S ARK TO THE CROSS: ICON, INDEX AND SYMBOL

As is well known, second-century Christians etched and painted numerous signs of their faith in the catacombs outside of Rome. Many people—Christian and non-Christian alike—would be surprised to learn, however, that no crosses appear in the catacombs. In contrast, signs of Noah's ark occur forty-one times.[23] Why might this be? Perhaps because the interpretants of early believers established the cross as an icon rather than a symbol. As an icon, the cross would picture for them something historical: the torture device upon which Jesus Christ sacrificed his life in atonement for human sin.

The perception of cross as icon explains the electrifying shock I got as a child when I heard a preacher say, "If Jesus had been incarnated in the 1960s, we would have images of electric chairs atop our church steeples." I had become so used to the comfortable symbolism of the cross—the sign of my redemption and eternal life with Jesus—that I had lost all sense of its function as an icon: that it looks like the killing mechanism used by ancient Romans.

Perhaps this is why early Christians did not use the sign of the cross until several hundred years after the resurrection: it reminded them of the grotesque torture and death of their Lord. They wanted, instead, to focus on the victory of Christ's exit from the tomb, as symbolized by Noah exiting the ark. The Noah story, for them, was therefore an index pointing to the resurrection. The creators of the catacomb arks therefore show little concern for biblical accuracy in the ark's proportions. While the dimensions outlined in Genesis 6:15 suggest that Noah's ark looked like a "gigantic grandfather clock floating on its back,"[24] many of the catacomb ark images look like modern day washing-machines, with Noah popping out the lids on top.

By the third century, Origen was describing the ark as a "truncated pyramid" that "floated directly upon" the flood waters. In his mind, such an unlikely shape demonstrated God's ability to save the righteous from the

---

[23]Jack P. Lewis, *A Study of the Interpretation of Noah and the Flood in Jewish and Christian Literature* (Leiden, Netherlands: Brill, 1968), p. 11. Richard Viladesau notes that, while Constantine made the cross popular in the fourth century, "portrayals of the crucifixion itself are rare before the fifth century." See *The Beauty of the Cross: The Passion of Christ in Theology and the Arts—From the Catacombs to the Eve of the Renaissance* (New York: Oxford University Press, 2006), p. 43.

[24]David C. Downing, *What You Know Might Not Be So: 220 Misinterpretations of Bible Texts Explained* (Grand Rapids, MI: Baker, 1987), p. 137. For the collateral experience that contributed to ancient images of the ark, see Crystal Downing and Sharon Baker, "Readers of the Lost Ark," *Books and Culture* 14, no. 3, May/June 2008, pp. 15-17.

floods of sin, for only God can make a pyramid float.[25] In other words, the ark for Origen functioned as an *index* pointing to God's saving power. While humans can construct navigable boats, they cannot construct their own means of salvation. This truth, then, supercedes any biblical details about the ark's presumed dimensions.

Unlike Origen, Augustine honored the ark's dimensions presented in Genesis, but he interpreted the elongated image as an icon, not of the resurrection, but of Christ himself. In *The City of God* he writes, "For even its very dimensions, in length, breadth, and height, represent the human body in which He came. . . . And its having a door made in the side of it certainly signified the wound which was made when the side of the Crucified was pierced with the spear: for by this those who came to Him enter."[26]

Seven centuries later, Hugh of St. Victor (ca. 1078-1141) interpreted the ark not as an icon of Christ, but as a *symbol* of how Christians should live, writing a treatise *On the Moral Interpretation of the Ark of Noah*. And though Hugh argued that the literal ark had to have a hull in order to float, many Christians illustrated the ark as a lidded box, sometimes with legs like a fancy cedar chest, well into the seventeenth century.[27]

INTERPRETANTS IN OUR OWN TIMES:
ARK AS SCIENCE VERSUS ARK AS TRUTH

For much of the history of the church, then, different interpretants saw the object—Noah's ark—as representamens of different truths. This is a vastly different approach than that of Young Earth Creationists today who regard only a literal, scientifically accurate reading of Genesis as "true." Some have even funded searches for remnants of Noah's ark in order to "prove" the Bible's authenticity.

Such Christians might be surprised to discover that their emphasis on scien-

---

[25]Grover A. Zinn Jr., "Hugh of St. Victor and the Ark of Noah: A New Look," *Church History* 40 (1971): 262-63. The illustrated *Vienna Genesis* of the fourth century makes the ark out to be a Sumerian pyramid, or ziggurat. Pyramidal arks appear at least through the middle of the fifteenth century, not only in psalters or as miniatures, but most famously in Ghiberti's panel illustrating the flood for the Baptistery at Florence.

[26]Quoted in John Gardner, *The Construction of the Wakefield Cycle* (Carbondale: Southern Illinois University Press, 1974), p. 43.

[27]It wasn't until the twelfth century that the ark as it is usually depicted today—a house with a peaked roof on a hull—became popular. See Zinn, "Hugh of St. Victor and the Ark of Noah," pp. 261-72. For pictures of chest-like arks, most likely influenced by "the Ark of the Covenant," see Downing and Baker, "Readers of the Lost Ark," p. 15.

tific accuracy reflects the signs of their times more than signs of ancient Christianity. Indeed, the idea that the "greatest" truths are scientifically accurate came to fruition in the nineteenth century, along with the theory of evolution. God-denouncing evolutionists and God-defending creationists, in other words, are merely opposite sides of the exact same coin: on one side Christians use science to prove a Creator; on the other side atheists use science to disprove a Creator. In contrast, great fathers of our faith stood on the edge, refusing to elevate the "literal" above the "spiritual." As Augustine puts it in his treatise on signs, "whatever appears in the divine Word that does not *literally* pertain to virtuous behavior or to the *truth of faith* you must take to be figurative."[28]

Peirce would agree with Augustine, suggesting that behavior and long-lasting belief are *indexes* of truth: behavior and belief *point to* the reality that cause them. For both Augustine and Peirce, "the conduct of life" validates truth far better than bits of Noah's ark gathered from the snowy slopes of Ararat.[29] In fact, Peirce explicitly criticizes "those who are over-anxious about the details of evidence in religion. They forget that . . . belief still depends on an internal impulse"—and this is as true for scientists as for Sunday school teachers.[30]

SIGNS OF SALVATION: THE EUCHARIST

If something as simple as Noah's ark can generate such diverse depictions and interpretations, we should not be surprised at the different ways people see one of the most mystically profound signs of Christian truth: the Eucharist. Once again, Peirce might help us assess change to the sign. But first we need to consider the multiple meanings within the word *Eucharist* itself, since, like pyramidal and lidded arks, the word *Eucharist* is no longer used by most Protestants, who prefer *Communion* or *the Lord's Supper*.

Eu-, from the Greek, means "good." Hence a funeral usually includes *eulogies* (good words) about the dead, along with *eu-phonious* (good-sounding) music, and in some churches, the sacrament of *Eu-charist*, which means good gift. (*Gifts* of the Spirit like tongues and prophecy are emphasized by "*charismatic*" Christians.) The word *Eucharist* was coined in the second century by

---

[28]Augustine, *On Christian Doctrine*, book 3, para. 14, p. 88, emphasis mine.

[29]C. S. Peirce, "The Essentials of Pragmatism," in *Philosophical Writings*, p. 252.

[30]C. S. Peirce, "A Treatise on Metaphysics," in *Peirce on Signs: Writings on Semiotic by Charles Sanders Peirce*, ed. James Hoopes (Chapel Hill: University of North Carolina Press, 1991), p. 19.

Ignatius, Bishop of Antioch (d. circa 107), signaling that, by taking the bread and wine, we make a good gift of ourselves to Christ in thankfulness for the good gift he gave to us. Eucharist should therefore fill us with *eu-phoria* (good feelings), for it signals a miraculous gift: the union of God and human—both in Christ and through Christ with us. (This gift will be explored more fully in chapter nine.)

According to Anselm of Canterbury (ca. 1033-1109), Eucharist also celebrates the substitution of the perfectly good man, Jesus as the Word of God, for fallen humanity.[31] For Anselm, the substitutionary atonement celebrated by Eucharist parallels, on a cosmically transcendent scale, the function of *euphemism:* the substitution of a good term for a sullied one (as when I asked the British woman for the "bathroom"). Eucharist signals a divine euphemism: the Word become flesh was substituted for our sullied flesh, the sign of the crucified Christ standing for the si(g)ns of humanity.

THE SEMIOSIS OF EUCHARIST: FROM SYMBOL TO ICON TO INDEX

The sign of Eucharist was instituted, of course, through the (re)signing of Jesus. Resigned to the importance of celebrating a Jewish Passover meal with his disciples, Jesus nevertheless re-signed how the angel of death might pass over the children of God:

> While they were eating, Jesus took a loaf of bread, and after blessing it he broke it, gave it to the disciples, and said, "Take, eat; this is my body." Then he took a cup, and after giving thanks he gave it to them, saying, "Drink from it, all of you; for this is my blood of the covenant, which is poured out for many for the forgiveness of sins." (Mt 26:26-28)

According to my interpretant, molded by "habits" of my Protestant community, Jesus was speaking metaphorically, since his flesh and blood were still intact as he talked to his disciples. He created a *symbol* in Peirce's sense, turning bread and wine not into flesh and blood but into a sign (something that stands for something else) of his upcoming sacrifice. Augustine, in his treatise on signs, suggests the same thing:

> "Except you eat," [Jesus] says, "the flesh of the Son of man, and drink his blood, you shall not have life in you." He seems to commend a crime or a vice.

---

[31]In chapter ten I will once again consider Anselm, discussing changes in theories of the atonement throughout Christian history.

It is therefore a *figure,* admonishing communion in the Passion of Our Lord, and sweetly and usefully concealing a *memorial* of the fact that His flesh was crucified and wounded for us.[32]

Not long after the resurrection, however, Christians began treating the sign of the Last Supper as an *icon* in Peirce's sense, holding meals called "love feasts" that *resembled* the Passover meal in which Jesus made his prophetic announcement. Therefore, just as the meal in the upper room certainly had more food stuffs than bread and wine, so also did the "love feasts" of early Christians. Paul's first letter to the Corinthians, in fact, expresses concern about abuses to the feast, some people eating or drinking their fill before others were served (1 Cor 11:20-21). Paul therefore tells the Corinthians that they should not treat "the Lord's supper" (v. 20) as an *icon,* in imitation of Passover feasts: "Do you not have homes to eat and drink in?" (1 Cor 11:22). Instead, they should consider the supper as an *index* of what initiated it: "For as often as you eat this bread and drink the cup, you proclaim the Lord's death until he comes" (1 Cor 11:26). Celebrating the Lord's Supper is a sign that points to what caused it.

TRANSUBSTANTIATION: FROM REPRESENTAMEN TO OBJECT

By the second century, however, church leaders were echoing Christ's famous words—"This is my body"—to suggest the "real presence" of Christ in the bread and wine. Justin Martyr (100-165) is still quoted to this purpose: "In the same way that through the power of the Word of God Jesus Christ our Saviour took flesh and blood for our salvation, so the nourishment consecrated by the prayer formed of the words of Christ . . . is the flesh and blood of this incarnate Jesus."[33]

Even before Justin, Christians began to regard the Eucharist bread and wine no longer as signs—representamens *standing for* objects—but as elements containing the object itself: the body and blood of Christ. In other words, the priestly blessed elements became "one substance" with Christ. The word *transubstantiation* (Latin *transubstantiatio*) was therefore coined in the eleventh century to capture this long-held belief that bread and wine transform during mass into the substance of Christ.

In his *Summa Theologica,* Thomas Aquinas (ca. 1225-1274) asks "whether

---

[32]Augustine, *On Christian Doctrine,* book 3, para. 24, p. 93, emphasis mine.
[33]Quoted in "St. Justin Martyr," *Catholic Encyclopedia,* on the New Advent website, www.newadvent .org/cathen.

the body of Christ be in this sacrament in very truth, or *merely as in a figure or sign?*" (my emphasis). He asks this rhetorical question to make the point that Eucharist is far more than a mere representamen. For him, as for his Latin predecessors, bread and wine are indexes that transform into their objects. Therefore, after astutely outlining four objections to the real presence, Aquinas states, "The presence of Christ's true body and blood in this sacrament cannot be detected by sense, nor understanding, but by faith alone, which rests upon Divine authority."[34] Note how he appeals to what Peirce calls the interpretant: the elements are representamens that transubstantiate into the objects of blood and body, but it is a presence seen only with God-guided faith. And faith, as Peirce notes, "is the vigour of that part of the mind which is in communication with the eternal verities. By this, mountains are moved,"[35] just as Eucharist elements are changed.

CHANGING EUCHARIST: CONSUBSTANTIATION

Though many people assume Martin Luther changed the sign of Eucharist in the sixteenth century as part of his Reformation, the semiosis—as is always the case—occurred in a step by step process. Even before /transubstantiation/ was coined in the eleventh century, leaders in the Western church were arguing about it, some questioning whether the bread totally transformed into the physical body born of Mary. A monk named Ratramnus asserted that the body of Christ was present in the bread not physically, but only spiritually. When the theologian Berengarius of Tours confirmed Ratramnus's view in 1047, he was imprisoned by the church until he recanted.[36]

In order to discourage such (re)signing of ancient truth, the Western church made transubstantiation an official doctrine in 1215, so that challengers could be officially excommunicated. Nevertheless, John Wyclif openly questioned transubstantiation in 1380, calling the blessed bread (or Host) "an effectual *sign*" rather than the object itself.[37] For him, the representamen contained the "real presence" of Jesus, but did not transform into the literal *object* of Christ's flesh.[38]

---

[34]Thomas Aquinas, "Question 75: The Change of Bread and Wine into the Body and Blood of Christ," *Summa Theologica, Catholic Encyclopedia,* on the New Advent website.

[35]Peirce, "A Treatise on Metaphysics," p. 20.

[36]"Berengarius of Tours," *Catholic Encyclopedia,* on the New Advent website.

[37]Quoted in "John Wyclif," *Catholic Encyclopedia,* on the New Advent website.

[38]As discussed in chapter one, the Church was so disturbed by Wyclif's (re)signing of the Eucharist

Wyclif's views anticipate what has been called "consubstantiation": the idea that the representamen contains the real presence of Jesus without turning into the *object* of Christ's flesh and blood. Consubstantiation, as later taught by followers of Luther, could be interpreted according to Peirce's categories as follows: while the interpretant sees the real presence of Christ's body and blood in the bread and wine, those elements maintain their unchanged status as representamens.[39]

THE EVANGELICAL SIGN OF COMMUNION: HOLY CORPUS OR HOCUS-POCUS?

And the semiosis continues. While Lutherans gave up on the idea that, during Eucharist, the representamen transubstantiates into the object itself, most evangelicals have given up on the idea that the representamen contains the real presence of Jesus. They, instead, regard the elements as *symbolic,* in Peirce's sense, of Christ's sacrificial act. The sign symbolizes an action, as referenced by the italicized word: "Behold the blood and body of Christ *sacrificed* for you" (see fig. 7.5).

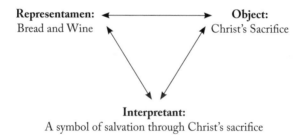

Representamen: ← → **Object:**
Bread and Wine   Christ's Sacrifice

Interpretant:
A symbol of salvation through Christ's sacrifice

Figure 7.5. Eucharist as triadic sign

Because of this difference, transubstantiation has elicited contempt from many Protestants, the sign /hocus-pocus/ aligned with the Eucharist.[40]

(as well other challenges to traditional doctrine) that it commanded his body be exhumed from its grave and burned. In other words, since Wyclif refused to accept the literal body of Christ in the sacred Host, the Church refused to accept his literal body in the sacred ground of a church cemetery.

[39]Kenneth Burke uses /consubstantiality/ to indicate the "identification" a rhetor must make with her audience in order to be persuasive: "you give the 'signs' of such consubstantiality by deference to an audience's 'opinions.'" See *A Rhetoric of Motives* (New York: Prentice-Hall, 1950), p. 55.

[40]Raised as a Unitarian, but converting to Protestantism in order to marry an Episcopal woman, Peirce expresses disturbing contempt for transubstantiation. See "How to Make Our Ideas Clear," in *Philosophical Writings,* pp. 30-31.

During the Latin Mass, a priest holds up the bread before the congregation and says *"Hoc est Corpus meum"*—"This is my Body"—before the element transforms into the flesh of Christ. Around 1694 a Protestant preacher therefore conjectured, "In all probability those common juggling words of *hocus pocus* are nothing else but a corruption of *hoc est corpus*, by way of ridiculous imitation of the priests of the Church of Rome in their trick of Transubstantiation" *(OED)*. The *OED* suggests that this etymology reveals the anti-Catholic prejudices of the preacher more than the history of the term. Instead, hocus-pocus is most likely related to the words "joke" (from the Latin *jocus*) and "hoax."[41]

Such dismissal of Catholic signs makes Protestants little different from those Catholics who imprisoned Berengarius of Tours, disinterred Wyclif or excommunicated Luther: opposite sides of the same coin. How, then, do we stay on the edge? Peirce's triadic view of the sign might help with an answer. Rather than condemning different views of the Lord's Supper, we should communicate that different Christians read signs of the *same truth* differently. Resigned to the truth of Christ's atoning sacrifice, Christians re-sign the truth in diverse ways.[42] Consider, for example, the rhetorical approach taken by Cardinal Henri de Lubac.

ON THE EDGE WITH HENRI DE LUBAC (1896-1991)

A French Jesuit priest who became a Cardinal of the Roman Catholic Church, Henri de Lubac sought to balance on the edge between different views of the Eucharist. He did so in response to opposite sides of the coin:

- The medieval reduction of Christ's body to the transubstantiated Host

- The Protestant reduction of the Lord's Supper to a mere symbolic gesture[43]

---

[41]Eric Partridge, *Origins: A Short Etymological Dictionary of Modern English* (New York: Greenwich, 1983), p. 323.

[42]Of course, Roman Catholic and Eastern Orthodox Christians might say that this statement itself is a "Protestant" way of reading signs. For them, in contrast, there is only one way to read the signs of Christian truth: the way established by the most ancient traditions of Christian communion. But this assumption leads to problems, for Eastern Orthodox and Roman Catholic Christians often consider their own traditions as more fully tied to the origins of Christianity than those of the other.

[43]The editors of de Lubac's book on the Eucharist draw attention to opposite kinds of Eucharistic "fetishisation": that of the Host on the one hand, and that of the worshiping community on the other. See Laurence Paul Hemming and Susan Frank Parsons, "Editors' Preface" to Henri Cardinal de Lubac, S.J., *Corpus Mysticum: The Eucharist and the Church in the Middle Ages*, trans. Gemma Simmonds, C.J., et al. (Notre Dame, IN: University of Notre Dame Press, 2006), pp. xiii-xiv.

Astutely summarizing these two sides, theologian Hans Boersma captures de Lubac's position on the edge:

> de Lubac attempted to sail between two hazards: on the one hand, the Scylla of Protestant symbolism, for which the Eucharistic bread was simply an arbitrary symbol "X" referring to a distant reality "Y"; and, on the other hand, the Charybdis of a strict neo-scholastic focus on real presence that so identified symbol "X" with reality "Y" that the spiritual reality in no way exceeded the symbol.[44]

Note how Boersma returns us to the "X" that began our study of semiotics: differing views of the sign. De Lubac, then, balances on the edge between dualistic X versus Y thinking by focusing on a triad. In his book *Corpus Mysticum: The Eucharist and the Church in the Middle Ages*, he identifies "three bodies" that the sacrament conjoins:

- the historical body of Jesus, who walked the earth;
- the sacramental body of Jesus, present in the bread and wine;
- the ecclesial body of the Church universal.[45]

This list connects us (as it connected de Lubac) to the fifth-century theologian who was the first to explicitly "propose a 'general semiotics.'"[46] Augustine suggested that the body of Christ, as celebrated in the Eucharist, signals the real presence of Christ *in the body of the church*. When we participate in Eucharist, in other words, the Holy Spirit unites us into Christ's body. Such reclamation of Augustine might enable Protestants to communicate with Catholics on the edge of the coin. This certainly is the conclusion reached by Boersma:

> The common acceptance of the Lubacian view within Catholicism offers new prospects for fruitful dialogue. Just as the *Catholic* Church has begun to focus more strongly on the fellowship of the Church community, so it is time for *Protestants* to celebrate much more unambiguously the real presence of Christ in the Eucharist.[47]

---

[44]Hans Boersma, "The Eucharist Makes the Church," *Books and Culture*, November/December 2010, p. 23.

[45]De Lubac reiterates this triad throughout *Corpus Mysticum*, acknowledging the "evolution of Eucharistic theories" (p. 256).

[46]Eco, *The Limits of Interpretation*, p. 113. I also quote this description of Augustine in chapter three.

[47]Boersma, "The Eucharist Makes the Church," p. 24.

"Fruitful dialogue" occurs when Christians seek to understand each others' community-defined interpretants while acknowledging "the historicity implicit in semiotics."[48] In other words, to effectively communicate we must recognize how our historical location, both in space and time, shapes the way we understand truth. Furthermore, when communication is genuine—meaning "open to the other"—it welcomes change of the self as well as of the other. And, of course, change is the whole point of Eucharist: changing ourselves in response to the good gift of salvation.

SIGNS OF CHANGING AND CHANGING OF SIGNS

The apostle Paul repeatedly encourages change, reassuring his readers that God guides the process of semiosis. He tells the Philippians, for example, to "work out your own salvation with fear and trembling; for it is God who is at work in you, enabling you both to will and to work for his good pleasure" (Phil 2:12-13). As an adolescent, I disliked this verse, because it sounded like Paul was endorsing a "works orientation" rather than emphasizing salvation through grace. But now I understand the passage differently. For Peirce, "thinking is a kind of action," or work.[49] By "working out" my salvation, then, I am "working" my interpretant, seeking to understand what salvation means. But I do such work with "fear and trembling," knowing that others "work out" their understanding differently, depending upon the habits of the community with which they identify.

This, of course, leads to another problem: if God "is at work" in believers, why do Christians disagree? How might semiotics help Christians acknowledge their different interpretations without reducing belief to an insipid "let's agree to disagree" on the one hand, or vicious proclamations of heresy on the other? How do we know which beliefs we resign ourselves to as fundamental to the very essence of Christianity, and how do we know which beliefs we can or *should* re-sign? The last four chapters of this book will address these questions more fully.

---

[48]Webb Keane, "Semiotics and the Social Analysis of Material Things," *Language and Communication* 23 (2003): 420.

[49]C. S. Peirce, "'Pragmatism' Defined," in *Peirce on Signs: Writings on Semiotic by Charles Sanders Peirce,* ed. James Hoopes (Chapel Hill: University of North Carolina Press, 1991), p. 247.

8

PLACING THE COIN ON EDGE

Trinitarian Signs

I'll never forget the moment I heard a theologian proclaim, "Christians need to get rid of the Trinity!" Before I could raise my hand to ask why, the theologian continued, "/The Trinity/ is only a metaphor, and Muslims don't like it." I was chagrined to discover that the speaker (like other theologians today) wanted to re-sign a doctrine to which I was resigned. Questions began to ricochet in my brain like a pinball in an arcade machine:

- Have I been oblivious to directions of contemporary Christian theology?

- Am I holding on to the "same substance" of the Trinity the way many Christians have held on to the "same substance" of transubstantiation?

- Why have most Protestants I know given up on the latter but not the former?

- Is it possible to be "open to the other" while also communicating the necessity of the Trinity to Christian faith?

- Can I persuasively advocate the (re)signing of truth in relationship to doctrine about the Trinity?

The remainder of this book will grapple with this tension between resigning and re-signing, suggesting how semiotics enables us to respond intelligently. In this chapter I discuss how the theory of Charles Sanders Peirce helps Christians persuasively communicate the truth of the Trinity. Then, in part four, I will address the issue of religious pluralism, in order to make two important points relevant to my disturbing moment related above:

- "Openness to the other," as advocated by Derrida, *does not mean* altering or suppressing our beliefs for the sake of other religions or ideologies, whether Islam or Hinduism, Marxism or Capitalism.

- "Openness to the other" *means, instead,* that Christian communicators change signs of belief *for the sake of Christ.*

In the conclusion, I will pull together most of the ideas developed so far in order to suggest specific rhetorical strategies: "how to" advice about the (re)signing of truth.

THE COIN OF CHRIST: SEMIOLOGY VERSUS SEMIOTICS

In one of the Synoptic Gospels' most famous incidents, Christ's enemies attempt to "entrap" him by asking "Is it lawful to pay taxes to the emperor, or not?" In response, Jesus asks for a coin. Drawing attention to the *signs* on one side—the head and title of the emperor—he implies the coin belongs to Caesar (Mt 22:15-21). Indeed, Caesar had it coined. However, as everyone in the audience at the time must have realized, the coin also belonged to the person who handed it to Jesus, a person who would later use it to buy bread and wine. Jesus thus stayed on the edge, implying that there are two sides to every coin: our embeddedness in culture (the realm of Caesar) and our embrace of Christ, for whom bread and wine would become signs of salvation.

Saussure's semiology, as discussed in part three, generated many different theories about how to understand *one side* of this coin: our embeddedness in language and culture. But structuralists influenced by Saussure had no way to talk about the other side of the coin—our embrace of Christ—except to say that it is embedded in culture as well. For them, any language about the truth of Christ is generated by the speaker's culture. For the thorough-going structuralist, in other words, all religious language is merely a product of the system in which one is situated, cooked up out of the ingredients in one's linguistic cupboard. Some cupboards provide the ingredients for Christ, others the ingredients for Muhammad.

Of course, to a limited extent this is true. How can we talk about the divine apart from the metaphors that mold the way we think of it? Even Christian language varies from denomination to denomination (from shelf to shelf) as believers communicate the need for Christ differently:

- Are you born again?
- Have you found Jesus?

- Have you put your all on the altar?
- Have you asked Jesus into your heart?
- Have you heard of the "four spiritual laws"?
- Are you a baptized believer?
- Have you been baptized in the Spirit?
- Have you been washed in the blood?
- Do you have a personal relationship with Jesus?
- Have you made right with God?
- When were you baptized?
- When were you confirmed?
- When were you converted?
- When was your first communion?
- Are you redeemed?
- Have you prayed the sinner's prayer?
- Are you saved?[1]

Problematically, some Christians suspect the salvation of anyone who doesn't use one or another of these phrases, as though to say only *their* church's shelf has the right ingredients to ward off hell. Christian writer Dorothy L. Sayers didn't like it when people asked her, "When were you saved?" sometimes answering, "When Jesus rose from the dead!" She thought, quite rightly, that the evangelical emphasis on a dramatic conversion experience did not reflect the experience of all Christians; it was only one way to talk about salvation through Christ.

CHRISTIAN AND MUSLIM INTERPRETANTS: A TRANSCENDENT GOD

Despite these differences, Christians, like Muslims, believe that God exists beyond all cultural and linguistic cupboards. Unfortunately, Saussure's view of the sign gives us no way to talk about anything outside the structure of any one cupboard, except by acknowledging that other cupboards generate different signs of truth. This is a problem for anyone who believes that God transcends all sign systems. How might Christians justify their belief that

---

[1]Thanks to Theran Knighton-Fitt, a student in my semiotics class at Regent College, Vancouver, for contributing phrases to this list.

something transcendent to our structural system also entered into it—the way God entered into culture (the realm of Caesar) through the incarnation of Christ? This very belief, in fact, is what disturbs Muslims, who deny that a transcendent God would ever suffer the indignities that flesh is heir to. As David W. Shenk summarizes,

> According to Islamic theology, the sovereign, powerful Creator does not suffer. He is invulnerable and defends truth forcefully if necessary. This is why Muslims deny the crucifixion of Jesus. They believe Jesus is the Messiah, . . . [but] a crucified Messiah is impossible. Speaking of the Messiah, the Koran says, "But they killed him not nor crucified him, but so he was made to appear to them" (Nisaa [4]:157).[2]

Like Christians, Muslims believe there is only one God. For them, therefore, the Trinity suggests polytheism.[3]

"Openness to the other" means we take this criticism seriously. Why do we maintain belief in the Trinity when it alienates others? How do we communicate that belief so that it makes sense? How might we "fix" our beliefs? In other words, how do Christians cement (fix) beliefs into a solid foundation, and how do we repair (fix) beliefs that have started to crack?

FIXING BELIEF

In an essay entitled "The Fixation of Belief" (1877), Peirce talks about four ways that people approach their beliefs: either with tenacity, or according to authority, a priori reason or science.

Tenacity. Some people tenaciously hold on to an individual opinion no matter how much evidence to the contrary is offered. Think, for example, of someone who reports that he was abducted by aliens in a flying saucer, refusing to question the legitimacy of his experience. But think also of a Christian mystic convinced that she has experienced the divine in a way no other human understands. While Peirce parallels such tenacity to an ostrich with "its head in the sand,"[4] his later work provides a way we might distinguish between belief in space aliens and a mystical theophany. The difference,

---

[2]David W. Shenk, "Jesus and Muhammad: Two Roads to Peace," in *Where Was God on Sept. 11? Seeds of Faith and Hope,* ed. Donald B. Kraybill and Linda Gehman Peachey (Scottdale, PA: Herald Press, 2002), p. 54.

[3]The Koran repeatedly states that God has no Son. See, for example, 4:171; 10:68; 17:111; 19:88, 29.

[4]C. S. Peirce, "The Fixation of Belief," in *Philosophical Writings of Peirce,* ed. Justus Buchler (New York: Dover, 1955), p. 12.

for Peirce, would be in what each person's tenacious belief leads to, and to this end he quotes Jesus: "By their fruits ye shall know them."[5]

Peirce uses this famous verse to explain "pragmatism," a word that he "invented."[6] For him, action is "the finale of the symphony of thought, belief being a demicadence. Nobody conceives that the few bars at the end of a musical movement are the purpose of the movement. They may be called its upshot."[7] In other words, action (which includes the action of thought) is not the *purpose* of belief, it is the *result* of belief. This echoes that famous statement in the letter of James: "So faith by itself, if it has no works, is dead" (Jas 2:17). Faith without works is dead in the same way a symphony dies if an orchestra fails to play its finale. But note: a symphony implies a community of musicians acting together. For Peirce, the solo performances of those with tenacious belief produce, at their best, only "brilliant, *unlasting* success."[8] Better is "fixation of belief" endorsed by the community that shapes one's interpretants. But this can lead to problems as well.

Authority. Peirce sees many people internalizing their community's habits of perception without question. Such people form their beliefs based on the religious and political ideas of those with authority over them. On one level, this parallels the hegemony theory I discussed in chapter five. There we surveyed cultural materialists who argued that those with cultural hegemony (power) control the way the rest of society thinks and acts—evidenced every

---

[5]Mt 7:20 KJV, in Peirce, "Pragmatism in Retrospect: A Last Formulation," in *Philosophical Writings*, p. 271.

[6]Peirce makes this claim of invention in "The Essentials of Pragmatism" [*Philosophical Writings*, p. 252], a claim that William James, author of *Pragmatism: A New Name for Some Old Ways of Thinking* (1907), endorses. The *OED*, however, shows earlier usage (in 1860), though not with Peirce's meaning. In his *Critique of Pure Reason* (1781), which Peirce read, Immanuel Kant coined the phrase "pragmatic belief" to describe one among several kinds of belief. For Peirce, the *only* legitimate belief is that which is pragmatic, resulting in fruitful conduct, either of action or thought. In 1905 Peirce coined yet a new term—pragmaticism—in order to distinguish his thought from that of William James. For more details in accessible prose, see Louis Menand, *The Metaphysical Club: A Story of Ideas in America* (New York: Farrar, Straus & Giroux, 2001), pp. 227-29, 349-51.

[7]The *Collected Papers of Charles Sanders Peirce*, vols. 1-6, ed. Charles Hartshorne and Paul Weiss; vols. 7-8, ed. Arthur W. Burkes (Cambridge, MA: Harvard University Press, 1931-1958), vol. 5, para. 13n.1. Henceforth I will exercise the common practice of citing Peirce's papers as *CP*, followed by volume and paragraph numbers: *CP* 5.13n.1. Peirce's technical definition of pragmatism emphasizes the "rational conduct" of thought: "Consider what effects that might *conceivably* have practical bearings you *conceive* the objects of your *conception* to have. Then, your *conception* of those effects is the whole of your *conception* of the object." See "Critical Common-Sensism," in *Philosophical Writings*, p. 290, emphasis his.

[8]Peirce, "Fixation of Belief," p. 21, emphasis mine.

time someone buys something they do not need with money they do not have.

Though Peirce would agree that many people function like automatons controlled by the "moral terrorism" of cultural authority,[9] he also acknowledged the legitimacy of choice: individuals can choose to identify with a community's authority in order to collectively benefit society. He thus anticipates the "faithful presence" encouraged by James Davison Hunter in *To Change the World*.[10] As Hunter explains in a *Christianity Today* interview, "What history tells us is that the key actor in history is not the individual genius but rather the network and the new institutions that arise out of the network. This is not to undermine or undersell the importance of charismatic figures like Luther, Calvin, or Wilberforce. That kind of genius, courage, and charisma, however, cannot be understood apart from a network of similarly oriented people." Pragmatic change, for Hunter as for Peirce, always functions "in concert with the community."[11]

Peirce therefore encourages us to assess authority with questions that reflect his pragmatism: do the beliefs endorsed by religious or governmental authority result in the health and stability of an entire community or only in benefits to those with power? As Peirce scholar Robert Corrington summarizes, "Any method that helps to build up a genuine common consensus, but one that still remains open to self-correction and acknowledges its fallibility, is a pragmatic method."[12]

A priori reason. Some people appeal to reason as their justification for belief, saying that certain assumptions are so universally self-evident that they function as *a priori* truths (*a priori* means existing in the mind *prior* to education or experience). Peirce takes issue with a priori reason, anticipating Derrida and other poststructuralists who expose the cultural assumptions upon which many so-called a priori truths are built. Offering the example of cultures that assume polygamy to be universally reasonable, Peirce argues that belief in a priori reason differs little from belief based on authority.[13] All knowledge, in other words, reflects faith in traditional concepts, including

---

[9]Ibid., p. 20.

[10]James Davison Hunter, *To Change the World: The Irony, Tragedy, and Possibility of Christianity in the Late Modern World* (New York: Oxford University Press, 2010), pp. 238-72.

[11]James Davison Hunter, "Faithful Presence," an interview by Christopher Benson, *Christianity Today*, May 2010, www.christianitytoday.com/ct/2010/may/16.33.html, online pp. 2, 4.

[12]Robert Corrington, *An Introduction to C. S. Peirce: Philosopher, Semiotician, and Ecstatic Naturalist* (Lanham, MD: Rowman & Littlefield, 1993), p. 28.

[13]Peirce, "Fixation of Belief," p. 17.

the legitimacy of reason. As he explains elsewhere,

> Faith is not peculiar to or more needed in one province of thought than in another. For every premiss [*sic*] we require faith. . . . This is overlooked by Kant and others who draw a distinction between *knowledge* and *faith*. Wherever there is knowledge there is Faith. Wherever there is Faith (properly speaking) there is knowledge.[14]

This does not mean that Peirce denies the existence of universals. Instead, he asserts that human reason is *fallible* in its understanding of "the real," which does indeed exist apart from our thoughts about it.[15] To better understand "the real," then, humanity needs what he calls "science."

Science. Peirce uses the word "science" similar to the way Christian Scholastics employed it in medieval universities.[16] For them, science is about the search for truth by a community, its members engaging what is best about "tenacity," "authority" and "reason." For Scholastics, therefore, theology was "the Queen of the Sciences."

In his essay "Logic as Semiotic: The Theory of Signs," Peirce describes "'scientific' intelligence" as "intelligence capable of learning by experience."[17] As Corrington explains, "Both the scientist and the theologian rely on a common body of inferential strategies in coming to conclusions about the ultimate explanations of things."[18] In other words, both hold on to the fundamental beliefs of their community while also opening themselves to new ways of understanding reality, creatively suggesting new signs for old truths: signs that might change the very way the community perceives reality. In the physical sciences we have the example of Albert Einstein, whose emphasis on light as the universe's only constant changed the way physicists saw reality. In the theological sciences we have the example of St. Francis of Assisi, whose emphasis on God's love for every aspect of creation—"Father Sun" and "Sister Moon"—changed the way many Western Christians thought about their re-

---

[14]C. S. Peirce, "A Treatise on Metaphysics," in *Peirce on Signs: Writings on Semiotic by Charles Sanders Peirce,* ed. James Hoopes (Chapel Hill: University of North Carolina Press, 1991), p. 19.

[15]Peirce defines the "real as that which holds its character on such a tenure that it makes not the slightest difference what any man or men may have *thought* them to be, or ever will have *thought* them to be . . . but the real thing's character will remain absolutely untouched." *CP* 6.495.

[16]Peirce started studying the Scholastics in 1866. For the relation between Scholasticism and semiotics, see chapter three above.

[17]C. S. Peirce, "Logic as Semiotic: The Theory of Signs," in *Philosophical Writings,* p. 98.

[18]Corrington, *Introduction to C. S. Peirce,* p. 47.

lationship to nature. Indeed, St. Francis has been identified as the patron saint of ecologists.

Peirce called the new ideas of such scientists acts of "abduction," believing that abduction contributes to an evolving understanding of truth.[19] Peirce's "science" of abduction, then, is about the (re)signing of truth: committed to the beliefs of their community, creative thinkers challenge the limitations of those beliefs, as when St. Francis and Luther challenged habits of the Roman Church. Abduction is semiosis (a sign process) done on the edge of the coin, where a person refuses to fall onto one side or the other: either the "tenacity" of individualized assumptions or the robotic adherence to "authority."

(RE)SIGNING THE TRINITY

Significantly, the doctrine of the Trinity developed through a process of Holy Spirit guided abduction. Nowhere does the word "Trinity" appear in the Bible, although multiple passages suggest the plural nature of God. The most commonly cited example comes from the instructions Jesus gives his disciples at the very end of Matthew: "Go therefore and make disciples of all nations, baptizing them in the name of the Father and of the Son and of the Holy Spirit" (Mt 28:19). This verse, however, does not explicitly confirm that Father, Son and Holy Spirit are one substance as the church later defined it.

Furthermore, when the Gospels indicate that Jesus repeatedly called himself "the Son of Man," while others addressed him as "the Son of God," many scholars assume Gospel writers were probably appropriating Old Testament signs to establish Christ's authority rather than his union with God. "Son of God" aligned Jesus with King David and his successors, who were called "sons" of God.[20] And "Son of Man," which Jesus employs some eighty times in the Gospels, aligned him with multiple Old Testament prophets. The Gospels, then, establish that Jesus was (re)signing these terms, indicating not only that he fulfilled ancient Hebrew signs, but also that he re-signed what they meant, indicated by the addition of "the" in front of "Son of God": Jesus was *the* Son of God, enjoying a special relationship with the Father.[21]

---

[19]The *OED* credits Peirce with coining this new meaning of "abduction."

[20]See, for example, 2 Sam 7:14; Ps 2:7; 89:26-27. My understanding of "Son of God" and "Son of Man" comes from Larry W. Hurtado and David Jeffrey in *A Dictionary of Biblical Tradition in English Literature*, ed. David Lyle Jeffrey (Grand Rapids, MI: Eerdmans, 1992), pp. 723-27.

[21]"Some 92 times in Ezekiel the phrase 'son of man' appears as the title by which God addresses the prophet . . . and there is an intimation of this usage in Daniel 8:17." Ibid., p. 725.

This unique status seems most fully articulated by John, who (unlike the other Gospel writers) shows Jesus repeatedly employing "I am" statements: I am the bread, I am the door, I am the good shepherd, I am the vine. Written later than the other Gospels, John (re)signs truth by aligning Jesus with the sign of God, as pronounced to Moses: "I am Who I am." Significantly, four of Christ's "I am" statements occur in the same chapter were he states, "The Father and I are one" (Jn 10:30). The audacity of Christ's new signs, of course, made people in the audience want to stone him (Jn 10:31-33).

(RE)SIGNING THE TRINITY VERSUS HERESY

Though Tertullian coined /Trinity/ two centuries after the resurrection, the sign had not yet completed its process of semiosis. In 325 a council of church leaders met at Nicaea in order to determine the most faithful way to speak of Christ's relationship with the Father. At that first ecumenical council, the bishops declared that Christ was consubstantial with God. Seeking guidance from the Holy Spirit as they made this abduction, they coined a sign not found in the Bible: *homoousios,* a Greek word meaning "same substance/essence." In other words, they (re)signed truth.

Not all Christians were in favor of this (re)signing, however. Arius (ca. 250-336), a priest from Alexandria, denied that Jesus was coequal and coeternal with God. After all, in addition to the fact that /homoousios/ does not appear in the Bible, he could argue that a literal reading of /Son of God/, which *does* appear in the Bible—numerous times—establishes that God precedes Jesus the way a father precedes a son. Hence, followers of Arius, or Arians, could legitimately justify their position as thoroughly biblical. Why, then, was Arianism declared a Christian heresy? Perhaps because Arians were idolizing biblical signs rather than opening themselves up to an Other that exceeds all signs: God, the Object of our adoration. In this light, then, we might see the Council of Nicaea as an "Event" of deconstruction: a revelation of truth so far beyond the walls of biblical language to contain it that a new sign—*homoousios*—had to be coined.

This leads to a problem. If indeed, as David Lyle Jeffrey's *Dictionary of Biblical Tradition* puts it, "The orthodox doctrine of the Trinity was hammered out gradually over a period of three centuries or more,"[22] how can we

---

[22]Donald V. Stump and David L. Jeffrey, "Trinity," in *A Dictionary of Biblical Tradition*, p. 785. As the authors note, the orthodox doctrine of the Trinity wasn't finalized until the First Council of Constantinople in 381.

resign ourselves to it? Might not the doctrine change again—just as the theologian who began this chapter suggests?

To address these extremely serious questions, we need to once again extract a coin from Peirce.

THE EDGINESS OF (RE)SIGNING: TRIADIC COINHERENCE

Note how my image of the coin throughout this book is triadic: in order to avoid the coin falling onto one side or the other we must balance on the third part—the edge. Significantly, within his triadic view of the sign (*object + representamen + interpretant*) Peirce considers the interpretant the "Third." The place where "abduction" occurs, the place of the Third, keeps the process of semiosis rolling—like a coin on edge.

Peirce, in fact, was obsessed with threes—trichotomies, triplets, triads—as though the universe itself were created by a Trinity. Significantly, he once said that every sign functions as "a divine trinity," and that, "in many respects, this trinity agrees with the Christian trinity."[23] Indeed, just as Christian orthodoxy holds that no person of the Trinity created or reigns over any of the others, Peirce argues that no aspect of the triadic sign creates or determines the others. An object can only be known through its representamen as made accessible through the interpretant. Though distinct, the three interdependent elements make up one substance: the sign. We might argue, therefore, that the way humans perceive reality reflects the trinitarian nature of the God who created us. In fact, one Peirce scholar summarizes human perception using a word often employed to describe the Trinity: "while all thoughts are signs, so also all things are signs, and signs and things must necessarily and absolutely *coinhere*."[24]

The word *coinhere* goes back to 1836, its formation inspired by a term coined by poet Samuel Taylor Coleridge in 1824: coinherence *(OED)*. Charles Williams appropriated the word in the twentieth century to describe the relationships within the Trinity. As C. S. Lewis scholar David C. Downing explains it, coinherence for Williams

---

[23]This statement comes from one of Peirce's unpublished manuscripts, quoted in Donna M. Orange, "Peirce's Conception of God: A Developmental Study," *Peirce Studies* 2, September 10, 1984, 21.

[24]Charles Lock, "Peirce Unbound," *The Semiotic Review of Books* 4 (1993), on SRB archives at http://www.univie.ac.at/wissenschaftstheorie/srb/srb/unbound.html.

is built into the very fabric of reality, a reflection of the Trinity: Father, Son and Holy Spirit, three persons in one being, eternally expressing their natures in relation to the others. Coinherence leads to substitution, Christ's dying for all humanity in order that they may be lifted up. Redeemed humans coinhere in their Maker, living in the Spirit as he lives in them, and also with each other in a mystical body.[25]

How appropriate, then, that the very way signs work—through the coinherence of object, representamen and interpretant—should be trinitarian as well! As Peirce himself put it in 1902, "To believe in a god at all, is not that to believe that man's reason is allied to the originating principle of the universe?" And he concludes that "man is made after his maker's image."[26] However, by theorizing an Object that exists apart from any interpretant, Peirce also implies that no single understanding can exhaust the fullness of the reality of that Object. Similarly, no single interpretant can capture the full reality of the being and becoming of God. Nevertheless, Christians believe that some representamens point more faithfully, by the grace of God, to the Object of our adoration than others.

Perhaps this explains why Peirce's triadic view of the sign resembles that of Augustine, who wrote books discussing not only the sign (see chapter three above), but also the Trinity (*De Trinitate*, ca. 400 c.e.).[27] Augustine argues, like Peirce, that human consciousness reflects the Triune God in whose image we were created. For example, Augustine offers not only the interdependence of mind, knowledge and love, but also the coinherence of memory, understanding and will: "not three substances, but one substance."[28]

Significantly, like both Augustine and St. Francis, Peirce had a mystical experience of Christ's real presence that affected the way he understood how signs work.

PEIRCE'S MYSTICAL EXPERIENCE

In April of 1892, reviled for his financial and sexual indiscretions, Peirce

---

[25]David C. Downing, *Into the Region of Awe: Mysticism in C. S. Lewis* (Downers Grove, IL: InterVarsity Press, 2005), p. 48.

[26]*CP* 2.24, 34.

[27]T. L. Short, *Peirce's Theory of Signs* (Cambridge: Cambridge University Press, 2007), p. 24. Though establishing a similarity, Short has found no evidence that Peirce read Augustine (p. 23).

[28]Quoted from *De Trinitate,* in Diarmaid MacCulloch, *Christianity: The First Three Thousand Years* (London: Viking Penguin, 2010), p. 310.

wandered into St. Thomas's Episcopal Church in New York City. There he mystically felt "the direct permission of the Master" to take Eucharist. In a letter to the rector of the church recounting the experience, Peirce explained his life-long struggle to reconcile "notions of common sense and of evidence with propositions of the creed." But on that April morning, "I found myself carried up to the altar rail, almost without my own volition." After taking Eucharist, "that which seemed to call me today seemed to promise me that I should bear a cross like death for the Master's sake, and he would give me strength to bear it. I am sure it will happen. My part is to wait."[29]

Peirce's mystical experience led him to theorize a coinherence to the entire universe. As one of his biographers explains, "I believe that, for Peirce, semeiotic should be understood, after his mystical experience, as the working out of how the real is both immanent and transcendent and of how the infinite speaker may be said to practice semeiosis, the action of signs, in creating our universe."[30] Transcending all signs, God nevertheless reveals God's-self through the semiosis of signs on earth.

TRIADIC RHETORIC: SUPPORTING THE TRINITY

Christians, then, can use the coinherence operative within Peirce's triadic sign as a rhetorical strategy, arguing that the very way humans perceive reality endorses the doctrine of the Trinity. Here's how an argument supporting belief in the Trinity might run:

- Resigned to the ancient Jewish understanding of the one true God who transcends all signs of creation, Christians believe that Jesus re-signed how transcendence became imminent within creation.

- Responding to Christ's (re)signing, New Testament writers established that Jesus expressed God's love for the world through his death and resur-

---

[29]Joseph Brent, *Charles Sanders Peirce: A Life*, rev. ed. (Bloomington: Indiana University Press, 1998), pp. 209-10. Though he valued the Christian Scholastics, Peirce was also influenced by mystic Emanuel Swedenborg (1688-1772). Believing that God created evil, Swedenborg saw the Trinity not as three persons making up one substance, but rather different aspects of Jesus. Brent notes, however, that Peirce "rejected" Swedenborgian ideas in the last three years of his life (p. 345).

[30]Ibid., p. 212. Peirce's theology is so ambiguous that scholars interpret it in radically different ways. Some align Peirce with process theology (see Orange, "Peirce's Conception of God," pp. 62, 28, 76-78), while others describe him as a panentheist (see Michael L. Raposa, *Peirce's Philosophy of Religion* [Bloomington: Indiana University Press, 1989], p. 50).

rection, making possible the reconciliation of creatures with their Creator (Jn 3:16).

- The gift of reconciliation, what Tyndale called "at-one-ment," confirms that God is Love, for love, by definition, means relationship (1 Jn 4:7-12).[31]

- However, if we say that loving God can be relational only through interaction with created beings, we compromise the transcendence to which we are resigned, for we have made God's character dependent on creation.

- Therefore, through God-guided acts of (re)signing, early church leaders established God's transcendent character itself as inherently relational: Father, Son and Holy Spirit in constant communion with each other, coinhering as one transcendent God.

- Nevertheless, if love is inherent to God's very nature, it only makes sense that God desires to also be in communion with creation, for love is about relationship.

- We as fallible humans, however, can only recognize a loving relationship through signs, as when our loved ones offer us gifts of affection, praise, attention, mercy and merchandise.

- Like all signs, we perceive signs of love triadically, implying that the *imago Dei*—the image of God within us (Gen 1:27)—is manifest at the very level of perception. The trinitarian God, in other words, created humans to function like God's own self.[32]

- We can therefore argue that our inherently relational God guided the church, through a process of semiosis, to understand our relationship with Transcendent Love triadically as well: The Father is the ultimate *Object* of our devotion; the Son is the *Representamen* of God to us and us to God; and the Holy Spirit guides our *Interpretants* as we seek to understand our relationship to God through Christ.

This final point does not mean that Jesus represents God the way smoke represents fire. To think this way would reduce Jesus to an index, pointing to

---

[31]Even when someone says they love their car, or they love to ski, they are admitting to a relationship with that item or activity.

[32]The *imago Dei* passage from Genesis, as H. David Brumble notes, "is at the heart of St. Augustine's *De Trinitate*, where he attempts to discover what he can about God by examining the *imago Dei*. The most important way in which humanity images the triune God, argues Augustine, is in his mind." See "Imago Dei," in *A Dictionary of Biblical Tradition*, p. 372.

what caused him: an Arian reduction that Peirce does not endorse. Even before his mystical experience, Peirce thought Christians should believe "that Christ is now directing the course of history and presiding over the destinies of kings, and that there is no branch of the public weal which does not come within the bounds of his realm."[33] This belief, he knew, results from a centuries-long process of semiosis, guided by abductions made in multiple ecumenical councils.

When the First Council of Nicaea (325 c.e.) pronounced, and the First Council of Constantinople confirmed (381 c.e.) that Father and Son were one substance *(homoousios)*, and when the Council at Chalcedon added in 451 the double nature of Jesus—both fully God and fully human simultaneously—our predecessors established the coinherence of the Trinity. The Son is not only God's incarnated representamen on earth, but is also one being with the Object to whom we become reconciled, as fully divine as the Father. And the Spirit, who conceived the Son in a womb of flesh, connects the divine with the human—not only in Christ but also for us, through guidance of our interpretants. The Redeemer is therefore no less the Object of our belief and loving adoration than is the Creator, for the two are one: the coinherence of God's transcendent reality and immanent presence in the person of Jesus Christ.[34]

THE COUNCIL AT CHALCEDON: TWO NATURES IN CHRIST

To understand the Chalcedonian abduction about Christ's two natures—an idea many people consider outrageous—think of the following analogy. When I have speaking engagements in Europe, I take my laptop, which connects me not only to my scholarship, but also to my friends and family back in America. My laptop, then, represents various aspects of who I am. But for the laptop to work, I need to plug it in to an invisible source of power: electricity, which I cannot see but I know is there, bringing light and energy to the world. However, in England I cannot connect to that invisible source of

---

[33]Quoted in Orange, "Peirce's Conception of God," p. 14.

[34]In an essay arguing the significance of Peirce for evangelicals, Amos Yong writes that "there are fruitful insights to be gained in any effort to understand the doctrine of the Trinity if close attention is paid to Peirce's triadic categories. . . . Much more thought needs to be given to these matters." I have taken up Yong's challenge in this chapter. See Amos Yong, "The Demise of Foundationalism and the Retention of Truth: What Evangelicals Can Learn from C. S. Peirce," *Christian Scholar's Review* 29, no. 3 (Spring 2000): 581.

power without an adapter. Even if my laptop plug could fit the wall outlets in England, which is impossible, the different kind of power surges would quickly burn out my computer. A good adapter, however, can connect with my laptop on one end and plug into British wall sockets on the other end, while mediating between the different electrical charges.

The doctrine established at Chalcedon, then, determined that Christ's role is like that adapter: as both fully God and fully human, Jesus was able to mediate between the invisible source of power in the universe and the time-bound laptops of human existence. Only as a mediator can Jesus connect sinful flesh to transcendent righteousness.

Of course, this analogy is problematic on many different levels, not least of which is comparing Persons of the Trinity to wall sockets. For an analogy that employs the idea of personhood, picture a woman who stands between her white-haired father and her disobedient ten-year-old while holding their hands. The woman connects her father with her tear-stained ten-year-old through her body as each holds one of her hands. Jesus is like that woman, the hand of his divinity grasping the divinity of the Father, and the hand of his flesh grasping our fallen flesh. As children, then, we connect to the Father through Jesus. However, we only recognize this connection when prompted by the Holy Spirit, at which point, we reach out to join our free hand with that of the Father, who has been waiting, hand extended, for us to regret our disobedience and turn in his direction.

As a fleshly picture for a spiritual mystery, this analogy is woefully deficient as well. But it is more like the signs we see in art museums, where God is painted like a white-bearded old man, sometimes holding up the cross on which Jesus is nailed, with the Holy Spirit approaching as a dove. Nevertheless, this image, like all human-made imagery, cannot capture the Triune One who transcends all signs. This, of course, explains why God took on the sign of flesh to dwell among us. And in that flesh, Jesus gave us another sign, /Father/, to give our minds a picture of the One who transcends all signs of sex and gender. Like every sign, that sign is triadic, mirroring a Triune God who brought all signs of the universe into being.

SIGNIFYING HERESIES

In light of the triadic sign reinforcing the doctrine of the Trinity, we might therefore regard heresies about Jesus as based in a dyadic (X $\rightarrow$ Y) rather than triadic view of the sign. For example, Docetism (chapter two) saw Jesus as merely an apparition of God on earth: a ghostly signifier of the unreachably transcendent God. In contrast, Arianism regarded Jesus as enfleshed, but still a mere signifier pointing to the signified God of Love. Both views, failing to offer the mediation necessary for reconciliation with God, might be charted as in figure 8.1.

signifier (Jesus) —————————▶ SIGNIFIED (GOD)

Figure 8.1. Arian and Docetic signifiers

In the nineteenth century, Higher Critics argued from the other side of the coin, regarding Jesus as entirely human, pointing to God only insofar as he modeled the behavior that God desires for all of humanity (see fig. 8.2).

SIGNIFIER (JESUS) —————————▶ signified (God)

Figure 8.2. Higher Critics' signifiers

While the first diagram refers to people who place the emphasis on the reality of God, the second diagram represents those who put their entire focus on Jesus as moral exemplar. In contrast, the bishops at the multiple ecumenical councils stood on the edge, rolling the coin in a process of interpretation that reflected the coinherence inherent to a trinitarian concept of the sign. For them, Father and Son are two fully real persons of God made known to us through the third: the Spirit.

DIFFERING INTERPRETANTS: EAST VERSUS WEST

Nevertheless, different parts of the church generated different interpretants as to how the Trinity functions. Eastern Orthodox Christians tend to see the Trinity as diagrammed in figure 8.3.

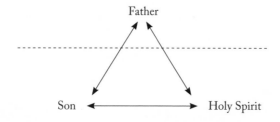

Figure 8.3. Eastern Orthodox Trinity

The dotted line signifies that the Father transcends all signs. At the same time, the Father connects with creation, the realm of signs, through his coinherence with the Son and Spirit. The Son entered into creation at a particular time and place, and the Spirit continues to connect us to the Father as our interpretants reach out to God.

The interpretant of the Western Church, however, caused doctrine to branch out in a different direction. In 589, bishops at the Third Council of Toledo echoed language used by Augustine in *De Trinitate* by adding the Latin word *filioque*, which means "and the Son," to the Nicene Creed. Doing so they (re)signed a centuries-long doctrinal statement. Rather than "[We believe] in the Holy Spirit, the Lord, and giver of life, who proceeds from the Father," the Creed now reads "[We believe] in the Holy Spirit, the Lord, and giver of life, who proceeds from the Father *and the Son*." To the minds of Eastern Orthodox Christians, this changed the sign of the Trinity (see fig. 8.4).

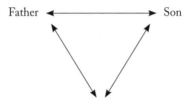

Father ◄————————————► Son

Holy Spirit, who proceeds from Father and Son

Figure 8.4. Trinity after *filioque* addition

This change so disturbed Christians in the East that it contributed to a growing division between the Western and Eastern church, resulting in a definitive break in 1054. Known as the East-West Schism, the church still hasn't resolved the filioque controversy.[35]

CHRISTIAN DISAGREEMENT

How do we explain the schism between the East and West? If, indeed, Christians truly submit themselves to the guidance of the Holy Spirit, who coinheres with us at the site of our interpretants, shouldn't signs of truth be the same to all?

---

[35]Poet Scott Cairns explained this distinction to me, noting that Eastern Orthodox scholars often draw triangles, as I have, to denote the change that the filioque clause represents to believers in the East.

Furthermore, why do Christians perceive the Son of God differently? Some see Jesus as a sign of submission to hegemony ("Render unto Caesar"); some see Jesus as a sign of counter-hegemonic action (healing on the sabbath); some see Jesus as a sign of pacifism ("Turn the other cheek"); some see Jesus as a sign of born-again grace ("not because of works"); some see Jesus as a sign of social justice ("Do this unto the least of them"); some see Jesus as endorsing socialism ("Sell all that you own and distribute it"); some see Jesus aligned with capitalism.[36] Where is the Holy Spirit in all of this? Opposite sides of the coin respond in opposite ways.

One side of the coin: Holy Spirit as **our** *interpretant.* Some Christians respond to the pluralism within Christianity by assuming that only *their* particular denomination has been guided by the Holy Spirit. The only truth is truth as they understand it. All other Christians are wrong and may even go to hell because they have resisted the guidance of the Holy Spirit. For example, I met someone who regularly preaches about the evils of the Christian college where I teach because our science professors do not believe that the world was created in 4004 B.C. She considers me, as well, to have been duped by the devil, because I teach the history of the English language by tracing its origins to ancient Indo-European language roots rather than to the Tower of Babel.

The other side of the coin: Holy Spirit as human construction. Because there are so many different interpretations of Christian doctrine, some people discard the idea of the Holy Spirit altogether, regarding it as a human "invention" that Christians use to justify practices that serve their own best interests. In fact, for some people, a doctrine about the Holy Spirit—the *filioque* clause—helps undermine the Holy Spirit. For if there were a Holy Spirit shaping interpretants of Christian truth, wouldn't all Christians agree? Especially about the Trinity?

Christians on the edge: Holy Spirit in relationship with human spirits. Christians on the edge attempt see the best in both sides of the coin. On the

---

[36]For an example of exegesis in support of capitalism, consider this statement by pastor Lyman Abbott: "Jesus did not say 'Lay not up for yourselves treasure upon earth.' He said 'Lay not up for yourselves treasures upon earth where moth and rust doth corrupt and where thieves break through and steal.' And no sensible American does. Moth and rust do not get at Mr Rockefeller's oil wells, and thieves do not often break through and steal a railway." Quoted in C. K. Ogden and I. A. Richards, *The Meaning of Meaning: A Study of the Influence of Language upon Thought and of the Science of Symbolism* (New York: Harcourt, Brace & World), p. 16.

one side they affirm that God has been uniquely revealed in Christ, who made reconciliation with God possible through the death and resurrection of Jesus. This truth distinguishes Christianity from all other religions. However, on the other side of the coin, they recognize the multiple ways Christians understand how salvation functions, such that theology does, indeed, seem to be shaped by humans. Some Christians, for example, are "exclusivists," arguing that only those who proclaim their "born again" status (Jn 3:3-7) will be in heaven (thus eliminating many Roman Catholic and Eastern Orthodox Christians). Some Christians are "universalists," believing that all humans will ultimately join God in heaven (see 2 Pet 3:9). Some Christians, disturbed by the certitude implied in both these positions, balance between them as "inclusivists," citing the sheep and goats passage from Matthew 25, where Jesus suggests that certain unbelievers will be included in heaven, while some people who expect to be there "will go away into eternal punishment" (Mt 25:46).[37] These divergent theologies result from different interpretants responding to the exact same Bible.

FALLIBILISM AND CHRISTIAN COMMUNICATION

Christians on the edge therefore constantly balance between God's truth and human formulations of that truth, knowing that we understand the former through the lens of the latter: the two coinhere. To deny this is to say that we have attained the mind of God, which would be sheer arrogance, if not blasphemy. As Christian philosopher Merold Westphal succinctly puts it, "The Logos is absolute; we are not."[38] Peirce calls such a condition "fallibilism": a human trait shared by both scientists and theologians.

In light of our fallibilism, then, how can we possibly have enough confidence to communicate our understanding of Christian truth? Coinherence might help us develop a rhetorical strategy. If relationship is indeed constitutive of God—Father, Son and Holy Ghost in constant communion with each other—it makes sense that humans, created in the image of God, reflect the

---

[37]For a discussion of C. S. Lewis's inclusivism, see Crystal Downing, *How Postmodernism Serves (My) Faith: Questioning Truth in Language, Philosophy and Art* (Downers Grove, IL: IVP Academic, 2006), pp. 202-6.

[38]This statement, made during a public lecture at Messiah College, January 19, 2010, distills what Westphal says elsewhere: "perspectivism is the relativism that insists that we are not God, that only God is absolute." See Merold Westphal, "Onto-theology, Metanarrative, Perspectivism, and the Gospel," *Christianity and the Postmodern Turn: Six Views,* ed. Myron B. Penner (Grand Rapids, MI: Baker, 2005), p. 152.

imago Dei through the coinherence of communion: not only with God but also with each other. In Peirce's terms, the *imago Dei* means that we are an *index* of the Trinity: a sign that points back to what created it.[39] And our *communion* with each other, if even only a shadow of the image of God among us, is fulfilled in *communication*.

Words, like all signs for Peirce, are communal as well: object, representamen and interpretant in "tri-relative" communion with each other.[40] And since "all thought whatsoever is a sign,"[41] the communion of the sign reflects the perception of the community that gives it value. A community molds the interpretants by which its members understand the Truth that transcends all human signs. As Peirce puts it, "The very origin of the conception of reality shows that this conception essentially involves the notion of a COMMUNITY, without definite limits, and capable of an increase in knowledge."[42] This explains why Jesus surrounded himself with a community of disciples in order to communicate the gospel message. This explains why Paul emphasized to the Romans and the Corinthians that Christians should perceive themselves as one body with many members: the communion of many in one (Rom 12:4-8; 1 Cor 12:12-31). This explains why leaders of the early church convened ecumenical councils—where they often communicated through passionate argumentation—to develop "an increase in knowledge" about God's character and relationship to creation. This explains why Christians continue to worship together: bodies of believers communing and communicating with and through God while communing and communicating with each other.

Peirce, in fact, suggested that community establishes personhood: "The individual man, since his separate existence is manifested only by ignorance and error, so far as he is anything apart from his fellows, and from what he and they are to be, is only a negation."[43] Personhood is negated without community. Or, as Eastern Orthodox Bishop Kallistos Ware puts it, "There is no true personhood without relationship."[44]

---

[39]Note how Brent defines "mysticism" in Peirce: "our temporal existence is an index of the eternal" (*Charles Sanders Peirce*, p. 354).

[40]Peirce, "Pragmatism in Retrospect," p. 282.

[41]Peirce, "The Essentials of Pragmatism," p. 258.

[42]C. S. Peirce, "Some Consequences of Four Incapacities," in *Philosophical Writings*, p. 247.

[43]Quoted in Brent, *Charles Sanders Peirce*, p. 338.

[44]Kallistos Ware is titular bishop of the Greek Orthodox Ecumenical Patriarchate. His statement is from an essay in which he parallels the thought of C. S. Lewis with Eastern Orthodox theology:

PERSONHOOD AND THE HOLY SPIRIT

Both Peirce and Ware, like many Christians, believe that relationship is necessary for personhood. Would we be true "persons," however, if we all thought the same? Doesn't our personhood reflect the contexts in which God has placed us, different communities generating habits of interpretation that inevitably affect the way we read signs? If all Christian communities came to the exact same conclusions on every theological issue, wouldn't we all function like robots programmed by the Holy Spirit? Do robots have personhood?

Instead, God, through the Holy Spirit, affirms our personhood through relationship: God meeting us where we are, both in time and space. Some Christian communities meet God through the sacraments, some through speaking in tongues. Some draw closer to God by separating from the world in order to meditate, some by going out into the world to preach the gospel. Instead of despairing over such differences, we should glory in God's affirmation of our personhood. As James K. A. Smith repeatedly emphasizes in *The Fall of Interpretation,* "interpretation is constitutive of human be-ing and creaturehood."[45] Or, to connect the language of Peirce with that of Bishop Ware, the Holy Spirit engages our personhood at the site of community-informed interpretants.

RESIGNED TO THE TRINITY

Using this rhetorical strategy, we communicate resignation to the Trinity as an essential Christian truth. Admittedly, it took four centuries for the doctrine of the Trinity to develop through a process of semiosis. But, as Peirce notes, "truth's independence of individual opinions is due . . . to its being the predestined result to which sufficient inquiry would ultimately lead"—despite the inevitable fallibility of human knowledge.[46] We might therefore communicate that the semiosis is complete when our sense of truth accords with the very way we perceive reality: according to the coinherence of the triadic sign. God's "progressive revelation," we might say, occurs at moments when a COMMUNITY is drawn away from dyadic, dualistic thinking in order to embrace the coinherence of three-in-one

---

"God of the Fathers: C. S. Lewis and Eastern Christianity," *The Pilgrim's Guide: C. S. Lewis and the Art of Witness,* ed. David Mills (Grand Rapids, MI: Eerdmans, 1998), p. 67.

[45]James K. A. Smith, *The Fall of Interpretation: Philosophical Foundations for a Creational Hermeneutic* (Downers Grove, IL: InterVarsity Press, 2000), p. 26.

[46]Peirce, "Pragmatism in Retrospect," p. 288.

that pervades the very universe—as happened at the first several ecumenical councils.[47]

THE COINHERENCE OF ETHICAL COMMUNICATION

In addition to helping us develop arguments for belief in the Trinity, the co-inherence of the triadic sign should also affect our everyday rhetoric. As Peirce writes in "The Essentials of Pragmatism," the "meaning of every proposition . . . becomes applicable to human conduct."[48] Perhaps, then, we should see the way we conduct our communication as an extension of our belief in the Trinity.

In their book *Semiotics Unbounded*, Petrilli and Ponzio describe Peircean-inspired semiotics with language that harmonizes with the coinherence of trinitarian theology. For them, effective communication necessitates an "interpretant of answering comprehension." Let's say, for example, that after seeing the burqa-clad woman in the airport (as described in chapter seven), I find myself seated next to her on the airplane. Rather than simply "identifying the interpreted"—Muslim woman, perhaps a terrorist in disguise—an "interpretant of answering comprehension . . . installs a relationship of involvement" with the person; "it responds to the interpreted and takes a stand in relation to it."[49] I therefore communicate with the Muslim representamen in such a way that my interpretant might change. I discover that under the burqa are signs of a wife, or a teacher, or a bird-watcher, or a writer: signs that similarly define me. My interpretant therefore changes by standing "in relation" to signs that we share. Petrilli calls this "semioethics": an ethical response to the signs of others.[50]

Jesus, of course, calls his followers to semioethics, most famously in the Golden Rule: "Do to others as you would have them do to you" (Lk 6:31). Or, in the language of semioethicists, we exercise an "interpretant of answering comprehension" by which we open ourselves to understanding the other. For

---

[47]I am (re)signing the term "progressive revelation," which has long been associated with evangelical scholars. See, for example, Bernard Ramm, *Protestant Biblical Interpretation: A Textbook of Hermeneutics*, 3rd ed. (Grand Rapids, MI: Baker, 1980), p. 101.

[48]Peirce, "The Essentials of Pragmatism," p. 261.

[49]Susan Petrilli and Augusto Ponzio, *Semiotics Unbounded: Interpretive Routes Through the Open Network of Signs* (Toronto: University of Toronto Press, 2005), p. xviii. The authors' phrase "answering comprehension" is inspired by Bakhtin, the subject of chapter ten below.

[50]Susan Petrilli, *Sign Crossroads in Global Perspective: Semioethics and Responsibility*, ed. John Deely (Piscataway, NJ: Transaction, 2010).

only by doing so can we expect them to open themselves to us, seeking to understand the communication of our belief in the Trinity and the mediation of the Holy Spirit between God and human.

Furthermore, because the Trinity is inherently relational, we are called, through the Holy Spirit, to respond to Christ with "answering comprehension"; we are called to take a stand in relationship with the Trinity by communicating with God through prayer: a communication that will change our interpretants. At the same time, the Holy Spirit engages with our personhood, not only through the perceptual habits of our Christian communities, but also through our collateral experiences. (Re)signing Christians therefore open themselves to experiences that aid in the development of their interpretants: reading up on church history as well as through the Bible; listening to political commentary as well as sermons; assessing the products of culture, via the media and the arts, that reflect the signs of the times. Communication is effective only when it participates in the communion of answering comprehension.

AGAPISM: (RE)SIGNING LOVE

For Peirce, "belief is partly determined by old beliefs and partly by new experience": beliefs to which we are resigned, and experiences that lead us to resign them.[51] The process of (re)signing therefore follows his "first rule of logic" (F.R.L.): "in order to learn, one needs to desire to learn and desire it without resting satisfied with that which one is inclined to think."[52] After his mystical experience, Peirce perceived God to be part of this process, guiding the evolution of semiosis. He called this divine guidance "agapism," from *agape,* one of the Greek words for love employed in the New Testament.

In an essay entitled "Evolutionary Love," Peirce acknowledged three (of course!) types of evolution: Darwinian chance, Hegelian necessity and, surmounting them both, "creative love."[53] This love embraces that which is "most bitterly hostile and negative to itself,"[54] reminding us not only of Der-

---

[51]C. S. Peirce, "What Is a Leading Principle?" in *Philosophical Writings,* p. 130.
[52]C. S. Peirce, "F. R. L." (First Rule of Logic), in *CP* 1.135.
[53]C. S. Peirce, "Evolutionary Love," in *Philosophical Writings,* pp. 364-55. Peirce's emphasis on evolution can be used to endorse progressivism at the expense of tradition. For this reason I do not give Peirce the last word. Mikhail Bakhtin, discussed in chapter ten, keeps us on the edge of the coin.
[54]Peirce here quotes what he calls the "sublime" words of William James. Ibid., p. 362.

rida's "hostipitality" (chapter six), but also of the Love that embraced us: "But God proves his love for us in that while we still were sinners, Christ died for us" (Rom 5:8). This, of course, is a fundamental doctrine of Christianity. But, even then, different Christians have different interpretations as to what this means (as will be explored more fully in chapter ten). When earnest believers respond to the Holy Spirit with "answering comprehension," their interpretants inevitably reflect their personhood, molded by diverse environments that generate different "habits" of perception.

Unfortunately, some readers may interpret this to mean that Christians have no right to question the interpretants of others, that tolerance is the highest goal of a faith-filled life. The next chapter addresses this issue, showing how tolerance and intolerance are, in fact, opposite sides of the exact same coin. (Re)signing Christians, as we shall see, balance on the edge by following the example of Jesus.

Part IV

Communication in a
Pluralistic World

9

SI(G)NS OF COMMUNICATION

(In)tolerance Versus the Gift

The signs /tolerance/ and /intolerance/ have become as problematic in our culture as /liberal/ and /conservative/. Those Christians who preach a single way to heaven are denounced by other Christians as *intolerant*. In response, the so-called intolerant Christians say advocates of religious pluralism honor the god of *tolerance* more than Jesus Christ. While the former see themselves committed to "truth," the latter see themselves committed to "love."

As opposite sides of the exact same coin, both kinds of Christians can easily fall into hypocrisy. Advocates of "truth" often ignore the history of Christianity, reluctant to educate themselves about how and when the truths they hold dear came into being. So much for the love of Christian truth! Similarly, advocates of "love" often preach it as an intellectual abstraction without practicing it, failing to disturb their comfortable lifestyles by donating significant time and money to people other than friends and family. So much for the truth of Christian love! Even the non-Christian Peter Singer, a famous utilitarian ethicist, argues that persons who do not give at least ten percent of their income to the needy are selfish. Imagine what he would say about the statistic discussed by Ron Sider in *The Scandal of the Evangelical Conscience:* that less than ten percent of "born-again" Christians tithe![1]

Equally problematic are Christians who assume that, by voting for a particular political party, they have fulfilled their commitment to love or truth, tolerance or intolerance. What an easy way to absolve oneself of personal re-

---

[1]Peter Singer, "What Should a Billionaire Give—and What Should You?" *New York Times Magazine*, December 17, 2006. Ronald J. Sider, *The Scandal of the Evangelical Conscience: Why Are Christians Living Just Like the Rest of the World?* (Grand Rapids, MI: Baker, 2005), p. 21.

sponsibility! But note: this is a self-directed sermon. I can be the most hypocritical Christian around. This chapter, in which I confess many sins, explores how Christians might negotiate the edge, balancing between blind intolerance and bland tolerance. How might we keep from falling down onto one side or the other? The answer, as you might have guessed, depends on one's view of the sign. I will argue that the structuralism generated by Saussure perpetuates the problematic extremes of tolerance and intolerance. In contrast, I will show how Peirce might keep us on the rhetorical edge, where we can persuasively argue for the truth of Christianity.

TOLERANCE OF SAUSSURE: COOKING UP SIGNS

In chapter three, I compared Saussure's concept of system, or *langue*, to a kitchen cabinet: a structure containing ingredients that can be cooked up into new signs. Hence, just as the cabinets in different kitchens contain ingredients that produce different foods, so different *langues* produce different signs of truth.[2] People often respond to these multiple cabinet structures in opposite ways: either with tolerance for all or by tolerating only one.

Let's apply this idea to religious truths. Advocates of tolerance would say that we have no right to condemn the signs cooked up from any religious cabinet, drawing an analogy with ethnic food: Ethiopian restaurants produce fare that tastes quite different than that produced in Mexican, Italian or Chinese restaurants, because each uses different ingredients. But, they would argue, that doesn't mean one kind of cuisine is superior to all the others. Though dissimilar in appearance and taste, each food provides nutrients that feed the body. So also with linguistic cabinets: they contain dissimilar ingredients that produce very different religious truths and practices, but each religion provides signs that feed the soul. One might prefer Ethiopian over Italian food, but it's more a matter of taste than right and wrong. The truly tolerant person therefore seeks to broaden her tastes, sampling the best signs from all religions.

Anyone employing such an argument, however, runs into a conundrum: if

---

[2]As in chapter three, I credit Paul Cobley and Litza Jansz for suggesting the metaphor of a "cupboard" to explain Saussure's system of differences, or *langue*. However, they oversimplify when they say that "*Langue* can be thought of as a communal cupboard, housing all the possible different signs which might be pulled out and utilized in the construction of an instance of *parole*." The cupboard doesn't contain the signs; rather, it contains a collection of ingredients that can produce signs. I therefore change the metaphor slightly, calling each system a "cabinet." See Paul Cobley and Litza Jansz, *Introducing Semiotics* (Duxford, UK: Icon, 1999), p. 15.

we cannot judge the truths produced by other cabinets, except by saying they do not conform to our own cabinet's products, what right do we have to ban distasteful products cooked up from the ingredients in certain cabinets?

Here's a real-life example. I met someone quite outspoken about the need to teach "tolerance for all viewpoints" in his college. To verify his commitment, he told a story about his Composition class: when one of his students wanted to write her persuasive research paper arguing why women should not be pastors, he refused to let her do it. Wanting to teach his "fundamentalist" student tolerance, he forced her to choose another topic. (I am not making this up!)

As in this example, people who advocate "tolerance" based on a structuralist view of competing sign systems inevitably become inconsistent. They preach tolerance as though their own linguistic cabinet contains just the right ingredients to produce accurate signs of what should and should not be tolerated. By thus implying the superiority of their own system of truth, they differ little from the "intolerant" fundamentalists they denounce, for both assume that their cabinet produces the most accurate signs of truth.

By exposing this inconsistency I have "deconstructed" what Homi Bhabha, a theorist influenced by Derrida, calls "well-intentioned moralist polemics against prejudice and stereotype."[3] In the spirit of both Derrida and Bhabha, I have deconstructed "tolerance" by showing that something outside of it—intolerance—is actually a part of it.

INTOLERANCE OF OTHER CABINETS

Christians intolerant of all cabinets but their own are more consistent, believing that only their signs can possibly bake up the "bread of salvation." Some will begrudgingly admit that their cabinet has different shelves: an Eastern Orthodox shelf, a Roman Catholic shelf, a Pentecostal shelf, a Southern Baptist shelf and so on. Nevertheless, many think only one of these shelves contains just the right ingredients for salvation. Any other shelf, not to mention all other cabinets, provides ingredients unf(l)avorable to God.

---

[3]Homi K. Bhabha, "The Commitment to Theory," in *The Norton Anthology of Theory and Criticism*, ed. Vincent B. Leitch et al., 2nd ed. (New York: Norton, 2010), p. 2368. While advocating the notion of "cultural difference," Bhabha takes issue with the problematic structuralist notion of "cultural diversity," for it naively assumes "the separation of totalized cultures that live unsullied by the intertextuality of their historical location" (ibid.).

This idea greatly disturbed my husband, David, while in middle school. He still remembers the day his Sunday school teacher announced that anyone who doesn't ask Jesus into their heart will go to hell. "What about all those people living in South America before Christian missionaries brought them the gospel?" David asked. "After all, they never had a chance to ask Jesus into their hearts!" The Sunday school teacher smugly responded, "Well, David, God knew in advance all those people who would reject his truth, and he put them in places that missionaries would never reach."

Fortunately, few Christians today would endorse such a warped view of God: a view not at all supported by the Bible. Even the idea of predestination is questioned by many evangelicals, due to ambiguities in Scripture about "election." But how much different from David's Sunday school teacher are those who assume that God will burn up all signs but their own?

THE VIOLENCE OF INTOLERANCE

The disdain of signs produced from other cultural cabinets can easily become violent, as illustrated by a shameful incident during my grade school days. One summer weekday, a neighbor girl invited me to walk with her to the local Catholic church where her family worshiped. Inside, after splashing holy water as though frolicking at a pool party, we bowed to the statue of Mary, lit all the candles at the front of the church, climbed into adjacent confession booths where we whispered silly nothings through the conjoining window, and then ran atop the oak pews, jumping across the aisles from one pew to another, pretending to be Superwoman. At the time, I felt not a shred of shame, mainly because I did not value the signs I had desecrated. If anything, I felt self-righteous: I was confirming the truth of Protestantism by demeaning the signs of Roman Catholicism. For me, the Holy Water was anything but holy; it was a sign of empty ritual rather than a reminder of baptism. The confessional booths signaled not the biblical injunction to "confess your sins"; they signaled legalism. The statue of Mary was not an image of the Mother of God; it was a sign of idolatry.

While this incident might be credited to the immaturity of ten-year-old girls, my irresponsible behavior differs little from Taliban adults who, in March 2001, destroyed ancient images of Buddha that had been carved into cliff walls in Afghanistan. For them, signs of the Buddha gesture toward the profane: that which is outside of (*pro-*) the sacred structure of *their* cabinet of truth (the word *fane* denotes a sacred structure). Signs of the "other" have no value for them.

Such physical attacks parallel the ferocious verbal attacks generated by many Democrats and Republicans in our own country, both disdaining signs of the other's belief. As becomes obvious during every election, political "true believers" become positively religious in their goal to exchange their political sign-system for that of the party currently in power. They want to exchange one cabinet *(langue)* for another.

The concept of *exchange* that motivates much religious and political rhetoric is fundamental to *a structuralist view of the sign.* This concept is important to understand, for it is the very idea of *exchange* that perpetuates simplistic notions of tolerance versus intolerance.

SIGNS OF EXCHANGE: MONEY

To understand the logic of exchange implied by Saussure's structuralism, think of monetary exchange. Money is a sign that can be exchanged for lattes, loofahs, lozenges and love. Originally functioning like Peirce's "index" (smoke indexes fire), money once pointed to a nation's gold and silver reserves. Today, however, money functions more like Peirce's symbol: a conventional sign endorsed and maintained by national governments.

As a symbol, currency has no absolute value in itself, functioning only according to differences within and between systems. I experience this every time I go to England. One summer an American dollar will buy two pounds; several summers later it buys only a pound and a half. In fact, the difference can vary from day to day. In the 1980s, when my husband and I led twenty students to England for semester-long study programs, we would watch for bank postings, attempting to exchange money for our living expenses on days when the exchange rate was in our favor. We could "lose" dozens of dollars if we exchanged on the wrong day. Monetary signs had no absolute value.

Saussure's sign is like money that has no value except from the national banking system that produces it.[4] The sign of a peso works only in a Mexican system; the sign of a pound works only in a British system. Hence, Saussure's

---

[4]Saussure makes the analogy of monetary exchange explicit, using the example of "a five-franc piece" in order to show how "a word can be exchanged for something dissimilar, an idea." See Ferdinand de Saussure, *Course in General Linguistics,* trans. Wade Baskin (New York: Philosophical Library, 1959), p. 115.

signs function according to "a code regulating exchange relations between signifiers and signifieds."[5] Here's an example: when I use the signifier "hat," I get in exchange the signified concept of an object worn on the head. Of course, my dear friend Cathy, as a child, used to walk around her parents' house with a live duck on her head: an object I would hesitate to call a hat. This goes to show that the signifier "hat" can be exchanged only for a particular signified, just as a single dollar bill can be exchanged only for particular objects: for candy, say, but not for a car.

Derrida therefore uses the word "exchangist" to describe the structuralism that Saussure set into motion.[6] Semioticians Susan Petrilli and Augusto Ponzio follow suit, calling the Saussurean sign model "equal exchange semiotics," and they note how it was influenced by economic theory. This, however, disturbs them: "When the study of language follows the same path as the study of the marketplace in an ideal state of equilibrium, the result is a static conception of sign."[7] Christians should be disturbed as well, for the concept of economic exchange runs counter to the gospel message, undermining the dynamic *gift* of salvation.[8]

EXCHANGE VERSUS THE GIFT

Many of us have caught ourselves wondering why someone gave us a gift, questioning what the giver wants in exchange. I felt this way when high school or college guys I barely knew took me on extravagant dates. What did they expect from me in return? I think we all know what some of them expected. But not all were this way. Some were lavishing me with elegant dinners and expensive concert tickets because they liked me. End of story. Unfortunately, having become suspicious from several bad experiences, I failed to read their signs as gifts. It reminds me of television moments when a woman responds to her husband's presentation of a gorgeous bouquet with "What did you do now?!" Rather than a sign of love, the roses function in her

---

[5]Susan Petrilli and Augusto Ponzio, *Semiotics Unbounded: Interpretive Routes Through the Open Network of Signs* (Toronto: University of Toronto Press, 2005), p. xviii.

[6]Jacques Derrida, *Given Time: I. Counterfeit Money*, trans. Peggy Kamuf (Chicago: University of Chicago Press, 1994), p. 76.

[7]Petrilli and Ponzio, *Semiotics Unbounded,* pp. 74, xvii. The authors explain that "the Saussurean sign model is heavily influenced by the marginalistic theory of economic value as developed by the School of Lausanne" (p. xvii).

[8]Kathryn Tanner makes a similar point in *Economy of Grace* (Minneapolis: Fortress, 2005), pp. 56-57.

mind as compensation for some vagary. The roses, for her, signal what Derrida calls "an economy of exchange."[9]

This, in fact, illuminates one of my many failings in life: I tend to read signs according to an economy of exchange rather than according to the goodness of grace. For example, I once destroyed a birthday gift I had given to my generous friend Anita: not physically but economically. When she expressed joy upon opening the package, I immediately gloated, "Oh good; now we're even!" At the time, I interpreted the look she gave me as a sign of my tackiness: one doesn't express such things out loud. Only now do I recognize that Anita was hurt because I had reduced my gift to an economy of exchange. Thus, my gift was no longer a gift. Furthermore, by regarding my own present as payback for all the wonderful things Anita had given me, I had rejected the grace behind her gifts.

When I read *The Gift of Death* by Derrida, I felt him haunting Anita's birthday party. Like a specter from the past he was speaking to me about my economic sin:

> The moment the gift, however generous it be, is infected with the slightest hint of calculation, the moment it takes account of knowledge *[connaissance]* or recognition *[reconnaissance]*, it falls within the ambit of an economy: it exchanges, in short it gives counterfeit money, since it gives in exchange for payment.[10]

The phrase "counterfeit money" alludes to an earlier work, *Given Time*, in which Derrida discusses a short narrative (titled "Counterfeit Money") by French poet Charles Baudelaire (1821-1867). The narrator of Baudelaire's tale describes a friend who admits that the coin he gave a beggar was "counterfeit." In response, the narrator states, "I then saw clearly that [the friend's] aim had been to do a good deed while at the same time making a good deal; . . . to win paradise economically; in short, to pick up gratis the certificate of a charitable man."[11] Derrida builds upon this tale to suggest that any gift given in hope for something in exchange—whether it be the reputation for charity or the gratitude of the recipient—is "counterfeit coin."

---

[9]Jacques Derrida, *The Gift of Death*, trans. David Wills (Chicago: University of Chicago Press, 1995), p. 102.

[10]Ibid. The translator bracketed Derrida's original French to foreground his pun.

[11]Derrida, *Given Time*, p. 32. *Given Time* provides multiple complex interpretations of Baudelaire's tale that exceed the point of my chapter.

Derrida thus returns us to the primary metaphor of this book: a coin on edge. To stay on the edge, Christians cannot offer the coin of communication the way Saussure's signifiers are offered in exchange for their signified meaning. To communicate the salvation message in exchange for something else—God's favor, heaven, self-righteous satisfaction—is to offer the needy a counterfeit coin. Why? Because the message itself is about a gift.

THE GIFT OF SALVATION

The New Testament repeatedly emphasizes that salvation does not function according to "a code regulating exchange relations." Eternal life is a gift made possible through the death and resurrection of Jesus: a gift freely offered to all willing to accept it. Of course, to accept a gift, one must not only *believe* that the giver has offered it, but also have *faith* that the gift is offered in love, with no strings attached. For as soon as we perceive strings attached, we no longer see it as a gift. We see it operating according to an economy of exchange.

As Derrida notes in *The Gift of Death*, Jesus repeatedly teaches against such economic thinking: "You have heard that it was said, 'An eye for an eye and a tooth for a tooth.' But I say to you, Do not resist an evildoer. But if anyone strikes you on the right cheek, turn the other also. . . . For if you love those who love you what reward do you have? Do not even the tax collectors do the same?" (Mt 5:38-39, 46).[12] Derrida's commentary on these verses helps explain Christ's reference to the reward as well as to tax collectors:

> If you love only those who love you and to the extent that they love you, if you hold so strictly to this symmetry, mutuality, and reciprocity, then you give nothing, no love, and the reserve of your wages will be like a tax that is imposed or a debt that is repaid, like the acquittal of a debt. In order to deserve or expect an infinitely higher salary, one that goes beyond the perception of what is due, you have to give without taking account and love those who don't love you.[13]

For me, this helps explain the disturbing verse that closes Matthew 5: "Be perfect, therefore, as your heavenly Father is perfect" (Mt 5:48). For decades this idea oppressed me. But that is because I was thinking according to an economy of exchange: to be worthy of God's favor I needed to be as perfect as

---

[12]Derrida, *Gift of Death*, pp. 102, 106. The translator uses the KJV, which I have changed to the NRSV.
[13]Ibid., p. 106.

God, which, of course, is impossible.[14] But considering the context of Matthew 5, perfection simply means love: God is love, which does not function according to an economy of exchange; and neither should we. To be perfect, then, is to offer the gift of love with no expectation of return.

Numerous examples from the Gospels reinforce this message.

THE PRODIGAL—OR ECONOMICALLY IRRESPONSIBLE—SON

People often forget that the story of the prodigal son appears in the midst of parables related to economic issues. Luke 15 begins with denunciations of Jesus by Pharisees and scribes because he dined with tax-collectors and sinners. Christ's critics implied that unclean people had not *earned* a right to eat with him. In response, Jesus tells multiple tales, first about a shepherd who leaves 99 sheep untended in order to look for one that has become lost. This certainly could not be economically astute, for the shepherd might lose several untended sheep to predators while searching for only one. Quite clearly, however, the story does not endorse the fiscal responsibility of an economy of exchange.

The woman in the next story seems more fiscally savvy, not putting her assets into jeopardy. Having lost one of her ten silver coins, she searches her whole house until she finds it. But then, like the shepherd in the first story, "she calls together her friends and neighbors, saying, 'Rejoice with me, for I have found the coin that I had lost'" (Lk 15:9). Such rejoicing, however, implies a party. She therefore may have spent more than one coin celebrating her discovery of the one she had lost. Such fiscally frivolous behavior certainly harmonizes with the idea behind Christ's next story.

In the third parable of Luke 15, a son asks his father for his inheritance, taking all his assets to "a distant country," where he parties with abandon. After "he squandered his property in dissolute living," a famine reduces him to such squalor that even pig food looks appetizing. So he decides to return

---

[14]Significantly, Derrida considers a pure gift impossible. This is because any time someone consciously has a reason for giving, she operates according to exchange: "In giving the reasons for giving, in saying the reason of the gift, it signs the end of the gift" (*Given Time*, p. 148; see also p. 123 on the issue of "intention" behind the gift). For Derrida, the perfect gift is made unwittingly, the giver unaware she is giving. Later in his writings, however, Derrida also aligned "the Impossible" with God. This lends piquancy to Christian orthodoxy: the impossible gift is made possible by *the* Impossible. And I believe that the more Christlike we become, our charitable actions become so automatic that we are not conscious of them as gifts—thus approximating Derrida's notion of "the gift."

to his father with an offer of economic exchange: food for labor. However, before he can deliver his planned speech—"I am no longer worthy to be called your son; treat me like one of your hired hands"—his father, seeing him at a distance, runs to welcome him home. Then, like the shepherd and the woman in the preceding two parables, the father does something fiscally irresponsible: he throws a party! Only this case is much worse, for the prodigal son does not deserve to be showered with so much love. Indeed, the older son recognizes the injustice of it all, telling his father, "For all these years I have been working like a slave for you, and I have never disobeyed your command; yet you have never given me even a young goat so that I might celebrate with my friends." The older son thinks according to an economy of exchange: celebration should signify reward for obedience.

But Christ's whole point is that the father's love does not operate according to such an economy. He offers grace to his son not as a reward but as a gift, fulfilling those famous words to the Ephesians: "For by grace you have been saved through faith, and this is not your own doing; it is the gift of God—not the result of works" (Eph 2:8-9). The father is therefore as prodigal as the son, only for opposite reasons: the son's prodigality was selfish, serving his own interests; the father's prodigality was an excess of love, serving the needs of the other.[15]

Perhaps this story should be renamed "The Economically Responsible Son," for the older brother displays the characteristics of many people today— including me. As my closest friends will tell you, I complain about academicians with higher salaries who work half as much as I do, about professors who get second-rate books published just because of the prestige of their schools, about students who expect to get good grades without doing excellent work. In my mind, only people who work hard and work smart should be rewarded.

Father forgive me, for I know what I do: I grumble like the economically responsible son. He and I parallel workers in a parable told only in Matthew: the story of laborers who protest when everyone hired gets paid the same. Whining to the owner of the vineyard who recruited them, they complain, "These last worked only one hour, and you have made them equal to us who

[15]Catholic philosopher Jean-Luc Marion, a former student of Jacques Derrida, discusses the Prodigal Son parable to the same end. See *God Without Being*, trans. Thomas A. Carlson (Chicago: University of Chicago Press, 1991), p. 97.

have borne the burden of the day and the scorching heat" (Mt 20:12).

Such desire for justice seems only natural, explaining why so many religions function according to an economy of exchange: make the right sacrifices, practice the right rituals, believe the right things, use the right signs (like /born again/) and you'll get salvation in return. But Jesus has the landowner respond to his grumbling laborers by defying an economy of exchange: "I choose to give to this last the same as I give to you. Am I not allowed to do what I choose with what belongs to me? Or are you envious because I am generous?" (Mt 20:14-15). Laborers—like the scribes and Pharisees that begin Luke 15—want an economy of fair exchange rather than the generosity of the gift. Communication theorist John Durham Peters calls this "the eternal complaint of economics against love."[16]

THE ECONOMIC IRRESPONSIBILITY OF THE DISHONEST MANAGER

Luke 16 begins with this "eternal complaint." We are told of a rich man who discovers that his manager "was squandering his property" (Lk 16:1). The Greek word for "squandering" here is the same word used in Luke 15:13 to describe the "squandering" of the prodigal son: a clue that might help us interpret this strange story.

Jesus narrates that the manager learns his job is in jeopardy. The manager therefore goes to his master's debtors, requiring each of them to repay only a portion of what they owe. Then we read,

> And his master commended the dishonest manager because he had acted shrewdly; for the children of this age are more shrewd in dealing with their own generation than are the children of light. And I tell you, make friends for yourselves by means of dishonest wealth so that when it is gone, they may welcome you into the eternal homes. (Lk 16:8-9)

Huh? Dishonesty commended? How unfair is that?

Precisely! As with the prodigal son and the vineyard laborers, our Master does not function in terms of economic exchange. This may give new meaning to the famous statement four verses later: "You cannot serve God and wealth"

---

[16]John Durham Peters, *Speaking into the Air: A History of the Idea of Communication* (Chicago: University of Chicago Press, 1999), p. 55. Peters discusses the parables of Luke 15 in order to distinguish two approaches to communication: the emphasis on interpersonal dialogue modeled by Socrates in Plato's *Phaedrus,* and the idea of dissemination (scattering the seed) modeled by Jesus in the Gospels.

(Lk 16:13). In other words, the realm of wealth operates according to economies of exchange; but the realm of God functions according to the gift. This, I believe, is also the point of the Good Samaritan.

THE GOOD—OR ECONOMICALLY IRRESPONSIBLE—SAMARITAN

Jews reviled Samaritans as impure, due to their complicity with pagan invaders. This occurred during the Assyrian invasions seven hundred years before Christ, when Jews in the Northern Kingdom of Samaria made economically advantageous marriages with their conquerors. Such fiscally motivated behavior may provide a backdrop for the fiscally irresponsible Samaritan in the famous parable.

The context is significant. Jesus has just complimented a lawyer for knowing the key to eternal life: "You shall love the Lord your God with all your heart, and with all your soul, and with all your strength, and with all your mind; and your neighbor as yourself" (Lk 10:27). But when the lawyer proceeds to ask, "Who is my neighbor?" Jesus tells the tale of a mugged traveler lying at the side of a road. When a Jewish priest and then a Levite pass by the beaten and stripped body, both walk wide of the victim, probably due to Jewish purity laws: touching a bloody man of questionable origins would make them unclean—like Samaritans! In contrast, a Samaritan stranger not only cleans and bandages the sufferer's wounds, but also pays an inn keeper to care for him, getting nothing in exchange.

But then Jesus puts a strange twist on the tale. We expect him to point out that the victim of violence is the "neighbor" the lawyer should love. But instead, Jesus establishes the Samaritan—an impure ethnicity made all the more impure by touching a bloody man—as the "neighbor": "Which of these three, do you think, was a *neighbor* to the man who fell into the hands of the robbers?" In response, as Harold Lindsell notes, "the lawyer could not bring himself to use the word 'Samaritan,'" so reviled was the sign.[17] Instead, the lawyer answers, "The one who showed him mercy" (Lk 10:36-37).

Significantly, /mercy/ is etymologically related to the words mercantile, merchant, market, merchandise and mercenary—all coming from a Latin root meaning "goods." All the words except *mercy*, however, allude to goods received through an economy of exchange: you give me money, I'll give you

---

[17]Harold Lindsell, ed., *Harper Study Bible* (Grand Rapids, MI: Zondervan, 1965), p. 1552.

merchandise; you give me money, I'll kill your enemies. Mercy, however, grants goods—or "the good"—totally apart from economic exchange: as did the Good Samaritan. Mercy, in other words, is a gift.

By pronouncing the Samaritan a "neighbor," then, Jesus taught the lawyer (and us) two things:

1. "Eternal life" (Lk 10:25) comes to those whose love of God and neighbor avoids an economy of exchange.

2. We must regard as our "neighbor" anyone who exercises such love, even if we consider them impure in their beliefs and practices.

These conclusions might help us resolve the tolerance/intolerance issue. Rather than think according to the structuralism instigated by Saussure, wherein we feel the need to either tolerate all religious cabinets or denounce any but our own, we need to think according to Peirce's trinitarian sign. By using the word "neighbor" for the Samaritan, for example, Jesus was changing the lawyer's interpretant: how he *saw* his neighbor.

THE GOOD SAMARITAN: SAUSSURE VERSUS PEIRCE

Let's consider the parable semiotically. It begins with the lawyer's question about the economy of eternal life: "what must I *do* to inherit eternal life?" It would appear that the lawyer was thinking like Saussure. As Susan Petrilli and Augusto Ponzio explain, for Saussure "the sign is caught within a synchronic framework, one dominated by the logic of perfect correspondence between that which is given and that which is received"; and this logic appeals "to a code regulating exchange relations between signifiers and signifieds."[18] We might chart it as illustrated in figure 9.1.

Figure 9.1. Exchangist thought

Rather than answering with a simple signifier, however, Jesus responds with a question: "What is written in the law?" (Lk 10:26). When the lawyer (presumably versed in the law) answers with scriptural truths about love of

---

[18]Petrilli and Ponzio, *Semiotics Unbounded*, p. xviii.

God and neighbor, Jesus finally says, "Do this" (Lk 10:28). But note, how does one "do" love? Love does not function according to an economy of exchange, but according to gifts of unmerited favor. The lawyer is therefore unsatisfied, still desiring an identifiable signifier that might be exchanged for the signified of eternal life. So he asks, "Who is my neighbor?" (Lk 10:29), which could be charted as in figure 9.2.

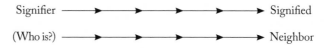

Figure 9.2. Saussure's dyadic sign applied to neighbor

Jesus, however, triangulates the sign by giving competing definitions of neighbor (see fig. 9.3).

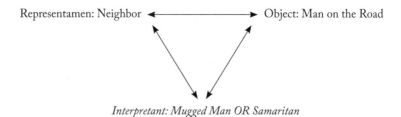

Figure 9.3. Triangulated sign of neighbor

Which man on the road is the sign of one's neighbor? Clearly not the priest or the Levite, who avoid the mugged man the same way they avoid Samaritans. But note, Jesus (re)signs the lawyer's understanding of "neighbor" by appealing to his interpretant: there are different ways of interpreting "neighbor." Not only are victims of social injustice our neighbors, but so also are people outside our religious systems—like Samaritans.

Rather than responding with tolerance for all cabinets or intolerance of any but our own, Jesus answers the question "what must I do to inherit eternal life?" by appealing to our interpretants, implying that the scriptural "law" of love should mold the way we see others. He thus deconstructs an easy correspondence between signifiers and signifieds. In other words, Jesus does not interpret signs of salvation according to an economy of exchange: this signifier gets that signified. Instead he endorses salvation as a gift.

Unlike Jesus, many religious people function according to an economy of exchange: "do this" and you "get that." Buddhists, in fact, call such exchange "karma," which the *OED* defines as follows: "the sum of a person's actions in one of his successive states of existence, regarded as determining his fate in the next." We might chart it as in figure 9.4.

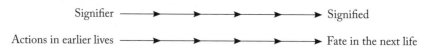

Figure 9.4. Saussure's dyadic sign applied to salvation

In contrast, we might chart the Christian sign of salvation triadically (see fig. 9.5).

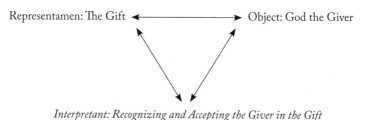

Figure 9.5. Triangulated sign of salvation

THE FALL INTO EXCHANGIST THOUGHT

Unfortunately, humans tend to fall into economies of exchange when it comes to their religious practices. In fact, "the Fall" could be interpreted as the result of economic thinking. In the Genesis story, the serpent tempts Eve not just with a tasty bit of ripe fruit; he tempts her with what she will get *in exchange* for eating it: "when you eat of it your eyes will be opened, and you will be like God, knowing good and evil" (Gen 3:5). In contrast, having read the entire Bible, our interpretants should be trained to see God's warning against eating from "the tree that is in the middle of the garden" as a prediction of natural consequences rather than as a statement of what one gets in exchange.

So what is the difference between consequence and exchange? Here's how I think of it: when a child is told he will "suffer the consequences" if he does not wash his hands, he could interpret this to mean that hygiene police regularly roam bathrooms, ready to slap anyone who fails to soap up. Such an interpretation would reflect exchangist thought: one gets a slap in exchange for failing to follow an arbitrary law. (Remember that signs in the exchangist thought of Saussure are arbitrary.) Instead, of course, consequences reflect the way we were created and have evolved: failure to wash hands allows germs to spread, causing sickness and perhaps even death. Similarly, God's laws reflect what is best for us. Rather than punishing us in exchange for breaking arbitrary laws, our loving God wants us to avoid the consequences of sin.

Let's take this idea back to the garden. God does not say to Eve, "I will punish you if you eat of that tree." Rather, God communicates something like "Just as you will get burned if you touch fire, so 'you shall die' if you 'touch' the tree" (Gen 3:3). Confirming this interpretation is the way Satan tempts Jesus in the wilderness. When the first two temptations do not work, Satan ups the ante by displaying splendid "kingdoms of the world" and then stating, "All these I will give you, *if* you will fall down and worship me" (Mt 4:8-9). Notice how the devil uses the language of giving, but immediately undermines it with the concept of exchange. One could conclude, then, that temptation is based on exchangist thought: if I cheat on my test I'll get in exchange a better grade; if I cheat on my taxes I'll get in exchange more spending money; if I cheat on my spouse I'll get in exchange erotic gratification. But the consequences of such exchangist thought might be a sickness of the soul that leads to the death of all God intended for us.

While theologians might easily align such exchangist attitudes with the Fall, anthropologists actually *do* align exchangist attitudes with the human condition (which, in the Judeo-Christian tradition, is pretty much saying the same thing). In an extremely influential book called *The Gift* (1925), French anthropologist Marcel Mauss argues that numerous cultures operate according to systems of exchange, where gifts serve the interests of givers as much as the needs of the recipients.[19] Influenced by Mauss, structural anthropologist Lévi-Strauss (see chapters four and six) extended the idea of exchange even to marriage rites. For him the incest taboo had nothing to do with biological or psychological health. Instead, laws against sex among family members had to do with an economy of exchange: women are like coins traded among different tribes and therefore need to remain available for reciprocal gift-giving. Like Saussure's semiology that inspired him, Lévi-Strauss's structuralism operates according to an economy of exchange.

---

[19]Marcel Mauss, *The Gift: The Form and Reason for Exchange in Archaic Societies,* trans. W. D. Halls (New York: Norton, 1990). In *Given Time,* Derrida repeatedly challenges *The Gift,* discussing how Mauss fails to question the idea of reciprocity.

Significantly, Lévi-Strauss regarded such exchange to be a form of communication. Christians therefore need to assess our own understanding of communication, especially the communication of our faith. When do our signs fall into similar economies of exchange?

THE HOCUS-POCUS OF EXCHANGE

As we saw in chapter seven, Protestants sometimes criticize Roman Catholics for hocus-pocus thinking, wherein signifiers can magically be exchanged for signified blessings. For example, in the medieval era, many churches had reliquaries, elaborate golden boxes inlaid with gems, each of which contained a holy object: a piece of the cross, bone chips or eyelids of a saint. Pilgrims would travel for days to see the famous contents of a reliquary, believing that they would get something in exchange: healing, shorter time in purgatory, a successful crop. It was like magic!

But how is this any different from evangelicals who think they can magically avoid hell simply by appropriating the sign /born again/? Without an ensuing commitment to follow the sacrificial example of Christ, the phrase "I accept Christ" becomes mere hocus-pocus language, getting one into heaven the same way Ali Baba used "Open Sesame" to get into a treasure cave.

Like the snake in the garden, exchangism tempts all seekers after God. In fact, one could argue that a logic of exchange motivated many of the greatest behavioral problems in Christian history: problems that skeptics love to foreground in order to denounce Christianity. The Crusades provide an obvious example. As Rodney Stark makes very clear in *God's Battalions: The Case for the Crusades,* church leaders recruited knights to fight the Muslims by promising that, in exchange, all their former sins would be forgiven (and perhaps their future sins, considering the number of prostitutes that joined crusader camps, offering sex in exchange for money). As a result, when crusaders lost both land and battles, many exchanged their Christianity for the religion of the winners. As Philip Jenkins notes, "what turned Christians to Islam was 'the common acceptance by Muslim and Christian alike of the error that the favor of God is shown by worldly success.'"[20] One can't help wondering how

---

[20]See especially chapter five of Rodney Stark, *God's Battalions: The Case for the Crusades* (New York: HarperOne, 2009); Philip Jenkins, *The Lost History of Christianity: The Thousand-Year Golden Age of the Church in the Middle East, Africa, and Asia—and How It Died* (San Francisco: HarperOne, 2008), p. 224.

this logic of exchange differs from Christians today who say God will bless America *only if* its citizens maintain certain beliefs and practices!

Note how the economy of exchange functions in each of these examples: rather than accept reconciliation with God as a gift available to any taker, religious people feel the need to do or say something in exchange for God's favor, believing that their extra efforts will earn them grace. Believing so, they undermine the very concept of grace. Even worse, as philosopher Bruce Ellis Benson puts it, "To follow Christ because one will profit in some anterior way is to set up an idol, to put something in Christ's place."[21]

LUTHER AND ECONOMIC EXCHANGE

Martin Luther was so disgusted by economies of exchange within Christendom that, in 1517, he placed a challenge to the entire Church on the door of one particular church. Significantly, his 95 theses nailed to that Wittenberg door primarily address a practice of economic exchange: the buying and selling of indulgences. Like a coupon for fifty cents off one's next purchase of Tide detergent, an "indulgence" might give a paying customer fifty days off the cleansing tide of purgatory. Remission from sin had become a purchasable commodity.

One contemporary of Luther, a professional "pardoner" named Johann Tetzel, actually used advertising to sell his indulgence papers. He wrote a jingle similar in tactics to those used in 1960s television commercials: "As soon as the coin in the coffer rings, / The soul from purgatory springs!"[22] Rather than keeping their coins on edge, Christians were giving up their coins to get better passage to heaven. Indulgences had come to signal merchandizing more than mercy.

Resigned to Christ's mercy, Luther committed himself to re-signing the five-hundred-year tradition of indulgences: he committed himself to the (re) signing of truth. He believed that the only indulgence humans need is that freely offered by God and made available through the resurrection of Jesus Christ. God indulges us with the gift of salvation the same way the prodigal father indulged his returning son.

---

[21]Bruce Ellis Benson, *Graven Ideologies: Nietzsche, Derrida and Marion on Modern Idolatry* (Downers Grove, IL: InterVarsity Press, 2002), p. 138.
[22]Alister E. McGrath, *In the Beginning: The Story of the King James Bible and How It Changed a Nation, a Language, and a Culture* (New York: Doubleday, 2001), p. 48.

When Luther was accused of heresy, he amplified his theses rather than revoking them, emphasizing justification by faith alone, as validated by Scripture alone. Repeatedly pressured by the Church to renounce his views, Luther committed himself all the more to re-signing the teachings of Christianity. After a 1520 bull condemned his multiple "errors," he wrote *The Babylonian Captivity of the Church,* finally resigning from the Church hierarchy and his adherence to the seven sacraments.

Martin Luther, then, exemplifies one of the fundamental principles upon which (re)signing must rest: a commitment to the gift of salvation rather than to economies of exchange. Unfortunately, Luther, like many of his followers, so emphasized the paradigm of "grace through faith," that he fell into structuralist (cabinet) thinking rather than semiotic (interpretant) thinking. For him the cabinet of the Roman Church contained the antichrist (the pope) and must be repudiated. Furthermore, he became so rigid about "grace through faith" that he denounced one of the books of the Bible, calling it "a book of straw." Why? Because the book of James teaches that "faith by itself, if it has no works, is dead" (Jas 2:17). Luther's repudiation of James might be schematized as in figure 9.6.

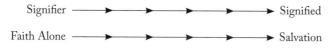

Figure 9.6. Dyadic sign applied to Luther's "faith alone"

By leaving no room for alternate ways of seeing the relationship between salvation and faith, this dyadic sign ignores teachings of Jesus that emphasize how we treat our neighbor. We have already considered Christ's neighborly answer to the lawyer's question about "eternal life." We could also cite Christ's more daunting answer to the rich young ruler who asks, "what must I do to inherit eternal life?" First Jesus tells him to "sell all that you own and distribute the money to the poor," then to "follow me" (Lk 18:18, 22).

FAITH AND WORKS: OPPOSITE SIDES OF THE SAME COIN

Inattentive readers might assume I am preaching works here, but that would obviously go against everything I have been saying so far in this chapter. Instead, I am encouraging triadic rather than dyadic thinking: I am encouraging the semiotic of Peirce over the semiology of Saussure. People who read signs dyadically reduce salvation to one way or the other, as illustrated by figure 9.7.

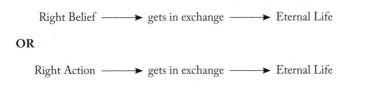

Right Belief ⟶ gets in exchange ⟶ Eternal Life

OR

Right Action ⟶ gets in exchange ⟶ Eternal Life

Figure 9.7. Faith and works as either/or

In contrast, a semiotic view of the sign puts us in a third place: on the edge of the coin, maintaining balance between both. The third place is Peirce's interpretant, which recognizes that the representamen of salvation—like the neighbor on the road—should be seen both ways. Because the interpretant is a sign in the mind, it becomes triadic as well, open to a new interpretant. We could make a chart similar to the one in chapter seven about the burqa-clad woman (see fig. 9.8).

Both branches reflect acceptance of God's gift. Rather than either/or, it is a both/and response.

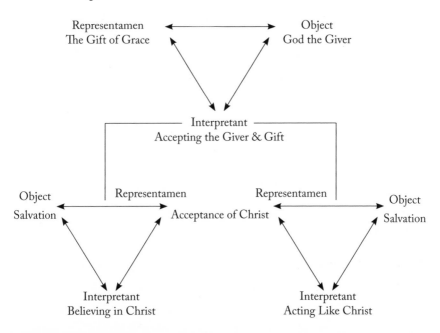

Figure 9.8. Action and belief as branching interpretants

The process of semiosis, of course, will continue to branch out as different Christians develop different interpretants of what "believing in Christ" and "acting like Christ" might look like. Branches on the side of belief (to the left) correlate to the different ways various Christian denominations signal their belief, with representamens like sacraments, Bible studies, tongues, adult baptism, icons. Branches on the side of action (to the right) correlate to Paul's description of the body of Christ in Romans 12: some act "in ministering," some act "in teaching," some act "in generosity" (Rom 12:7-8). The interpretant of "acting like Christ," in other words, develops different "signs" guided by the Holy Spirit: some are called to be feet, some are eyes, some are ears (1 Cor 12:12-26). As discussed in chapter eight, we believe the third person of the Trinity meets us at the third point of the sign—the interpretant—to engage with our personhood.

Endorsement of such branching semiosis is implied by famous words to the Philippians: "work out your own salvation with fear and trembling" (Phil 2:12). This clear allusion to process is followed by a reference to God's involvement: "for it is God who is at work in you, enabling you both to will and to work for his good pleasure" (Phil 2:13). The repetition of "work," then, is not about "works," lest anyone should boast. Instead, we are inspired "to will and to work" due to the unearned gift of salvation. We respond to that gift with our own gifts of salvation: caring for people who have not *earned* or deserve our care.

Unfortunately, some people may trip over this idea and fall into exchangist thought, as in "I owe God good works because of the gift of salvation." But to think this way destroys not only God's gift, but also our own, just as I destroyed Anita's gift when I pronounced that my present to her finally made us "even."

Rather than "an economy of exchange," we are called to "follow" Jesus. Our gifts follow his gift, in both senses of *follow*. To follow is to follow Christ's example by giving the gift of salvation: saving the deprived from both spiritual and physical poverty. As we have seen, right before Jesus tells the rich young ruler to "follow me," he says, "sell all that you own and distribute the money to the poor." In other words, the ruler is to radically follow the example of the gift. This, I believe, is what the book of James is all about. It's not a matter of either/or thinking: either I'm saved through grace or I'm saved through works. Instead it's matter of both/and semiosis: to follow

Christ is to follow his example with gifts of salvation. Our gifts, then, are like the talents described in Matthew 25.

ON THE EDGE OF THE TALENT

In the parable of the talents (Mt 25:14-30), Jesus once again puts a coin on edge. A master gives different amounts to his various slaves, praising those who multiply their coins, castigating the slave who protects his one talent by burying it.

Because our English word *talent* came from the Greek *talanton* via this parable, we tend to interpret the parable in terms of either using or hiding our God-given abilities, especially in light of verse 15: "to one he gave five talents, to another two, to another one, *to each according to his ability.*" But millennia before the word *talent* denoted special abilities, the talents of Matthew 25 had been interpreted by Christians in myriad ways: as offices of the Episcopate, as insightful comprehension of Scripture, as merits of the saved, as an endorsement of capitalism and so on.[23] Signs of the times, in other words, affect how we read the parable.

I would therefore like to suggest another reading: perhaps the servant who buried his talent thought only in terms of exchange. His master gave him a talent that he planned to return; for him it was an assiduously honest transaction. The other servants, however, gifted their master with more than he required or requested, bringing him "joy" (Mt 25:21, 23). "Works," then, should be seen as our gifts to the Master: works are talents never required, never earning anything in exchange.

WORKS *AS* GRACE

One loving work is (re)signing. Since a talent, like any coin, is a sign, we should consider how we multiply signs. Do we increase signs of God in our culture through making new ones, or do we prevent our signs from changing by burying them, protecting them from the signs of the times, as when nineteenth-century Christians resisted abolition? The process of (re)signing encourages investment in new signs so that they create increased "interest" in the gift of salvation. (See my conclusion for examples.)

The work of (re)signing, like all gifts, should therefore be a work of love.

---

[23]Manfred Siebald, "Unprofitable Servant, Parable of the," in *A Dictionary of Biblical Tradition in English Literature,* ed. David Lyle Jeffrey (Grand Rapids, MI: Eerdmans, 1992), p. 800.

As the great Christian theologian Thomas Aquinas (1225-1274) notes,

> A gift is literally a giving that can have no return, i.e. it is not given with the intention that one be repaid and it thus connotes a gratuitous donation. Now the basis of such free giving is love; the reason we give something to others freely is that we will good to them. Therefore what we give first to others is the love itself with which we love them. And so it is manifest that love has the quality of a first gift, through which all other free gifts are given.[24]

Significantly, Derrida scholar John D. Caputo quotes this passage from the *Summa Theologica* to illustrate what deconstruction came to mean in the thought of Jacques Derrida: it is a "desire for the *gift* beyond economy, for the *justice* beyond the law, for the *hospitality* beyond proprietorship, for *forgiveness* beyond getting even."[25]

DECONSTRUCTING "ALL RELIGIONS ARE THE SAME"

Some regard "the gift" as a new development in Derrida's thought,[26] but as early as 1967 Derrida was challenging economies of exchange. By deconstructing Saussure's view of the sign, Derrida was defying the "exchangism" represented by the dyadic sign, wherein a signifier is exchanged for a signified. Making way for "the gift," Derrida thus helps us expose the simplicity of many current conversations about religious pluralism. Let me give one recent example.

Not long ago I heard a theologian give a talk on Islam. Attempting to make his Christian audience more sympathetic with Muslims—an admirable goal—he argued that Muslim fundamentalists are just like Christians: both have killed people with different beliefs; both have tortured people within their belief system for failure to conform; both have oppressed women. To make this argument, however, the theologian repeatedly compared the excesses of contemporary Muslim radicals with those of Christians from 200 to 1,200 years ago. Doing so, he operated according to Saussure's logic of exchange, regarding the contents of a twenty-first-century Taliban cabinet as comparable to those from the Spanish Inquisition five hundred years earlier.

---

[24]Quoted in John D. Caputo, *The Weakness of God: A Theology of the Event* (Bloomington: Indiana University Press, 2006), p. 210.

[25]Caputo, *Weakness of God*, p. 111, emphasis his, to foreground diction employed by Derrida.

[26]See, for example, Marion Grau, "Erasing 'Economy': Derrida and the Construction of Divine Economies," *CrossCurrents* 52, no. 3 (Fall 2002): 363.

In contrast, Peirce, whom Derrida aligned with deconstruction, would have us concentrate on gifts of abduction—new ways of thinking, like universal suffrage or the abolition of slavery—which have improved conditions for all of humanity. These improvements, then, become integrated into Christian understanding of truth, such that we now regard obedience to God as including efforts to maintain universal suffrage and to abolish slavery, even though the Bible does not advocate either.

In Peirce's perception, "If the universe never advances or develops at all, or if there is merely an alternate flow and ebb of progress then there is no absolute in creation."[27] For him, to believe in God is to believe in "Evolutionary Love," a philosophy "that makes the principle of growth a primordial element of the universe." Unlike atheistic approaches to evolution, "a genuinely evolutionary philosophy . . . is so far from being antagonistic to the idea of a personal creator that it is really inseparable from that idea."[28] God, in other words, guides the process of semiosis through gifts of abduction, enabling the development of new signs down through the centuries.

This should entirely change our rhetorical strategies. Anyone who compares despicable behavior in the twenty-first century to similar behavior over five hundred years ago, can be countered by saying that all of humanity in the twenty-first century should be held accountable to increased understanding of human rights. At the same time we can challenge anyone who dismisses Christianity today because of its abuses in the past, pointing out that all signs, including signs of faith, should be assessed in terms of their contexts. During the Inquisition, we might argue, Christians were acting according to the understanding of truth in their own day: people must be severely punished if they fail to conform to the hegemonic understanding of truth. Significantly, as Diarmaid MacCullough notes in his *History of Christianity*, the Inquisition was often less abusive than secular law. In the thirteenth century, for example, "secular courts were much more likely than inquisitors to impose death penalties."[29] In context, then, the Inquisition

---

[27]Quoted in Donna M. Orange, "Peirce's Conception of God: A Developmental Study," *Peirce Studies* 2, September 10, 1984, p. 35.

[28]*Collected Papers of Charles Sanders Peirce*, vols. 1-6, ed. Arthur Burks, Charles Hartshorne and Paul Weiss; vols. 7-8, ed. Arthur W. Burkes (Cambridge, MA: Harvard University Press, 1931-1958), vol. 6, para. 157.

[29]Diarmaid MacCulloch, *Christianity: The First Three Thousand Years* (London: Viking Penguin, 2010), p. 408.

manifested more grace than signs of the times in which it occurred.

This does not mean I am defending the Inquisition. Its "fall" into an economy of exchange is an insult to the gospel message. I am simply deconstructing the argument of those people who refuse to take Christianity seriously because of the Inquisition. For by implying that the cabinet of medieval Christianity can be exchanged for the cabinet of twenty-first-century Christianity—or any other twenty-first-century religion—they are operating by an economy of exchange as well.

By getting away from the economy of exchange encoded by structuralism, we get away from simplistic notions of tolerance and intolerance. On the edge of the coin, we should be intolerant of Inquisition tactics based on the standards of our own day, but we should be tolerant of the Inquisitors based on the standards of their own era. Furthermore, we should be all the more impressed that, guided by the Spirit on the edge of the coin, Christians have challenged abusive practices in their own day, as when nineteenth-century believers took leadership in causes such as women's suffrage and the abolition of slavery. With the expectation of nothing in return, these people offered communication as a gift. Professor of communication John Durham Peters would endorse such a perspective: "Taking gifts as our analogy for communication shows that something more than reciprocity must prevail."[30]

COMMUNICATING SALVATION: RHETORIC SHAPED BY THE GIFT

This, then, should entirely change the way we communicate our faith: according to the gift rather than an economy of exchange. Persuasive rhetoric about the gospel message, then, might look something like this:

- We communicate the problem with both tolerance (all faith-signs are legitimate) and intolerance (only *my* signs of faith are legitimate), showing how both reflect simplistic cabinet thinking in which signs function according to an economy of exchange.

- Rather than an economy of exchange, we appeal to the universal thirst for love, noting that the truest sign of love is the gift: favor unmerited, unearned, unqualified.

- We therefore communicate the profundity of faith based on love and the gift rather than a religion based on an economy of exchange.

---

[30]Peters, *Speaking into the Air*, p. 59.

- We then reference the repeated signs of the gospel message: that a God of love offers reconciliation with humanity as a gift, a gift sent special delivery by God in human form.

- We communicate the power of the love behind this gift by our own gifts of love, refusing to reduce Christianity to an economy of exchange in which God requires certain words, beliefs, rituals or practices for salvation.

- Hence, we also avoid rhetoric that reduces the gift of Christ's atoning death to an economic metaphor, as in "Christ paid the price for our redemption."[31] Instead, we say that "God so loved the world that he *gave* his only Son, so that everyone who believes in him may not perish but may have eternal life" (Jn 3:16).

- We thus help people conceptualize belief not as the purchase-price for salvation, but as the necessary response to a gift that has been offered. *For one can accept a gift only if one believes it has been offered as a gift.*

Belief, then, functions through the interpretant in Peirce's triadic sign (see fig. 9.9).

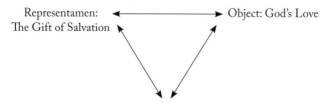

Representamen: ←——————————→   Object: God's Love
The Gift of Salvation

Interpretant: Recognizing and Accepting the Giver in the Gift

Figure 9.9. Triadic sign of belief

If we identify the interpretant in Peirce's triadic sign as the place where the Holy Spirit guides our understanding (chapter eight), we have a way to recognize God's leading: new signs confirm not only the Trinity but also the gift of salvation. Or, to put it in the language of this book, resigned to the Trinity

---

[31]While the word "gift" appears nearly 40 times in the New Testament, the idea of being "bought" by Christ appears only three times: 1 Cor 6:20; 7:23; 2 Pet 2:1. And all three times it occurs in a passage exhorting Christians to avoid enslaving themselves to the ways of the world, as in "fornication" or "licentiousness." In context, then, the idea of the "price" Christ paid has to do more with how precious we are in God's eyes than with an economy of exchange. I will discuss this issue more in chapter ten.

and the gift, we can re-sign our faith to make these basic truths of Christianity understandable to contemporary culture. With such a notion of (re) signing, we can persuasively argue that *not all interpretations of God are equally legitimate.* While most religious people, including many Christians, fall into exchangist thought, *truth is verified by signs that endorse the gift.*

Significantly, Peirce argues that the triadic (trinitarian) basis of the universe is best illustrated through gift-giving. As Robert S. Corrington summarizes, "the triad of A gives B to C is irreducible to any dyadic pairing. This formal relation mirrors the deeper ontological structures of the world. Any event, from a protoplasmic cell to the divine life, will function according to the primal triadic structures that are ubiquitous."[32]

PERSONAL APPLICATION

To be effective communicators, we must assess our response to signs of the times with these questions:

- Rather than judgmentalism (which Scripture repeatedly denounces), do I react to the human representamens around me with an interpretant that offers the gift of love: seeing the best of them, their religion, their culture?

- Do new signs in the church result from an interpretant that loves or rejects? Christians who resist new signs often reject change for the future, while Christians who advocate change often reject truths of the past. How might our love be more inclusive, like that of Jesus, who loved signs of the past even as he changed them?

- How will such inclusive love affect the way we communicate our belief in the Trinity and the gift of salvation?

For the last, though never final, word on these issues, the next chapter introduces a Christian semiotician who synthesizes the best insights discussed so far: Mikhail Bakhtin.

---

[32]Robert S. Corrington, *An Introduction to C. S. Peirce: Philosopher, Semiotician, and Ecstatic Naturalist* (Lanham, MD: Rowman & Littlefield, 1993), p. 129.

10

ANTISEPTIC BAKHTIN

Healing Signs of the Body

When I would scrape a knee as a young child, one of my parents took from the medicine cabinet a small green bottle filled with an antiseptic called Bactine. And though it stung quite a bit, I was told it was good for me because it killed germs.[1] I was told something similar about Jesus, who cleansed me from the germs of sin at the moment I felt the sting of death. After that moment, the germs were gone: "Where, O death, is your sting?" (1 Cor 15:55).

For over a thousand years, most Europeans regarded Christ as the only effective antiseptic for the germs of culture. During the so-called Enlightenment, however, many intellectuals began to regard Christianity as part of society's wound that must be cured by the antiseptics of reason and science. C. S. Peirce, in fact, once described his rearing around Harvard University as "an antiseptic" against belief in transcendent realities. After his mystical experience, however, he thankfully acknowledged "that some cultured bacilli, some benignant form of the disease was implanted in my soul."[2]

The current New Atheists, of course, feel less than benign about the disease of religion. In 1997 Richard Dawkins, the famous evolutionary psychologist, asserted that "faith is . . . comparable to the smallpox virus but harder to eradicate." And in 2004 he called religion a "malignant infection."[3]

---

[1]I borrowed these first two sentences from the opening of my essay "Antiseptic Bakhtin: The Dialogic Christian," *Pacific Coast Philology* 34, no. 1 (1999): 18. The rest of this chapter, however, bears little resemblance to that essay.

[2]C. S. Peirce, "The Law of Mind," in *Philosophical Writings of Peirce,* ed. Justus Buchler (New York: Dover, 1955), p. 339. Peirce's father, Benjamin, taught mathematics at Harvard for fifty years.

[3]Quoted in H. Allen Orr, "A Passion for Evolution," review of *A Devil's Chaplain: Reflections on*

Such wounding words cannot be salved—or solved—with Bactine. This chapter offers, instead, Bakhtin: a critic studied by rhetoricians as well as literary and cultural theorists.

BAKHTIN ON EDGE

Russian-born Mikhail Bakhtin (1895-1975) provides a foothold on the edge of the (re)signing coin, synthesizing the most intriguing ideas we have covered so far. Saussure and his structuralist followers emphasized the *system* that gives a coin/sign value. Emphasizing, like Saussure, synchronic contexts, Bakhtin nevertheless challenged both structuralism and cultural materialism, as did Derrida. Scholars have therefore paralleled Bakhtin with Peirce, whose *triadic* sign allows for an edge on which interpretation might roll, balancing between signs and the objects to which they refer. Bakhtin completes the metaphor (and this study) by emphasizing the body that stands on the edge of the coin: the body that also balances between tradition and change.

In this chapter I will therefore apply Bakhtin to the body—not only the physical body but also the body of believers—explaining how he can help us heed and heal changes in Christianity and culture. Before we analyze Bakhtin's antiseptic, however, we first need to consider signs of the body within contemporary culture.

SEX AND THE SIMULACRUM

Western culture today seems obsessed with the body, especially the sexualized body. The popularity of "sexting" has led to a new kind of crime, "sextortion," where "predators catch victims in embarrassing situations online and threaten to expose them unless they create sexually explicit photos or videos for them."[4] In Switzerland, lawmakers have advocated the production of "extra-small condoms" for twelve-year-old boys in order to combat increasing teen pregnancies. In June of 2008 *Time* magazine reported on a "pact" among females at Gloucester (MA) High School—"none older than sixteen"—to get pregnant "and raise their babies together" without males in their lives.[5]

Hope, Lies, Science and Love, by Richard Dawkins, *New York Review of Books,* February 26, 2004, p. 28.

[4]"Prosecutors File More Charges in Man's 'Sextortion' Case," *The Patriot-News* (Harrisburg, PA), September 15, 2011, A11.

[5]"Swiss Promote Extra-Small Condoms for Preteen Boys," AOLNews.com, March 4, 2010, www .aolnews.com/2010/03/04/swiss-promote-extra-small-condoms-for-preteen-boys/ (accessed March

Linguistic signs, of course, perpetuate such attitudes and behavior. For many, intercourse is no longer called "making love"; it is "hooking up." Sexual consummation is no longer reserved for one's spouse or even "significant other"; instead teenagers have "friends with benefits" or "sex buddies." These trends, of course, are encouraged by images on movie and television screens, which rarely show the physical or psychological consequences of "hooking up." And next to the tooth-decaying candy in most supermarket check-out lines is chastity-decaying eye-candy, multiple magazine covers blaring out celebrity affairs du jour.

The change in sexual signs has been noted by secular theorists. The editors of one college textbook state that "sexual desire is no longer a response to a person whom we meet and know face-to-face. Rather, sexual desire is stimulated by images promulgated by the media, and we strive to remake our bodies to fit those images."[6] People have thus substituted signs for reality, submitting themselves to what cultural critic Jean Baudrillard (1929-2007) calls "simulacra": copies of reality for which no original exists.[7]

Think of those magazines in checkout lines, for example. Many have gorgeous women on their covers, often with boldfaced lies, oops, I mean boldface type proclaiming things like "How to be as sexy as this model" or "Achieve this celebrity's perfect figure." Ironically, of course, most of the cover models are merely simulacra: signs of "perfection" for which no originals exist. That is because their wrinkles, pimples and sometimes even extra fat have been airbrushed out, and their gorgeously full and shiny hair did not hold its style for many minutes longer than the photo-shoot. Each model is a simulacrum: a sign of extravagant beauty that does not exist. Or, in the language of Peirce, each model is a representamen cut off from its object. Nevertheless, our interpretants want to believe that the gorgeous object is a living model of perfection. This perpetuates a longing for simulacra more than for intelligence and character. As a result females reduce themselves to the simulacra they think men desire, buying products that promise the signs, without the sub-

25, 2010); Kathleen Kingsbury, "Pregnancy Boom at Gloucester High," *Time*, June 18, 2008, online: www.time.com/time/magazine/article/0,9171,1816486,00.html.
[6]Vincent B. Leitch et al., eds., "Jean Baudrillard," in *The Norton Anthology of Theory and Criticism*, ed. Vincent B. Leitch et al., 2nd ed. (New York: Norton, 2010), p. 1554.
[7]Jean Baudrillard, *Simulacra and Simulation*, trans. Sheila Faria Glaser (Ann Arbor: University of Michigan Press, 1994).

stance, of beauty.[8] Ironically, then, our culture's obsession with the body often leads to a denial of the body, offering simulacra instead.

DENYING THE BODY: SIGNS OF CELIBACY

Many religions have advocated a denial of the body, a teaching that marred Christianity almost from its start. Eusebius (ca. 263-339), an early Christian historian, reports that the second-century theologian Origen castrated himself to honor Christ's words, "there are eunuchs who have made themselves eunuchs for the sake of the kingdom of heaven. Let anyone accept this who can" (Mt 19:12).

Though the prevalence of Christian castration is contested among historians, early believers most certainly valued celibacy as a sign of faith. First of all, persecution promoted a denial of the body. Rowan Williams notes that martyrs regarded their ability to withstand suffering as "a *sign* of the presence of divine power," identifying them as "outsiders in the imperial structure."[9] Then, to reinforce their God-inspired countercultural status, Christians also denied their flesh sexually. Thus, celibacy signaled the denial of the body that persecution made necessary. As Williams explains, "up to the fourth century at least, the high standard of sexual continence evident in Christian communities was put forward as an argument for a unique level of divine assistance given to believers."[10]

Hence, when Constantine put an end to persecution in the fourth century, virginity became all the more important as a sign of Christian distinctiveness. As Williams puts it, "the virginal body becomes an analogue of the martyred body; consumed by God and unviolated by humanity, it is a localised channel of power."[11] In other words, without martyrdom to unite believers, sexual purity became intensified as a *sign* of Christian commitment.

By the eleventh century, the Western Church was only ordaining unmarried men, and in 1139 a council in Rome "declared all clerical marriages not only unlawful but invalid."[12] Even the laity were cautioned. In the thir-

---

[8]For an example of simulacra, go to www.youtube.com/watch?v=tbb8D-u8ues. There you will see how an average-looking woman gets a PhotoShop makeover to transform her into cover-model material.

[9]Rowan Williams, *Why Study the Past? The Quest for the Historical Church* (Grand Rapids, MI: Eerdmans, 2005), pp. 38, 34, emphasis mine.

[10]Ibid., p. 38, emphasis mine.

[11]Ibid., p. 39.

[12]Diarmaid MacCulloch, *Christianity: The First Three Thousand Years* (New York: Viking, 2010), p. 373.

teenth century, Vincent of Beauvais, a Dominican Friar "who wrote the most widely esteemed compendium of knowledge of the high Middle Ages," argued that "excessive love for one's own wife" is "shameful," such that a man "who loves his wife rather eagerly is an adulterer" (!).[13]

Celibacy, quite clearly, was a sign of truth that changed. And Protestants changed it again. Despite having taken vows of celibacy before God when he became an Augustinian friar, Luther got married after the Roman Church excommunicated him. Though seeming only "natural" to Protestants today, married clergy are the result of semiosis. But it is semiosis on the edge: looking to both past and future. For Luther's new sign (married priests) looks to the early centuries of the church, when clergy did marry. Luther's (re)signing is thus based upon signs from the past: what cultural materialist Raymond Williams calls "residual" values (chapter five). And the residual value to which Luther appeals is the biblical endorsement of embodiment, with sex as part of God's creative plan.

THE BIBLE AND THE BODY

The Hebrew Scriptures start with explicit details about the creation of human bodies, bodies blessed with sex: "God blessed [Adam and Eve], and God said to them, 'Be fruitful and multiply'" (Gen 1:28). Reflecting this divine commandment about sexual relations, Old Testament genealogies meticulously delineate how one body descended from earlier bodies, culminating in the genealogy of Jesus (Mt 1:1-17). Sex, then, did not cause the Fall, as many biblically illiterate people assume. In fact, it's just the opposite: as a result of the Fall, Adam and Eve felt shame over their naked bodies and hence their sexuality (Gen 3:7).[14]

To redeem humanity from the Fall, God takes human form: an endorsement of body that appalls people in other religions. As noted by historian Diarmaid MacCulloch, "Christianity affirms the positive value of physical human flesh in the incarnation of Christ, while Buddhism has at its centre nothingness and the annihilation of the self."[15] And we have al-

---

[13]Quoted in ibid., p. 314. One Christian sect in Russia, lasting well into the twentieth century, encouraged males to castrate themselves and women to cut off their breasts "to achieve purity" (ibid., pp. 545-46).

[14]In the Hebrew Scriptures "to uncover the nakedness" of someone alludes to intercourse (see Lev 18:16-18).

[15]MacCulloch, *Christianity*, p. 201.

ready seen that Muslims repudiate the idea that God would take on flesh (chapter eight).

Rather than condemning such views, we must note how closely they parallel a belief that developed within Christianity several decades after the crucifixion: docetism. As we have seen in chapters two and eight, docetists assumed that Jesus only "appeared" to have a human body: an interpretation that reflects signs of the times. In fact, according to Rowan Williams, most Christians in the first and second centuries often "played down the humanity of Jesus." Under persecution and torture, they focused instead on the divinity of their lord, seeing him as "the earthly form of some great angelic power": a power that could help them transcend the suffering of their bodies.[16]

SIGNS OF GNOSTICISM

Docetism was reinforced by a philosophy that had strong pull in Greek culture: Gnosticism.[17] Gnostics believed that the body was either completely evil or mere illusion, blinding individuals to authentic spiritual realities. In their minds, a spiritually transcendent God would never take the form of a human. In fact, Gnostics went so far as to distrust the Jewish creation account in Genesis. Because "the world of senses is such an inferior state of being," they assumed "it could not possibly have been created by a supreme God."[18] Gnostics even disdained Christian martyrdom: for them, the body wasn't important enough to sacrifice in the name of truth.[19] Marcion, the second-century bishop discussed in chapter two, went so far as to denounce the incarnation, calling it "a disgrace to God" because the human body is "stuffed with excrement."[20]

Early in church history, then, a tension between things of the spirit and things of the body developed: opposite sides of the coin of faith. The first four ecumenical councils sought the leading of the Holy Spirit on these issues

---

[16]Williams, *Why Study the Past?* p. 43.

[17]See MacCulloch, *Christianity*, pp. 121-40.

[18]Ibid., p. 122.

[19]MacCulloch writes, "Not only is there a total absence of stories of gnostic martyrs, but there is positive evidence that gnostics opposed martyrdom as a regrettable self-indulgence and were angry that some Christian leaders encouraged it" (*Christianity*, p. 125).

[20]Jaroslav Pelikan, *The Christian Tradition: A History of the Development of Doctrine*, vol. 1: *The Emergence of the Catholic Tradition (100-600)* (Chicago: University of Chicago Press, 1971), p. 75. Marcion, however, as discussed at the start of chapter two, was declared a heretic for his views.

as they struggled to develop doctrine on the edge. By 451, they had established a theology of the incarnation wherein Christ was both fully God and fully human: both/and rather than either/or thinking. As explored in chapter eight, then, Christians believe that God's Spirit guided the semiosis of doctrine as it rolled closer and closer to the Truth that transcends all signs.[21]

And we can learn from their example. Rather than either/or thinking, a (re)signing Christian stands on the edge with both/and thinking: believing in a God who, though transcending all signs, works in and through bodies in their contexts—bodies, at least, open to the Other. Derrida, as we have seen, considered this Other "impossible" because if something or someone is Wholly Other it must exceed all human signs (chapter six). Nevertheless, Christians can argue that we get glimpses of that Other through signs themselves, which function triadically (chapter eight), like the One who created them. Furthermore, Christians believe that the Transcendent Other took on flesh to connect with humanity in the realm of signs. We can therefore argue that Christianity has developed a much more robust view of the body than many people today, who often prefer simulacra to real bodies.

This, then, prepares us for Bakhtin: a believer in the Trinity who emphasized that the communication of truth relies upon the body.

THE CHRISTIAN BODY OF BAKHTIN

Bakhtin mirrors Antonio Gramsci, whose theory of "cultural hegemony" appears in chapter five. Born four years apart, both studied linguistic and cultural signs, and both were punished for their beliefs in 1929. However, while Gramsci was arrested by Italian fascists for communist activities, Bakhtin was arrested by Soviet communists for Christian activities.

Educated in the classics at Petrograd University (St. Petersburg), Bakhtin taught school in the provinces after the Russian Revolution, returning to Leningrad in 1924, the year Stalin took power. Accused of ties to the Christian underground, Bakhtin was arrested on Christmas Eve, 1928: a sign, perhaps, of his refusal to take the Christ out of Christmas. After ten days of interrogation, he was released, only to be arrested again three months

---

[21]MacCulloch argues against current attempts to celebrate the so-called Gnostic Gospels, saying it is "unwise to rebrand gnostic belief as a more generous-minded, less authoritarian alternative to the Christianity which eventually became mainstream." He goes on to comment, "Still less plausible is a view of gnostic belief as a form of proto-feminism" (*Christianity*, p. 124).

later. Admitting that he hosted and attended theological discussions, Bakhtin was exiled to Kazakhstan until 1934.

Bakhtin, then, suffered for his faith.[22] However, unlike pre-Constantinian Christians who "played down the humanity of Jesus," Bakhtin's suffering seems to have reinforced his incarnational view of truth. Though we do not know details about his theology—due to Stalinist suppression of Christian signs—Bakhtin's belief in the importance of the body grounds his view of the sign.[23]

BAKHTIN'S PHILOSOPHY OF LANGUAGE

In 1929 a book titled *Marxism and the Philosophy of Language* was published in Russia, with the name V. N. Voloshinov, a friend of Bakhtin, on its title page. Lucidly outlining the semiotic theories of its day, this book has generated controversy over its authorship. Some scholars think Bakhtin wrote it, substituting Voloshinov's name for his own so Stalin would not ban the book the way he had banned Bakhtin's body. Others believe the work to be a collaboration between Voloshinov and Bakhtin, even though the first English edition (1973) places Voloshinov's name as the sole author.

The debate parallels controversies over the authorship of Shakespeare's plays. Whether the man from Stratford on Avon wrote the plays or not matters less than their brilliant content, and most scholars use the sign /Shakespeare/ to describe the fertile imagination that created *Hamlet, Lear, Macbeth, Othello* and all the rest. Similarly, I follow the lead of many Bakhtin scholars and communication theorists by using the sign /Bakhtin/ to describe the mind that generated the semiotic insight of *Marxism and the Philosophy of Language.*[24]

---

[22]Jonathan Hill notes that "It is often said that there were more Christian martyrs in the twentieth century than in all the previous nineteen centuries put together, and a good proportion of those who died were killed in the Soviet Union." See *What Has Christianity Ever Done For Us? How It Shaped the Modern World* (Downers Grove, IL: InterVarsity Press, 2005), p. 31.

[23]Significantly, Julia Kristeva, who aligned "the semiotic" with the body (chapter four), is largely responsible for introducing Bakhtin's work to the French-speaking world.

[24]Patricia Bizzell and Bruce Herzberg, for example, attribute the work entirely to Bakhtin in *The Rhetorical Tradition: Readings from Classical Times to the Present* (Boston: Bedford/St. Martin's, 2001), pp. 1206-9. Bakhtin scholar Michael Holquist also attributes the book to Bakhtin, noting that Bakhtin himself claimed authorship (*Dialogism: Bakhtin and his World,* 2nd ed. [New York: Routledge, 1990], p. 8). Though I will attribute quotations in my chapter to Bakhtin, I will nevertheless cite the first English edition in my footnotes as Voloshinov, since that is the name that appears on the title page: V. N. Voloshinov, *Marxism and the Philosophy of Language,* trans. Ladislav

In the book, Bakhtin argues against two popular views about signs: *individualistic subjectivism* and *abstract objectivism*. Both these trends reflect the modernist emphasis on autonomy that dominated the first half of the twentieth century:[25]

Individualistic subjectivism focuses on "the individual creative act of speech."[26] Like painters who transcend their culture by creating entirely original works of art, autonomous individuals creatively invent new forms of speech. In this view, established language is like the inert crust that forms over a volcano crater. Different cultures are like different volcanoes, with most people conforming their signs to the hardened crust. But the molten imaginations of people with genius create utterances that break through society's conformist crust, changing the lava of language. Eventually, however, those new signs eventually harden into another crust as people standardize those new signs.[27] Take, once again, the example of Shakespeare, who erupted into sixteenth-century English culture with numerous original words and phrases that we now take for granted: *lonely, laughable, bump, monumental, critic, fancy-free, to fall to blows, the mind's eye, to breathe one's last.*

Abstract objectivism looks not to the autonomy of creative individuals, but to the autonomy of each system of language: systems create signs, not people. Such systems are autonomous not only in relation to each other, but also in relation to their own past. The linguist therefore studies the sign system of a particular culture at a particular time. This should sound familiar. The autonomous linguistic systems of abstract objectivism are the separate cabinets of Saussure, who had quite a following in the Soviet Union.[28]

COOKING SAUSSURE'S BOOKS: COMMUNICATION GENRES

Bakhtin disliked the semiology of Saussure because it studies *langue* (each

---

Matejka and I. R. Titunik (New York: Seminar Press, 1973).

[25]For a brief history of modernist autonomy, see Crystal Downing, *How Postmodernism Serves (My) Faith: Questioning Truth in Language, Philosophy and Art* (Downers Grove, IL: IVP Academic, 2006), pp. 53-83.

[26]Voloshinov, *Marxism and the Philosophy of Language*, p. 48.

[27]Bakhtin aligns the origin of this view with German linguist Wilhelm von Humboldt (1767-1835) and sees it perpetuated by Italian philosopher Benedetto Croce (1866-1952), as well as by theorists in his native USSR.

[28]Michael Holquist notes, "In those early years Saussure's impact in the Soviet Union was greater than in any other country" (*Dialogism*, p. 43).

cabinet) rather than the actual humans who cook up new signs out of a cabinet's ingredients. Simply put, Saussure emphasizes systems over people. Furthermore, Bahktin felt that Saussure failed to recognize the role of "genres" in cooking up speech acts. As he explains in an essay called "The Problem of Speech Genres," Saussure "ignores the fact that in addition to forms of language there are also *forms of combination* of these forms, that is, he ignores speech genres."[29]

Think of it this way: very few people bake cakes without recipes; even when they experiment they usually follow a basic recipe to which they might add new ingredients from their cabinets. Similarly, people follow certain recipes—what Bakhtin calls "genres"—when they communicate. For example, we all recognize that *kidding* one's brother is a different genre of communication than *exhorting,* or *tempting,* or *comforting* him. For each italicized genre, we combine the ingredients of our signs differently, with distinctive spicing of intonation, inflection and facial gesture. Furthermore, we learn the recipes for such combinations from other human beings, having watched them joke, exhort, tempt and comfort. Every word, then, has been embodied by someone else first.

STERILIZING SAUSSURE: GARGLE FOR GARGOYLES

This does not mean that Bakhtin regards communication as the robotic reading of someone else's script. He, in fact, disliked the structuralism that developed out of Saussure's semiology, where minds are programmed by linguistic codes. Structuralists seemed to regard people as gargoyles at the end of cathedral water spouts through which flows the rain (and reign!) of signs. As Saussure's structuralist disciple Roland Barthes (1915-1980) once put it, "only language acts, 'performs,' and not 'me,'" an assumption applicable to even the most volcanic author: "it is language which speaks, not the author."[30] Barthes therefore celebrates what he calls "The Death of the Author." In other words, structuralists like Barthes believe that the signs of a cultural system precede and hence constitute thought, leading to the "death" of authority as it has traditionally been known: authors do not authorize their

---

[29]M. M. Bakhtin, *Speech Genres and Other Late Essays*, trans. Vern W. McGee, ed. Caryl Emerson and Michael Holquist (Austin: University of Texas Press, 1986), p. 81, emphasis his. We are certain that Bakhtin wrote the essays collected in this volume.

[30]Roland Barthes, "The Death of the Author," trans. Stephen Heath, in *The Norton Anthology of Theory and Criticism*, ed. Vincent B. Leitch et al., 2nd ed. (New York: Norton, 2010), p. 1323.

language.[31] They, like all people, are merely gargoyles spouting out the reign of signs.

Bakhtin provides an antiseptic gargle to sterilize such ideas. As he puts it, "the word does not exist in a neutral and impersonal language (it is not, after all, out of a dictionary that the speaker gets his words!), but rather it exists in other people's mouths, in other people's contexts, serving other people's intentions."[32] Bakhtin thus emphasizes the *incarnational* aspect of language. This does not mean, however, that Bakhtin endorsed individual subjectivism, wherein humans generate autonomous thoughts that erupt into new lava of language. Quite the contrary. He saw individual subjectivism and abstract objectivism as opposite sides of the exact same coin: a coin that emphasized autonomy. For Bakhtin, however, "no work, no 'sign' is independent and autonomous."[33]

In *Marxism and the Philosophy of Language*, Bakhtin states that he seeks a "dialectical synthesis" between the "thesis" of individual subjectivism and the "antithesis" of abstract objectivism.[34] Publishing under Stalin's regime, it makes sense that Bakhtin would invoke signs that Marxists had appropriated from the Hegelian dialectic: *thesis-antithesis-synthesis* (chapter one). As a matter of fact, however, Bakhtin was "militantly anti-Hegelian," for Hegel emphasized consciousness over the body.[35] Bakhtin's semiotic theory focuses, instead, on human relationships. "The usable sign" for Bakhtin, as Raymond Williams (chapter five) approvingly summarizes, "is a product of this continuing speech-activity between real individuals who are in some continuing social relationship."[36]

BAKHTIN'S CONSUMMATION OF THE BODY

For Bakhtin, we cannot fully know truth—even about ourselves—without interacting with other bodies. For example, when I stand in front of my students, they see me in ways I cannot see myself, for they see the black-

---

[31]I use very similar language in my book *Writing Performances: The Stages of Dorothy L. Sayers* (New York: Palgrave, 2004), p. 141. But I authorize the borrowing.

[32]M. M. Bakhtin, *The Dialogic Imagination*, trans. Caryl Emerson and Michael Holquist, ed. Michael Holquist (Austin: University of Texas Press, 1981), p. 294.

[33]Anthony Ugolnik, *The Illuminating Icon* (Grand Rapids, MI: Eerdmans, 1989), p. 162.

[34]Voloshinov, *Marxism and the Philosophy of Language*, p. 82.

[35]Holquist, *Dialogism*, pp. 16, 18.

[36]Raymond Williams, "Language as Sociality," in *The Raymond Williams Reader*, ed. John Higgins (Oxford: Blackwell, 2001), p. 201.

board that frames my face. If I turn around to look at the blackboard, they still see me as I cannot see myself, for they look at the back of my head framed by the blackboard. As Bakhtin explains in a 1970 interview, "one cannot even really see one's own exterior and comprehend it as a whole, and no mirrors or photographs can help; our real exterior can be seen and understood only by other people, because they are located outside us in space and because they are others."[37]

Signs of the self, like all signs for Bakhtin, are situated in particular contexts. In the example of my classroom, Bakhtin might point out that students sitting to the right and to the left of me see the blackboard framing my face at a slightly different angles. If I had written on the board, "To be or not to be that IS the question," as I often do, students facing the board on the right side of the room might only see "that IS the question" since my head blocks out the quotation's beginning. Students sitting on the left side of the room, of course, might see only "To be or not to be." And students in the middle of the room might see "To be" and "the question" on either side of my head. Each group sees me framed differently, at least in that moment.

This, of course, is merely an analogy for a much larger issue: I am seen differently by different people, as when my godson Jude sees me as a master-builder of blanket forts, while my students see me as a ferociously hard grader. Even my colleagues see me differently, some as a cultural theorist, some as a Sayers scholar, others as specialist in poststructuralism (depending upon which publications they have read). Each person "consummates" me in different ways.

When Bakhtin uses the word "consummate," he avoids its limited sexual connotations. In today's culture, sexual consummation is often reduced to an economy of exchange, people giving pleasure in order to get it in return. For Bakhtin, to consummate another person is a gift: we enrich a person's sense of self by drawing attention to our perception of their embodied contexts.[38] Consummation is a gift of *communion* within *community*. The /mun/ within these italicized words means, in fact, "gift," as seen in the word *munificence*.[39] For Bakhtin, then, effective *communication* functions as a gift (see chapter nine).

---

[37]Bakhtin, *Speech Genres*, p. 7.

[38]Tony Ugolnik, explains Bakhtin's theory with these words: "For each of us, the self is a gift of the other" (*Illuminating Icon*, p. 172).

[39]John Durham Peters, *Speaking into the Air: A History of the Idea of Communication* (Chicago: University of Chicago Press, 1999), p. 7.

CONSUMMATION AND COMMUNICATION: PARTICIPATORY OUTSIDENESS

By emphasizing "the material embodiment of signs,"[40] Bakhtin avoids the problem of Saussure's semiology, in which different linguistic systems (cabinets) produce a pluralism of equally legitimate truths (chapter nine). For Bakhtin, it is perception, not truth, that is pluralistic. Like a flesh and blood material body, truth is identifiable, or, as Peirce might put it, there is an Object that exceeds its representamens and interpretants. None of my students, for example, see a carburetor at the front of the classroom—or even a wizened old lady (at least not yet). Nevertheless, they still see me differently depending on where they are positioned. But only through "participatory outsideness" can they consummate me. Bakhtin's word "participatory" is key. A student who repeatedly sleeps or Twitters in the back of the room may be positioned outside me, but his lack of participation creates no connection between us.

Consummation therefore necessitates the gift of communication.[41] For a relevant (if somewhat constrained) example, think of the evaluations my students fill out at the end of the semester. The college requires this form of communication, encouraging me to see myself from the "outsideness" of student perspectives. Indeed, evaluations give me a sense of how I am perceived by struggling as well as A+ students, by introverts as well as extroverts, by males as well as females, by majors as well as nonmajors: a pluralism of perspectives that enriches my sense of teaching effectiveness, and hence my sense of the vocation that defines me. I know the truth about my teaching only through openness to others (chapter six).

THE TRIADIC COMMUNION OF COMMUNICATION

Regarding truth as relational, Bakhtin, like Peirce, sees signs triadically: a communion of three in one.[42]As he puts it in "The Problem of Speech

---

[40]Voloshinov, *Marxism and the Philosophy of Language*, p. 86.

[41]Bakhtin scholar Caryl Emerson summarizes, "I cannot 'analyze' the content of another consciousness at all. I can only *address* it—that is, offer to change it a little, and to change myself a little as well, by *asking* a question of it. To know a given content, therefore, I must, from my own outside position, participate in it, *converse* with it, and assume that in turn I will be altered by my *interaction* with it." See Caryl Emerson, "Bakhtin at 100: Art, Ethics, and the Architectonic Self," *Centennial Review* 39 (Fall 1995): 406, emphasis mine.

[42]Though Bakhtin makes no reference to Peirce in *Marxism and the Philosophy of Language*, his translators argue that Bakhtin's "pivotal interests overlap with questions that had challenged the

Genres," "any word exists for the speaker in three aspects":

1. as a neutral word of a language, belonging to nobody;

2. as an *other's* word, which belongs to another person and is filled with echoes of the other's utterance;

3. as *my* word, for, since I am dealing with it in a particular situation, with a particular speech plan, it is already imbued with my expression.[43]

Think of it this way: even if words can be found in a dictionary, where they belong "to nobody," words always carry with them the presence of other bodies: people who have used them in the past, giving them the meanings that we intend when we employ them for communication. This explains why the *OED*, like many other dictionaries, includes the author and the year when a word first appeared in print: the word reflects embodied others.

Bakhtin's idea is especially obvious in young children, who learn not just vocabulary words, but also specialized meanings that they get from others. For example, during a chat with Kalaina, the four-year-old daughter of my pastor, I discovered she learned to read before kindergarten. When I told her that I could not read until first grade, she put her hand on her hip and responded, "You can *not* be serious!" Exercising my best theatrical skills, I refrained from laughing at Kalaina's adorable gesture, assuring her that I was, indeed, serious. What filled me with delight, of course, was the recognition that her utterance carried "the other" in it: Kalaina was reproducing how her mother expressed amazement.

According to Bakhtin, all utterances are this way: bearing signs of embodied others. The way we talk about our faith, for example, reflects language we hear in church and home, utterances which themselves reflect previous signs of faith: "Any utterance is a link in a very complexly organized chain of other utterances."[44] While in dialogue with others, we are simultaneously in conversation not only with their predecessors but also with our own. For Bakhtin, then, language is a medium that inherently (re)signs, offering new applications of old meanings.

---

profound inquisitiveness of Charles Sanders Peirce and had stimulated his epoch-making contribution to the general theory of signs." Ladislav Matejka and I. R. Titunik, "Translators' Introduction," to Voloshinov, *Marxism and the Philosophy of Language,* p. 3. See also Holquist, *Dialogism,* p. 50.

[43]Bakhtin, *Speech Genres,* p. 88. I added the numbers, but the words are all from Bakhtin.
[44]Ibid., p. 69.

DIALOGISM AND CHRONOTOPE

Scholars have coined the word "dialogism" to describe Bakhtin's recurring emphasis that language, like perception, arises from *dialogue* with embodied others. And this includes others long dead. As Bakhtin puts it, "the utterance appears to be furrowed with distant and barely audible echoes," such that "each individual utterance is a link in the chain of speech communication."[45] Every utterance looks both to the past and to the future: the speaker uses words shaped by the past, hoping to elicit a response in the future, if even the immediate future of the addressee's reaction.

Even context is triadic for Bakhtin, comprised of

1. the shared, or "common," physical location of the speaker and listener;

2. their "common [shared] knowledge and understanding of the situation";

3. their "common [shared] evaluation of that situation."[46]

Bakhtin's repeated word "common" forces us to change the image of our rolling coin. At least two bodies balance on the edge of Bakhtin's coin, rolling communication along. For him, truth is understood relationally.

Truth, in other words, is dialogic, as is the source and creator of all truth, the inherently relational Trinity (chapter eight). Indeed, Christian tradition endorses dialogism. The revelation of God in Christ was not magically written on a wall by a divine finger, as in the story recounted in Daniel. Instead, as discussed in chapter two, the temple walls in Jerusalem were (re)signed, the incarnate Christ becoming a walking, talking temple that communicated with embodied others. And the significance of that incarnated temple was revealed dialogically, first through the apostle Paul who wrote letters to embodied people with particular concerns and difficulties. Then the Gospels were written, named after disciples who walked and talked with Jesus. Moreover, because they were embodied, the writers didn't always get their details straight, as in the death of Judas and the number of women who visited the empty tomb.[47] Even the doctrine of the incarnation and the Trinity were established not through writing on the wall but through dialogism, leaders in

---

[45]Ibid., p. 93.
[46]Quoted in Holquist, *Dialogism*, pp. 62-63.
[47]For Judas's death see Mt 27:5-8 and Acts 1:18-19; for the women at the tomb, see Mt 28:1-10; Mk 16:1-6; Lk 24:1-10; and Jn 20:1-18. Despite these discrepancies, the essential truth about the empty tomb was clearly established.

the church guided by the Holy Spirit as they argued over the nature of God's revelation in Christ (chapter eight).

Rather than feel apprehensive about fallible humans being part of the process, we should rejoice, knowing that the very semiosis of doctrine reflects God's endorsement of embodied communication. When the church established that Jesus was fully God and fully human simultaneously, it established that Truth becomes known relationally, God revealing God's own self through embodiment.

Embodiment, however, implies that signs of truth are consummated differently in different places, for bodies are always constrained by the time and space in which they are situated. Thus some signs of truth important to early Christians—like the necessity of refraining from sex with one's spouse—do not strike most Christians as important today. This does not mean that early Christians were unenlightened compared to us—or vice versa. Instead, it means that the "chronotopes" of Christian contexts have changed.

By "chronotope," Bakhtin means the time and place where an embodied self is located. It is "one of the few non-Russian words Bakhtin uses as part of his technical vocabulary," thus making its Greek meaning—"time-place"—explicit for readers in many different languages.[48] Admittedly, Bakhtin tends to use /chronotope/ to describe the time-place that situates characters in literary texts. For example, it is no coincidence that Mary Shelley's famous character, Dr. Frankenstein, creates a "monster" in early nineteenth-century Europe just as people were discussing the life-changing potential of electricity. Nevertheless, Bakhtin makes clear that literary chronotopes reflect the condition of all human knowledge, based on "the actual chronotopes of our world," as he puts it. Embodiment in time and space, then, affects the way humans perceive and communicate truth.[49]

THE CHRONOTOPE OF THE WORD: TRANSLATING THE BIBLE

The Gospel that says, "In the beginning was the Word," also tells us that the embodied Word is "the way, and *the truth*, and the life" (Jn 1:1; 14:6). Because he was embodied, Jesus, like all signs of truth, was affected by the shaping of

---

[48]Holquist, *Dialogism*, p. 109.
[49]Mikhail Bakhtin, "Forms of Time and Chronotope in the Novel," in *The Dialogic Imagination*, p. 253. The connection of "chronotope" to embodiment is reinforced by the fact that Bakhtin first heard the word used by a physiologist. See Holquist, *Dialogism*, pp. 109, 153.

space and time—the chronotope—which inevitably affected the signs he
used. Why did Jesus say, for example, "I lay down my life for the sheep" (Jn
10:15) and not "I lay down my life for the koala bears"? Quite obviously, the
latter would have made no sense in first-century Palestine.

Chronotopes challenge Bible translators. Those who care about effective
communication must repeatedly consider whether to maintain metaphors
from ancient Hebrew culture that make no sense to indigenous cultures
today. For example, when the United Bible Societies translated Scripture into
Mayan for Guatemalan believers, they employed an image that reflected the
Mayan chronotope: a metaphor for life called the "eating bowl." Hence, for
Proverbs 1:12, "like Sheol let us swallow them alive / and whole, like those
who go down to the Pit," translators substituted "may he fall into our eating
bowl." And for Psalm 109:13, "may his name be blotted out in the second
generation," they substituted "may his eating bowl be overturned."[50] Seeking
to communicate scriptural truth to bodies embedded in cultural contexts, the
translators (re)signed truth.

Bible translators thus deal not only with spatial differences—Guatemala
(eating bowl) versus ancient Israel (the Pit)—but also with temporal differences. For example, the seventeenth-century translators hired by King James
to produce a new Bible translation put signs into Holy Writ that mean quite
different things today. When their Epistle of James states, "And ye have respect to him that weareth the gay clothing, and say unto him, Sit thou here in
a good place" (Jas 2:3 KJV), they had no idea how many of their words would
change meaning or fall out of usage.[51] (Perhaps this explains why my Grandma
Tuty refused to acknowledge new meanings of /gay/: the old meaning was
scriptural! After all, she also justified her use of the King James Bible with the
fact that it offered "mansions" in heaven, whereas readers of newer translations
only got "dwelling places" [Jn 14:2]. Why give up a mansion?!)

THE GUTENBERG CHRONOTOPE AND MARTIN LUTHER

Even the idea that the Bible should be translated reflects one's chronotope.

---

[50]Robert Bascom, a translation specialist with the United Bible Societies, provided me with this
example. Willis Barnstone reports that "Translators of the Bible into Eskimo Have Resorted to
the Phrase 'Seal of God' for 'Lamb of God.'" See *The Poetics of Translation: History, Theory, Practice*
(New Haven: Yale University Press, 1993), p. 41. Thanks to my student Kinley Zook for alerting
me to Barnstone's work.

[51]The RSV, NRSV and NIV substitute "fine" for the KJV "gay."

Jerome's fourth-century Latin translation—the Vulgate—was considered the sacred language of truth for a thousand years. Then signs of the times changed, quite literally, with the invention of the printing press in the mid-fifteenth century. Before Gutenberg's movable type, only monasteries and the very rich could afford to own Bibles, which had to be hand-copied. Truth was therefore in the hands, quite literally, of those bodies that could read, necessitating a view that salvation came only through the Roman Church: the home of literate priests. Rather than denounce this view, Protestants should regard it with the eyes of participatory outsideness, seeing it as a necessary reflection of the times.

However, contexts change, such that movable type energized a dramatic (re)signing of Christianity: the Protestant Reformation. It is important to realize that Gutenberg's printing press printed more than Gutenberg Bibles. It allowed the production of indulgence coupons by the score, making it easier for reprobate entrepreneurs to market them like scalpers selling tickets outside a concert (see chapter seven). One need merely purchase a printed indulgence coupon to get special passage through purgatory. Luther's protests nailed to the Wittenberg door, therefore, reflected a change in culture—the printing press—that made it easier for people to sell indulgences.

Rather than repudiate the printing press, Luther established a dialogic relationship with the new technology. First, the printing press enabled copies of Luther's Ninety-five Theses to be reproduced and distributed by the thousands after he nailed them to the Wittenberg door. Second, thanks to the printing press, Luther could now argue for "the priesthood of all believers" rather than absolute dependence upon the pope. This is because many more believers could now afford to purchase Bibles for their own reading, enabling them to be part of the "priesthood." And it is no coincidence that after a Bull of Excommunication was launched against him in 1521, Luther threw himself into translating the Greek New Testament into German, the language of the common people. Within two months after Luther completed his translation, five thousand printed copies had been sold.

As printing technology spread throughout Europe in the fifteenth century, so did vernacular Bibles, printers sensing a "ready market" and potential for "large sales." Diarmaid MacCulloch, in fact, notes that a recent biography of John Calvin "has suggested this huge increase in Bibles created the Reformation rather than being created by it."[52] Though this statement glosses over multiple economic and political factors that contributed to the Reformation, it makes clear that signs of the times—movable type—helped transform signs of Christianity.[53]

SEEING THE LIGHT OF THE WOR(L)D

Like signs of the Bible as Word of God, signs of Jesus as Word of God are seen differently in different eras. This does not reduce Jesus to a projection of human desire. Just the opposite! It is Jesus who projects the light of truth to us, but we see the light differently, depending upon our chronotopes.

Think of the way the North Star has projected its light for millions of years, guiding thousands of ships to their destinations. However, depending upon where each ship is floating, a crew will see the star in relationship to their location differently: at certain times the star appears off the starboard bow, at other times it is directly behind them. And under certain conditions—fog, rain, interfering land masses—the crew does not see the star at all; but the light nevertheless continues to shine beyond the obstructions. Even when the star is readily apparent, the kind of boat and the sea in which it navigates will affect how the crew will apply the light of "true north" to their behavior: in some instances sails will be furled; in others fires will be fed coal; in still others, computations will be made on computers. Finally, the way different ships search for "true north" differs from era to era. In the earliest days of navigation, humans had to rely on the naked eye, whereas today navigators have highly complex technological devices to ascertain true north. Even though technology has changed the mediums of perception over the centuries, it's still the same star, no matter how sophisticated human devices become.[54]

Similarly, perceptions of Jesus reflect the chronotopes of the perceivers: their own embodied contexts in space and time. And no matter how sophisticated our devices of theological language become, it is still the same Christ directing us today that directed the course of Christians in the catacombs—

---

[52]MacCulloch, *Christianity*, pp. 569-70. MacCulloch cites Bernard Cottret, *Calvin: A Biography*, trans. Wallace M. McDonald (Grand Rapids, MI: Eerdmans, 2000 [1995]), pp. 93-94.

[53]For a concise overview of contributing factors to the Protestant Reformation, see James Davison Hunter, *To Change the World: The Irony, Tragedy, and Possibility of Christianity in the Late Modern World* (New York: Oxford University Press, 2010), pp. 64-70.

[54]I thank Gary Deddo, my editor at IVP Academic, for suggesting this fertile metaphor.

even before the ecumenical councils. In the language of Bakhtin, the words of different eras consummate the Word differently.

Theologian Kevin Vanhoozer invokes Bakhtin's chronotope to argue, as I do, that, "while God's truth is eternal, our theologies inevitably show the signs of the times in which they were conceived."[55] Or, to use the guiding metaphor of this book, even though the Holy Spirit joins us on the edge of the coin as we balance between the immutable Word and our mutable words, the surface upon which we roll the coin changes with time. Consider, for example, one of the key doctrines of Christianity: the atonement.

CHANGING SIGNS OF THE ATONEMENT

Since the resurrection, Christians have developed multiple theories about the atonement: the means by which Christ's bodily death and resurrection reconcile us to God. In *Mere Christianity,* C. S. Lewis acknowledges these many different theories, arguing that one does not need to understand how the atonement works in order to accept the *gift* of salvation: "The central Christian belief is that Christ's death has somehow put us right with God and given us a fresh start. Theories about Christ's death are not Christianity; they are explanations about how it works. . . . [N]o explanation will ever be quite adequate to the reality."[56] Nevertheless, many Christians believe their particular interpretation to be "the Truth," regarding other theories as heretical. Bakhtin can help us understand where these competing theories come from, enabling us to accept them as expressions of an incarnational faith: faith that recognizes God's radical endorsement of embodiment, expressed through the incarnation.

The dominant theories about Christ's atoning work might be summarized as follows:

- **Ransom theory:** Traditionally attributed to Irenaeus, a second-century bishop, this theory was (re)signed by Origen (in the third century) and Gregory of Nyssa (in the fourth century). It conceived of Christ as a "ransom" paid to Satan who, as Augustine puts it, "held humanity in his captivity."[57] Gregory the Great (pope from 590 to 604) embellished the

[55]Kevin J. Vanhoozer, *The Drama of Doctrine: A Canonical-Linguistic Approach to Christian Theology* (Louisville: Westminster John Knox, 2005), p. 345.
[56]C. S. Lewis, *Mere Christianity* (New York: Macmillan, 1960), p. 57.
[57]Quoted in Richard Viladesau, *The Beauty of the Cross: The Passion of Christ in Theology and the*

theory, using the image of a baited hook. As Alister McGrath summarizes, "Christ's humanity is the bait, and his divinity the hook. The devil, like a great sea-monster, snaps at the bait and then discovers, too late, the hook."[58] We might compare it to the action in kidnapping movies. Detectives bait the criminals with a false ransom, like a suitcase full of tube socks rather than money, and the kidnappers discover the deception only after it's too late. Similarly, in order to ransom humanity, God sent Jesus to be killed by the devil, who discovers he has been tricked when God raises Jesus from the dead. As Bruno of Segni approvingly noted 500 years later, "It was fitting only to Wisdom, that is, to the Son of God, to wisely deceive the devil."[59]

- **Satisfaction theory:** Bothered by God's deceptive actions in the ransom view of atonement, Anselm of Canterbury (1033-1109) advocated something more honorable. In fact, God's honor is key to Anselm's theory. In 1097 c.e., he argued that God's righteous honor was insulted when humanity chose sin over obedience. Just as a knight who has dishonored his lord is obligated to rectify their relationship through an act of restitution, humanity must satisfy the Lord God's honor through an act of reconciliation. However, unlike the honor of an earthly lord, God's righteous honor so far transcends humanity that it can not possibly be satisfied by any human action. Only God in human form can satisfy the requirements. As McGrath explains it, "a 'God-man' would possess both the ability (as God) and the obligation (as a human being) to pay the required satisfaction."[60]

- **Moral influence theory:** Peter Abelard (1079-1142) offered another theory of atonement, perhaps bothered by the economy of exchange that is key to the other two theories. While in the ransom theory God sets up an economic transaction with Satan, in the satisfaction theory Christ exchanges himself for sinful humanity to restore God's honor. In contrast, Abelard emphasized salvation as God's *gift* to humanity. As an act of love rather than exchange, Christ took the sins of the world on himself, pro-

---

Arts—From the Catacombs to the Eve of the Renaissance (New York: Oxford University Press, 2006), p. 69.

[58]Alister E. McGrath, *Historical Theology: An Introduction to the History of Christian Thought* (Malden, MA: Blackwell, 1998), p. 134.

[59]Quoted in Viladesau, *Beauty of the Cross*, p. 71.

[60]McGrath, *Historical Theology*, p. 136.

viding an example of sacrificial obedience that influences those who turn to him. As Abelard puts it, "The Son of God took our nature, and in it took upon himself to teach us by both word and example, even to the point of death, thus binding us to himself through love."[61] Christ's loving gift thus influences us to make gifts of ourselves to God, as well as to a needy world.

Later views of the atonement tend to rework one of these basic theories:

- **Penal substitution theory:** Anselm's theory was (re)signed by Calvinists, who replaced the sign of God's honor with the sign of God's moral law. Because humans break God's law, they deserve to die. God, however, sent Jesus to take punishment in our place, so that a sinless human pays the price rather than sinful humanity. As fully-God, Jesus then conquered death through the resurrection.

- **Demythologizing theories:** Scholars influenced by the anti-supernaturalism of the so-called Higher Criticism, (re)signed Abelard's moral influence theory to say that Jesus gave us an example of the sacrificial love that humans should follow. Demythologizers would therefore argue that the resurrection is a symbolic reflection of Christian practice, as in, "I resurrect Christ every time I act Christlike." As discussed in chapter one, such anti-supernatural theology came to prominence in the early nineteenth century through the work of the Young Hegelians. It reached its apex in the mid twentieth century with the demythologizing of Rudolf Bultmann (1884-1976), who saw the crucifixion as modeling "victory over inauthentic existence and unbelief." Similarly, theologian Paul Tillich (1886-1965) held that Christ's martyrdom symbolizes how we might conquer "existential forces which threaten to deprive us of authentic existence."[62] In other words, Christ's sacrificial act models for us truly authentic living.

- **Christus Victor:** Disturbed by the anti-supernaturalism of demythologizers, a Swedish bishop named Gustaf Aulén (re)signed the ransom theory in a 1931 book called *Christus Victor.* However, rather than endorsing a "bait" and switch game with the devil (as in the traditional ransom view), or making God subservient to honor or the moral law (as

---

[61]Quoted in ibid., p. 139.
[62]Ibid., p. 287.

in satisfaction and penal substitution theories), Aulén argues that Christ achieved victory over evil not through his death but through the resurrection (hence *Christus Victor*). Furthermore, Aulén says the Christus Victor theory was advanced by some of the earliest fathers of Christianity (such as Irenaeus), and should be considered the "classic" view of the atonement. His desire to promote the "classic" theory, however, is undermined by the fact that Christians throughout history, from the earliest centuries until now, have not always agreed about which view is most "true."

How might we negotiate among these various theories about atonement?

ROLLING ON THE EDGE OF ATONEMENT WITH BAKHTIN: HETEROGLOSSIA

Bakhtin's word to describe multiple theories like this is "heteroglossia": a word he coined from Greek meaning "different tongues." But his theory of heteroglossia does not assume the economy of exchange discussed in the previous chapter. There we saw that Saussure's idea of multiple systems (cabinets) leads to arguments either for tolerance of all religions or for intolerance of all but one. Bakhtin, instead, would have us respond according to the gift of "participatory outsideness." In other words, my position outside of the times in which these theories were formulated enables me to perceive how each manifests "signs of the times."[63]

Theories of atonement, in other words, reflect the contexts, or chronotopes, of the Christians that develop them:

• The ransom theory, with its duel between God and Satan, arose when Christians were under persecution by Roman emperors. Life for them felt like a battle between forces of good and evil: an idea that echoed contemporary Manicheism, a Persian religion based on the mortal combat between a spiritual world of light and a material world of darkness. Though most Christians declared Manicheism heretical, it was merely an extreme form of the Gnosticism that held sway over many Christians in the early centuries.

---

[63]Vanhoozer also discusses the changes to theories of atonement, avoiding (as I do) an evolutionary understanding of the views. Nevertheless, he responds to the various theories differently than do I (*Drama of Doctrine*, pp. 380-94).

• Anselm's renunciation of the Manichean-like duel of the ransom theory similarly reflects his own chronotope. Embedded in a feudal culture in which knights pledged fealty to their lords, whose honor they must defend, Anselm naturally thought in terms of "satisfying" the honor of our Lord God. He therefore (re)signed the idea of "satisfaction"—a word early church fathers applied to penance—by applying it to his contemporary environment: a "world of feudal chivalry, with its incipient 'code of honor.'"[64] McGrath suggests that the idea of "satisfaction" could derive *either* "from the Germanic laws of the period, which stipulated that an offense had to be purged through an appropriate payment," *or* from the Catholic practice of penance, wherein priests required penitent sinners to "satisfy" God by going on pilgrimage or doing charitable works.[65] In the spirit of Bakhtin, I would suggest a heteroglossia to Anselm, in which both concepts influence his theology.

• By the Reformation, of course, Christians no longer assumed feudal fealty as "natural." Living in a century that showed increasing interest in universal applications of the law to rich and poor alike, Protestant (re)signers of Anselm therefore considered "satisfaction" in relationship to the moral law rather than to a lord's offended honor. John Calvin (1509-1564), a name usually associated with the "penal substitution theory," reflects his training in criminal law when he writes that Christ was "made a substitute and a surety in the place of transgressors and even submitted as a criminal, to sustain and suffer all the punishment which would have been inflicted on them."[66] The title of his watershed theological work that presents his view of atonement, *Institutes of the Christian Religion* (1536), anticipates the title of a watershed legal work published a century later: *Institutes of the Lawes of England* by Sir Edward Coke (1552-1634). As Kathryn Tanner notes, "it is very hard to avoid entirely the suggestion [in Calvin's *Institutes*] that grace and liberality are simply being made to fit a context of legal requirement."[67]

• The resulting emphasis on equal rights under the law fed the "Enlightenment" commitment to reason: just as all humans have equal access to the

---

[64]Viladesau, *Beauty of the Cross*, p. 73. He asserts that the "satisfaction" of penance is taught by both Tertullian and Augustine (p. 71).

[65]McGrath, *Historical Theology*, p. 136.

[66]John Calvin, *Institutes*, 2.16.1.

[67]Kathryn Tanner, *Economy of Grace* (Minneapolis: Fortress, 2005), p. 49.

law, so all humans have equal access to reason. The centuries-old hierarchy of the Catholic Church, with power in the hands of the pope and his cardinals, therefore seemed more feudal than egalitarian, feeding a growing Enlightenment assumption that belief in the supernatural was feudal as well. The development of science as an increasingly important source of truth about nature abetted this view. The rationalism and empiricism necessary for scientific research and technological development made belief in supernatural realities seem all the more antiquated and anti-intellectual. By the twentieth century, then, Rudolf Bultmann could say with impunity, "We cannot use electric lights and radios and, in the event of illness, avail ourselves of modern medical and clinical means and at the same time believe in the spirit and wonder world of the New Testament."[68] And his view of the atonement reflects such hope in science.

• By the 1970s, however, poststructuralists were deconstructing such naive hope in science and technology, arguing that belief in the beneficence of human reason is as much a faith position as belief in Christ's resurrection. Of course, many Christians throughout the reign of demythologizing theology maintained belief in the supernatural power of the cross. But just as believers in the resurrection like Irenaeus, Gregory, Anselm, Abelard and Calvin developed different views of the atonement, so today theologians, aided by their openness to the supernatural "Other," continue the tradition of (re)signing. Resigned to salvation made possible through Christ's death and resurrection, they wish to re-sign how we understand it—in dialogue with the signs of our times.

(RE)SIGNING A NONVIOLENT ATONEMENT

Just as Anselm felt uncomfortable with the deception by God demonstrated in the ransom theory, and Calvinists felt uncomfortable with the feudal assumptions behind Anselm's satisfaction theory, many Christians today feel uncomfortable with the violence of God implied by penal substitution. The theory can strike unbelievers as presenting a God who requires the brutal suffering of his son *in exchange for* salvation.

---

[68]Rudolf Bultmann, "New Testament and Mythology: The Problem of Demythologizing the New Testament Proclamation," in *New Testament and Mythology and Other Basic Writings*, ed. and trans. Schubert M. Ogden (Philadelphia: Fortress, 1984), p. 4.

This is especially problematic in our own times, when religious fanatics endorse violence as part of an economy of exchange: murdering the enemy in exchange for bliss in the afterlife. Some theologians therefore argue for a perspective that avoids the economy of exchange that defines so many world religions. They focus, instead, on what distinguishes Christianity from generic religious behavior: the gift. Arguing that human sin, not God, put Jesus on the cross, these theologians (re)sign Aulén's Christus Victor theory by saying salvation functions not through Christ's death but through his resurrection.[69] Christ triumphed over the violent consequences of sin by conquering death. His victory over sin, then, is a gift we accept once we believe the gift has been offered.[70]

DIALOGIZING HETEROGLOSSIA

Rather than tolerating all atonement theories or repudiating all but one, Bakhtin expects us to dialogize the heteroglossia. In other words, after understanding how each theory dialogues with signs of its times, we critically assess how the theories dialogue with our own times. Since the Bible has been used to support them all, we ask ourselves which ones best communicate *to people today* the truth of salvation through Christ. Doing so we place God's desire to be in relationship with all of creation—at-one-ment—above our desire to protect the signs with which we feel most comfortable.[71]

But the dialogism does not stop there. I still need these theories to dialogue with my theological assumptions, to make me aware of prejudices reinforced by my own chronotope. How might Anselm help me think about ways that I dishonor God? How might Abelard focus my attention on following the example of Christ's loving sacrifice? How might Calvin remind me that I can acknowledge salvation as a gift only when I recognize that I deserve punishment? How might the demythologizers help me value the

---

[69]Viladesau argues that Anselm limits salvation to "the single moment of Christ's death. The incarnation itself is reduced to the necessary condition for the sacrifice; the resurrection is reduced to a consequence" (*Beauty of the Cross*, p. 75). Problematically, Anselm's theory reinforced a "commercial analogy" in which "one could pay someone else to satisfy one's penitential obligation, or could in place of it pay to have a certain number of masses celebrated" (p. 71): an economy of exchange.

[70]For a collection of theologians who are working on nonviolent atonement theory, see Brad Jersak and Michael Hardin, eds., *Stricken by God? Nonviolent Identification and the Victory of Christ* (Grand Rapids, MI: Eerdmans, 2007).

[71]Scot McKnight uses the metaphor of a golf bag with multiple clubs to illustrate the multiple views of atonement. Under different conditions different clubs are chosen to best keep the truth in play. See *A Community Called Atonement* (Nashville: Abingdon, 2007).

Enlightenment sensibilities that continue to shape American democracy? How might interest in nonviolent atonement explain contemporary wrestling with the doctrine of hell?[72]

This latter question, of course, is the most controversial. Nevertheless, Bakhtin would want us to dialogue with it rather than ignore it. We might do so by asking ourselves even more questions: In an era when suicide bombing expresses genuine faith for many, how might Christians communicate the distinctiveness of a religion based on the gift of salvation rather than upon the economy of exchange represented by traditional views of hell? How might we resign ourselves to the doctrine of hell even as we re-sign it?[73]

We must ask ourselves these questions with openness to the otherness of the past—as though the past is a foreign country. Here's how Bakhtin explains such openness:

> We raise new questions for a foreign culture, ones that it did not raise itself; we seek answers to our own questions in it; and the foreign culture responds to us by revealing to us its new aspects and new semantic depths. Without one's own questions one cannot creatively understand anything other or foreign.[74]

We seek new semantic depths in the desire for words that can deepen our relationship with the Word that walked among us. We dialogue with the foreign in the hope that, together, we can get a better fix on the light revealed, through the Word, to the world.

THE DIALOGISM OF PAST, PRESENT AND FUTURE

For Bakhtin, every sign worth using is situated in a "dialogic" relationship not only between human bodies, but also with past, present and future. When John the Baptist describes Jesus as "the lamb of God," for example, he reflects

---

[72]The most popular examples are Rob Bell, *Love Wins: A Book About Heaven, Hell, and the Fate of Every Person Who Ever Lived* (San Francisco: HarperOne, 2011); and Brian McLaren, *The Last Word and the Word After That: A Tale of Faith, Doubt, and a New Kind of Christianity* (San Francisco: Jossey-Bass, 2005).

[73]Christians who want to totally eliminate the doctrine of hell look only in one direction, embarrassed by the way horrific images of despicable torture have been used to scare people into heaven. (Re)signing Christians are equally disgusted with any message that reduces the gift of salvation to an economy of exchange: "become a Christian and you get in exchange the bliss of Heaven rather than the torments of Hell." Nevertheless, they resign themselves to scriptural precedents for hell *even as* they re-sign the way we think and talk about the afterlife. For a good example of (re)signing hell, see Sharon L. Baker, *Razing Hell* (Philadelphia: Westminster John Knox, 2010).

[74]Bakhtin, *Speech Genres*, p. 7

his present chronotope: a time and place in which mutton sustained society. But he also alludes to an ancient practice of Jewish religion: the sacrifice of an unspotted lamb. John's phrase encompasses not only the bodies of his contemporaries who eat lambs to live, but also the bodies of priests who have been communicating for centuries the significance of sacrificial lambs. And in the process he prepares his listeners for the future, when Jesus would say to his disciples: "This is my body; take and eat."

For Bakhtin, then, effective communication requires that I recognize the chronotope of persons I address: their contexts past and present. For instance, if I desire to share my faith with a Jewish friend, I don't use the offensive cliche "the Jews killed Jesus." Even if I believe that scribes and Pharisees had something to do with Christ's arrest, I recognize that the sign "Christ-killer" has led to centuries of anti-Semitism, fueling pogroms and genocide. Even if I innocently mean to state a fact, "many Jews wanted to get rid of Jesus," the statement is not innocent. And my use of it, failing to consider the chronotope of my Jewish listener, is a selfish act: I'm thinking of myself and the value of my signs more than of the embodied person to whom I am speaking. Such selfishness leads to diseased communication.

COMMUNICATIVE DISEASES

It's easy to recognize diseased communication in hate-speech, pornography, slander, cursing, propaganda and lies. But there are more subtle forms of communicative dis-ease that infect many people:

1. People who refuse to converse with anyone whose opinions and/or beliefs differ from their own

2. People who only say things that they know their interlocutors want to hear

I have encountered both kinds of people, the first reflecting the "dis," the second the "ease" of /dis-ease/. Type #1 considers ideas more important than people, "dissing" anyone who disagrees with them. Type #2 values "ease" over truth, communicating opposite things to different people, often saying something different to a person's face than behind her back. While we call type #1 a fundamentalist (chapter one), type #2 has become so common that a new sign has been develop for it: /frenemy/. Though seeming very different from each other, #1 and #2 are merely different sides of the exact same coin. Why? Because both shut down conversation, the first by attacking those who disagree, the second by superficially agreeing with everyone.

Communicators on the edge, in contrast, commit to the far more difficult balancing act of genuine conversation. They are honest about their perspectives even as they seek to understand the chronotopes of their addressees, developing new signs that communicate firm belief in original ways. Such communicators, in other words, (re)sign, applying antiseptic Bakhtin to communicative diseases. Committed to dialogism, they are open to changing their own perspectives even as they hope to change the views of others.

Bakhtin explains his philosophy of communication with an image that anticipates my two-sided coin:

> Orientation of the word toward the addressee has an extremely high significance. In point of fact, *word is a two-sided act.* It is determined equally by *whose* word it is and *for whom* it is meant. As word, it is precisely *the product of the reciprocal relationship between speaker and listener, addresser and addressee.* Each and every word expresses the "one" in relation to the "other."[75]

On the edge of this two-sided coin, I use signs that look to my own past—the way "the community to which I belong" has traditionally employed the sign[76]—and to the past of the other as I seek to understand how the sign makes meaning to the community to which she belongs. I value, in other words, embodiment in place and time.

After all, how can I encourage belief in the embodiment of God-in-Christ if I refuse to value the embodiment of my audience, whether one person or a group of thousands?

INCARNATIONAL DIALOGISM:
INTERPERSONAL AND PUBLIC COMMUNICATION

A Christian rhetor, then, reflects belief in the incarnation by acknowledging the embodied chronotope of the addressee(s). Those who practice incarnational dialogism, as I call it, communicate value for the other—both people as other and ideas as other—while still maintaining their own beliefs. Here's how incarnational dialogism might function in relation to controversial issues:

Interpersonal communication. When a person says something that dis-

---

[75]Voloshinov, *Marxism and the Philosophy of Language,* p. 86, italics his.
[76]Ibid.

turbs me, rather than mount an attack, I need to first repeat back what they have said in my own words. When I respond, "What I hear you saying is . . . ," I operate according to the gift rather than an economy of exchange: I gift them with attentiveness, and I give them an opportunity to clarify their thought. This communicates that I value them enough to listen, but also prevents arguments that might develop from either my own misunderstanding or their failure of articulation. I then follow up with another gift: expressing what I like about their opinion before I present my alternate perspective.

Take for example, the aphorism, "if you're a conservative when you're young, you have no heart; if you're a liberal when you're old you have no head." If someone repeats this to me, I might respond, "you are right to foreground the dichotomy between head and heart in our culture." But then I follow up with a position on the edge: "Do we have to settle for either/or thinking? How might we exercise both brain and heart together?" I invite them onto the edge with me, communicating that together we might discuss issues apart from political cliches. And in the process I might introduce the limitations of /liberal/ and /conservative/ (chapter one).

Here's another example that happened to me recently. I was sitting around a table with a group of Caucasian acquaintances when one of them started denouncing affirmative action, saying, "blacks have gotten so many privileges in our country that whites are being discriminated against. I went to a mostly black school, and I was terrified to go to the bathroom, never knowing when I would get harassed." Rather than starting an argument about affirmative action, I acknowledged the speaker's embodied experience, saying, "that must have been very traumatic for you; how did that experience influence your perspective today?" In other words, I encouraged my interlocutor to talk about his chronotope. I then imaginatively put myself in his position by acknowledging the many abuses made in the name of affirmative action. Only at this point did I feel free to provide a different perspective, communicating a love for the person over a love for my own views. And, in the spirit of incarnational love, I had to be as willing to do what I wanted my conversationalist to do: change perspectives. Otherwise, my approach would have been merely condescending, if not hypocritical.[77]

---

[77]As an American contemporary of Bakhtin explains, one can successfully persuade an audience "only insofar as he yields to that audience's opinions in other respects. Some of their opinions are

Even when my interlocutor resorts to name calling, I must try to understand his chronotope. Rather than operating by an economy of exchange,
returning insult for insult, I give the gift of openness to the other. For example, when a student used a term bandied about in the 1990s by radio personalities—"femi-nazi"—I tried to engage rather than react: "What do you
mean by 'femi-nazi'?" When the student couldn't define the term, I helped,
explaining that some people use the sign /nazi/ to describe anyone who
pushes their agenda—whether female-rights or states-rights—by denouncing
people who disagree with them. After showing that I heard him, I then began
to ask about /nazi/, encouraging the student to reflect on the sign itself: "How
might the sign shut down communication rather than open it up? How might
employment of /femi-nazi/ end up doing the same thing that quite rightly
disturbs you?"

Without using the elitist term /deconstruction/, I thus deconstruct my interlocutor's argument. Something he thought was outside his house of
belief—the arrogant certitude of femi-nazis—might actually be inside it
when he denounces a whole group of people by using that dismissive term
(see chapter six). *By discussing the signs employed,* an argument can be transformed from heated antagonism to genuine communication.

Lest you think I claim to be a master of interpersonal communication, I do
not. Inspired by Bahktin's communication theory, I hold up incarnational
dialogism as a goal rather than an attainment.

Public communication. Incarnational dialogism is easier in small group or
one-on-one settings than in public speeches before scores of people. When
we are close enough to touch our interlocutors' bodies or see emotional nu-
ances expressed on their faces we are less likely to resort to name-calling—at
least until we lose control by falling into economic thinking, exchanging
insult for insult. But public speaking, often by necessity, turns an audience
into a mass of anonymous figures. How, after all, can a speaker consider the
chronotope of each embodied person within a group of a hundred or more?

Audience anonymity becomes quite literal for speakers on radio and television shows, who must direct their attention merely to a microphone and/or
camera. This explains the incivility of many media pundits these days. Re-

---

needed to support the fulcrum by which he would move other opinions." Furthermore, the rhetor
"will be more effective" if the shared opinions are "genuine." Kenneth Burke, *A Rhetoric of Motives*
(New York: Prentice-Hall, 1950), p. 56.

garding their political agendas as more important than embodied people, they often denounce whole groups through name-calling. Within Bakhtin's system of dialogized heteroglossia, such pundits are *not* communicators; they are warriors feeding ammunition to those who already agree with them. Their violent denunciations close down heteroglossia rather than dialogize it.

Synthesizing the insights of many communication theorists, Paul Graham has created a "hierarchy of disagreement" that establishes "name-calling" as the most degraded (and degrading) kind of argumentation.[78] Christians committed to incarnational dialogism therefore avoid name-calling not only in their own rhetoric, but also in their listening habits. Refusing to use simplistic slurs like "bleedin'-heart liberal" or "right-wing wacko," they also refuse listening to pundits who employ such signs. After all, if radio personalities lower themselves to name-calling, how can we trust that their political insights are not equally simplistic?

Only slightly better than name-calling, according to Graham's hierarchy, are *ad hominem* arguments: attacking the character or intelligence of one's opponents. When speakers employ statements like "all college professors are liberal elitists" or "anyone who disagrees with gay marriage is homophobic," they mirror each other: opposite sides of the same coin. Such ad hominem indictments shut down communication by slapping down the coin in order to silence those on the other side. The incarnational Christian rises above such simplistic denunciations by standing on the edge, attempting to understand alternate viewpoints without using dismissive signs.

Incarnational dialogism in public communication can be illustrated by the "I Have a Dream" speech of Martin Luther King Jr. Rather than resort to ad hominem slurs like "bigots" and "white-supremacists," which many victims of racism in his audience might have cheered, King presented a vision of hope without downplaying the injustices faced by African Americans. But to communicate these injustices, King (re)signed on the edge of the coin: resigned to the glory of America's constitutional democracy, King re-signed how his audience might think about America's commitment to its own ideals. He thus honored the chronotopes of people in the past as well as those in the present. For example, he could have indicted the slave-owning Thomas Jefferson, denouncing inhumane practices from America's beginnings. Instead, he quite

---

[78]Paul Graham, "How to Disagree," March 2008, on his personal website: www.paulgraham.com/disagree.html.

rightly said, "When the architects of our republic wrote the magnificent words of the Constitution and the Declaration of Independence, they were signing a promissory note." Thus honoring the architects of our country, he went on to say that "America has defaulted on this promissory note. . . . America has given the Negro people a bad check, a check which has come back marked 'insufficient funds.'"[79] By coining this and several other intriguing metaphors, King got people to think about racism in new ways. But he didn't leave his audience mired in these visions of failure; he developed a litany of new signs for the future, as demonstrated by his multiple repetitions of "I have a dream . . ." (see chapter four).

King, like any good public speaker, acknowledged problems but did not wallow in them. As he encouraged becoming new, he coined new signs so that his rhetoric practiced what it preached. Doing so, he reflected his Christian assumptions: that life in Christ is about becoming new.

CHANGING SIGNS: BECOMING VERSUS BEING

Committed to changing signs of truth, Bakhtin advocates "becoming" over the stasis of "being." People committed to "being," because they fear change, are like someone who slaps down one side of the coin—whether the right side or the left side—standing on it as the only way to understand reality. This, of course, applies to religious fundamentalists as well as to those who assert that, instead of truth, all we have are plural concoctions cooked up from different cabinets.

Considering such semiological, multi-cabinet thinking as semi-logical, Bakhtin believes there is absolute truth, but that we perceive it differently depending on our contexts—which inevitably change. For him, language is "a social phenomenon that is becoming in history." Therefore, as he states in *The Dialogic Imagination,* "The ideological becoming of a human being, in this view, is the process of selectively assimilating the words of others."[80]

Bakhtin's word "selectively" is key to (re)signing. Balancing on the edge of the coin implies a constant dialogue between signs of the past and signs of the present, selectively assimilating those that can keep Christianity and justice rolling into the future. This balance enables us to avoid falling into funda-

[79]Martin Luther King Jr., "The I Have a Dream Speech," in U. S. Constitution Online at www .usconstitution.net/dream.html.
[80]Mikhail Bakhtin, "Discourse in the Novel," in *The Dialogic Imagination,* p. 341.

mentalism on one side or the other: the side that refuses to consider new signs of belief versus the side that refuses to consider beliefs of the past. Once the coin falls on one side or the other, dialogism ends.[81]

BAKHTIN'S RELATIONAL SEMIOTIC

For Bakhtin, then, the dialogized word is the source of becoming. And Jesus incarnated the dialogized Word, such that his death on "the cross is the origin of all life, of all becoming."[82] "Being" a Christian is therefore a static concept, like standing on one side of a coin. Instead, believers are called to "become" like Christ in a process of sanctification. Eastern Orthodox Christians have a special word for sanctification—*theiosis*—by which they mean drawing closer and closer to God.[83]

The "-iosis" in *theiosis* means "process," as does the "-iosis" in *semiosis*. Bakhtin encourages the becoming of both, by inventing new words and pressing "old words into new service."[84] His coinages—outsideness, heteroglossia, chronotope—get us to think in new ways about ancient truths. He thus practices the principle of this book: the (re)signing of truth. For him, "Christ's truth is real, but," as Caryl Emerson summarizes, "truth always involves more work and more risk than dogma or propositions require of us." This is because "any truth we might achieve in life is available only as a relationship."[85] Just as God gave the Word new form—the body of Jesus—in order to draw us into relationship, so we give words new form in order to draw others to "the source of all becoming." Communication, like communion, is a gift of becoming.

THE BECOMING OF NEW SIGNS

To offer communication as a gift, then, we must practice the following principles:

- We avoid the arrogant mystification of ourselves as more enlightened than people in the past.

---

[81]As Bakhtin notes, "The semantic structure of an internally persuasive discourse is not *finite*, it is *open;* in each of the new contexts that dialogize it, this discourse is able to reveal ever newer *ways to mean*" (ibid., p. 346).

[82]Quoted in Caryl Emerson, "Russian Orthodoxy and the Early Bakhtin," *Religion and Literature* 22 (Summer-Autumn 1990): 112.

[83]Though most people write "theosis," I employ another accepted spelling to emphasize the parallel between the words *theiosis* and *semiosis*.

[84]Wayne C. Booth, "Introduction" to Mikhail Bakhtin, *Problems of Dostoevsky's Poetics*, ed. and trans. Caryl Emerson (Minneapolis: University of Minnesota Press, 1984), p. xxxv.

[85]Emerson, "Russian Orthodoxy," p. 113.

- We avoid naive idealizations of the past as more authentic than the present.

- On the edge between these first two options we humbly recognize that all humans, past and present, communicate out of their embodied contexts.

- Reflecting Christian belief in the incarnation, we work toward incarnational dialogism.

- Committed to "becoming" over "being," we advance the (re)signing of truth.

Bakhtin's dialogism is a communion between past and future, between resigning and re-signing. For him, as Caryl Emerson notes, "Everything that belongs only to the present dies along with the present."[86] Happily for us, the incarnate Jesus belongs not just to present times, whether the "present" of first-century Palestine or our own twenty-first-century "present." Though put to death in a particular present, Jesus transcended that chronotope through the resurrection, becoming present for all times. In all these presents we are offered the gift.

In response to the gift of the resurrected Word, Christians offer the gift of new words. On the edge of the coin, in other words, we coin other words. This, then, is the key to (re)signing. By coining new signs, we roll through our historical contexts while trusting that God not only transcends all contexts but also verifies their importance through the embodiment of the incarnation.

The next and final chapter offers guidelines for how to keep our coin(age)s on edge.

---

[86]Ibid., p. 4.

11

COMMUNICATION ON THE EDGE

A Conclusion

Like many people, I often prefer doing things the way I have always done them, surrounding myself with familiar signs. One incident during my grade school years could represent a general pattern in my life. During a class visit to the school library, Don, a fellow fourth-grader, mocked me for going straight to the "easy skinny books": ones dominated by pictures, like *Cat in the Hat*. Out of sheer pride (and a bit of infatuation) I followed Don to a place in the library that had turquoise-blue "fat books": biographies of famous people that contained (yikes!) absolutely no pictures. Daunted by the numerous words crowded on each page, I nevertheless checked out a book merely to impress Don. At home that night, I discovered, with a shock to my system, that written signs can create pictures in the human imagination far more exciting than anything drawn by Dr. Seuss.

My resistance to the signs in "fat books" serves as an analogy for how many people operate in culture: resisting change. In the 1820s, for example, the development of the railroad in England met fierce opposition, people arguing that "cows would cease to give milk, hens would be prevented from laying, and horses would become extinct" if the new technology were allowed to advance.[1] And, unfortunately, some used Christian rhetoric to denounce the railroad, mirroring other Christians who repudiated cultural innovations like dining forks, telephones and tea.[2]

---

[1]David Damrosch and Kevin J. H. Dettmar, eds., *The Longman Anthology of British Literature: The Victorian Age,* 3rd ed. (New York: Pearson Longman, 2006), p. 1140

[2]Diarmaid MacCulloch, *Christianity: The First Three Thousand Years* (New York: Viking, 2010), p. 545.

This is quite ironic, since the Christian life is all about change: we repent of our sins, we turn to Christ, we seek to grow closer to God through a process of sanctification, and we desire to help others change by attracting them to the same process. Unfortunately, all too many Christians limit such change to the spiritual realm, forgetting God's endorsement of embodiment. In contrast, those who believe that God took on flesh commit themselves not only to change the bodily conditions of those suffering around us, but also to recognize the inevitable change to cultures in which our bodies are situated. This, however, is the very thing that challenges us: how do we know whether we should resist the tides of change or go along with the flow?

In this concluding chapter I will analyze resistance to new signs before summarizing how the information covered in this book might help Christians surmount such resistance while at the same time avoiding the opposite error of indiscriminate endorsement of all cultural change. Encouraging effective communication through the (re)signing of truth, I end with ten guiding principles to keep us balanced on the edge of the coin.

I start, therefore, with an edgy Christian communicator, Dorothy L. Sayers, whose (re)signing changed lives.

THE (RE)SIGNING OF DOROTHY L. SAYERS

In 1940 the British Broadcasting Corporation (BBC) asked Sayers—by then a famous detective fiction novelist—to write a series of radio plays about the life of Jesus. In order to advertise the broadcasts, Sayers read passages from her finished work during a press conference in December of 1941. Journalists, looking for a scandal (imagine that!), played up the fact that Sayers put slang into disciples' mouths. Adding insult to injury, they lamented that Sayers sometimes employed—get ready for a shock—*American* slang.

Upset that Sayers did not use King James English for conversation among the disciples, several Christian groups mounted a censorship campaign, sending petitions to both Winston Churchill and the Archbishop of Canterbury, seeking to ban the plays. In the protesters' minds, creating new signs for the gospel message was a betrayal of the "Authorized Version" of truth.[3]

Fortunately, the BBC resisted tremendous pressure to censor the radio productions—and certainly benefited from the free advertising. Sayers's

---

[3]For an extended discussion of this incident see my book *Writing Performances: The Stages of Dorothy L. Sayers* (New York: Palgrave Macmillan, 2004), chap. 5.

twelve plays were broadcast as scheduled, thousands of people tuning in precisely because of the scandal. What they got, however, was a vivid and thoughtful account of Christ's death and resurrection communicated with new signs.

Sayers, in fact, received letters from scores of listeners testifying that, for the first time in their lives, the Bible made sense to them; that they finally understood how Christ could be relevant to regular slang-slinging, working-class individuals like themselves. Dozens of people made decisions to follow Christ because Sayers took the risk of (re)signing.

Even Christians benefited from Sayers's new signs. C. S. Lewis was so moved by the BBC play-cycle that he read the printed version, *The Man Born to Be King,* as part of his Lenten devotions every year until he died. The Spirit moves in mysterious ways, standing with (re)signers on the edge of the coin.

RESISTING THE IDOLATRY OF SIGNS

Sayers used the phrase "singular piece of idolatry" to describe Christian attacks on her radio plays.[4] A knowledge of semiotics helps explain her comment. Because a sign is "something that stands for something else," we see that a sign becomes an idol when it is valued more than that for which it stands. As Augustine noted in *On Christian Doctrine,* "He is a slave to a sign who uses or worships a significant thing without knowing what it signifies."[5] Like golden calves described in the Hebrew Scriptures, idols blind us to the dynamic nature of the deity, who meets us in the midst of changing "signs of the times," taking on different signs for different times.

Meeting Moses in the burning bush, for example, God used a verb rather than a noun for self-identification—"I am Who I am" or "I will be what I will be" (Ex 3:14)—as though endorsing that Moses' faith, in response, should be a verb rather than a noun. Indeed, God calls on Moses to take action, to challenge the status quo by leading the Israelites out of Egypt (Ex 3:10). Moses, however, focuses only on signs of his inadequacy: "Who am I that I should go to Pharaoh? . . . What shall I say to them? . . . But suppose they do not believe me? . . . O my Lord, I have never been eloquent, *neither*

---

[4]Dorothy L. Sayers, *The Man Born to Be King: A Play-Cycle on the Life of Our Lord and Saviour Jesus Christ* (Grand Rapids, MI: Eerdmans, 1979), p. 3.
[5]Augustine, *On Christian Doctrine,* trans. D. W. Robertson Jr. (New York: Liberal Arts Press, 1958), book 3, para. 13, p. 86.

in the past nor even now" (Ex 3:11, 13; 4:1, 10). In the language of Bakhtin (chapter ten), Moses resists change by appealing to his "being" rather than opening himself to God-guided "becoming." His initial "Who am I?" inverts God's dynamic name—"I am"—as though preferring stasis over change. Moses, in other words, clings to signs of the past to avoid (re)signing truth. It is no wonder that "the anger of the LORD was kindled against" him! (Ex 4:14).

Ironically, once he submitted to God-empowered "becoming," Moses witnessed the same kind of resistance to change among those he was called to lead. After he guided the Hebrews out of Egypt, Moses climbed Mount Sinai, where God (re)signed truth on tablets of stone. But the people who remained at the base of the mountain found comfort during Moses' absence by setting up an inert golden calf: an idol that kindled Moses' wrath.

And so the pattern continues. When Jesus actively (re)signed truth by substituting his body for temple sacrifice (chapter two), many people below the cross found comfort, instead, in the inaccessible Holy of Holies that enshrined the Ten Commandments. When the Council of Nicaea actively (re)signed truth by coining the word *homoousios* to establish that Jesus was one substance with the Father (chapter seven), Arians found comfort, instead, by thinking of the Son as below the Father in origin. When Tyndale actively (re)signed truth by coining the word *atonement* to describe the work of the cross, people who thought English too far below the sacred truth of Scripture found comfort, instead, in the Latin Bible (chapter one). When Dorothy L. Sayers actively (re)signed truth by putting slang into the mouths of the disciples, people below the BBC radio towers found comfort, instead, in the English of Tyndale, which makes up much of the King James Bible.

In sum, one generation's (re)signing becomes a future generation's idol. As Roman Catholic Cardinal Henri de Lubac asserts, "Preserving the *status quo* in theories and viewpoints has never been and can never be an adequate means of safeguarding the truth."[6] Thoroughly agreeing with this idea, Sayers went so far as to align the stubborn preservation of theories and viewpoints with the character of Judas.

---

[6]Henri de Lubac, S.J., *Corpus Mysticum: The Eucharist and the Church in the Middle Ages,* trans. Gemma Simmonds, C.J., et al., ed. Laurence Paul Hemming and Susan Frank Parsons (Notre Dame, IN: University of Notre Dame Press, 2006), pp. 258-59.

THE IDOLATRY OF JUDAS

In her eighth play of *The Man Born to Be King*, Sayers (re)signs the character of Judas. As she notes in the introduction to the published cycle, "simple-minded people" who regard Judas as a "creeping, crawling, patently worthless villain," end up "cast[ing] too grave a slur upon the brains or the character of Jesus."[7] In other words, radical vilification of Judas implies that Jesus was either too naive to recognize the disciple's evil intentions, or else too manipulative (using an evil man to achieve his purposes) to warrant our adoration.

Sayers therefore makes Judas "the most intelligent of all the disciples," fully understanding and intensely devoted to his Lord's sacrificial mission.[8] Grasping the truth of Christ better than any other disciple, Judas's strength becomes his greatest weakness: his passionate commitment to the Son of God turns into a certitude about his *ability to understand the signs* of that truth. He becomes so committed to *his own interpretation* of God's will that he stops trusting Jesus when the latter uses different signs than Judas regarded as "true."

In Sayers's play, Judas loses confidence in Jesus during the "triumphal entry": the moment when Jesus rides an ass into Jerusalem. Because jubilant crowds wave palm branches and shout "Hosanna," Judas comes to the conclusion that Jesus has "sold himself" to a political revolution. Out of commitment to "the truth," therefore, Judas willingly betrays Christ, telling Caiaphas, "Jesus is corrupt to the bone. . . . I believed in his pretensions. I supported his claim. . . . I sincerely thought he had sufficient character to resist temptation. I suppose I was a fool to trust him."[9] Reading the signs of the times according to his prejudices, Judas came to the conclusion that Jesus was a false Messiah.

Ironically, the actions that Judas regarded as signs of corruption actually prove the purity of Christ's purposes. In Sayers's fictionalized scenario, Judas does not realize that, earlier in the day, Jesus had received a note from "Baruch, the Zealot" stating,

> In the stable of Zimri, at the going-up into the City, is a war-horse saddled and ready. Set yourself upon him, and you shall ride into Jerusalem with a thousand spears behind you. But if you refuse, then take the ass's colt that is tied at the vineyard door, and Baruch will bide his time till a bolder Messiah come.[10]

---

[7]Sayers, *Man Born to Be King*, p. 15.
[8]Ibid., p. 52.
[9]Ibid., p. 220.
[10]Ibid., p. 203.

By choosing the colt, then, Jesus was refusing to instigate a political revolution. His decision to follow God rather than Baruch led to the cross rather than a coup, to resurrection rather than insurrection.

In her imaginative reconstruction of biblical events, then, Sayers establishes that the idolatry of signs leads to the betrayal of Jesus. Certain that *he understood exactly how* Jesus functioned as "the way, the truth, and the life," Judas rejected new signs of Christ. He saw only the colt, not realizing the dedication to God it represented—just as, two millennia later, those protesting Sayers's plays saw only the slang, not realizing the dedication to Christian truth it represented.[11] They, like Judas, resisted the (re)signing of truth.

BETRAYING TRADITION

One critic seeking to censor the BBC broadcasts went so far as to align Sayers's plays with current events of World War II. Suggesting that Singapore fell to the Axis powers due to the BBC broadcast, he demanded that the plays be taken off the air "before a like fate came to Australia."[12] For him, Sayers's betrayal of tradition became a treasonous act, contributing to the downfall of the country.

Ironically, the word *tradition* is etymologically related to the word *treason*. Coming from the Latin *traditio*, the word contains connotations of betrayal, as in the related words *traitor* and *traduce*. Why would this be? Isn't tradition exactly what we hold on to rather than betray? Significantly, *traditio* means "the 'handing over,'" as when one generation hands over ancient truths to another. However, when one generation "hands over" a tradition to another, the earlier group no longer has control of it, allowing for the possibility of change and hence betrayal of ancient interpretations. Indeed, "betrayal" is how papal powers interpreted the (re)signing of Wyclif, Tyndale and Luther, all of whom they regarded as "traitors" to the faith.

As Dale T. Irvin notes in his book *Christian Histories, Christian Traditioning*, the Greek word for "handing over"—*paradidōmi*—is used in the New Testament to describe radically different events. The verb describes not only Christ's communication of truth—its handing over—to his disciples,

---

[11]I similarly recount Sayers's interpretation of Judas in "Theopoetics: Si(g)ns of Copulation," *Cross-Currents* 60, no. 1 (March 2010): 51-52.
[12]James W. Welch, "Foreword," to *The Man Born to be King*, by Dorothy L. Sayers (London: Gollancz, 1946), p. 15.

but also the actions of Judas and Pilate as they hand over Jesus to his murderers. These two senses come together in one of the most familiar passages in the New Testament. Providing instructions for the Lord's Supper, Paul writes to the Corinthians, "For I received from the Lord what I also *delivered* *(paredoka)* to you, that the Lord Jesus on the night when he *was betrayed* *(paredideto)* took bread" (1 Cor 11:23).[13] Paul's pun, whether intentional or not, implies that the tradition he is handing over—the Lord's Supper—is meaningful not *in spite of* but because of what happened *after* the supper: the Lord was handed over to his enemies.

Irvin therefore coins a new sign to capture the double meaning of *traditio:* /traditioning/. Similar to my concept of (re)signing, "Christian traditioning" is a "constructive activity," expressing ancient truths in new ways, making them relevant to and for contemporary culture.[14] Traditioning, then, fulfills Andy Crouch's call for "culture-making" (see introduction) as when Sayers created a tremendously successful radio drama by (re)signing the gospel message. It also alludes to deconstruction (chapter six). As Derrida once explained in an interview, "We have gotten more than we think we know from 'tradition,' but the scene of the gift also obligates us to a kind of filial lack of piety, at once serious and not so serious, as regards the thinking to which we have the greatest debt."[15] For Derrida, then, "the gift" is opening ourselves to new signs even as we recognize that tradition molds how we understand truth.

Sayers's "filial lack of piety" through the "gift" of her plays generated a scandal. As reflected in the double meaning of "handing over," many religious people react to (re)signing as though it betrays truth. As Irvin notes,

> In every act of authentic traditioning there remains something of an act of treason, otherwise it would not be an authentic act of handing over, of change. Without a bit of treason performed in the act of handing over, the tradition remains inseparably bound to the world in which it was formed, hence not only irrelevant but incomprehensible.[16]

Problematically, as we saw in chapter one, "the world in which [truth] was

---

[13]I have quoted the passage as presented in Dale T. Irvin, *Christian Histories, Christian Traditioning: Rendering Accounts* (Maryknoll, NY: Orbis, 1998), p. 41, emphasis added.
[14]Ibid., p. 29.
[15]Quoted in John D. Caputo, *The Prayers and Tears of Jacques Derrida: Religion Without Religion* (Bloomington: Indiana University Press, 1997), p. 184.
[16]Irvin, *Christian Histories*, p. 41.

formed" often becomes mystified by people who idealize the past. Sayers recognized this problem, describing her attackers as people who seemed to believe that

> Christ wasn't born into history—He was born into the Bible (Authorized Version)—a place where nobody makes love, or gets drunk, or cracks vulgar jokes, or talks slang, or cheats, or despises his neighbours, but only a few selected puppets make ritual gestures symbolical of the sins of humanity. No wonder the story makes so little impression on the common man. It seems to have taken place in a world quite different from our own—a world full of reverent people waiting about in polite attitudes for the fulfillment of prophecies.[17]

Sayers, then, was accused of treason because she wanted to make the salvation message both relevant and comprehensible to 1940s audiences. On the edge of the coin, she "handed over" tradition through the (re)signing of truth. Doing so, she fulfilled the ancient concept of *invention*. When early rhetoricians encouraged *inventio,* their Latin word implied "finding again, or reassembling from past performances."[18] Sayers's newly invented signs helped people rediscover—find again—the ancient truth of salvation.

(RE)SIGNING TODAY: FROM COMPOSITION TO CONSERVATION

Readers may now be thinking, "but I am no Sayers—let alone a Luther, Tyndale or Wyclif, all of whom seem extraordinarily brilliant and gutsy. What can I possibly do to change the way people think about Christian truth?" My answer is simple: start with the simple signs of everyday communication.

As a teacher, for example, I have discovered that using new words can make writers think in new ways about essay composition. Early in my career, I noticed that college students would get either restless or bored when I taught about "interesting introductions," "a precise thesis" and "effective transitions," a resistance made manifest in their less-than-stellar essays. At first I got mad, writing stern notes at the bottom of their papers, chiding them for ignoring my wonderfully insightful teaching. But my anger at their recalcitrance did nothing to change their writing. In fact, my comments seemed to alienate them all the more from any desire to compose articulate papers.

And then, one day, I figured it out: my students had heard the words "intro-

[17]*The Letters of Dorothy L. Sayers,* ed. Barbara Reynolds (Cambridge: Carole Green, 1997), 2:354.
[18]Edward Said, *Humanism and Democratic Criticism* (New York: Columbia University Press, 2004), p. 140.

duction," "thesis" and "transition" for so long that the signs had not only lost their effectiveness, but had also begun to create distaste for the composition process. So I decided to change my signs. Rather than "introduction" I began to use the word "funnel," drawing a picture on the board of a funnel to show how an effective paper starts with an intriguing statement to draw readers' interest, then slowly narrows down the topic until it gets to the lip of the funnel—the "thesis"—that should snugly fit into the "jar" of the paper. And rather than the worn-out term "transitions," I tell my students to create "hooks" between paragraphs, drawing fish-hooks on the board with demonstrations of what a new paragraph might best "hook on to" in the preceding paragraph. It sounds silly, but it worked. Course essays improved remarkably, my new signs having jolted students into thinking differently about their composition process. Resigned to the importance of good writing, I had re-signed how to achieve it.

In other words, changing signs can change behavior. This happened quite literally at the University of Colorado at Boulder several decades ago.[19] Multiple signs posted in front of a college lawn demanded "KEEP OFF THE GRASS." Students nevertheless crisscrossed the lawn in defiance of the postings. Consequently much of the grass had disappeared, lines of hardened dirt etching pathways between buildings. And then one day the signs changed. Now the postings, in green and white rather than black and white, pled (rather than demanded), "Give Mother Earth a Chance." By the end of the year, so many students had heeded the signs that grass had begun to overtake the dirt pathways. Note what happened here. The sign-posters had not changed their message; instead they changed their form of communication to match the interests of those they wanted to change: students much more responsive to environmental conservation than to the "authoritarian" rules of institutions. As rhetoric specialist Maurice Charland notes, "the artful deployment of language . . . has real effects upon language itself, upon meaning, and finally, upon what humans do."[20]

THE RULE OF METAPHOR

Charland also notes that, in rhetorical theory, "the metaphor is fundamental

---

[19]This change was observed by my husband, David C. Downing, during his undergraduate days at Boulder.

[20]Maurice Charland, "Rehabilitating Rhetoric: Confronting Blindspots in Discourse and Social Theory," in *Contemporary Rhetorical Theory: A Reader,* ed. John Louis Lucaites, Celeste Michelle Condit and Sally Caudill (New York: Guilford, 1999), p. 465.

to the creation of new meaning."[21] Notice how both my above examples of change—writing good papers and righting bad lawns—rely on metaphors: comparisons that turn introductions into kitchen funnels, transitions into fishing hooks, nature into a mother. The history of rhetoric, in fact, might be considered the history of discussions about metaphor: a word coined by Aristotle from the Greek *meta-* (beyond) and *phor* (carry). New metaphors *carry us beyond* stale, cliched forms of communication.

In his book *The Rule of Metaphor,* Paul Ricoeur defines metaphor as "that strategy of discourse by which language divests itself of its function of direct description in order to reach the mythic level where its function of discovery is set free."[22] For *direct description,* think "Keep off the grass"; for *mythic* description think "Give Mother Earth a chance." Obviously, earth isn't really a mother with head, hands and heart. Instead, the metaphor has mythic associations: the Earth that nurtures and sustains humanity desires our loving response, as do the human mothers that gave us birth. Hence, when university officials employed the metaphor "Give Mother Earth a Chance," student "discovery" was "set free": the lawn they had been abusing needed their loving respect. Even "funnels" become mythic for my students, setting free a process of discovery through an image—a kitchen funnel—that illustrates both the purpose and effective construction of introductions.

METAPHORIC COPULAS

More often than not, metaphors rely on the "to-be" copula: Earth *is* a mother; introductions *are* funnels; "I *am* the vine, you *are* the branches" (Jn 15:5). Of course, when Jesus uses this metaphor, he doesn't mean that his feet are hairy roots planted in soil and that we hang off his body with grapes sprouting on our limbs. Instead, his copula means both "am" and "am not," both "are" and "are not." While Derrida's call to put the copula under erasure seems edgy (chapter six), we see that metaphors have always put their copulas under erasure:

I a~~m~~ the vine, you a~~re~~ the branches.

Ricoeur describes this metaphoric doubleness as "tension in the relational

---

[21]Ibid., p. 468.
[22]Paul Ricoeur, *The Rule of Metaphor: Multi-disciplinary Studies of the Creation of Meaning in Language,* trans. Robert Czerny et al. (Toronto: University of Toronto Press, 1981 [1975]), p. 247.

function of the copula: between identity and difference in the interplay of resemblance."[23]

In *The Rule of Metaphor*, in fact, Ricoeur discusses Derrida's critique of theorists who naively think of metaphors as candy-coated signs in contradistinction to *real* truth.[24] For example, "funnel" might seem like a trite substitution for the seriously referential word "introduction." But to think in such a way ignores the fact that *introduction* is itself a metaphor, related to the words *aqua duct, conductor, reduction, abduction* and even *duke*. The Latin *duc-* means "to lead": an aqua duct leads water, a conductor leads an orchestra, a reduction leads something back to an earlier state, a duke leads his country, and C. S. Peirce appropriated the word "abduction" to describe a sign that leads the mind in a new direction (chapter eight). *Introduction*, then, means "to lead into," which is exactly what a funnel is designed to do. So when I substitute "funnel" for "introduction," I am simply updating a metaphor that has become flat, stale and unprofitable.[25]

The same point can be made about theological language. As C. S. Lewis notes,

> We can, if you like, say "God entered history" instead of saying "God came down to earth." But, of course, "entered" is just as metaphorical as "came down." You have only substituted horizontal or undefined movement for vertical movement. We can make our language duller; we cannot make it less metaphorical.[26]

Lewis, then, would agree with Ricoeur and Derrida—that there is no escaping metaphoric language in order to get at pure unadulterated truth; we always understand reality through the metaphors we use. And this is as true for atheists as it is for Christians.

To this end, both Derrida and Ricoeur quote the German philosopher Friedrich Nietzsche (1844-1900). Fascinated with the poetic power of lan-

---

[23]Ibid.

[24]Ibid., pp. 284-89.

[25]My research assistant, Abigail Long, came up with another good example. When people argue, "I want ideas explained in clear nonmetaphoric language," they are oblivious to the fact that their word "explain" is itself a metaphor. *Plain* means *to make flat*, like a plain. We cannot avoid metaphor. For a book-length discussion about the innate metaphoricity of language, see Owen Barfield, *Poetic Diction: A Study in Meaning* (Middletown, CT: Wesleyan University Press, 1973).

[26]C. S. Lewis, "Is Theology Poetry?" in *Screwtape Proposes a Toast and Other Pieces* (London: Fontana, 1965), pp. 53-54.

guage, Nietzsche argued that truth is composed of "worn-out metaphors which have become powerless to affect the senses, coins which have their obverse effaced and now are no longer of account as coins but merely as metal."[27] We thus return to the metaphor that ties this book together: a metal coin. By standing on the edge of the coin, Christians can see when signs of faith, having been worn away through overuse, need to be re-signed. From that position, Christians roll the coin into new places by coining new signs.

COINING NEW SIGNS: THE STRONG POET

Richard Rorty (1931-2007), a philosopher influenced by Peirce's pragmatism, argues that people can challenge the status quo by coining new signs. He calls such people "strong poets." For him,

> The line between weakness and strength is . . . the line between using language which is familiar and universal and producing language which, though initially unfamiliar and idiosyncratic, somehow makes tangible the blind impress all one's behavings bear.[28]

By "blind impress" Rorty refers to the way signs become imprinted on our psyches, like the impress made by hand stamps at theme parks. Inevitably, people become blind to how such impressions affect their attitudes and behavior, as when those with power in the Late Middle Ages suspected all village-dwellers, or "villains," of criminal activity (chapter five).

For a biblical example of "blind impress" think of the apostle Paul. He had to be literally blinded on the Damascus Road before he could recognize how traditional signs of his day had "impressed" his "behavings" toward the Christians he persecuted. However, once he accepted the radical new sign of a resurrected Christ, he became a strong poet. In *Paul Among the People*, Sarah Ruden, a specialist in classical Latin and Greek, argues that Paul transformed the Greek language of his day in order to communicate Christianity's new understanding of God. As she explains, "it's as if [Paul] were giving vocabulary lessons, reforming the language of his correspondents right before their

---

[27]Ricoeur, *Rule of Metaphor*, p 286; Jacques Derrida, "White Mythology," trans. F. C. T. Moore, *New Literary History* 6, no. 1 (1974): 15.

[28]Richard Rorty, *Contingency, Irony, and Solidarity* (Cambridge: Cambridge University Press, 1989), pp. 20, 28-29. Rorty borrowed the term "strong poet" from literary critic Harold Bloom.

eyes."[29] No longer committing organized violence on Christians, Paul creates poetry as Roman Jakobson (chapter four) defines it: "organized violence committed on ordinary speech."[30]

Communicators who seek to follow Paul's example should do the same. Indeed, as theologian Scott Holland argues, "rhetorical innovation" may well "become the chief instrument of cultural and political change."[31] For a contemporary example, consider Jim Henderson, executive director of "Off the Map," a website for "a community of spiritual anthropologists." Like me, he puns on the words "resigned" and "re-signed," although with a different purpose. Henderson invokes the passive sense of "resigned" in order to describe women stuck in churches that fail to encourage their gifts. Rather than give up on the church, he exhorts women to "re-sign up": to use their strengths as vehicles of change within their home churches. By seeking to transform churches from within, Henderson's activities fulfill the "counter-hegemonic" vision of Antonio Gramsci (chapter five).[32]

A more famous example is the *New York Times* bestseller *The Shack*. Though my friends have warned me that the novel is so poorly written that it will make me want to scratch my eyeballs out, I cannot help noticing the impact it has made, causing people to think about God in new ways. As the author William Paul Young reports,

> To me, the beauty of what the book's done is it's given people a language to talk about God in a way that's not religious. . . . All of a sudden people in the same family or friends are having a conversation that they've never had before because they didn't have a language for it. All they knew was religious language.[33]

---

[29]Interview with Sarah Ruden by John Wilson, "The Apostle of the Golden Age," Christianity Today, September 2010, online at http://www.christianitytoday.com/ct/2010/september/26.44.html. The full title of Ruden's book is *Paul Among the People: The Apostle Reinterpreted and Reimagined in His Own Time* (New York: Pantheon, 2010).

[30]Roman Jakobson, "Two Aspects of Language and Two Types of Aphasic Disturbances," in *Fundamentals of Language,* ed. Roman Jakobson and Morris Halle, 2nd ed. (The Hague: Mouton, 1971), p. 75.

[31]Quoted in Matt Guynn, "Theopoetics: That the Dead May Become Gardeners Again," *CrossCurrents* 56, no. 1 (Spring 2006): 109.

[32]For a summary of Jim Henderson's project, see "Are You Resigned, Have You Resigned, or Did You Re-sign?" posted April 28, 2010, on the Emerging Women Blog Archive, www.emergingwomen.us/2010/04/28/are-you-resigned-have-you-resigned-or-did-you-re-sign/. Jim Henderson's posting on the Off The Map website (April 26, 2010), is at http://offthemap.com/2010/04/26/are-you-resigned-have-you-resigned-or-did-you-re-sign/. Thanks to Valerie Weaver-Zercher for calling my attention to Henderson's re-signing.

[33]Quoted in David Yonke, "'Shack' Author Enjoys Book's Impact on Readers," *The Patriot-News*

Young's novel demonstrates that people hunger and thirst for the (re)signing of truth.

Whether by coining new metaphors or by re-forming contemporary language, the strong poet gets people to think in new ways. And I would argue that even the most humble Christian today can—and should—do the same, flexing linguistic muscles in order to (re)sign truth. As philosopher Gilles Deleuze and psychoanalyst Felix Guattari have exhorted, "Since the language is arid, make it vibrate with a new intensity."[34]

This is certainly what Sayers was seeking to do in her radio plays about Jesus, believing that by quenching aridity with the living water of new signs, Christians fulfill the *imago Dei:* the image of God described in Genesis 1:27. As she argues in *The Mind of the Maker,* when we create something new we imitate our Creator.[35]

What follow, then, are some examples of aridity in Christian language that need quenching—in both senses of the term. Like quenching a smoking fire, we sometimes must quench old signs that hinder people's vision. Meanwhile, by creating new signs, we quench the scorched earth around the fire so that new life might grow from the same ground.

/BORN AGAIN/ BORN AGAIN

For many people, the phrase "born again" has become arid. This became apparent several Christmases ago, when my brother-in-law found himself in a long line at the post office. Watching tinsel trickle down from evergreen boughs over the windows, he (like everyone else in line) overheard a loud conversation between two package-toting customers complaining about their in-laws. Each trying to trump the other with a story of in-law dysfunction, one finally said, "and then she became a *born-again-Christian.*" Ten people standing in line all groaned in unison.

Rather than transmitting "the aroma of Christ . . . among those who are perishing" (2 Cor 2:15), /born again/ was creating a stink.[36] Why? Perhaps

---

(Harrisburg, PA), April 25, 2010.

[34]Gilles Deleuze and Felix Guattari, "What is a Minor Literature?" in *Out There: Marginalization and Contemporary Cultures,* ed. Russell Ferguson et al. (Cambridge, MA: MIT Press, 1990), p. 61. I thank my student Karissa Graybill for drawing my attention to this essay.

[35]See Dorothy L. Sayers, *The Mind of the Maker* (San Francisco: HarperSanFrancisco, 1979). Significantly, Sayers wrote much of this book while she was composing her radio plays (1940).

[36]Not all translations interpret the Greek phrase in Jn 3:3 with "born again." The New Revised Standard Version and the Jerusalem Bible both write "born from above."

because the sign had lost touch with its original radical implications. Its coinage is well known. The Pharisee Nicodemus approached Jesus at night saying, "Rabbi, we know that you are a teacher who has come from God; for no one can do these *signs* that you do apart from the presence of God" (Jn 3:2). Recognizing Nicodemus's openness to new signs, Jesus coined /born again/ to explain how Nicodemus might "see the kingdom of God." However, the coinage was so idiosyncratic that Nicodemus needed clarification: "Can one enter a second time into the mother's womb and be born?" (Jn 3:3-4). Jesus had created such an outrageous metaphor that a Pharisee well-acquainted with "salvation" (a term appearing in different forms at least 119 times in the Hebrew Scriptures) had trouble processing it. Jesus, of course, was not rejecting the truth of the Hebrew Scriptures; instead he was (re) signing it, implied when he says to Nicodemus, "Are you a teacher of Israel, and yet you do not understand these things?" (Jn 3:10). His radical new sign, in other words, was still connected to ancient truths about reconciliation with God.

Unfortunately, due to its overuse and abuse, /born again/ has been emptied of its exciting reference to new life.[37] Instead, it often operates like an old coin that people hold on to like a good-luck charm. This was confirmed for me by a 2002 study that said only 6 percent of self-proclaimed "born again" Christians tithed. In 2006, however, a study established that 91 percent of regular churchgoers give four times as much money to charity than do those who avoid church.[38] It would seem, then, that many who use /born again/ do not regularly attend church, their sign a mere identifying tag—like the graffiti gang members use to mark their territories—rather than signaling a desire to sacrificially follow their savior.

It is time for Christians to re-sign /born again/ in order to re-infuse it with its life-altering implications. To do so we might appropriate a definition of

---

[37]Steve Chalke similarly notes that /born again/ "has become the basis for one of the most confused, misused and abused, misunderstood and despised ideas in the history of the Church." See Steve Chalke and Alan Mann, *The Lost Message of Jesus* (Grand Rapids, MI: Zondervan, 2003), p. 147.

[38]Ronald J. Sider, *The Sandal of the Evangelical Conscience: Why Are Christians Living Just Like the Rest of the World?* (Grand Rapids, MI: Baker, 2005), p. 17; Arthur Brooks, *Who Really Cares: The Surprising Truth About Compassionate Conservatism* (New York: Basic Books, 2006). See also chapter thirteen of Robert D. Putnam and David E. Campbell, *American Grace: How Religion Divides and Unites Us* (New York: Simon & Schuster, 2011), pp. 443-92, which reports that churchgoers are considerably more likely than nonchurchgoers to volunteer both time and money to secular as well as religious causes.

metaphor invoked by Ricoeur: "presenting an idea under the *sign* of another idea more striking or better known."[39] Of course, awareness of something "striking or better known" necessitates familiarity with signs of the times. To invoke the language of Bakhtin (chapter ten), we must be sensitive to an audience's "chronotope": its location in time and space. Effective communication considers cultural contexts as well as human need.

Here's an example. Rather than putting up a sign stating "You Must be Born Again!" a church placed over its front door a sign stating "Servants' Entrance."[40] Rather than merely copying culture with a sign like "Got Jesus?" the church was thus counter-hegemonic (chapter five), for the idea of a "servants' entrance" is something that makes most people uncomfortable today. The sign therefore disturbs people, making them wonder what is going on, especially when "Servants' Entrance" is placed over the main door. Wondering, then, can lead to questioning, which can lead to answers: Christians are called to follow the example of Christ, "who, though he was in the form of God," became a servant (Phil 2:6-7).

(RE)SIGNING THE BIBLE

It is relatively easy to communicate the salvation message without using /born again/. A harder sign to eliminate is /the Bible/, for Scripture is the authoritative guide to Christian faith and practice, making clear the gift of salvation. Nevertheless, when non-Christians hear the phrase "According to the Bible, . . . " many stop listening, often due to prejudices against "Bible-thumpers," if not against Christianity itself. There is no excusing prejudice, of course. But a good communicator acknowledges its existence and then seeks to get around it—by (re)signing truth. Recognizing that the Bible is essential to a life in Christ, (re)signers simultaneously recognize that /the Bible/ (i.e., the *sign itself*) is not essential to communicating this truth.

To get non-Christians to think about the content of the Bible rather than the sign /the Bible/, a (re)signer might say something like, "in an effort to understand human psychology, I use a manual of case studies. One intriguing story tells of religious people who ignore a victim of assault at the

---

[39]Ricoeur quotes a definition of metaphor offered by rhetorician Pierre Fontanier in the early nineteenth century (*Rule of Metaphor,* p. 294).

[40]This example was given me by Carl Friesen, a student in the semiotics course I taught for Regent College, Vancouver, July 2011.

side of the road." The listener might then respond, "Yes; that's the trouble with religious people! What happened to the victim?" The communicator is thus invited to re-tell the Good Samaritan story, perhaps even avoiding the sign /Good Samaritan/.

In another context, a (re)signer might say, "A book that has helped me understand the love of God contains this interesting story of a son who spends his entire inheritance on self-indulgent partying . . ." Using signs that appeal to rather than alienate our addressees, we demonstrate a love that entices them toward the God of Love. To insist on the sign /the Bible/—rather than on what the sign stands for—is to turn a well-worn coin into an idol.

Another phrase we must reconsider is "biblical Christian." What exactly does that mean? After all, the Amish follow biblical prescriptions far more exactly than many people who describe themselves as "biblical Christians." Committed to resurrection through Christ, the Amish do not participate in the "unbibilical" practice of hiring pastors (see chapter one), but instead ordain ministers based on the biblical concept of casting lots as a sign of God's will.[41] Taking very seriously Paul's citation of Isaiah 52, "be separate" (2 Cor 6:17), the Amish also fulfill prescriptions about head-coverings for women (1 Cor 11:4-10), foot washings (Jn 13:14-15) and, most famously of all, turning the other cheek (Lk 6:29). They seem to deserve the sign "biblical Christian" far more than do many evangelicals. Perhaps, then, the phrase should be abandoned, not only due to its inaccuracy, but also because some Christians worship it as a golden calf.

In sum, while never giving up on the Bible as our God-inspired guide to faith and practice, we need to re-sign how we talk about it in order to break both idols and communication barriers. After all, as discussed in chapter two, the Bible itself offers numerous examples of (re)signing. The Holy Spirit who inspired its writers joins our interpretants on the edge of the coin, clarifying its relevance to our own day and age.

How, then, do we know which signs *not* to change? Which signs do we resign ourselves to as unalterably essential to our faith?

---

[41]Lev 16:8; Josh 18:6-10; 1 Chron 24:31; 25:8; 26:13-14; Neh 10:34; 11:1. Each Amish man nominated for minister selects a hymnal from a pile; the man who happens to take the book that hides a slip of paper is considered chosen by God. Significantly, the paper is inscribed with Proverbs 16:33, usually in Luther's German, that translates "The lot is cast into the lap, but the decision is the Lord's alone."

RESIGNED TO A TRINITY OF TRUTHS

Changing Signs of Truth has established three fundamental doctrines as essential to Christianity: the Trinity, the incarnation and the gift of salvation through Christ's atoning work. Furthermore, through an exploration of semiotics and its heirs, the book has provided rhetorical strategies to argue for these irreducible minimums of orthodox Christianity:

- While Saussure's sign operates according to an economy of exchange, Peirce's sign suggests that world religions (including Christianity!) should be assessed according to the idea of **Salvation as a Gift**, rather than according to simplistic notions of tolerance and intolerance.

- Peirce's triadic sign reinforces the doctrine of the **Trinity**, the coinherence of three-in-one giving Christianity more explanatory power than other religions.

- Diversity of belief within Christianity—both diachronically and synchronically—reinforces one of its distinctive doctrines: the **Incarnation.**

The three intertwine to form the basic beliefs of Christian faith: the death and resurrection of the incarnated Son reconciles us to the Father through the gift of salvation. We are led to the gift by the Holy Spirit, who not only directed the formation of the biblical canon as a reliable guide for faith and practice, but also, through that Word, convicts us of our need for the gift. The conviction, of course, comes with the awareness of sin: self-centeredness, idolatry, hardheartedness, dishonesty, refusal to forgive. All these, in fact, might be encapsulated with the help of Derrida's famous phrase: sin is a refusal to be "open to the other." Accepting the gift, then, is a choice: a turn (*conversion* means "with a turn") from self-serving to serving the Other who transcends all signs.

Creative acts of re-signing, then, should be made in resignation to these basic Christian beliefs. Different Christians, of course, will re-sign differently, depending on their bodily contexts. Think about the charts drawn in earlier chapters to capture Peirce's concept of semiosis. Because the interpretant becomes a sign in the mind, that sign generates another interpretant, causing perception to branch out in different ways as different people understand words, and the Word, differently. Now let's apply that idea of multiple branches to Christ's fruitful metaphor quoted earlier: "I am the vine, you are the branches."[42]

---

[42]On the opening page of a chapter called "Nature of the Linguistic Sign," Saussure draws a tree. But for him, the tree is a static sign, determined by one's *langue*. For Peirce, the sign grows through

PRUNING AND (IM)PROVING CHRISTIANITY: THE TREE OF FAITH

Jesus invites us in John 15:1-8 to think of the incarnate Christ as a grape vine whose branches have spread out from the trunk in fruitful splendor. The atonement—"at-one-ment," as Tyndale coined it—occurs at the place where all branches unite into one. But—switching the picture of trunk and branches to that of a tree—just as each branch of the tree joins the trunk at a different spot, so the various branches of Christianity connect to atonement in different ways (chapter ten). Nevertheless, it is the same atonement—united to the same trunk—made possible through the death and resurrection of Jesus. Indeed, the trunk grew from the seed of Christ, dying that life might be reborn (1 Cor 15:35-47).

This metaphor might help us see the proliferation of branches in the church as a gift of God, providing far-reaching shade that might attract many different kinds of seekers. To lop off all branches but one would not only make a woeful-looking tree, but also probably kill it. At the same time, as any horticulturist can tell you, a tree needs periodic pruning for successful growth. Especially problematic are tiny off-shoots on the tree's trunk called suckers, since they suck off strength that should go into the larger branches and leaves.

This is how we might regard our early church fathers: as horticulturists, snipping away strength-sapping suckers of heresy. Practicing incarnational dialogism, they met face to face in ecumenical councils while praying for the rain and reign of Truth. Even then, they still didn't always agree about which new branches needed to be lopped off for the good of the tree (sometimes attacking each other with their pruning shears). Nevertheless, we believe that the Holy Spirit—part of the coinherence of the Trinity that established the coinherence of the sign—entered into this process, guiding the decision-making conversation so that essential truths about God's nature became dominant. The same Spirit guided the canon-formation, establishing the Bible as the definitive guidebook about the truth of the tree and its best tending.

Significantly, our word for the doctrines that developed out of this process, "orthodoxy," comes from Greek roots which mean "straight" (as in *ortho-dontia*, straight teeth) and "opinion." To invoke the language of Charles Sanders Peirce, we might say that the Spirit guided the interpretants *(opinions)*

---

branching interpretants. Ferdinand de Saussure, *Course in General Linguistics,* trans. Wade Baskin (New York: Philosophical Library, 1959), p. 65.

of leaders at the ecumenical councils so that the church might grow *straight* toward the light of Truth. C. S. Lewis, like many other Protestant Christians, believed that orthodoxy was established by the fourth ecumenical council—at Chalcedon in 451—and that the tree of Christianity branches out in multiple directions after that important year.[43]

This, then, might explain the three biggest branches of the church— Eastern Orthodox, Roman Catholic and Protestant—all of which, as in any beautiful tree, have multiple forks with numerous off-shoots. Some people, believing that only Protestants, or only the Eastern Orthodox, or only Roman Catholics are authentic Christians, apparently want to lop off the other two main limbs as unhealthy growths from the trunk. But wouldn't it be more productive to direct our time and energies to nurturing the entire tree so that it grows higher and stronger?

At the same time, we must protect the trunk, for branches are dead wood without a trunk. Enlightenment rationalists like Thomas Jefferson (chapter one), and demythologizers like Rudolf Bultmann (chapter ten) attacked the trunk with the buzz saw of anti-supernaturalism, refusing to believe that Jesus could be both fully human and fully divine simultaneously. In many people's minds, they nearly killed the tree—at least until poststructuralists like Derrida pointed out the deficient horticultural credentials of Enlightenment rationalism.[44]

What, then, holds up the trunk?

A TRINITARIAN ROOT

As we have seen (chapter seven), Charles Sanders Peirce developed a triadic view of the sign, establishing that all knowledge is trinitarian: the coinherence of object, representamen and interpretant. Christians can therefore argue that the process of human perception reinforces the doctrine of the Trinity: the coinherence of Father, Son and Holy Ghost. In other words, God created humanity to understand reality in a way that reflects God's own nature. The coinherence of the Trinity, like the coinherence fundamental to human knowledge, reflects what it means to be human. We might therefore

---

[43]Suzanne Bray, "C. S. Lewis as an Anglican," in *Persona and Paradox: Issues of Identity for C. S. Lewis, His Friends and Associates* (Cambridge: Cambridge Scholars Publishing, 2012).

[44]See Crystal Downing, *How Postmodernism Serves (My) Faith: Questioning Truth in Language, Philosophy and Art* (Downers Grove, IL: IVP Academic, 2006).

see the Trinity not only as the three tap roots from which the incarnational trunk grows, but also as the earth, sun and rain that nurtures the tree: God both imminent within the tree and transcendent to it.

Of course, theories of the Trinity developed over time as early Christians sought to understand how God nurtured the gift of salvation through Christ (chapter eight). But just as a tree grows through *osmosis*—the absorption of nutrients in earth, light and rain—so our understanding of truth grows through *semiosis*, the absorption of knowledge as signs change. This is how I answer Christians who argue that we need to eliminate the doctrine of the Trinity because it is an out-worn human construction not supported by Scripture. I would point out that such arguments differ little from those of Christians who naively assume that the doctrine of the Trinity is clearly outlined in Scripture. As opposite sides of the same coin, both positions ignore the semiosis that nurtures the growth of truth. Peirce, in fact, believed "the principle of growth" to be such "a primordial element of the universe" that it *endorses* "the idea of a personal creator."[45]

With the help of Peirce, Christians on the edge of the coin can therefore endorse a process of God-guided "becoming" (the *-osis* of *osmosis* and *semiosis* means, of course, *process*), by which the great doctrines of the faith developed through history. And though different branches of the church might conceptualize the truth differently, they will grow larger and fuller if they stay connected, at the site of at-one-ment, to the incarnational trunk and the trinitarian roots.

THE LIMITS OF SIGNS

As an example of (re)signing, my tree metaphor is, alas, just that: a metaphor. Like all signs, my metaphor cannot fully capture the Truth that transcends all signification. Nevertheless, humans are limited to signs, which function like the mirror described in First Corinthians: "For now we see in a mirror, dimly, but then we will see face to face. Now I know only in part; then I will know fully, even as I have been fully known" (1 Cor 13:12-13). Any mirror reflects the one who looks into it, just as Peirce's sign reflects the presence of the interpretant. But, at the same time, Peirce's sign contains more then the interpretant: there is an object beyond both representamen and interpretant—

---

[45]C. S. Peirce, "The Law of Mind," in *Philosophical Writings of Peirce*, ed. Justus Buchler (New York: Dover, 1955), p. 350.

One whom we will someday meet face to face. Furthermore, just as some mirrors reflect reality better than other mirrors, so some signs reflect the light of truth better than other signs.

Despite its obvious limitations, then, my tree metaphor seeks to re-sign how we think about the Trinity, the incarnation, and atonement as a gift, suggesting that branches of faith that deny these three essentials impede healthy growth of the tree. The metaphor also implies that signs of these three essentials vary in appearance at different eras in the history of the church, just as a one-year-old tree looks quite different than a fifty-year-old tree: same tree, different signs of growth. Finally, the metaphor allows for the fact that Christians will inevitably disagree on issues concerning the relationship between orthodoxy and culture, their opinions colored by the particular location of their branch in time and space.

Changing Signs of Truth therefore does not resolve the controversies of our day. Instead, it provides principles of communication by which Christians on different branches can seek to confirm the salvation message, such that the tree flourishes with such beauty that people outside our faith are drawn to seek rest under its shade. With delight we recognize that different people will stand under different branches, eventually grafted into the tree as they accept the gift. There they will become part of the entire tree, contributing to its growth and change by sprouting new signs: "By their fruits ye shall know them."[46]

STAYING ON THE EDGE: TEN FERTILE PRINCIPLES

(Re)signing truth, then, is about the healthy growth of Christianity. Guiding the process are ten principles suggested by this book:

1. Like a beautiful historic house, the dwelling place of Christianity will remain standing *only if* we replace outworn elements with healthy new signs, as exemplified by Augustine, St. Francis, Wyclif, Tyndale, Luther, Sayers and so many others. Peirce, in fact, believes that any vibrant philosophic system requires radical repairs in order to maintain the beauty of the original edifice: "This is like partially rebuilding a house. The faults [in construction] that have been committed are, first, that the repairs of the dilapidation have generally not been sufficiently thorough-going, and

---

[46]Peirce quoting Mt 7:20 (KJV) in "Pragmatism in Retrospect," in *Philosophical Writings,* p. 271.

second, that not sufficient pains have been taken to bring the additions into deep harmony with the really sound parts of the old structure."[47] By maintaining the house of Christianity, our goal should be hospitality, welcoming "the other"—in the form of both persons and perspectives—to join us inside (chapter six).

2. "Openness to the other" should include "openness" to the "otherness" of the past. Just as we hesitate to support Christians who refuse change of any sort, we should also hesitate to promote movements that, in the name of progress, reject all signs of the past. As opposite sides of the same coin, both have narrow perspectives. Those who resist change reveal ignorance about the changing history of Christianity; those who repudiate the past seem unaware that all knowledge is based on signs from the past. (Re)signers function on the edge: resigned to historical understandings of truth, they re-sign them to make sense amidst current signs of the times.

3. (Re)signing should reflect the fundamental premise of Christianity: salvation comes as the charitable gift of God rather than through an "economy of exchange." We should not seek to exchange one sign for another out of self-interest, but to make a gift to culture of new signs. A gift, by its very definition, expresses love, not hate. We therefore seek to love culture by infusing it with new signs, signs that attract people to the love of God, manifest in the gift of Christ. Furthermore, the concept of "the Gift" enables us to communicate why we believe Christianity reflects God's truth better than the mirrors of other religions (chapter nine).

4. We believe that God gave the gift of the Holy Spirit, whom we welcome on the edge of the coin through a triadic (Peircean) rather than dyadic (Saussurean) view of the sign. While Saussure's sign functions according to an economy of exchange between signifier and signified, Peirce's sign endorses the relational coinherence of three-in-one: object, representamen, interpretant. Christians can therefore argue that (1) our perception of reality reflects the Three-in-One who created all signs; (2) the Holy Spirit guides our interpretants on the edge of the sign, aiding us as we roll into new contexts and hence into new ways to see and communicate God's truth.

---

[47]C. S. Peirce, "The Architecture of Theories," in *Philosophical Writings*, p. 315.

5. We believe that the Spirit gave the gift of the Bible, which contains signs that must be interpreted in context. The signs of God's Word should not be treated as idols, precious for their own sake. Instead, like all signs, they generate value from their contexts even as they communicate to our own: past and present in dialogic relationship (chapter ten). The significance of context, what Bakhtin called our "chronotope," is established by a fundamental doctrine of Christianity: that God became flesh.

6. Reflecting Christian endorsement of embodiment, we regard the pluralism within Christianity itself as a gift. Christians placed in different contexts will endorse different signs: speaking in tongues versus penance, immersion versus sprinkling, Beatification versus Bible-memorization, icons versus flags in church. What Bakhtin calls "heteroglossia" should therefore guide our communication (chapter ten). Not only do we attempt to see truth in its contexts to better understand why Christians in different times and places understand truth differently, but we also attempt to understand non-Christians in their contexts in order to better dialogue with them.

7. Rather than obsessing over political power, we recognize that effective cultural change usually comes from the margins, in counter-hegemonic moves. Cultural materialists (chapter five) believe that political hegemony rarely produces long-lasting change in ideology. As we see happening in almost every election, people on opposite sides of the political coin tend to put more energy into getting hegemony, or attacking those who have it, than into altering perception. Change is reduced to an economy of exchange (chapter nine), manifest when a new party takes power by flipping the political coin from one side to the other. In contrast, as Antonio Gramsci and Raymond Williams argue, there is more power to change society through cultural signs than through political signs. This, of course, does not mean that Christians should avoid politics. It means that politics does little to alter culture except when politicians generate new signs that help people think in new ways.

8. Even in our daily communication we can counter hegemony by coining new signs: signs that might change culture. For example, a group of believers in the 1960s noticed that many of their college peers dismissed Christianity as part of the "Establishment"—the same "Establishment"

that put up authoritarian signs like "KEEP OFF THE GRASS." In order to communicate to the "hippie" generation, these believers developed a new sign, calling themselves "Jesus People" rather than "Christians": same content, new sign. And despite some controversies (similar to those that marked the early church), Jesus People USA (established 1972) is still going strong, its members living together in community in order to better spread the love of Jesus to people on the margins of society. In addition, for the past twenty-five years, Jesus People USA has sponsored a music festival that continues to draw between ten and twenty thousand Christians from all over the world to engage in counter-hegemonic communication.

9. As exemplified by Jesus People USA, (re)signing functions best in a community committed to collaboratively understanding and practicing the love of God. As reiterated in chapter eight, Peirce aligned the branching process of semiosis with community, capitalizing the word due to its importance: "the very origin of the conception of reality shows that this conception essentially involves the notion of a COMMUNITY, without definite limits, and capable of a definite increase of knowledge."[48] This provides another way to think about Christ's fertile metaphor "I am the vine, you are the branches": the branches continue to grow, producing more and more fruit.

10. In addition to branching out with the fruit of new signs, followers of Christ are called to *be* signs of truth. While witnessing with our words via the employment of new signs, we must also witness with our bodies, using them to communicate the Christ we follow. God's people, in other words, are called to be representamens of the Object of our belief: God's incarnated Love. Thus, "If I coin new signs with the tongues of mortals and of angels, but do not have love, I am a noisy gong or a clanging cymbal. And if I have prophetic powers, and understand all mysteries and all contexts, and if I have all faith, so as to change ancient signs, but do not have love, I am nothing" (1 Cor 13:1-2, Crystal Downing Version). Augustine put it more simply in his treatise on signs: "Scripture teaches nothing but charity."[49]

---

[48] *Collected Papers of Charles Sanders Peirce*, vols. 1-6, ed. Arthur Burks, Charles Hartshorne and Paul Weiss; vols. 7-8, ed. Arthur W. Burkes (Cambridge, MA: Harvard University Press, 1931-1958), vol. 5, para. 311.
[49] Augustine, *On Christian Doctrine*, book 3, para. 15, p. 88.

We exercise these principles knowing that (re)signing has been part of Christianity from its start. Rather than resisting new signs, then, we joyfully participate in a tradition begun by Jesus Christ: the mediator between God and humanity. Joining us on the edge of the coin, his Spirit guides our interpretants in the ancient practice of (re)signing truth.

Name and Subject Index

Scripture Index